Ctrl+Shift+

Mike Girvin

Holy Macro! Books
PO Box 82 Uniontown, OH 44685

Ctrl+Shift+Enter: Mastering Excel Array Formulas

Author: Mike Excelisfun Girvin

Editor: Kitty Wilson

Layout: Tyler Nash

Published by: Holy Macro! Holy Macro! Books, PO Box 82 Uniontown, OH 44685, USA

Printed in USA

First printing: July 2013

Tech Editor: Bob Umlas

Cover Design: Shannon Mattiza 6'4 Design

Indexing: Nellie J. Liwam

Distributed by: Independent Publishers Group, Chicago, IL

ISBN: 978-1-61547-007-5 (print)

ISBN: 978-1-61547-109-6 (mobi)

ISBN: 978-1-61547-209-3 (pdf)

ISBN: 978-1-61547-329-8 (epub)

Library of Congress Control Number: 2013938519

Contents

Dedications

To Amy Girvin, my wife, who puts up with all this "Excel stuff."

To Dennis Ho, my 17-year-old son, who likes to hang with his friends and play tennis.

To Isaac Girvin, my 7-year-old son, who likes to race BMX, play baseball, and go on adventures.

About the Author

In 2011, Mike Girvin published his first book and DVD, titled *Slaying Excel Dragons*. Since 2008, he has video blogged at the excelisfun channel at YouTube, which contains more than 2,000 Excel how-to videos and logs about 30,000 views per day. Since 2002, he has taught quantitative business classes at Highline Community College, using 100% Excel in all classes so that students get a working-world-ready business education. In the 1990s, he ran a boomerang manufacturing company called Gel Boomerangs.

Mike still remembers the awe he felt the first time he changed a formula input for an Excel income statement, and the whole thing updated. Since that inspiring, life-changing moment, Mike has tried to create the same feeling of Excel awe in every class, video, and book he has created.

Mike has won a number of awards for Excel video blogging, including the 2011 Highline Faculty of the Year Award, the 2012 Central Washington University Achieving the Dream Award, and the 2013 Microsoft Excel MVP Award.

Acknowledgements

Thanks to Steve Kavanaugh, the first person to show me Excel in the 1990s. Thanks to Bill "MrExcel" Jelen for inspiring me to learn Excel well with his books and podcasts, and thanks also to Mr Excel for noticing the videos I had posted on YouTube and inviting me to make videos with him and write books for his company. Thanks to Dusty Wilson for helping me with my matrix algebra. Thanks to the editors, Bob Umlas and Kitty Wilson, for helping me to make this a good book.

But wait…

The REAL thanks that I must give is to all the amazing Excel masters at the MrExcel Message Board. The MrExcel Message Board is where I *really* learned about advanced formulas and array formulas. This amazing source for information on how formulas really work is incalculably valuable. This book is simply my attempt to put the ideas that I have learned from the MrExcel Message Board masters together in a logical order. I'd like to thank the people from the MrExcel Message Board and YouTube comments section who have helped me over the years and who are the source of the ideas in this book.

Specifically from the MrExcel Message Board, I must say a few words about the masters I have learned from:

- Thanks to Aladin Akyurek for all the amazing formula knowledge and always helping me and many others to "robustify" our formulas. As so many people write, it all starts with Aladin!
- Thanks to barry houdini for some amazing date formulas and other cool formula stuff.
- Thanks to Charles "Fast" Williams for his amazing articles on how to speed up calculation time.
- Thanks to Domenic for always answering my detailed array formula questions.
- Thanks to DonkeyOte for amazing formulas, including two awesome reverse lookup formulas!
- Thanks to pgc01 for amazing statistical formulas and VBA!

And thanks all the people who have answered my posts at the MrExcel Message Board: Aladin Akyurek, Andrew Poulsom, barry houdini, Bill "MrExcel" Jelen, Charles "Fast" Williams, circledchicken, Colin Legg, Dave Patton, Domenic, DonkeyOte, HOTPEPPER, jeffreybrown, Jon von der Heyden, Marcelo Branco, Norie, Peter_SSs , pgc01, Richard Schollar , Ron Coderre, Smitty, T. Valko, Tom Urtis, VoG, xenou, Yogi Anand, Teethless mama, BigC, Boller, Beate Schmitz, bosco_yip, c_m_s_jr, crimson_b1ade, Domski, edokhotnik, Erdinç E. Karaçam, erik.van.geit, Fazza, gavinkelly, GlennUK, HalfAce, Haseeb Avarakkan, hiker95, hkaplan2, iknowu99, iliace, James006, jasonb75, jbeaucaire, jindon, jonmo1, krn6264, Latchmaker, lenze, Lweiy, Makrini, Mark O'Brien, Matty, MickG, mikerickson, MrKowz, mvptomlinson, NateO, nbrcrunch, Oaktree, PaddyD, PCL, pto160, RalfA, ravishankar, robind21283, RomulusMilea, RoryA, sanrv1f, schielrn, scottylad2, shemayisroel, shg, sous2817, stanleydgromjr, Starkman, steimel386, texasalynn, timorrill, Travis, tusharm, UniMord, Weaver, wigi, and wsjackman.

Thanks also to a few amazing YouTube Excelers who have helped me tremendously: circledchicken, krn14242, hamy72, AThehos, SchultzesBlues, and dmr450.

Go, Excel online team!!!

Introduction

Why in the world would you read a book about array formulas?

Seriously, array formulas are rarely needed and can be insanely difficult. Here are some potential reasons you might want to read a book about them:

- You love Excel magic and wizardry. Your idea of fun is making Excel do the impossible with a formula.

- You know how to create formulas and want to take the next leap in Excel, into the upper echelon of creating advanced formulas.

- You have heard about array formulas and know that in some situations, they are the most efficient solution, but you have no idea how to create them.

- You use array formulas and are aware of some of the drawbacks they present (such as slow formula calculation time), and you would like to learn how to create more efficient array formulas.

Why are array formulas important tools to have in your Excel toolkit?

Here are some reasons array formulas may be useful to you:

- Sometimes using array formulas is the only way to accomplish a given task. See Figure IN.1

- Array formulas can replace intermediate steps and provide a single-cell solution. See Figure IN.2

- In general, the advantage of using formulas over using Excel features such as sorting, filtering, and PivotTables is that when you change a formula input, the formulas update instantly. By learning about array formulas, you increase your range of formula skills and are less limited when it comes to building Excel solutions. See Figure IN.3.

- If you understand how array formulas work, you understand the true beauty and power of Excel formulas! See Figure IN.4.

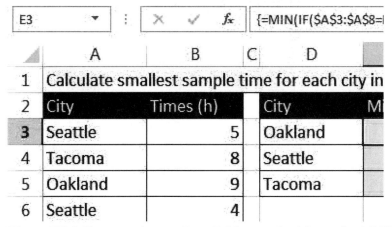

Figure IN.1 *If you can't use a PivotTable, you don't have the AGGREGATE Excel 2010 function, and you need to copy the formula down a column (you can't use DMIN function), using the array formula in cell E3 is an efficient solution. See how to create this formula in Chapter 4.*

| G7 | ▼ | : | × | ✓ | fx | =SUMPRODUCT(SUMIFS(G3:G5,F3:F5,B3:B7)) |

⯊	A	B	C	D	E	F	G
1	Lookup and add all costs associated with products.					**Lookup Table:**	
2	Date	ItemSold	Price	Cost		Product	Cost
3	10/17/2012	Product 1	22	12.5		Product 1	12.5
4	10/17/2012	Product 2	36	19		Product 2	19
5	10/17/2012	Product 1	22	12.5		Product 3	5.75
6	10/17/2012	Product 3	14	5.75			
7	10/17/2012	Product 2	37.5	19		Total	68.75
8			Total	68.75			∧ ∧ ∧
9						Single Cell Method	
10						(saves space)	

Figure IN.2 *If you want to avoid using the lookup formula in column D before calculating the total costs, you can use the array formula in cell G7 as an efficient single-cell solution. See how to create this formula in Chapter 6.*

| G8 | ▼ | : | × | ✓ | fx | =IF(ROWS(G$8:G8)>$F$3,"",INDEX(A$6:A$13,AGGREGATE(15,6,(ROW($A$6:$A$13)-ROW($A$6)+1)/ (($A$6:$A$13>=$B$3)*($A$6:$A$13<=$C$3)*($B$6:$B$13=$D$3)),ROWS(G$8:G8)))) |

⯊	A	B	C	D	E	F	G	H	I	J	K	L
1	Extract records automatically when criteria in cells is changes.											
2	Criteria:	Date	Date	Region		Count						
3		2/1/12	5/31/13	East		2						
5	Date	Region	Customer	Units								
6	7/29/13	West	WFMI	929		**Extract Area:**						
7	2/7/12	East	SW	681		No	Date	Region	Customer	Units		
8	9/23/12	Midwest	K	1393		1	2/7/12	East	SW	681		
9	4/14/12	West	WFMI	530		2	7/26/12	East	WFMI	1058		
10	7/26/12	East	WFMI	1058		3						

Figure IN.3 *When the criteria for record extraction changes often, it can be beneficial to use formulas rather than the Filter feature. The array formula in cell G8 is an efficient solution for extracting with three criteria. See how to create this formula in Chapter 15.*

| B4 | ▼ | : | × | ✓ | fx | =SUMPRODUCT(--(TEXT(ROW(INDIRECT(B2&":"&B3)), "dddd dd")="Friday 13")) |

⯊	A	B	C	D
1	How Many Friday 13th between these two dates?			
2	Start	12/9/2012		
3	End	11/9/2014		
4	Count How Many Fri, 13ths:	3		

Figure IN.4 *As shown in cell B4, this array formula does the seemingly impossible, counting how many "Friday the 13ths" there are between a start date and an end date. With the power and beauty of array formulas under your belt, almost anything is possible with formulas! See how to create this formula in Chapter 10.*

Why would Mike excelisfun Girvin write a book about array formulas?

Here are some potential difficulties with writing a book about the topic of Excel array formulas:

- It's a niche topic.
- It's a very difficult topic.
- Microsoft doesn't provide much documentation about array formulas.
- Excel users disagree about what an array formula is.
- There is no systematic listing of all the aspects of array formulas, and there is not a good set of rules or guidelines for array formulas.

Why would I, Mike excelisfun Girvin, write a book about Excel array formulas—especially when there are hundreds of Excel masters who are much smarter than I about Excel and Excel array formulas? As I always say at YouTube, "I am just a guy having fun with Excel!" I've written this book because I have long wished for a book that systematically lists the aspects, elements and guidelines for array formulas. What I have done in this book is just gather up what I have learned over the years from places like the MrExcel Message Board (mrexcel.com/forum) and other Excel sites, and I've tried to present the details I have gleaned in a systematic way. I do not promise that this book tells the complete story of Excel array formulas or even that it is 100% correct, but I do promise that I have done my best to present what I have learned about Excel array formulas.

About the Book

This book is similar to the first book I wrote, *Slaying Excel Dragons*, in that it is a story from beginning to end about efficiencies in Excel.

Whereas in *Slaying* I wrote about how to build a foundation of basic skills across all of Excel, this book concentrates on a set of guidelines for how to create efficient array formulas. That said, this book actually covers three topics: formulas, advanced formulas, and array formulas. Because an array formula is just a more narrow type of advanced formula or formula, much of what this book says can be applied across all three categories of formulas. This is good news because it means that this book is not just about building efficient array formulas, but it is about building efficient solutions using formulas. Further, throughout the book I compare and contrast a given potential array formula solution against other Excel features, such as filtering, PivotTables, and non-array formulas. This will help you understand the context or situation in which array formulas may be the most efficient solution.

Finally, this book is *not* just a listing of cool array formulas or of readymade solutions. Instead, it is a story that starts at the point of "no knowledge of array formulas" and builds, piece by piece, toward an endpoint of "now we have a set of guidelines and rules we can use to build our own array formulas." To this end, this book gradually builds a set of "Array Formula Efficiency Rules," one by one, which Chapter 14 lists all in one place. Then, in later chapters, you'll be able to create truly mega Excel formulas. In the early parts of this book, I give a lot of detail and move slowly through each topic, especially about how each individual part of a formula is working. As the book moves along, I give fewer details, move more quickly and show more examples.

A final note about this book: I think that I have done a less than stellar job with the writing in this book. I believe that sometimes as I was writing I got lost in the complexities of the topic and wrote in a somewhat less than optimal manner. However, if you can wade through the less than stellar writing, there are many valuable formula lessons in this book that can improve your formula creation abilities.

Files That Accompany the Book

As you read this book, you'll want to follow along with the examples, in many cases trying them out yourself. To make this easier for you, I've posted the Excel files that contain the finished examples from this book online. You can get them from the "Ctrl+Shift+Enter: Mastering Excel Array Formulas" section of this website:

http://people.highline.edu/mgirvin/excelisfun.htm

At this site you can download a zipped folder named FilesForCtrlShiftEnterBook. After you download the zipped folder, you will have to unzip the folder to get access to the files inside the zipped folder.

Inside the downloaded folder is a file named CtrlShiftEnterBookFinishedFile.xlsm. This file has all the finished examples from this book. To find the worksheet in this workbook that relates to the example you are interested in, simply navigate to the worksheet that has the same name as the figure number in the book. For example, if the figure number is IN.1, the sheet name you should look for is IN.1.

In addition to the workbook with the finished examples from the book, I've made available a number of other files with large data sets that have timing results for different formulas. In each section of the book that discusses timing results, I've provided the name of the corresponding file or files you should use.

> **Note:** If you are used to watching excelisfun videos at YouTube or if you have read the book *Slaying Excel Dragons*, please note that there is no Start file for this book. This is because most of the examples in the book are already completed for you. If you want to try the formulas as shown in the book, a good strategy would be to copy the file with the finished examples and then delete the formulas from the cells before you try the formulas on your own.

> **Note:** I have published both a book and a DVD titled *Ctrl+Shift+Enter: Mastering Excel Array Formulas*. The files that go along with this book and that DVD are not the same files. If you are reading the book, download the files that go along with the book.

The *Ctrl+Shift+Enter: Mastering Excel Array Formulas* DVD

The DVD *Ctrl+Shift+Enter: Mastering Excel Array Formulas* is a separate product from this book. The two products cover the same broad topics related to creating efficient array formulas. However, the video has kinetic visuals of how array formula work and less detail than the book. The book has a more complete story and systematic presentation of array formulas. If you really want to master array formulas, study both the book and the DVD.

Who This Book Is For

Because this is an advanced Excel formula book, it assumes that you have the basics of how to build formulas under your belt. In Chapter 1, I list the key formula concepts that you should be familiar with in order to get the most out of this book.

> **Note:** If you need a full refresher course on all the aspects of Excel formulas, pick up my DVD *Ctrl+Shift+Enter: Mastering Excel Array Formulas*, just described. The first video on this DVD is a one-hour powerhouse of 31 examples that can quickly get you up to speed before you move on to array formulas.

Special Formatting of Cells with Formulas, Labels, and Raw Data

All the Excel examples in this book use fill colors to indicate cell contents:

- A pale green fill color indicates a cell that contains a formula.
- A dark blue fill color indicates a cell that contains a label.
- Cells that contain raw data or formula inputs have no fill color added.

I follow these conventions here and in my YouTube videos to make it clear which cells contain formulas, labels, and raw data. For tasks outside this learning process, other formatting conventions are usually preferred. Although this book is in black and white, you can see this convention in the Excel workbook that accompanies the book.

Remembering the Old Conditional Sum Wizard

I still remember the first array formula I created, using the Conditional Sum Wizard dialog box from the old Tools menu in earlier versions of Excel. In those days, I could get the wizard to work and get the correct result. But after the formula was entered into the cell through the dialog box, mysterious curly braces would appear in the cell with the formula. Then if I tried to edit the cell without using the Conditional Sum Wizard dialog box, I would get an error. Looking back at the Conditional Sum Wizard dialog box now, I can see that the dialog box itself was pretty easy to follow, but it didn't mention the term *array formula*, and it didn't mention the need to enter Ctrl+-Shift+Enter with an array formula. If only there had been better instructions.

Hopefully this book will provide better guidance than the old Conditional Sum Wizard. To start, let's move on to Chapter 1 and take a look at the key concepts involved in building formulas.

Chapter 1: Formula Basics

Excel Files

To follow along with the examples in this chapter, you can download the accompanying files, as explained in the Introduction.

What This Book Assumes

This book assumes that you already know how to create formulas. This chapter presents a condensed list of what you should know before starting on the examples in this book. If you feel that you need a review, check out the free Excel Basics Series at the excelisfun channel at YouTube (https://www.youtube.com/course?list=EC3FBEE51974F03CCF) or purchase the DVD *Ctrl+-Shift+Enter: Mastering Excel Array Formulas* (a separate product from this book). The first video on this DVD contains 31 examples that demonstrate all the formula basics you need in order to succeed with this book.

Excel's Golden Rule

Excel has a Golden Rule: If formula input data can change, put it in a cell and refer to it with cell references. If data will not change, you can hard code it into a formula. Examples of data that does not change are things like 24 hours in a day and the number 1 in a formula to calculate the complement of a tax rate.

The Golden Rule is the original idea that Dan Bricklin and Bob Frankston had in mind when they invented the first spreadsheet, VisiCalc. Formulas instantly update when you change the value in a cell; this is the leading advantage of formulas over other features in Excel, such as filters and PivotTables.

Formula Elements

To become skilled in creating array formulas, you need to understand the different elements that can go into formulas. Here is a list of the types of things you can put into formulas:

- Equal sign (starts every formula as the first character in a cell)
- Cell references (including defined names, sheet references, workbook references, and table nomenclature)
- Math operators
- Comparative operators
- The join operator (&)
- Functions (for example, IF, MATCH, INDEX, COUNTIF, and so on)
- Function argument elements (such as a 0 in the third argument of MATCH to tell the function to do an "exact match" lookup)
- Numbers (if the number will not change)
- Text within quotation marks (for example, "The PMT is")
- Array constants (for example, {1,2,3})

Math Operators

You use math operators to make math calculations. Here is a list of the math operators in Excel:

Operator	Description
+	**Addition**
-	**Subtraction** or **negation**
*	**Multiplication**
/	**Division**
^	**Raising to an exponent**
( )	**Parentheses**

Comparative Operators

You use comparative operators to make comparative calculations. Here is a list of the comparative operators in Excel:

Operator	Description
=	**Equal**: Are two things equal?
<>	**Not equal**: Are two things not equal?
>	**Greater than**: Is the thing on the left greater than the thing on the right?
>=	**Greater than or equal to**: Is the thing on the left greater than or equal to the thing on the right?
<	**Less than**: Is the thing on the left less than the thing on the right?
<=	**Less than or equal to**: Is the thing on the left less than or equal to the thing on the right?

Types of Formulas

When designing Excel formula solutions, it is useful to have a clear understanding of the different types of formulas you can create in Excel. The following are some of the types of formulas:

- A **calculating formula** calculates a number answer (for example, formulas that do addition).
- A **logical formula**\ gives you a logical value, either TRUE or FALSE (for example, formulas that say whether two accounts are in balance).
- A **text formula** delivers a word or text to a cell (for example, a formula that uses the LEFT function).
- A **lookup formula** looks up an item in a table (for example, looking up a price for a product).
- An **array formula** is an advanced formula that acts on an array (range) rather than on individual cell references, or a formula that delivers more than one item. Array formulas can deliver results that are calculating, logical, text, or lookup.

How Formulas Calculate: Order of Precedence in Excel

Understanding how Excel evaluates or calculates formulas is particularly important when you start building large formulas that have many elements. Excel evaluates or calculates a formula in the following order:

1	**Parentheses**: ( )
	Example: (10-4)*5 = 6*5 = 30
2	**Reference operators**: colon, space, comma
	Example of a colon to indicate a range of cells: =SUM(A1:A4)
	Example of the intersection operator: =E12:G12 F10:F15 (retrieve what is in F12)
	Example of a comma (union): =SUM(E10:G10,E14:G14)
3	**Negation**: -
	Example: = -2^4 = 16
	Example: = -(2^4) = -16
	Example: --2+1 = 3
4	**Converts**: **%** (1% to .01)
5	**Exponents**: (^)
	Example: 4^(1/2) = 2
	Example: 3^2 = 9
6	**Multiplication** (*) and **Division** (/), left to right
7	**Addition** (+) and **Subtraction** (-), left to right
8	**Ampersand**: &
9	**Comparative symbols**: =, <>, >=, <=, <, >

Number Formatting Is a Façade

One of the most common mistakes that Excel users make concerns number formatting. What you see is not always what is in the cell, so it is crucial to understand number formatting if you are to become really good with formulas. Keep in mind the following points:

- What you see on the face of a spreadsheet can be different from the underlying number in the cell.
- There can be a disconnect between what you see in a cell with your eyes and what is actually stored in the cell as content.
- Calculations are made on the underlying number, not on the number format that you see on the face of the spreadsheet. For example, you can use the Decrease Decimal button to show fewer decimal places, but that does not remove the decimal places for calculation purposes. As another example, dates such as 12/1/2012 are serial numbers. Although you see 12/1/2012 on the face of the spreadsheet, the cell actually contains the serial number 41244. Formulas calculate on the underlying serial number 41244, not on the date 12/1/2012.

Default Alignment for Data in Excel

Understanding default alignment in Excel can be very helpful for tracking down errors and for understanding how complex formulas work. Here is a list of the default alignment for data:

1. **Text** is left-aligned.

2. **Numbers** are right-aligned.

3. **Logical values**, or **Boolean data**, are center-aligned.

4. **Error values** are center-aligned.

Chapter Summary

Having a grasp of the formula concepts listed in this chapter will greatly help you understand the remaining chapters in this book, especially when you get to the larger, more complicated mega-formulas.

In this book's Introduction, I mentioned that this book builds a series of "Array Formula Efficiency Rules" to give you a set of guidelines for creating efficient array formulas. Each one appears as a sidebar in the chapter where it's first discussed. The first rule appears below. Use it and the rest of the rules throughout this book to become an Excel formula master. And remember that you can find a complete list of the rules in Chapter 14.

Array Formula Efficiency Rule 1

In order to be proficient at creating formula solutions, you must know (1) Excel's Golden Rule, (2) the formula elements, (3) the math and comparative operators, (4) the types of formulas, (5) Excel's order of precedence when calculating formulas, (6) number formatting principles, and (7) default alignment in Excel.

In this chapter you learned some of the formula prerequisites that you should understand before you move forward in this book. Chapter 2 introduces array formulas.

Chapter 2: Introduction to Array Formulas

Excel Files

To follow along with the examples in this chapter, you can download the accompanying files, as explained in the Introduction.

What Is an Array?

An **array** is a collection of two or more items. This is the logical starting point for the book. Everything else follows from this.

Array Formula Efficiency Rule 2

An *array* is a collection of two or more items.

The Types of Arrays in Excel

There are three types of arrays in Excel:

- A **reference array** contains more than one cell. Examples include a range of cells, a worksheet reference, and a defined name.
- An **array created by a formula element**, also called a *resultant array*, is an array of items created by the array operation.
- An **array constant** is an array of values hard coded into a formula.

Array Formula Efficiency Rule 3

There are three types of arrays in Excel: a reference array, an array created by a formula element, and an array constant.

What Is An Array Formula?

An *array formula* is a formula that contains an operation (math, comparative, join, or function argument) on an array of items rather than on single items, and, the operation delivers a resultant array of items rather than a single item. This operation is called an *array operation* and is distinguish from an *aggregate operation*, which delivers a single item. The resultant array of items (also called an array created by a formula element) can be used as a formula element in a larger formula, or it can be the final answer that the array formula delivers to a range of cells. The final answer from an array formula can either be a single item or an array of items.

Array Formula Efficiency Rule 4

An *array formula* is a formula that contains an operation on an array of items rather than on single items, and, the operation delivers a resultant array of items rather than a single item.

Performing an Operation on an Array of Items Rather Than on Single Items

To understand what it means to perform an operation on an array of items rather than on single items, let's first look at an operation on single items. Figure 2.1 shows a table of opening and closing stock prices. The goal of the formula in this case is to calculate the change between the close prices and open prices.

	A	B	C	D	E	F
1	Calculate change in stock value.					
2	Stock	Date	Open	Close	Change	
3	GOOG	10/1/12	759	762	3	< Formula =D3-C3
4	GOOG	10/2/12	765	757	-8	
5	GOOG	10/3/12	756	763	7	
6	GOOG	10/4/12	762	768	6	
7						
8				Max	7	

Figure 2.1 *A math operation on single items.*

The formula in Figure 2.1 operates on single items. Here are the details:
- Cell E3 contains a formula that subtracts the value in cell C3 from the value in D3.
- The operation is the math operation subtraction.
- The single items being operated on are the numbers in cells D3 and C3.
- This is not an array formula because the operation being performed is being performed on single items only, and the result from the operation is a single item.

Figure 2.2 shows another table of opening and closing stock prices. In this case, the formula goal is to calculate the maximum stock value change over the four-day period.

D8		:	× ✓ f_x	{=MAX(D3:D6-C3:C6)}				

	A	B	C	D	E	F	G	H
1	Calculate maximum stock change.							
2	Stock	Date	Open	Close				
3	GOOG	10/1/12	759	762				
4	GOOG	10/2/12	765	757				
5	GOOG	10/3/12	756	763				
6	GOOG	10/4/12	762	768				
7								
8			MAX	7	< Formula {=MAX(D3:D6-C3:C6)}			

Figure 2.2 *A math operation on an array of items.*

The formula in Figure 2.2 operates on an array of items. Here are the details:

- Cell D8 contains a formula that subtracts the values in the range C3:C6 from the values in D3:D6.
- The operation is the math operation subtraction.
- The two arrays being operated on are the numbers in the ranges D3:D6 and C3:C6.
- This is an array formula because the operation is being performed directly on an array of items. I always think of it as "Is the operator touching the array?" (The function argument operation and array functions examples later in the book are slight variations on this idea.) In this case, the subtraction operator is touching the range (an array), and therefore it is performing an operation on an array. In addition, as you will see in the next section, this operation will produce a resultant array of numbers.

Here is the comparison between operations on single items and operations on arrays:

This formula contains an operation on single items: =D3-C3
This formula contains an operation on two arrays: D3:D6-C3:C6

Let's now move on and examine the previous two examples in more detail.

First Example: Single-Cell Array Formula or Helper Column?

In Figure 2.3, which shows a table of opening and closing stock prices, the formula goal is to calculate the maximum stock value change over the four-day period

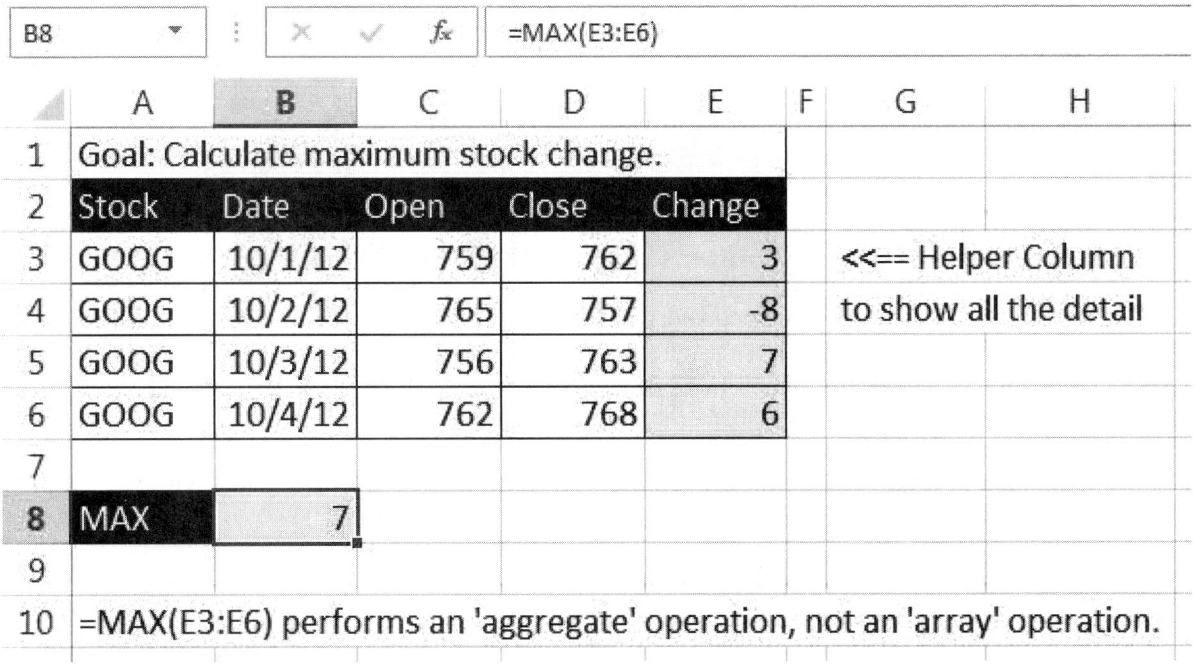

Figure 2.3 *If the goal is to see all the individual calculations and then calculate the maximum change, using a helper column is a great idea.*

Figure 2.3 shows four individual formula calculations made in the Change column. This column is called a **helper column** because it helps you get the values needed to calculate the maximum stock change. In cell B8, the MAX function looks through the values 3, -8, 7, and 6 and picks out the maximum value, which is 7. This calculation made by the MAX function is called an **aggregate operation** because it looks through all the values and calculates one answer; it is not an array operation, even though it deals with more than one item.

If your project requirements mandate that you show all the individual changes, then the helper column and the MAX function aggregate calculation is a great solution. But what if you do not want to see all the detail, and you just want to calculate the maximum change? Or what if you have thousands of rows of data, and you cannot afford to use the spreadsheet real estate to create an extra column? In such a situation, it would be useful to have a single-cell formula solution.

How do you get *all* those individual stock change calculations into a single-cell formula? Look again at Figure 2.3 and notice that the current MAX function is looking at the values 3, -8, 7, and 6. If you could create that helper column in your single-cell array formula, you would have your solution. With an array calculation, you can accomplish exactly that!

	A	B	C	D	E
1	Goal: Calculate maximum stock change.				
2	Stock	Date	Open	Close	Change
3	GOOG	10/1/12	759.05	761.78	2.73
4	GOOG	10/2/12	765.2	756.99	-8.21
5	GOOG	10/3/12	755.72	762.5	6.78
6	GOOG	10/4/12	762.75	768.05	5.3
7					
8	MAX	=MAX(D3:D6-C3:C6)			
9		MAX(**number1**, [number2], ...)			

Figure 2.4 *Creating an array calculation in the MAX function number1 argument.*

As shown in Figure 2.4, when you create the array calculation, you highlight the entire Close column range, then type a subtraction operator, and then highlight the entire Open column range inside the MAX function's number1 argument.

Using the "Evaluate Formula Element" Trick to Show the Resultant Array

Before you enter a formula, you want to prove to yourself that the array calculation delivers a resultant array of numbers that simulates the helper column shown in Figure 2.3. In order to prove this to yourself, you can evaluate your array calculation while the formula is still in Edit mode.

As shown in Figures 2.5, the first step in evaluating the array operation is to highlight the entire array operation. You do this by clicking the number1 argument in the ScreenTip (the gray prompt below the formula being created in Edit mode).

8	MAX	=MAX(D3:D6-C3:C6)
9		MAX(**number1**, [number2], ...)

Figure 2.5 **I**n *order to highlight the array operation while the formula is in Edit mode, click the number1 argument in the ScreenTip.*

Goal: Calculate maximum stock change.					
Stock	Date	Open	Close	Change	
GOOG	10/1/12	759	762	3	<<== Helper Column
GOOG	10/2/12	765	757	-8	to show all the detail
GOOG	10/3/12	756	763	7	
GOOG	10/4/12	762	768	6	
MAX	=MAX({3;-8;7;6})				
	MAX(**number1**, [number2], ...)				

Figure 2.6 *In order to see the resultant array of numbers created by the array operation, you press the F9 key to evaluate the selected formula element.*

As shown in Figure 2.6, the next step is to press the F9 key. You do this to evaluate the selected formula element. When you evaluate the array operation, you can see that the array operation *does* simulate the values in the helper column. That is amazing! What a space saver! You have created the numbers you need inside the formula without using extra cells in the spreadsheet.

Notice that the formula element D3:D6-C3:C6 creates the array of values {3;-8;7;6}. Remember from the list of the different types of arrays you can have in Excel that {3;-8;7;6} is an example of an array created by a formula element; it is the resultant array delivered by the array operation.

> **Note:** In Chapter 7 you will learn about the syntax used when the formula element D3:D6-C3:C6 is evaluated to {3;-8;7;6}. The term used to describe this array of values is **array constant**. In an array constant, curly braces house the array, a semicolon indicates a row, and a comma indicates a column.

However, after you press the F9 key, you must immediately undo the formula element evaluation because you do not want to leave the resultant array hard coded into the formula. As shown in Figure 2.7, you undo the evaluation by using the keyboard shortcut for undo: Ctrl+Z.

8	MAX	=MAX(D3:D6-C3:C6)	
9		MAX(**number1**, [number2], ...)	

Figure 2.7 *Don't forget to undo the evaluation by using Ctrl+Z.*

This ability to evaluate a formula element and see what the resultant array will be before you enter the formula into the cell is a monumentally important trick for creating array formulas. It allows you to check whether your formula creation is on the right track. I like to call this trick the "Evaluate Formula Element" trick. These are the steps in the trick:

1. Select the formula element.

2. Press F9.

3. Look at the resultant array and check whether your formula creation is on the right track.

4. Press Ctrl+Z to undo the evaluation.

This trick is particularly useful with mega-formulas that have many formula elements.

Array Formula Efficiency Rule 5

You can use the Evaluate Formula Element trick to see what an array operation evaluates to before you enter the formula into the cell by following these steps: (1) Select the formula element, (2) press F9, (3) look at the resultant array and check to see if the formula creation is on the right track, and (4) press Ctrl+Z to undo the evaluation.

By using the Evaluate Formula Element trick, you can see the simulated column of values in a single cell. With an array operation, you can create a column of values in a single cell. This ability to skip over a helper column and create an array of values in a single cell can be revolutionary for formula creation: It means that whenever you have a column of calculations and you either don't care about all the individual calculations or you can't afford the spreadsheet real estate, it is almost certainly possible to just do away with the column of calculations and instead create an array calculation in a single cell.

Later in this book, you will consider what pushing the calculations from a helper column to a single cell will do to calculation time.

Array Formula Efficiency Rule 6

Whenever you have a column of calculations and you either don't care about all the individual calculations or you can't afford the spreadsheet real estate, it is almost certainly possible to just do away with the column of calculations and instead create an array calculation in a single cell. The caveat is that you must also consider formula calculation time for single-cell calculations.

Entering an Array Formula into a Cell

In the example you've been working on in this chapter, once you have proven to yourself that the array calculation simulates the column of stock value changes, you need to enter into the cell the MAX function with its array calculation in the number1 argument. Then you press Enter. Figure 2.8 shows that you get a #VALUE! error. By sending you this #VALUE! error, Excel is telling you that you did not enter the array formula correctly. (Yes, there are correct and incorrect ways of entering an array formula into a cell!)

8	MAX	#VALUE!
9		

Figure 2.8 *Using Enter to put the MAX function with its array calculation into the cell does not work.*

You need to consider whether the function argument that the array calculation sits in can innately handle array operations. (Only four functions have arguments that can innately handle array operations without Ctrl+Shift+Enter: SUMPRODUCT, LOOKUP, AGGREGATE, and INDEX. You'll learn more about them later in this chapter.)

Figure 2.9 shows that the array calculation is housed in the number1 argument in the MAX function. The number1 argument in the MAX function is not programmed to innately handle array operations. Therefore, you must tell Excel that this argument contains an array calculation and that you would like Excel to perform that array calculation. You say this to Excel by using the special keystroke Ctrl+Shift+Enter. With the formula in Edit mode, the best way to enact this keystroke is to hold down Ctrl and Shift and then press the Enter key.

Figure 2.9 *The array calculation is housed in the number1 argument in the MAX function.*

| B8 | ▼ | : | × | ✓ | *fx* | {=MAX(D3:D6-C3:C6)} |

	A	B	C	D	E
1	Goal: Calculate maximum stock change.				
2	Stock	Date	Open	Close	Change
3	GOOG	10/1/12	759	762	3
4	GOOG	10/2/12	765	757	-8
5	GOOG	10/3/12	756	763	7
6	GOOG	10/4/12	762	768	6
7					
8	MAX	7			

Figure 2.10 *For an array calculation in the number1 argument in the MAX function, you must enter the formula with Ctrl+Shift+Enter.*

Figure 2.10 shows that when you use Ctrl+Shift+Enter, you successfully enter the formula into cell B8. You can see that the MAX function correctly selects the value 7 from among the values 3, -8, 7, and 6.

After you enter an array formula with Ctrl+Shift+Enter, you should immediately shift your eyes up to the formula bar and look to determine whether a left curly brace has been placed at the beginning of the formula and a right curly bracket has been placed at the end of the formula. Figure 2.11 shows what the formula should look like after you press Ctrl+Shift+Enter. Notice the curly braces in the formula. How did those curly braces get there, if you didn't type them in? Excel automatically places those curly braces when you press Ctrl+Shift+Enter. By placing those curly braces, Excel tells you that it understands that this is a formula with an array calculation and that you would like Excel to calculate it correctly.

{=MAX(D3:D6-C3:C6)}

Figure 2.11 *The curly braces indicate that Excel knows that this formula contains an array calculation.*

In terms of entering an array formula into a cell, so far you have learned the following:

- If the function argument does not innately handle array operations, you must enter the formula with Ctrl+Shift+Enter.
- After you enter a formula with Ctrl+Shift+Enter, Excel places curly braces at the beginning and end of the formula. If you try to type in the curly braces, they will appear as text, not as part of an array formula.
- If you don't use Ctrl+Shift+Enter, you may get a #VALUE! error.

Note: If you press Ctrl+Shift+Enter on a non-array formula your formula will calculate correctly and it will have curly braces around it which are not necessary.

But this is not the whole story. The #VALUE! error is not the only answer you can get if you forget to use Ctrl+Shift+Enter. Figure 2.12 shows the formula =MAX(D3:D6-C3:C6) entered into eight cells. Seven of the cells contain formulas entered *without* using Ctrl+Shift+Enter. Only in cell B8 is the array formula entered correctly with Ctrl+Shift+Enter. The formulas entered next to the Open and Close columns of data show numeric answers from a process called **implicit intersection**. All these answers are incorrect except for the one cell that corresponds to the opening and closing numbers that calculate the correct maximum stock change. If the formula is entered without Ctrl+Shift+Enter in a cell that is not next to the Open and Close columns of data, a #VALUE! error is displayed. This phenomenon happens on the left or right of a vertical data set and above or below a horizontal data set.

A common array formula error is to forgetfully enter an array formula (that requires Ctrl+Shift+Enter) next to a vertical data set *without* using Ctrl+Shift+Enter and then to mistakenly interpret the numeric answer as correct. However, seeing a numeric answer or not seeing a #VALUE! error is not proof that a formula has been entered correctly. For a formula that requires Ctrl+Shift+Enter, curly braces are the best proof that the formula has been entered correctly. To avoid the pitfall of implicit intersection, it is always best to immediately check the formula bar to see if the curly braces are in place.

	A	B	C	D	E	F	G
1	Goal: Calculate maximum stock change.						
2	Stock	Date	Open	Close		#VALUE!	< Formula =MAX(D3:D6-C3:C6)
3	GOOG	10/1/12	759	762		3	< Formula =MAX(D3:D6-C3:C6)
4	GOOG	10/2/12	765	757		-8	< Formula =MAX(D3:D6-C3:C6)
5	GOOG	10/3/12	756	763		7	< Formula =MAX(D3:D6-C3:C6)
6	GOOG	10/4/12	762	768		6	< Formula =MAX(D3:D6-C3:C6)
7						#VALUE!	< Formula =MAX(D3:D6-C3:C6)
8	MAX	7	< Formula {=MAX(D3:D6-C3:C6)}				
9							
10			#VALUE!	< Formula =MAX(D3:D6-C3:C6)			

Figure 2.12 *Be careful of an implicit intersection answer when creating array formulas. Only the formula in cell B8 is correct.*

Notes About the Formula =MAX(D3:D6-C3:C6)

The following table shows a summary of the MAX array formula you just learned about.

Impetus for Creating an Array Formula:

To save space, you want a single-cell formula with no helper column.

You don't need all the detail, just the one number that is biggest.

Calculation Summary:

1. =MAX(D3:D6-C3:C6)

The two arrays are the ranges D3:D6 and C3:C6.

You are performing a math operation (subtraction) on two arrays.

This is an array formula because you are performing an operation on an array, and the operation produces a resultant array.

2. =MAX({762;757;763;768}-{759;765;756;762})

The two columns need to have corresponding numbers subtracted.

3. =MAX({759-762;765-757;756-763;762-768;})

The corresponding numbers are subtracted.

4. =MAX({3;-8;7;6})

The array operation D3:D6-C3:C6 evaluates to {3;-8;7;6}.

The array operation D3:D6-C3:C6 delivers the resultant array {3;-8;7;6}.

{3;-8;7;6} is an example of an array created by a formula element.

The formula element D3:D6-C3:C6 delivers the array {3;-8;7;6} to the MAX function.

5. The formula delivers the single value 7.

Entering a Formula into a Cell:

The array calculation is located in the number1 argument in the MAX function. This argument is not innately programmed to handle array operations. To get the array calculation to calculate correctly, you must press Ctrl+Shift+Enter to enter the formula into the cell.

This is the formula as it appears in the formula bar after you enter it with Ctrl+Shift+Enter: {=MAX(D3:D6-C3:C6)}

If you do not use Ctrl+Shift+Enter, you will get a #VALUE! error or potentially an incorrect answer caused by implicit intersection.

Conclusion:

If you do not want to use a helper column and you don't need to see all the detail, using this array formula is a great option.

Notes:

In Chapter 23, you will see an alternative to using the MAX array formula that uses the new Excel 2010 function AGGREGATE.

In Chapter 7 you will learn about the syntax used when the formula element D3:D6-C3:C6 is evaluated to {3;-8;7;6}. This is an array constant, and you will see that curly braces house the array, a semicolon indicates a row, and a comma indicates a column.

For the array formula =MAX(D3:D6-C3:C6), you had to enter the formula using Ctrl+Shift+Enter and then verify that the formula was entered correctly by looking at the formula bar to see if the curly braces were automatically added. But must you always enter array formulas by using Ctrl+Shift+Enter? No.

Four functions have arguments that can innately handle array operations without Ctrl+Shift+Enter: SUMPRODUCT, LOOKUP, AGGREGATE, and INDEX. To complete our discussions about how to enter an array formula into a cell, you need to understand how these types of functions handle array operations. The next section looks at SUMPRODUCT. (You'll learn much more about SUMPRODUCT and these other functions in later chapters.)

SUMPRODUCT Array Operations

Figure 2.13 shows the same data set you have been working with, but in this example, you would like to add all the stock changes rather than find the maximum stock change. Figure 2.13 shows how you could use the non-array formula =SUM(E3:E6) and a helper column. This method is good if you want to see all the detail and you can afford the spreadsheet space.

Figure 2.14 shows how you could use the formula =SUMPRODUCT(D3:D6-C3:C6). This method is good if you don't need to see all the detail or you can't afford you use the space in the spreadsheet.

	A	B	C	D	E	F	G
1	Goal: Add all stock changes.						
2	Stock	Date	Open	Close	Change		
3	GOOG	10/1/12	759	762	3		<<== Helper Column
4	GOOG	10/2/12	765	757	-8		to show all the detail
5	GOOG	10/3/12	756	763	7		
6	GOOG	10/4/12	762	768	6		
7							
8	Add		8	< Formula =SUM(E3:E6)			

Figure 2.13 *To see all detail, you can use a helper column and the SUM function.*

B8	▼	:	×	✓	fx	=SUMPRODUCT(D3:D6-C3:C6)

	A	B	C	D	E	F
1	Goal: Add all stock changes.					
2	Stock	Date	Open	Close		
3	GOOG	10/1/12	759	762		
4	GOOG	10/2/12	765	757		
5	GOOG	10/3/12	756	763		
6	GOOG	10/4/12	762	768		
7						
8	Add		8	< Formula =SUMPRODUCT(D3:D6-C3:C6)		

Figure 2.14 *If your goal is to add the individual stock changes in a single cell, the SUMPRODUCT array formula is great.*

Figure 2.15 gives you a closer look at the formula bar for the SUMPRODUCT formula in Figure 2.14. What do you notice? That's right: There are no curly braces!

fx		=SUMPRODUCT(D3:D6-C3:C6

Figure 2.15 *No curly braces and no Ctrl+Shift+Enter for SUMPRODUCT!*

In Figure 2.16, notice that the same array calculation that you used in the earlier MAX function is now located in the array1 argument of the SUMPRODUCT function. The difference here is that the array1 argument of the SUMPRODUCT function is programmed to innately handle array operations without requiring you to use Ctrl+Shift+Enter. You can simply create the formula and use Enter as you would do with any other formula.

The SUMPRODUCT function normally takes two or more arrays and multiplies the arrays and then adds. But because you are using only one argument here, SUMPRODUCT simply calculates the array operation and then adds the results.

Figure 2.16 *The SUMPRODUCT array argument can handle array operations without Ctrl+Shift+Enter.*

> **Note**: SUMPRODUCT is a function that normally takes two or more arrays (placed in the arguments array1, array2, and so on) and first multiplies the arrays (the PRODUCT part of SUMPRODUCT) and then adds the results (the SUM part of SUMPRODUCT). Because you are using only one argument here, you are not utilizing the PRODUCT part of SUMPRODUCT. However, you are using SUMPRODUCT to house your array calculation so that you don't have to use Ctrl+Shift+Enter to get the array calculation to calculate correctly.

The next section compares the SUMPRODUCT function and the SUM function.

Comparing SUMPRODUCT and SUM for Array Calculations

Figure 2.17 shows that you can use the SUM function with an array calculation, but because the number1 argument in the SUM function is *not* innately programmed to handle array operations, the formula requires Ctrl+Shift+Enter. If you have a choice between using SUM or SUMPRODUCT, as shown in Figure 2.17, it is more efficient to use the SUMPRODUCT version. Why? Beginners and advanced users alike occasionally forget to use Ctrl+Shift+Enter and get either an error or a potentially incorrect answer due to implicit intersection. Because of this, you should be polite to yourself (and other users who may use the spreadsheet) and use the version of the array formula that does not require Ctrl+Shift+Enter.

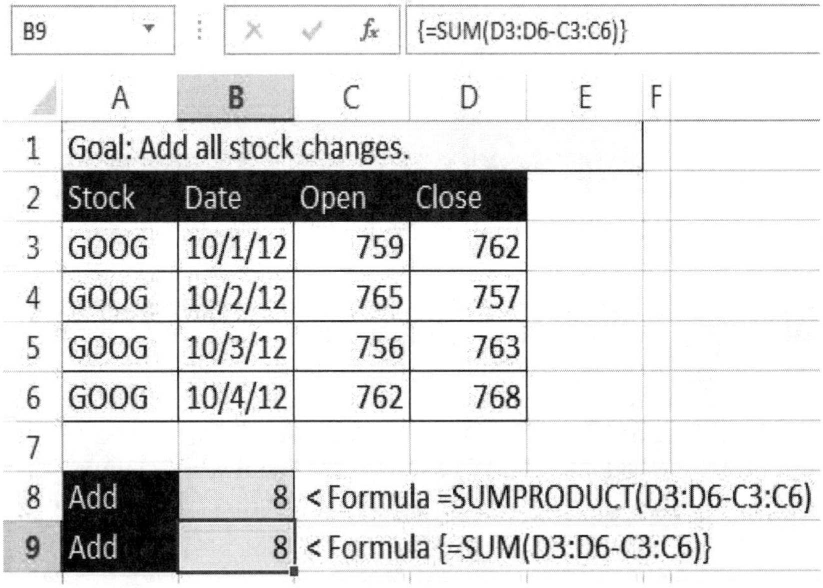

Figure 2.17 *SUM requires Ctrl+Shift+Enter; SUMPRODUCT does not.*

Array Formula Efficiency Rule 7

If you have a choice between two equally efficient array formulas and one requires Ctrl+Shift+Enter and one does not, you should choose the one that does not require Ctrl+Shift+Enter. A formula that does not require Ctrl+Shift+Enter does not run the risk of getting a #VALUE! or implicit intersection error.

Notes About the Formula =SUMPRODUCT(D3:D6-C3:C6)

The following table presents a summary of the SUMPRODUCT array formula you just learned about.

Impetus for Creating an Array Formula:
To save space, you want a single-cell formula and no helper column. You don't need all the detail but just want to add the differences.
Calculation Summary:
1. =SUMPRODUCT(D3:D6-C3:C6)
The two arrays are the ranges D3:D6 and C3:C6. You are performing a math operation (subtraction) on two arrays. This is an array formula because you are performing an operation on an array, and the operation produces a resultant array. Because you are adding the results of an array calculation, you choose to use SUMPRODUCT rather than SUM so that you don't have to use Ctrl+Shift+Enter.
2. =SUMPRODUCT({762;757;763;768}-{759;765;756;762})
3. =SUMPRODUCT({762-759;757-765;763-756;768-762})
4. =SUMPRODUCT({3;-8;7;6})
The array operation D3:D6-C3:C6 delivers the resultant array {3;-8;7;6}. {3;-8;7;6} is an example of an array created by a formula element. The formula element D3:D6-C3:C6 delivers the array {3;-8;7;6} to the SUMPRODUCT function.
5. The formula delivers the single value 8.
Entering a Formula into a Cell:
The array1 argument in the SUMPRODUCT function is programmed to handle array operations without Ctrl+Shift+Enter. Ctrl+Shift+Enter is not required when entering this formula into a cell.
Conclusion:
If you do not want to use a helper column and you don't need to see all the detail, this array formula is a great option.
Note:
SUMPRODUCT is a function that normally takes two or more arrays (placed in the arguments array1, array2, and so on) and first multiplies the arrays (the PRODUCT part of SUMPRODUCT) and then adds the results (the SUM part of SUMPRODUCT). Because you are using only one argument here, you are not utilizing the PRODUCT part of SUMPRODUCT. However, you are using SUMPRODUCT to house your array calculation so that you don't have to use Ctrl+Shift+Enter to get the array calculation to calculate correctly.

Later chapters talk much more about SUMPRODUCT and the other functions that do not need Ctrl+Shift+Enter. For now, realize that you decide whether to use Ctrl+Shift+Enter to enter an array formula based on the function argument that houses the array operation.

Array Formula Efficiency Rule 8

We can formalize the rules for entering an array formula into a cell like this:

- If a function argument does not innately handle array operations and you give it an array operation, you must enter the formula with Ctrl+Shift+Enter. The MAX function's number1 argument is an example of an argument that does not innately handle array operations, and therefore you need to press Ctrl+Shift+Enter when you place an array operation in the number1 argument. The SUMPRODUCT array1 argument is an example of an argument that *does* innately handle array operations and therefore does *not* require you to press Ctrl+Shift+Enter when you place an array operation into the array1 argument.

- After you enter a formula with Ctrl+Shift+Enter, Excel places curly braces at the beginning and end of the formula. If you try to type in these curly braces, they will appear as text, not as part of an array formula.

- If you don't use Ctrl+Shift+Enter for a formula that requires it, you will get a #VALUE! error or a potentially incorrect answer due to implicit intersection.

- Several caveats are discussed in later chapters: (1) Array constants usually do not require Ctrl+Shift+Enter (Chapter 7); (2) IF function array calculations always require Ctrl+Shift+Enter (Chapters 4 and 10); and (3) Defined names that contain array operations do not require Ctrl+Shift+Enter (Chapters 13 and 15).

Using a Helper Column or a Single-Cell Array Formula

In both the MAX function array formula and the SUMPRODUCT function array formula, you have the option of creating a helper column solution or a single-cell array formula. Which is preferred? The answer depends on your goal and the situational demands.

If you want to see all the detail and you can afford the spreadsheet space, the helper column method is preferred. If you cannot afford to use the space for a helper column or you don't want to see all the detail, a single-cell array formula is preferred. Later chapters also consider formula calculation time as a factor in whether to use a single-cell method or a helper column.

Array Formula Efficiency Rule 9

Points to think about if you are trying to decide between a single-cell formula or a helper column that contains a multistep solution:

- Use a helper column or a multistep solution when you want to see all the detail and can afford the real estate.

- Use a single-cell formula to save spreadsheet real estate and when you don't care about all the detail.

- Sometimes helper column solutions calculate more quickly than single-cell array formulas.

Advantages and Disadvantages of Array Formulas

As you progress through this book, you will consider the advantages and disadvantages of array formulas. You will also consider alternatives to each array formula that you consider. The following table lists the most important advantages and disadvantages of array formulas.

Advantages of Array Formulas
Array formulas can sometimes achieve what no other Excel method can achieve without using VBA code.
Array formulas can save spreadsheet space by reducing a multiple-column solution to a single-cell formula.
It is difficult to delete array formulas entered in multiple cells.
Given a desired formula result and the situational demands, an array formula is the best option.

Disadvantages of Array Formulas
Array formulas may slow down formula calculation time for a spreadsheet. This is a concern for spreadsheets that contain many formulas with large numbers of cell references and calculations.
Array formulas sometimes require Ctrl+Shift+Enter. For beginners and advanced users alike, remembering to use Ctrl+Shift+Enter can be difficult.
Other users of a spreadsheet may have a hard time using array formulas.
Not as much information is available about array formulas as about other topics in Excel, such as PivotTables, charts, filter, and so on.
Creating array formulas can sometimes be very complicated.

To determine whether other methods would be more efficient than using array formulas, consider the following (these topics will be covered through the book):

- Is there a built-in function that can do the same thing more efficiently?
- Could you use a helper column formula?
- Could you use a helper cell formula?
- Could you use Filter, Advanced Filter, or a PivotTable?
- Have you timed the various formula options? For spreadsheets that contain many formulas with large numbers of cell references and calculations, you might need to time different formula options to see if one is significantly faster.
- Is there an alternative array formula or non-array formula that is as efficient but does not require Ctrl+Shift+Enter?
- Could you use VBA code instead of an array formula? (This option is beyond the scope of this book.)
- Could you use a PowerPivot instead of an array formula? (This option is beyond the scope of this book.)

Calculation Time for Array Formulas and Large Data Sets

The most significant disadvantage of array formulas is that they can slow down calculation time. Most of the examples in this book are based on small data sets. A small data set makes it easy to see how a formula is put together and how it works. But a small data set is likely to calculate much more quickly than a large one. And the working world is full of large data sets. Therefore, it's important to consider how array formulas behave on larger data sets.

Array formulas make calculations on arrays. If your arrays are large, the time it takes to perform the array calculation will increase. If you are using array formulas on larger data sets, the formulas can contain large ranges of cells and perhaps many array calculations. The more cell references and calculations there are in a formula, the longer it takes for the formula to calculate. Array formulas are by their nature calculation intensive. Further, if the source data or formula inputs change, the formula has to recalculate, further increasing calculation time.

> **Note:** It is possible to set calculations to Manual and then recalculate by clicking the Calculate Now button in the Calculation group of the Formula Ribbon tab.

Given these considerations, if you have a workbook with a large data set that uses array formulas and in which the data changes often, you have the potential for a workbook that calculates slowly. Therefore, when you are considering which array formula to use from among a number of options, it can be advantageous to select the formula that calculates most quickly. Throughout the examples in this book, you will consider calculation time as a criterion for choosing the most efficient formula.

> **Note:** Throughout this book you will consider function choice, helper cells/columns, and array calculation construction to help speed up calculation time.

The *Ctrl+Shift+Enter: Mastering Excel Array Formulas* DVD shows the many timing tests that I performed while preparing this book. In this written book, I simply report the results from timing different formulas rather than go through how to time formulas. However, if you are interested in timing your own formulas, check out this amazing article by Excel MVP Charles Williams: http://msdn.microsoft.com/en-us/library/office/ff700515(v=office.14).aspx#Office2007excelPerf_MakingWorkbooksCalculateFaster. He discusses speeding up formula calculation time and includes free VBA code that you can download and use to time your formulas. Actually, Charles Williams is known as "Fast Excel" because he is a world leader in making spreadsheets go fast! Find him at www.decisionmodels.com.

If you use array formulas often, you should download Williams's code and time your own formulas. This is especially helpful because although in this book you will learn about some general rules for types of formulas that calculate quickly, your individual situation will vary, given factors such as size of data, data type, and computer calculation speed.

Summary of the Importance of Formula Calculation Time
For formulas with many cell references and/or many calculations, calculation time matters.
Timing formulas depends on the particular functions used, the construction of formulas, and the processing power of the computer.
If you are concerned about slow calculation time, it pays to time different methods for your particular situation. As mentioned above, Excel MVP Charles Williams has a great website and free code that is great for timing formulas.

Chapter Summary

In this chapter you have learned the basics of array formulas, including what they are, how to create them, and how to enter them into a cell. The array operation you saw in this chapter is a math operator. Chapter 3 looks at array operations with different operators, such as comparative, join, and function argument operations.

Chapter 3: Math Array Operations

Excel Files

To follow along with the examples in this chapter, you can download the accompanying files, as explained in the Introduction.

Array Operations

Now that you know that array formulas perform operations on arrays, you can consider the different types of array operations that you might see. This chapter looks at math array operations. Chapters 4, 5, and 6 look at comparative array operations, join array operations, and function argument array operations, respectively.

Math Operations

In Chapter 2 you saw an array formula that uses a math operator. Figure 3.1 shows one of the formulas you created. Notice that the array operation consists of an array, a subtraction operator, and an array.

f_x | =SUMPRODUCT(D3:D6-C3:C6)

Figure 3.1 *An array formula to add the differences between two ranges.*

If you were to watch the array calculation in Figure 3.1 evaluate, you would see this:

D3:D6-C3:C6
{762;757;763;768}-{759;765;756;762}
{762-759;757-765;763-756;768-762}
{3;-8;7;6}

Each number in the second array is subtracted from the corresponding number in the first array: four numbers minus four numbers. But what if you had an array of values and you wanted to subtract a single number from an array of numbers? Is this possible? Sure! Let's take a look at how to do this.

A Formula to Calculate Total Net Cost for a Group of Products

Figure 3.2 shows a data set that has cost values in the range B2:B5 and a net cost rate in cell B8. You want to calculate the individual net costs and then add them. One way to do this is to calculate the individual net costs in a helper column and then use the SUM function to add the net cost amounts. Figure 3.2 shows this method. But could you just do away with the column of calculations and instead create an array calculation in a single cell? Yes, you can, and Figure 3.2 gives you a hint about how to do it. Notice that cell B8 is multiplied by B2 to B5. It is as if you were taking a whole column and multiplying it by B8. From this you can create the array calculation: B2:B5*B8.

	A	B	C	D
1	Item	Cost	Net Cost After Discount	<= Helper Column
2	GG-234	12	10.2	< Formula =B2*$B$8
3	GG-419	27	22.95	< Formula =B3*$B$8
4	HG-977	9	7.65	< Formula =B4*$B$8
5	RG-327	18	15.3	< Formula =B5*$B$8
7	Discount	0.15		
8	Net Cost	0.85	< Formula =1-B7	
9	Total	56.1	< Formula =SUM(C2:C5)	

Figure 3.2 *A helper column with a SUM function to calculate total net cost.*

Figure 3.3 shows an array formula that uses the array calculation B2:B5*B8 (an array times a single item). Because the array calculation is sitting in the array1 argument in the SUMPRODUCT function, this array formula does not require Ctrl+Shift+Enter.

	A	B	C
1	Item	Cost	
2	GG-234	12	
3	GG-419	27	
4	HG-977	9	
5	RG-327	18	
7	Discount	0.15	
8	Net Cost	0.85	< Formula =1-B7
9	Total	=SUMPRODUCT(B2:B5*B8)	
10		SUMPRODUCT(**array1**, [array2], [array3], ...)	

Figure 3.3 *A single-cell array formula to calculate total net cost.*

If you were to watch the array calculation in Figure 3.3 evaluate, you would see this:

B2:B5*B8
{12;27;9;18}*0.85
{12*0.85;27*0.85;9*0.85;18*0.85}
{10.2;22.95;7.65;15.3}

The number 0.85 is multiplied by each number in the first array: four numbers minus one number.

Figure 3.4 shows how you could condense the formula one step further by calculating the net cost rate directly in the formula, thus eliminating the need for the intermediate calculation for the net cost rate.

⬧	A	B	C
1	Item	Cost	
2	GG-234	12	
3	GG-419	27	
4	HG-977	9	
5	RG-327	18	
7	Discount	0.15	
8	Total	56.1	< Formula =SUMPRODUCT(B2:B5*(1-B7))

Figure 3.4 *A single-cell array formula to calculate the total net cost directly from the discount rate.*

Notes About the Formula =SUMPRODUCT(B2:B5*(1-B7))

The following table presents a summary of the SUMPRODUCT array formula you just learned about.

Impetus for Creating an Array Formula:
You do not need all the detail but just want total net cost.
Calculation Summary:
1. =SUMPRODUCT(B2:B5*(1-B7))
The array is the range of cells B2:B5. You are performing a math operation (multiplication) on an array and a single value. This is an array formula because you are performing an operation on an array, and the operation produces a resultant array. Because you are adding the results of an array calculation, you choose to use SUMPRODUCT rather than SUM so that you don't have to use Ctrl+Shift+Enter.
2. =SUMPRODUCT(B2:B5*0.85)
3. =SUMPRODUCT({12;27;9;18}*0.85)
4. =SUMPRODUCT({12*0.85;27*0.85;9*0.85;18*0.85})
5. =SUMPRODUCT({10.2;22.95;7.65;15.3})
The array operation B2:B5*B8 delivers the resultant array {10.2;22.95;7.65;15.3}. {10.2;22.95;7.65;15.3} is an example of an array created by a formula element. The formula element B2:B5*(1-B7) delivers the array {10.2;22.95;7.65;15.3} to the SUMPRODUCT function.
6. The formula delivers the single value 56.1.
Entering a Formula into a Cell:
The array1 argument in the SUMPRODUCT function is programmed to handle array operations without Ctrl+Shift+Enter. Ctrl+Shift+Enter is not required when you enter this formula into a cell.
Conclusion:
If you do not want to use a helper column and you don't need to see all the detail, this array formula is a great option.

You just saw that you can subtract a single number from an array. But what about subtracting an array from a single number? Would that be possible? As you have probably guessed, the answer is yes. Let's take a look at how this would work.

Calculating Net Cost from Four Series Discounts in Four Separate Cells

This example involves calculating the net cost for a product when you are given a series of discounts. In Figure 3.5 you can see the series discounts in the range A2:A5. To calculate the net cost for the Quad boomerang with a retail price of $30.25, you must do the following:

1. Calculate the complement for each discount—that is, 1 minus the discount. See Figure 3.5.

2. Multiply the complements to get the net cost equivalent. Figure 3.5 shows that the PRODUCT function multiplies the numbers in the range and displays the results.

3. Multiply the net cost equivalent by the retail price. Figure 3.5 shows that the ROUND function rounds to the penny because its second argument contains a 2.

The problem with the setup in Figure 3.5 is that if the goal is to simply get the net cost, you do not need the intermediate steps in the spreadsheet. This is a perfect situation for a single-cell formula. In Figure 3.5 notice that the array of discounts is really being subtracted from 1. Creating an array formula to accomplish the same end result should not be too difficult.

	A	B	C	D	E
1	Series Discounts	Complement			
2	0.2	0.8	< Formula =1-A2		
3	0.05	0.95	< Formula =1-A3		
4	0.1	0.9	< Formula =1-A4		
5	0.2	0.8	< Formula =1-A5		
7	Net Cost Equivalent	0.5472	< Formula =PRODUCT(B2:B5)		
8	Product	Quad			
9	Retail Price	$30.25			
10	Net Cost	$16.55	< Formula =ROUND(B9*B7,2)		

Figure 3.5 *A multistep method like this one to calculate net cost is usually not desirable. However, it can be useful as the source idea for how to create your own single-cell array formula.*

Creating Your Own Array Formulas

After you have created a multistep solution, a useful trick for creating your own single-cell array formulas is to start in the final result cell and move backward through the multistep solution. Looking back to Figure 3.5, here is what you might do to create our own formula:

1. Notice in the formula =ROUND(B9*B7,2) that cell B7 is pointing toward a cell that contains the formula =PRODUCT(B2:B5).

2. Take the formula element PRODUCT(B2:B5) and paste it into the =ROUND(B9*B7,2) formula in place of the cell reference B7, like this: =ROUND(B9* PRODUCT(B2:B5),2).

3. Next, ask: "What is in the cells B2:B5?" These cells contain all the complement calculations. Because you can see an array of discounts that are subtracted from the number 1, you create the array operation 1-A2:A5.

4. Replace the range B2:B5 in the PRODUCT function with the array operation 1-A2:A5. To do so, put 1-A2:A5 into the =ROUND(B9* PRODUCT(B2:B5),2) formula in place of the range B2:B5, like this: =ROUND(B9* PRODUCT(1-A2:A5),2).

> **Note**: Notice that the PRODUCT function is inside the ROUND function. Placing a function inside another function is called **nesting** functions. Throughout this book, you will see quite a lot of this. Nesting is quite helpful t because it means you can combine the power of two or more functions in a single formula.

Array Formula Efficiency Rule 10

After you have created a multistep solution with different formulas in different cells, a useful trick for creating your own single-cell array formulas is to start in the final result cell and move backward through the multistep solution. You can also do this in the opposite direction, starting in the first cell and working your way forward though the multistep solution.

You need to determine whether you need to use Ctrl+Shift+Enter with the formula =ROUND(B9* PRODUCT(1-A2:A5),2). Figure 3.6 shows that the array calculation is in the number1 argument in the PRODUCT function. The number1 argument in the PRODUCT function is not programmed to innately handle array operations. If this argument contains an array calculation, the formula *does* require Ctrl+Shift+Enter.

Figure 3.6 *The number1 argument in the PRODUCT function is not innately programmed to handle array operations. You must enter the formula with Ctrl+Shift+Enter.*

After you enter the formula using Ctrl+Shift+Enter, you can see the curly braces in the formula bar.

B10	▼	⋮	✕	✓	*fx*	{=ROUND(B9*PRODUCT(1-A2:A5),2)}

	A	B	C
8	Product	Quad	
9	Retail Price	$30.25	
10	Net Cost	$16.55	< Formula {=ROUND(B9*PRODUCT(1-A2:A5),2)}

Figure 3.7 *After you press Ctrl+Shift+Enter, look at the formula bar to verify that the curly braces have been added for you.*

Notes About the Formula =ROUND(B9*PRODUCT(1-A2:A5),2)

The following table presents a summary of the net cost array formula you just learned about.

Impetus for Creating an Array Formula:
Without a single-cell formula, calculating net cost for a series discount would require many helper cells. This would clutter up the spreadsheet, especially if there were many calculations to perform, based on many different series discounts.
Calculation Summary:
1. =ROUND(B9*PRODUCT(1-A2:A5),2)
The array is the range of cells A2:A5.   You are performing a math operation (subtraction) on a single number and an array.   This is an array formula because you are performing an operation on an array, and the operation produces a resultant array.
2. =ROUND(B9*PRODUCT(1-{0.2;0.05;0.1;0.2}),2)
3. =ROUND(B9*PRODUCT({1-0.2; 1-0.05; 1-0.1; 1-0.2}),2)
4. =ROUND(B9*PRODUCT({0.8; 0.95; 0.9; 0.8}),2)
Array operation 1-A2:A5 delivers the resultant array {0.8; 0.95; 0.9; 0.8}.   {0.8; 0.95; 0.9; 0.8} is an example of an array created by a formula element.   The formula element 1-A2:A5 delivers the array {0.8; 0.95; 0.9; 0.8} to the PRODUCT function.
5. =ROUND(B9*0.5472,2)
PRODUCT({0.8; 0.95; 0.9; 0.8}) evaluates to 0.5472.
6. =ROUND(30.25*0.5472,2)
7. =ROUND(16.5528,2)
8. The formula delivers the single value 16.55.
Entering a Formula into a Cell:
The array calculation is located in the number1 argument in the PRODUCT function. This argument is not innately programmed to handle array operations. To get the array calculation to calculate correctly, you must press Ctrl+Shift+Enter to enter the formula into the cell.   This is the formula you see in the formula bar after you enter it with Ctrl+Shift+Enter: {=ROUND(B9*PRODUCT(1-A2:A5),2)}.   If you do not use Ctrl+Shift+Enter, you will get a #VALUE! error or a potential incorrect answer caused by implicit intersection.
Conclusion:
Because you don't want to use helper cells for the intermediate calculations, this single-cell array formula is a great option.
Note:
In Chapters 7 and 23, you will see an expanded single-cell array formula that can calculate net cost equivalent when the series discounts are listed in a single cell with the form 20/05/10/20.

How You Can Structure Array Operation with an Operator

Now that you have seen a number of array operations, think back to the definition of an array formula: "…a formula that contains an operation on an array of items rather than on single items…" With this in mind, you can list the three possibilities of how an array operation that uses an operator can be structured:

Array, operator, array
Array, operator, single item
Single item, operator, array

Array Formula Efficiency Rule 11

An array operation that uses an operator can be structured in three possible ways: array, operator, array; array, operator, single item; or single item, operator, array.

Throughout the rest of this book you will see many more examples of math array operations.

Chapter Summary

In this chapter you have learned about math array operations and the structure of array calculations. In Chapter 4 you will take a look at array calculations that use comparative operators and how to make aggregate calculations with criteria.

Chapter 4: Comparative Array Operations and Aggregate Calculations with One or More Conditions

Excel Files

To follow along with the examples in this chapter, you can download the accompanying files, as explained in the Introduction.

Comparative Operations

Remember that Excel offers the following comparative operators:

=	Equal
<>	Not equal
>	Greater than
>=	Greater than or equal to
<	Less than
<=	Less than or equal to

Aggregate Calculations Based on One or More Conditions

A number of functions commonly use comparative operators. Some examples are SUMIF, SUMIFS, COUNTIF, COUNTIF, AVERAGEIF, and AVERAGEIFS. These functions make aggregate calculations based on one or more conditions or criteria. The problem is that these functions can only sum, count, and average. Many times you want to make other conditional calculations such as finding the min or max value, based on criteria, or calculating the standard deviation based on criteria. In these cases, because there is not a built-in function to accomplish the goal, you have to invent an array formula. Often this involves using comparative operators on arrays. The first example in this chapter involves a conditional calculation using the MIN function.

Using an IF Function to Select Items in An Array Based on one condition

Figure 4.1 shows a column of city names and a column of times. You want to find the smallest sample time for each city. The condition for calculating will be city name. You can use the MIN function to find the minimum value from a column of numbers, but how do you isolate just the numbers for Oakland and then Seattle and then Tacoma as you copy a formula down the column? Because there is no built-in function called MINIF, you have to combine the IF function with the MIN function and invent your own array calculation to solve this problem.

	A	B	C	D	E
1	Calculate smallest sample time for each city in sample.				
2	City	Times (h)		City	Min Time
3	Seattle	5		Oakland	6
4	Tacoma	8		Seattle	4
5	Oakland	9		Tacoma	8
6	Seattle	4			
7	Tacoma	10			
8	Oakland	6			

Figure 4.1 *Formula goal: Calculate the minimum time for each city.*

As shown in Figure 4.2, you start the formula in cell E3 with the MIN function. But you cannot put all the time values from column B into the number1 argument of the MIN. You want just the values if they are from Oakland.

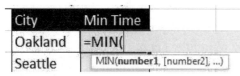

City	Min Time
Oakland	=MIN(
Seattle	MIN(**number1**, [number2], ...)

Figure 4.2 *Type "=MIN(".*

As shown in Figure 4.3, next you type "IF(" in the number1 argument for the MIN. You are nesting the IF inside the MIN.

City	Min Time
Oakland	=MIN(IF(
Seattle	IF(**logical_test**, [value_if_true], [value_if_false])

Figure 4.3 *Add an IF inside the MIN.*

As shown in Figure 4.4, with your cursor in the logical_test argument for the IF function, you highlight the range with all the city names and then lock the range (making the cell references absolute) by pressing the F4 key. You then type the comparative operator, the equal sign. Finally, you select the cell to the left of the formula, the relative cell reference with the city name. It is useful to think of this array operation as a question that you are asking of the range A3:A8. The question you are asking in this case is "Are any of the cities in the range equal to Oakland?"

	A	B	C	D	E	F	G
1	Calculate smallest sample time for each city in sample.						
2	City	Times (h)		City	Min Time		
3	Seattle	5		Oakland	=MIN(IF($A$3:$A$8=D3		
4	Tacoma	8		Seattle	IF(**logical_test**, [value_if_true], [value_if_false])		

Figure 4.4 *Create array operation in logical_test argument of IF function.*

Figure 4.4 shows that you have created an array operation using a comparative operator. Any time the operator for an array calculation is a comparative operator, the result will be an array of TRUEs and FALSEs or logical values. To see that this is true, you can click on the logical_test argument in the ScreenTip to highlight the array operation, and then to evaluate it, you press the F9 key. Figure 4.5 shows the result. The resultant array is an array of logical values that the IF function logical_test argument understands perfectly. Normally, you give the logical_test argument a single TRUE or FALSE, but because here you give it an array of TRUEs and FALSEs, it will be able to select the times from the Min Time column whenever it sees a TRUE.

City	Min Time
Oakland	=MIN(IF({FALSE;FALSE;TRUE;FALSE;FALSE;TRUE}
Seattle	IF(**logical_test**, [value_if_true], [value_if_false])

Figure 4.5 *Use F9 key to see resultant array.*

You must not forget to undo the Evaluate Formula Element trick by pressing Ctrl+Z. Figure 4.6 shows the undo to get you back to the array operation using cell references.

City	Min Time
Oakland	=MIN(IF($A$3:$A$8=D3
Seattle	IF(**logical_test**, [value_if_true], [value_if_false])

Figure 4.6 *Use Ctrl+Z to undo the evaluation.*

As shown in Figure 4.7, you type a comma to get to the value_if_true argument for the IF function and then enter the absolute (locked) range for the time values. The key here is that these are the values you want if a TRUE shows up in the logical_test argument. In addition, this range must have the same dimension as the array of logicals in the logical_test argument. You have entered an array of values into the value_if_true argument, but for the value_if_false argument, you want to enter nothing: You leave it empty. This forces a FALSE logical value into the positions in the time value array where the city is not Oakland. This is perfect because the MIN function is programmed to ignore logical values.

	A	B	C	D	E	F	G
1	Calculate smallest sample time for each city in sample.						
2	City	Times (h)		City	Min Time		
3	Seattle	5		Oakland	=MIN(IF($A$3:$A$8=D3,$B$3:$B$8		
4	Tacoma	8		Seattle	IF(logical_test, **[value_if_true]**, [value_if_false])		

Figure 4.7 *Enter range with numbers into value_if_true argument.*

As shown in Figure 4.8, you close off the IF function without putting anything in the value_if_false argument by typing a close parenthesis while the cursor is still at the end of the IF function value_if_true argument. Notice that the IF function formula element is complete, and it sits in the number1 argument in the MIN function.

City	Min Time
Oakland	=MIN(IF($A$3:$A$8=D3,$B$3:$B$8)
Seattle	MIN(**number1**, [number2], ...)

Figure 4.8 *IF sits in number1 argument on MIN function.*

To see that the IF function delivers an array of Oakland numbers and FALSE logical values to the MIN function, click the number1 argument ScreenTip and then press the F9 key. In Figure 4.9, you can see that MIN receives only the numbers from Oakland. This is an amazing use of the IF function to filter out values you do not want and to get just the numbers you want. You can use this method of using the IF function in other aggregate functions, such as MAX and STDEV.

City	Min Time
Oakland	=MIN({FALSE;FALSE;9;FALSE;FALSE;6}
Seattle	MIN(**number1**, [number2], ...)

Figure 4.9 *Use F9 key to see resultant array.*

As shown in Figure 4.10, you need to remember to use Ctrl+Z. You then type a close parenthesis for the MIN function. And for emphasis, you place your cursor back into the logical_test argument of the IF function. Notice that this is where the array calculation sits. The logical_test argument is not programmed to handle array operations without using Ctrl+Shift+Enter, so you must do so if you want this to calculate correctly.

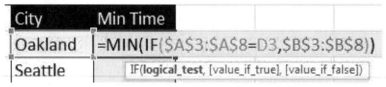

Figure 4.10 *Array operation in the logical_test argument of the IF function mandates that you use Ctrl+-Shift+Enter.*

> **Note:** For array calculations, the IF function's requirement to enter the formula with Ctrl+Shift+Enter trumps any other function's requirement to *not* use Ctrl+-Shift+Enter. More about this later.

Figure 4.11 shows that after you use Ctrl+Shift+Enter, Excel puts curly braces at the beginning and end of the formula.

| *fx* | {=MIN(IF($A$3:$A$8=D3,$B$3:$B$8))} |

Figure 4.11 *Formula bar shows the curly braces.*

Figure 4.12 shows that you can copy array formulas down a column, and the curly braces are also copied down.

| E5 | ▾ | : | ✕ | ✓ | *fx* | {=MIN(IF($A$3:$A$8=D5,$B$3:$B$8))} |

◢	A	B	C	D	E
1	Calculate smallest sample time for each city in sample.				
2	City	Times (h)		City	Min Time
3	Seattle	5		Oakland	6
4	Tacoma	8		Seattle	4
5	Oakland	9		Tacoma	8

Figure 4.12 *Copy array formula down the column.*

A significant advantage of a formula solution like the MIN/IF array formula you just created is that if the source city names and times change, the formulas will instantly update.

Notes About the Formula =MIN(IF($A$3:$A$8=D3,$B$3:$B$8))

The following table presents a summary of the MIN/IF array formula you just learned about.

Impetus for Creating an Array Formula:

You need to calculate the maximum value, based on a condition. You want a formula that you can enter and copy down a column and that will instantly update if the source data changes.

Calculation Summary:

1. =MIN(IF($A$3:$A$8=D3,$B$3:$B$8))

This is the first formula you have seen that has more than one array operation.

This is an array formula because you are performing an operation on an array, and the operation produces a resultant array.

The first comparative array operation is $A$3:$A$8=D3. The second is be the array created by the IF function.

You put the IF function inside the MIN function so that you can select only the values for Oakland. You want to filter the values inside the formula.

2. =MIN(IF({"Seattle";"Tacoma";"Oakland";"Seattle";"Tacoma";"Oakland"}="Oakland",$B$3:$B$8))

This formula asks whether any city names are equal to Oakland.?

3. =MIN(IF({FALSE;FALSE;TRUE;FALSE;FALSE;TRUE},$B$3:$B$8))

TRUE means the city is Oakland; FALSE means the city is not Oakland.

Array calculation 1: $A$3:$A$8=D3 delivers the resultant array {FALSE;FALSE;TRUE;FALSE;-FALSE;TRUE} to the logical_test argument of the IF function.

4. =MIN(IF({FALSE;FALSE;TRUE;FALSE;FALSE;TRUE},{5;8;9;4;10;6}))

The array of numbers in the value_if_true argument shows all the numbers.

Notice that you have not entered anything into the value_if_false argument.

5. =MIN({FALSE;FALSE;9;FALSE;FALSE;6})

Array calculation 2: IF($A$3:$A$8=D3,$B$3:$B$8) delivers the resultant array {FALSE;FALSE;9;-FALSE;FALSE;6} to the number1 argument of the MAX function.

Notice that if you leave the value_if_false argument empty, the IF function will put a FALSE into the resultant array any time the city is not Oakland.

You use the IF function to select from a column of numbers only the numbers that belong to Oakland and then dump them into the MIN function. The IF function filters the numbers, based on one condition.

5. The formula delivers the single value 6.

Entering a Formula into a Cell:

This array calculation is located in the logical_test argument in the IF function. This argument is not innately programmed to handle array operations. To get the array operation to calculate correctly, you must enter the formula using Ctrl+Shift+Enter.

This is the formula you see in the formula bar after you enter it with Ctrl+Shift+Enter: { =MIN(IF($A$3:$A$8=D3,$B$3:$B$8))}.

If you do not use Ctrl+Shift+Enter, you will get a #VALUE! error or an incorrect answer caused by implicit intersection.

Conclusion:

In the next section of the book, you will compare the array formula to the DMIN function and a PivotTable and see that this array formula is a great option if you want a single-cell formula that can be copied down a column and that updates instantly when source data changes.

Notes:

In Chapter 10 you will see an alternative to this MIN array formula that uses the new Excel 2010 function AGGREGATE.

You have just made a beautiful array formula. However, you should look at what other options are available in Excel to accomplish the same goal. You want to see the full context in which you are deciding to use an array formula. This way, you can chose which method will be most efficient for your situational demands. Next you will briefly look at database functions and PivotTables.

Understanding Database Functions

There is a group of 12 database functions (also known as D-functions) that can make calculations based on criteria. DMIN, DMAX, and DSUM are a few examples of D-functions. These functions are great when you have a single calculation to make and the data set has field names (column labels). Figures 4.13 and 4.14 show how you can use the DMIN function to calculate the minimum time for the city of Oakland. The advantage of D-functions is that if you have only a single calculation to make, such as the minimum for Oakland and not for Seattle or Tacoma, then the DMIN function is easier to create than a MIN-IF array formula, and it calculates quickly. (For large data sets and formulas with large ranges of cells, this matters; more later in chapters 5 and 10.)

The disadvantage of D-functions is that the criteria argument requires that you type the field name in a cell and type the criteria below that field name. This means two cells listed vertically, one on top of the other, must be typed for each calculation. Figure 4.15 shows this requirement. This is a disadvantage if you need to copy a formula down a column as you did back in Figure 4.12. Figure 4.15 shows the setup required to copy DMIN to other cells in order to make multiple calculations based on different criteria. In many cases, this setup would not be desirable.

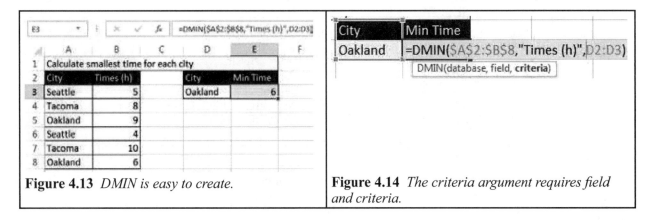

Figure 4.13 *DMIN is easy to create.*

Figure 4.14 *The criteria argument requires field and criteria.*

	A	B	C	D	E	F	G	H	I	J
1	Calculate smallest time for each city									
2	City	Times (h)		City	Min Time					
3	Seattle	5		Oakland	6	< Formula =DMIN($A$2:$B$8,"Times (h)",D2:D3)				
4	Tacoma	8		City	Min Time					
5	Oakland	9		Seattle	4	< Formula =DMIN($A$2:$B$8,"Times (h)",D4:D5)				
6	Seattle	4		City	Min Time					
7	Tacoma	10		Tacoma	8	< Formula =DMIN($A$2:$B$8,"Times (h)",D6:D7)				
8	Oakland	6								

Figure 4.15 *Coping D-functions down a column is cumbersome.*

Sometimes formula calculation time for a very large data set is a problem. Figure 4.16 shows a workaround that can take advantage of the D-functions' formula calculation time advantage over array formulas.

	A	B	C	D	E	F	G	H	I	J	K
1	Calculate smallest time for each city										
2	City	Times (h)		City	Min Time						
3	Seattle	5		Oakland	6	< Formula =DMIN($A$2:$B$8,"Times (h)",D2:D3)					
4	Tacoma	8									
5	Oakland	9			6	< Formula =E3					
6	Seattle	4		Oakland	6	< Formula {=TABLE(,D3)}					
7	Tacoma	10		Seattle	4	< Formula {=TABLE(,D3)}					
8	Oakland	6		Tacoma	8	< Formula {=TABLE(,D3)}					
9											

Data Table

Row input cell:

Column input cell: $D$3

OK   Cancel

Figure 4.16 *D-functions and data tables can work together to calculate a column of calculations.*

Here are the steps to create this data table solution:

1. Create the formula in cell E3.

2. Type all city names in the range D6:D8.

3. In cell E5, create a formula that points to cell E3.

4. Highlight the range D5:E8 and press Alt, D, T to open the Data Table dialog box (or select Data Table from Data Tools group in the Data Ribbon tab).

5. Enter D3 in the Column Input Cell text box.

Chapter 21 covers data tables in more detail.

Should You Use the DMIN Function or the MIN/IF Array Formula?

If you have a single calculation to make and a proper data set with field names, using DMIN is the way to go. It is easy to create and calculates quickly (which is important for large array formulas with many ranges and calculations). If you want to copy your formula down a column or if your data set does not have field names, using MIN/IF or another array formula may be the way to go. For large data sets with many calculations, you might want to consider using DMIN in combination with a data table (refer to Chapter 21).

Array Formula Efficiency Rule 12

Consider using D-functions as an alternative to array formulas if you have a proper data set with field names and you do not need to copy your formula down a column or across a row. The advantage of using D-functions is that they are easy to create and calculate formulas more quickly than most comparable array formulas. Using a D-function in combination with a data table is a workaround if you want a formula that you can copy down a column or across a row.

If you want a formula solution, DMIN or MIN/IF will work, but what if you do not need the immediate updatability that formulas bring? Then you can consider a PivotTable for aggregate calculations that have one or more criteria.

PivotTables

If you do not need the immediate updatability of formulas, you should consider using PivotTables any time you are creating aggregate calculations with one or more criteria. Why? Because PivotTables are quite easy to create, especially when there are many criteria. This section looks at a single-condition calculation. Figure 4.17 shows a completed PivotTable for the minimum calculation with one condition.

	A	B	C	D	E
1	City	Times (h)		City ▾	Min of Times (h)
2	Seattle	5		Oakland	6
3	Tacoma	8		Seattle	4
4	Oakland	9		Tacoma	8
5	Seattle	4			
6	Tacoma	10			
7	Oakland	6			

Figure 4.17 *Creating PivotTables can be fast and easy.*

Here are the steps to create this PivotTable solution:

1. Ensure that the data set has field names and that there are empty cells around the data set.

2. With a single cell in your data set, select PivotTable from the Table group of the Insert Ribbon tab.

3. In the PivotTable dialog box enter cell D1 in the Existing Worksheet Location text box. Drag the City field to Rows and the Times (h) field to Values.

4. Right-click a value in the PivotTable and click Value Field Settings,. Then in Value Field Settings dialog box, chose the MIN function.

5. Right-click PivotTable and click PivotTable Options. Then, in the PivotTable Options dialog box, on the Total and Filters tab, uncheck Grand Totals.

6. Select Tabular from the Report Layout group on the PivotTable Tools Design Ribbon tab.

Should You Use a PivotTable or an Array Formula?

One drawback to PivotTables is that they do not update immediately when source data from input cells is changed. Formulas do update immediately when source data changes. If the demands of a solution require immediate updatability, then formulas are a great answer. However, with Pivot-Tables, all that is required to update the PivotTable calculations is to refresh the PivotTable. You simply right-click somewhere in the PivotTable and click Refresh.

If you have multiple criteria for a calculation, a PivotTable is easier to create because you can simply drag and drop a field to the row or column area. With an array formula, you have to add a whole new array calculation. You will see how to do this later in this chapter.

If you want to change a function, in a PivotTable you simple right-click and point to Summarize Values By. With an array formula, you have to rebuild the formula.

Another consideration for whether to choose a PivotTable or an array formula is formatting and layout. The formatting and layout are more constrained with PivotTables than with formulas.

Finally, note that a PivotTable has only 11 functions available, whereas formulas have more than 350 functions available.

Next you will look at conditional calculations that have more than one criterion.

Array Formula Efficiency Rule 13

Consider using PivotTables as an alternative to array formulas. The following are advantages of PivotTables: Easy to create, especially if there are multiple criteria, and easy to change. These are some of the disadvantages of PivotTables: Do not update instantly (refreshing is easy, though), only 11 functions, and formatting is limited. Array formulas have a number of advantages: Instantly update when data changes and give you access to hundreds of functions.

Using the IF Function to Select Items in an Array Based on Multiple Criteria

You have seen that you can use the IF function inside the MIN function to select items in an array, based on a single condition. But what if you have more than one condition? In cases where you need to select items from an array based on multiple criteria, you can nest multiple IF functions together in one formula. If you have two criteria, you use two IF functions; if you have three criteria, you use three IF functions; and so on.

MAX Calculation with Two Criteria, Using Two IF Functions and Two Comparative Operators

Figure 4.18 shows the data set for this example. The goal here is to calculate the maximum sales amount for each sales representative in the west region. Further, you want a formula you can copy down the column, and you want the formula to automatically update if the source data changes. Using the MAX function with two nested IF functions will help you accomplish our goal of calculating MAX based on two criteria.

	A	B	C	D	E	F
1	Calculate the MAX value for each Sales Rep in the West					
2	Region	Sales Rep	Sales		Region	West
3	West	Chin	914			
4	Midwest	Sioux	355		Sales Rep	Sales
5	West	Sioux	590		Chin	
6	West	Chin	610		Moe	
7	Midwest	Moe	506		Sioux	
8	West	Moe	825			
9	Midwest	Chin	710			
10	Midwest	Sioux	280			
11	Midwest	Moe	363			
12	West	Sioux	685			

Figure 4.18 *Goal: Calculate maximum sales for each employee in the west.*

As shown in Figure 4.19, you start the formula in cell F5, and you nest the IF function in the number1 argument of the MAX function. The IF function will help you isolate only the values that meet your conditions.

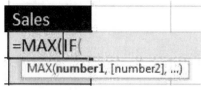

Figure 4.19 *Type "=MAX(IF(".*

As shown in Figure 4.20, in the logical_test argument of the IF function, you create an array operation (with absolute references) that asks "Is anything in the Region column equal to West?" Because you use a comparative operator, the array operation will evaluate to an array of TRUEs and FALSEs.

Region	West

Sales Rep	Sales
Chin	=MAX(IF($A$3:$A$12=$F$2
Moe	IF(**logical_test**, [value_if_true], [value_if_false])

Figure 4.20 *Enter array operation.*

Figure 4.21 shows that the next step is to type a comma to get to the value_if_true argument. Normally, you type the values you want in this argument, but because you have a remaining condition, you must type the next IF function.

=MAX(IF($A$3:$A$12=$F$2,
IF(logical_test, [**value_if_true**], [value_if_false])

Figure 4.21 *Type comma to get to value_if_true argument.*

As shown in Figure 4.22, when you type the second IF, a new ScreenTip for the second IF pops up. In the logical_test argument for the second IF, you create the second array operation that asks "Is anything in the Sales Rep column equal to the employee in the relative cell reference, one cell to my left?"

Sales Rep	Sales
Chin	=MAX(IF($A$3:$A$12=$F$2,IF($B$3:$B$12=E5
Moe	IF(**logical_test**, [value_if_true], [value_if_false])

Figure 4.22 *Add second IF function and array operation.*

Just to prove to yourself that a second IF is sitting in the value_if_true argument for the first IF, as shown in Figure 4.23, you can use your cursor to click in the value_if_true argument for the first IF. This trick of placing an additional IF function in the value_if_true argument is the key to nesting IF functions together when you multiple criteria. Prior to Excel 2007, you could nest up to seven IF functions; in Excel 2007 and later, you can have up to 64.

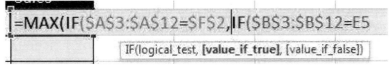

Figure 4.23 *Second IF sits in value_if_true argument of the first IF function.*

As shown in Figure 4.24, you can now add the Sales column to the value_if_true argument. The rule of thumb for nesting IF functions is to keep typing the IFs until you have no more conditions. Then you can enter the values for the value_if_true argument. In addition, you do not want anything to be typed into the value_if_false argument. If you leave it empty, the IF function will place FALSEs into the resultant array when the conditions are not met, which is perfect because the MAX function ignores logical values.

=MAX(IF($A$3:$A$12=$F$2,IF($B$3:$B$12=E5,$C$3:$C$12

825   IF(logical_test, **[value_if_true]**, [value_if_false])

Figure 4.24 *Enter range with numbers to value_if_true argument of second IF function.*

In Figure 4.25 you can see that you close the formula by typing three close parentheses. You can tell that you have finished typing your parentheses because the last one is black. Notice that there are two IF functions inside the MAX function number1 argument.

=MAX(IF($A$3:$A$12=$F$2,IF($B$3:$B$12=E5,$C$3:$C$12)))

MAX(**number1**, [number2], ...)

Figure 4.25 *Black closing parenthesis means formula is done.*

As shown in Figure 4.26, if you click on the number1 argument ScreenTip and then press the F9 key (evaluation key), you can see that the two nested IF functions deliver only the values that have met both criteria. The numbers 914 and 610 have been selected because they are numbers associated with the region West AND the sales rep Chin. The two IFs filter the numbers based on two criteria.

=MAX({914;FALSE;FALSE;610;FALSE;FALSE;FALSE;FALSE;FALSE;FALSE})

MAX(**number1**, [number2], ...)

Figure 4.26 *The two IF functions and two comparative array operations deliver a resultant array of filter values based on two criteria.*

> **Note:** The above criteria example demonstrates AND criteria. With AND criteria, all conditions must evaluate to TRUE. Later, in Chapter 11, you will differentiate this from OR criteria, where at least one must evaluate to TRUE.

How do the two IF functions do this? They look through each of the three arrays, and only when they finds a TRUE in the first array and a TRUE in the second array do they select the number from the third array. The formula looks like this:

=MAX(IF({**TRUE**;FALSE;TRUE;**TRUE**;FALSE;TRUE;FALSE;FALSE
FALSE;TRUE},IF({**TRUE**;FALSE;FALSE;**TRUE**;FALSE;FALSE;TRUE;FALSE;FALSE;
FALSE},{**914**;355;590;**610**;506;825;710;280;363;685})))

Figure 4.27 reminds you that you must immediately undo the Evaluate Formula Element trick by using Ctrl+Z. Now that you are ready to enter the formula, you must notice where the array calculation is located in the larger formula. Because it is in the logical_test argument of the IF function, and this argument is not programmed to innately handle array operations, you must use Ctrl+-Shift+Enter when you enter the formula into the cell.

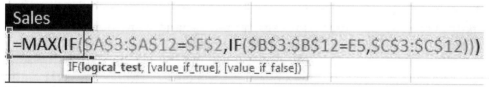

Figure 4.27 *Remember to undo the evaluation.*

> **Note:** For array calculations, the IF function's requirement to enter the formula with Ctrl+Shift+Enter trumps any other function's requirement to *not* use Ctrl+-Shift+Enter. More about this later in this chapter.

Figure 4.28 shows that after you enter an array formula with Ctrl+Shift+Enter, you must verify that the formula bar shows the curly braces at the beginning and end of the formula. Since they are there, you can copy the formula down the column.

> **Note**: if you usually copy formulas by using the mouse and the fill handle, you can copy the formula as usual. If you usually copy formulas using Ctrl+C and Ctrl+V, you have to make sure that the paste area does not include the copied cell. Select cell F6, Copy. Re-select F7:F8 and paste. If the paste area includes F6, Excel will deliver the cryptic "You cannot change part of an array" message.

fx   {=MAX(IF($A$3:$A$12=$F$2,IF($B$3:$B$12=E5,$C$3:$C$12)))}

Figure 4.28 *Formula bar shows curly braces after you enter formula with Ctrl+Shift+Enter.*

Figure 4.29 shows the finished spreadsheet.

Region	Sales Rep	Sales	Region	West
West	Chin	914		
Midwest	Sioux	355	Sales Rep	Sales
West	Sioux	590	Chin	914
West	Chin	610	Moe	825
Midwest	Moe	506	Sioux	685

Figure 4.29 *Finished spreadsheet.*

With the formula done, you can think about the larger Excel context: Are there other ways you could do this?

Figures 4.30 and 4.31 show how you could use the DMAX function and a PivotTable to make calculations based on two criteria. Because in this situation you need to copy the formula down a column and you want the formula to update instantly when the source data changes, the MAX with two IF functions is a good choice.

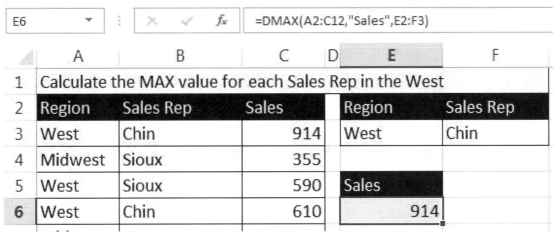

Figure 4.30 *DMAX can find maximum value with two criteria, but copying the formula is difficult.*

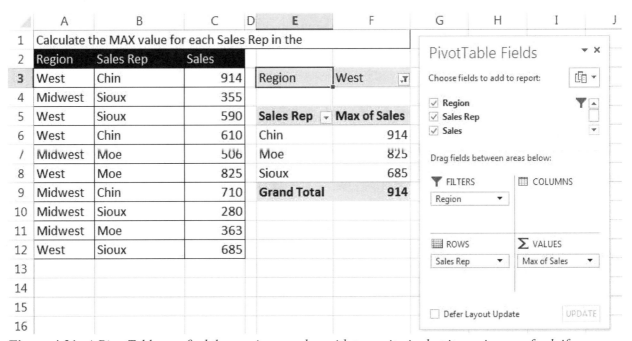

Figure 4.31 *A PivotTable can find the maximum value with two criteria, but it requires a refresh if source data changes.*

Notes About the Formula
=MAX(IF($A$3:$A$12=$F$2,IF($B$3:$B$12=E5,$C$3:$C$12)))

The following table provides a summary of the MAX/IF/IF array formula you just learned about.

Impetus for Creating an Array Formula:
You need to calculate the maximum value, based on two criteria. You want a formula that you can copy down a column and that will instantly update if the source data changes.
Calculation Summary:
1. =MAX(IF($A$3:$A$12=$F$2,IF($B$3:$B$12=E5,$C$3:$C$12)))
This formula has four array calculations.
This is an array formula because you are performing operations on arrays, and the operations produce resultant arrays.
You put the two back-to-back IF functions inside the MAX function so that you can select only the values for both West and Chin. You want to filter the values inside the formula.
2. =MAX(IF($A$3:$A$12="West",IF($B$3:$B$12="Chin",$C$3:$C$12)))
Question 1: Are any values in the Region column equal to West?
Question 2: Are any values in the Sales Rep column equal to Chin?
Array calculation 1: $A$3:$A$12="West" delivers the resultant array {TRUE;FALSE;TRUE;TRUE;-FALSE;TRUE;FALSE;FALSE;FALSE;TRUE} to the logical_test argument of the first IF function.
Array calculation 2: $B$3:$B$12="Chin" delivers the resultant array {TRUE;FALSE;FALSE;TRUE;-FALSE;FALSE;TRUE;FALSE;FALSE;FALSE} to the logical_test argument of the second IF function.
3. =MAX(IF({TRUE;FALSE;TRUE;*TRUE*;FALSE;TRUE;FALSE;FALSE; FALSE;TRUE},IF({TRUE;FALSE;FALSE;*TRUE*;FALSE;FALSE;TRUE; FALSE;FALSE;FALSE},",$C$3:$C$12)))
Array calculation 3: IF({TRUE;FALSE;TRUE;TRUE;FALSE;TRUE;FALSE;FALSE;-FALSE;TRUE},IF({TRUE;FALSE;FALSE;TRUE;FALSE;FALSE;TRUE;FALSE;FALSE;FALSE} delivers the resultant array {TRUE;FALSE;FALSE;TRUE;FALSE;FALSE;FALSE;FALSE;FALSE} to the logical_test argument of the first IF function.
4) =MAX(IF({TRUE;FALSE;FALSE;*TRUE*;FALSE;FALSE;FALSE;FALSE; FALSE;FALSE},{914;355;590;*610*;506;825;710;280;363;685}))
Only when there are corresponding TRUEs in the first and second IF calculations are you allowed to select a number. In this case, you select the first and fourth numbers.
5) =MAX({914;FALSE;FALSE;610;FALSE;FALSE;FALSE;FALSE;FALSE; FALSE})
Array calculation 4: IF($A$3:$A$12=$F$2,IF($B$3:$B$12=E5,$C$3:$C$12)) delivers the resultant array {914;FALSE;FALSE;610;FALSE;FALSE;FALSE;FALSE;FALSE} to the number1 argument in the MAX function.
The two IFs successfully dump just the numbers for West and Chin into the MAX function.
The two IFs filter the numbers based on two criteria.
5) The formula delivers the single value 914.
Entering a Formula into a Cell:
If the logical_test argument in the IF function contains an array operation, the formula requires Ctrl+-Shift+Enter. Verify that the curly braces have been entered at the beginning and end of the formula after you use Ctrl+Shift+Enter. If you do not see curly braces, the answer may be incorrect.
Conclusion:
If you do not want to create a PivotTable, and you need a formula that you can copy down a column, this array formula is a great option.

The next section describes how to use a NOT comparative operator and an amazing new Excel 2010 function that can perform some conditional aggregate calculations (like MIN and MAX) without requiring you to use Ctrl+Shift+Enter.

MIN Calculation with the NOT Condition and the Equating Condition

Figure 4.32 shows a data set with BMX bike racing times. The data set has the three columns: Track (the different tracks in different cities), BMX Racer (the name of a racer), and Times (s) (the time to make it around the track, in seconds). Your goal is to calculate the fastest time for each racer. However, because the PI track is very short and the other tracks are much longer, you want to exclude the PI times from the calculation. This means you have a MIN calculation with two conditions: BMX racer name and "not PI". Further, you need to be able to copy the formula down a column, so you can't use the DMIN function. And because this is a template where the data changes each week, you want the formula to automatically update, so you don't want a PivotTable.

	A	B	C	D	E	F
1	Calculate fastest time for each Racer NOT at PI track.					
2	Track	BMX Racer	Time (s)		Track	PI
3	PI	Zaine	34.5			
4	SeaTac	Logan	44.3		BMX Racer	Time (s)
5	Sumner	Zaine	49		Isaac	47.5
6	PI	Isaac	37.8		Logan	44.3
7	SeaTac	Isaac	47.5		Zaine	43
8	SeaTac	Zaine	43			
9	PI	Logan	35.9			
10	Sumner	Zaine	51			
11	Sumner	Logan	53.4			
12	Sumner	Isaac	55.6			
13	PI	Zaine	39			

Figure 4.32 *Goal: Calculate the fastest time for each racer for races not at the PI track.*

Based on what you learned in the last array formula example, you could use the MIN function with two IFs. Figure 4.33 shows this formula. The first IF selects only tracks that are not PI (notice that the NOT comparative operator is a less-than symbol and then a greater than symbol, <>), and the second IF selects the times for the racer Isaac. This formula will yield the correct answer, but because the array calculations are in the logical_test argument of the IF function, you need to use Ctrl+Shift+Enter.

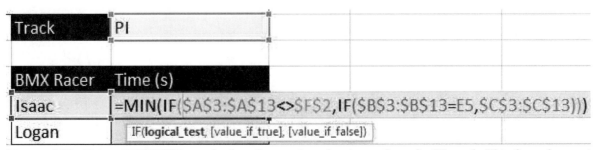

Figure 4.33 *Using MIN/IF/IF to calculate fastest time that is not from the PI track. This formula requires Ctrl+Shift+Enter.*

If there were a way to create a formula that would make this same calculation, but not require Ctrl+Shift+Enter, that would be preferable. If you have Excel 2010 or later, you can use the new AGGREGATE function to make this calculation without using Ctrl+Shift+Enter.

The AGGREGATE Function Array Argument

As mentioned in Chapter 2, when you compared the SUMPRODUCT and SUM functions for adding the results of an array calculation, if you have a choice between two equally efficient array formulas and one requires Ctrl+Shift+Enter and one does not, you should choose the one that does not require Ctrl+Shift+Enter. To this end, Excel 2010 offers a new function that can calculate MIN or MAX conditional array calculations without requiring Ctrl+Shift+Enter. This amazing new function is called the AGGREGATE function.

> **Note:** The AGGREGATE function has many different uses that this book does not cover. For a comprehensive 12-video series about the AGGREGATE function, go to www.youtube.com/course?list=EC95781BFAAB4162C0.

The formula goal is the same as in our last example: calculate the fastest time that is not from the track PI for each racer. As shown in Figure 4.34, if you start the formula in cell F5, you can see that the ScreenTip has two options. You use the top set of function arguments that shows the argument name array as its third argument. This third argument is what makes the AGGREGATE function useful for some array calculations because it can handle array operations without requiring the use of Ctrl+Shift+Enter. The version of AGGREGATE that you will use has four arguments: function_num, options, array, and [k].

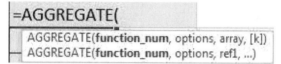

Figure 4.34 *Type "=AGGREGATE(" to start our formula to calculate the fastest time not from the PI track.*

The first argument of AGGREGATE allows you to choose from 19 different aggregate calculations. (See the following table for a full list.) Functions 1 to 13 *cannot* handle array operations. Functions 14 to 19 *can* handle array operations. It seems odd that function 5, MIN, cannot be used for a MIN array calculation, but you will get around this by using function 15, SMALL, and telling it to find the first smallest race time (k = 1). The second argument allows options. Option 6 will help your calculation because it will help you ignore the error values that the array operation will create when the two criteria are not met).

First Argument: function_num	
Value	Function
1	AVERAGE
2	COUNT
3	COUNTA
4	MAX
5	MIN
6	PRODUCT
7	STDDEV.S
8	STDDEV.P
9	SUM
10	VAR.S
11	VAR.P
12	MEDIAN
13	MODE.SNGL
14	LARGE
15	SMALL
16	PERCENTILE.INC
17	QUARTILE.INC
18	PERCENTILE.EXC
19	QUARTILE.EXC

Second Argument: options	
Value	What It Does
0	Ignores nested SUBTOTAL and AGGREGATE functions
1	Ignores hidden rows, nested SUBTOTAL, and AGGREGATE functions
2	Ignores error values, nested SUBTOTAL, and AGGREGATE functions
3	Ignores hidden rows, error values, nested SUBTOTAL, and AGGREGATE functions
4	Ignores nothing
5	Ignores hidden rows
6	Ignores error values
7	Ignores hidden rows and error values

As shown in Figure 4.35, you can choose function 15, SMALL, from the drop-down list for the function_num argument.

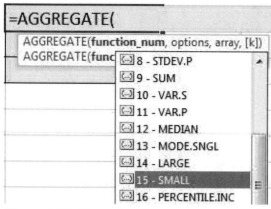

Figure 4.35 *From function_num argument drop-down select 15, the SMALL function.*

As shown in Figure 4.36, you can choose option 6, Ignore Error Values, from the drop-down list for the options argument.

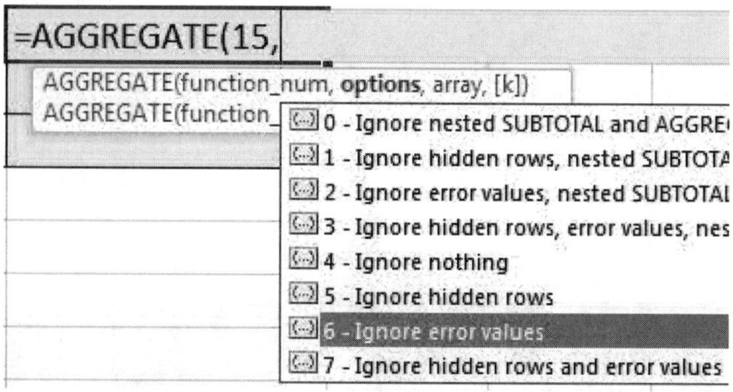

Figure 4.36 *From options argument drop-down select 6-Ignore error values.*

Figure 4.37 shows that after you type a comma, the array argument becomes bold. The array argument in the AGGREGATE function is programmed to handle array operations without using Ctrl+Shift+Enter for functions 14 to 19. This is the argument that can do array magic!

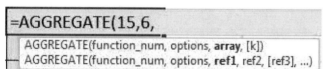

Figure 4.37 *Type a comma to get to the array argument. The array argument can handle array operations without having to use Ctrl+Shift+Enter.*

At this point, it is worthwhile to consider whether you can use the following formula element to create the array of values that match the two criteria:

IF($A$3:$A$13<>$F$2,IF($B$3:$B$13=E5,$C$3:$C$13))

As mentioned previously, if you have an array calculation in the logical_test argument of IF, the formula will require Ctrl+Shift+Enter no matter what—even if you place it in the array argument of AGGREGATE. The following section formalize this aspect of the IF function with a new rule.

The IF Function Ctrl+Shift+Enter Trump Rule

When you place array calculations in any of the IF function's arguments, the IF function's requirement to enter the formula with Ctrl+Shift+Enter trumps any other function's requirement to *not* use Ctrl+Shift+Enter.

Array Formula Efficiency Rule 14

If you have an array operation in the IF function, the formula requires Ctrl+Shift+Enter, regardless of where the IF function sits in the larger formula. This means that even if you put an IF function that contains an array operation into a function argument that can handle array operations (like the array arguments in the AGGREGATE or SUMPRODUCT functions), the formula will still require Ctrl+Shift+Enter. In some cases, rather than use the IF function with an array operation in a function argument that does not require Ctrl+Shift+Enter, it may be less ambiguous to not use the IF function and instead find an alternative formula.

To prove this to yourself, you can enter this formula:

=AGGREGATE(15,6,IF($A$3:$A$13<>$F$2,IF($B$3:$B$13=E5,$C$3:$C$13)),1)

You get a #VALUE! error. If you were to enter the formula using Ctrl+Shift+Enter, the formula would work, but it would defeat the goal of inventing an array formula that does not require Ctrl+Shift+Enter.

Therefore, if you are to remain faithful in your attempt to create a formula that does not require Ctrl+Shift+Enter, you need to adjust the formula element by removing the IF functions altogether. If you rearrange the two conditions and the range of numbers, you go from this formula element:

IF($A$3:$A$13<>$F$2,IF($B$3:$B$13=E5,$C$3:$C$13))

to this formula element:

$C$3:$C$13/(($A$3:$A$13<>$F$2)*($B$3:$B$13=E5))

Looking at the two-IF formula you just tried, notice that when you look left to right, the two conditions come first, and the numbers come last. With the array calculation for AGGREGATE, the numbers come first (in the numerator), and then you use division, and in the denominator you place the two conditional array calculations.

In addition, rather than use two IF functions to determine whether both conditions are met, you use multiplication. Multiplying two arrays of logical values is called **Boolean multiplication**, and only when there is a corresponding TRUE in the first array and a corresponding TRUE in the second array is the number from the numerator selected. The multiplication enforces an AND criterion where both conditions must be true. However, unlike when you use two IF functions, with Boolean multiplication, the resulting array is not filled with TRUEs and FALSEs but instead is filled with 1s and 0s (where 1 means TRUE, and 0 means FALSE).

Note: This is the first time in this book that you have seen that a math operation on a logical value converts TRUE to 1 and FALSE to 0. You will see this many more times in this book and learn more about it later, in Chapter 11.

If you were to evaluate the Boolean conditional array calculation for the AGGREGATE, you would see this:

$C$3:$C$13/(($A$3:$A$13<>$F$2)*($B$3:$B$13=E5))
{34.5;44.3;49;37.8;**47.5**;43;35.9;51;53.4;**55.6**;39}/(({FALSE;TRUE;TRUE;FALSE;**TRUE**;TRUE, FALSE;TRUE;TRUE;**TRUE**;FALSE})*({FALSE;FALSE;FALSE;TRUE;**TRUE**;FALSE;FALSE, FALSE;FALSE;**TRUE**;FALSE})
{34.5;44.3;49;37.8;**47.5**;43;35.9;51;53.4;**55.6**;39}/{0;0;0;0;**1**;0;0;0;0;**1**;0}
{#DIV/0!;#DIV/0!;#DIV/0!;#DIV/0!;**47.5**;#DIV/0!;#DIV/0!;#DIV/0!;#DIV/0!;**55.6**;#DIV/0!}

The resultant array contains only the numbers that meet both conditions (AND criteria). As with the two-IF construction, you have created an array of filter values! The difference here is that you have filtered out the values that do not meet the two conditions with #DIV/0! errors rather than FALSE values. The #DIV/0! errors are important because if you had a second instance of multiplication rather than division, the resultant array would contain zeros rather than errors; the MIN function would then pick a zero value as the minimum value rather than pick the correct racer's fastest time.

Further, #DIV/0! is not a problem for the AGGREGATE function because the options argument contains a 6, which instructs the function to ignore errors. Still further, the AGGREGATE function array argument performs the Boolean math and does not require Ctrl+Shift+Enter.

As shown in Figure 4.38, you place the Boolean conditional array calculation in the array argument of the AGGREGATE function. Notice in the denominator that because of Excel's order of precedence, you must add a set of parentheses for each comparative operator, and you also need an extra set of parentheses to force the multiplication to occur before the division.

	A	B	C	D	E	F	G	H	I
1	Calculate fastest time for each Racer NOT at PI track.								
2	Track	BMX Racer	Time (s)		Track	PI			
3	PI	Zaine	34.5						
4	SeaTac	Logan	44.3		BMX Racer	Time (s)			
5	Sumner	Zaine	49		Isaac	=AGGREGATE(15,6,$C$3:$C$13/(($A$3:$A$13<>$F$2)*($B$3:$B$13=E5))			
6	PI	Isaac	37.8		Logan	AGGREGATE(function_num, options, **array**, [k])			
7	SeaTac	Isaac	47.5		Zaine	AGGREGATE(function_num, options, **ref1**, ref2, [ref3], ...)			
8	SeaTac	Zaine	43						
9	PI	Logan	35.9						
10	Sumner	Zaine	51						
11	Sumner	Logan	53.4						
12	Sumner	Isaac	55.6						
13	PI	Zaine	39						

Figure 4.38 *The array argument of AGGREGATE contains the entire array formula element.*

As shown in Figure 4.39, you can finish off the conditional MIN calculation by typing a 1 into the [k] argument. By setting k = 1, you are telling the SMALL (function 15) to find the first smallest race time that matches the criteria.

Figure 4.39 *In the k argument of AGGREGATE type a one to get the maximum value.*

As shown in Figure 4.40, you do not need to enter the formula by using Ctrl+Shift+Enter.

| | fx | =AGGREGATE(15,6,$C$3:$C$13/(($A$3:$A$13<>$F$2)*($B$3:$B$13=E5)),1) |

	A	B	C	D	E	F
1	Calculate fastest time for each Racer NOT at PI track.					
2	Track	BMX Racer	Time (s)		Track	PI
3	PI	Zaine	34.5			
4	SeaTac	Logan	44.3		BMX Racer	Time (s)
5	Sumner	Zaine	49		Isaac	47.5
6	PI	Isaac	37.8		Logan	44.3
7	SeaTac	Isaac	47.5		Zaine	43

Figure 4.40 *The array formula does not need Ctrl+Shift+Enter.*

Notes About the Formula
=AGGREGATE(15,6,$C$3:$C$13/(($A$3:$A$13<>$F$2)*($B$3:$B$13=E5)),1)

The following table provides a summary of the AGGREGATE and Boolean conditional calculation array formula you just learned about.

Impetus for Creating an Array Formula:
You need to calculate the minimum value, based on two criteria. You want a formula that you can enter and copy down a column, that will instantly update if the source data changes, and that does not require Ctrl+Shift+Enter.
Calculation Summary:
1. =AGGREGATE(15,6,$C$3:$C$13/(($A$3:$A$13<>$F$2)*($B$3:$B$13=E5)),1)
You have Excel 2010 or later, so you choose AGGREGATE because the array argument can handle array operations without Ctrl+Shift+Enter.
The formula element $C$3:$C$13/(($A$3:$A$13<>$F$2)*($B$3:$B$13=E5)) contains four array calculations.
This is an array formula because you are performing operations on arrays, and the operations produce resultant arrays.
The array calculations filters the values based on the criteria "not PI" and Isaac.
2. =$C$3:$C$13/(($A$3:$A$13<>"PI")*($B$3:$B$13="Isaac"))
Question 1: Are any values in the Track column not equal to PI.
Question 2: Are any values in the BMX Racer column equal to Isaac?
Parentheses around the individual comparative operator calculations force the comparative operators to evaluate before the multiplication occurs.
Array calculation 1: ($A$3:$A$13<>"PI") delivers the resultant array {FALSE;TRUE;TRUE;-FALSE;TRUE;TRUE;FALSE;TRUE;TRUE;TRUE;FALSE}.
Array calculation 2: ($B$3:$B$13="Isaac") delivers the resultant array {FALSE;FALSE;-FALSE;TRUE;TRUE;FALSE;FALSE;FALSE;FALSE;TRUE;FALSE}.

3. =$C$3:$C$13/({FALSE;TRUE;TRUE;FALSE;TRUE;TRUE;FALSE;TRUE; TRUE;*TRUE*;FALSE}*{FALSE;FALSE;FALSE;TRUE;TRUE;FALSE;FALSE; FALSE;FALSE;*TRUE*;FALSE})

Next you must multiply the two arrays of logicals that were created by the array comparative operations. You use Boolean multiplication for the AND criteria. Only when you get TRUE*TRUE = 1 will the number in the numerator be selected.

Parentheses around the multiplication force the multiplication to occur before the division.

Array calculation 3: =$C$3:$C$13/({FALSE;TRUE;TRUE;FALSE;TRUE;TRUE;-FALSE;TRUE;TRUE;*TRUE*;FALSE}*{FALSE;FALSE;FALSE;TRUE;TRUE;FALSE;FALSE;FALSE;-FALSE;*TRUE*;FALSE}) delivers the resultant array =$C$3:$C$13/{0;0;0;0;1;0;0;0;0;1;0} to the denominator of the division calculation.

4. ={34.5;44.3;49;37.8;47.5;43;35.9;51;53.4;55.6;39}/{0;0;0;0;1;0;0;0;0;1;0}

Next you divide the two arrays. Only the numbers associated with a 1 will be selected.

Array calculation 4: ={34.5;44.3;49;37.8;47.5;43;35.9;51;53.4;55.6;39}/{0;0;0;0;1;0;0;0;0;1;0} delivers the resultant array {#DIV/0!;#DIV/0!;#DIV/0!;#DIV/0!;47.5;#DIV/0!;#DIV/0!;#DIV/0!;#DIV/0!;55.6;#DIV/0!} to the MIN calculation in the AGGREGATE function.

The division is the key concept when you make a minimum conditional array calculation because if you used multiplying instead, the zero values would cause the MIN function to incorrectly select a 0.

5. =AGGREGATE(15,6,{#DIV/0!;#DIV/0!;#DIV/0!;#DIV/0!;47.5;#DIV/0!;#DIV/0!;#DIV/0!;#DIV/0! ;55.6;#DIV/0!},1)

The array argument in AGGREGATE handles this without Ctrl+Shift+Enter.

The 15 in the function_num argument tells AGGREGATE to do a MIN calculation.

The 6 in the options argument tells the AGGREGATE to ignore errors.

The 1 in the [k] argument tells AGGREGATE to take the first smallest value.

6. The formula delivers the single value 47.5.

Entering a Formula into a Cell:

The array argument in AGGREGATE can handle array operations without Ctrl+Shift+Enter.

Conclusion:

If you have Excel 2010 or later, you do not want to create a PivotTable, you need a formula that you can copy down a column, and you want to avoid Ctrl+Shift+Enter, this array formula is a great option.

Should You Use AGGREGATE and Boolean Conditional Calculation or MIN/IF/IF?

The AGGREGATE and Boolean conditional calculation and the MIN/IF/IF array formula are similar in formula calculation time and in how they are created. Perhaps some will find the AGGREGATE and Boolean calculation a bit more complicated. The AGGREGATE does not require Ctrl+Shift+Enter. The MIN/IF/IF array formula does require Ctrl+Shift+Enter. In general, if two formulas are equally efficient, I tend to go with the one that does not require Ctrl+Shift+Enter. Nevertheless, Excel offers different options, and when formulas are close like these are, either one is fine.

Always keeping the larger context in mind, Figures 4.41 and 4.42 show how the DMIN function and data table or a PivotTable could be used to calculate the fastest times for each racer that are *not* from the PI track.

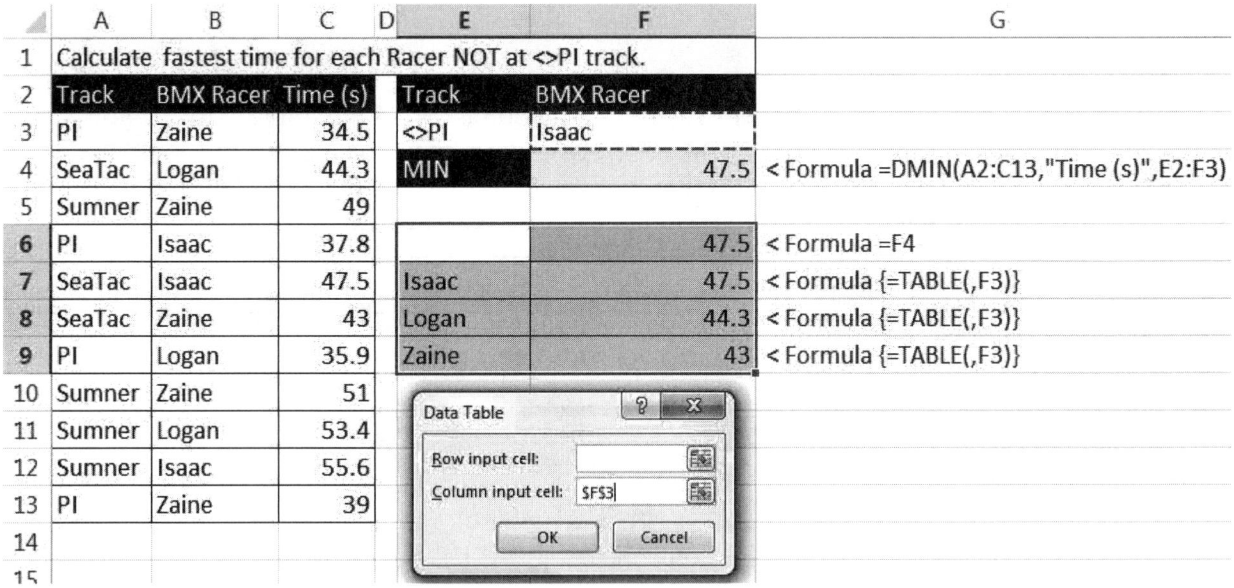

	A	B	C	D	E	F	G
1	Calculate fastest time for each Racer NOT at <>PI track.						
2	Track	BMX Racer	Time (s)		Track	BMX Racer	
3	PI	Zaine	34.5		<>PI	Isaac	
4	SeaTac	Logan	44.3		MIN		47.5 < Formula =DMIN(A2:C13,"Time (s)",E2:F3)
5	Sumner	Zaine	49				
6	PI	Isaac	37.8				47.5 < Formula =F4
7	SeaTac	Isaac	47.5		Isaac		47.5 < Formula {=TABLE(,F3)}
8	SeaTac	Zaine	43		Logan		44.3 < Formula {=TABLE(,F3)}
9	PI	Logan	35.9		Zaine		43 < Formula {=TABLE(,F3)}
10	Sumner	Zaine	51				
11	Sumner	Logan	53.4				
12	Sumner	Isaac	55.6				
13	PI	Zaine	39				
14							
15							

Data Table

Row input cell:

Column input cell: $F$3

OK   Cancel

Figure 4.41 *Notice that the <>PI criteria is typed in cell E3. You'll learn more about data tables in Chapter 21.*

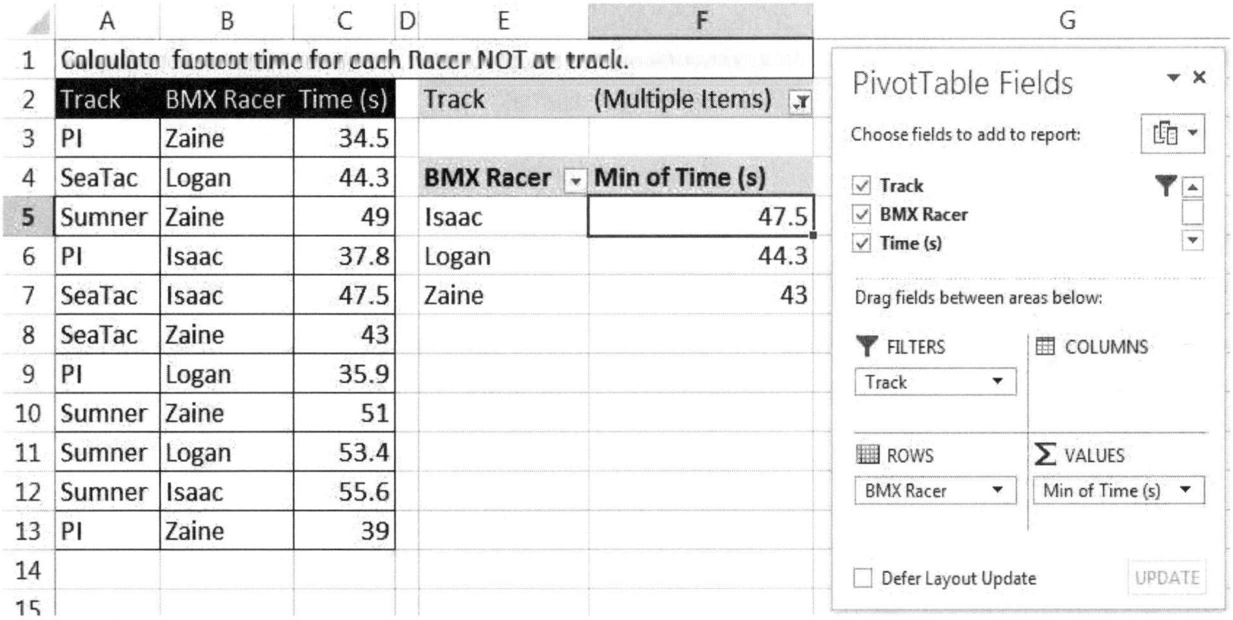

	A	B	C	D	E	F	G
1	Calculate fastest time for each Racer NOT at track.						
2	Track	BMX Racer	Time (s)		Track	(Multiple Items)	
3	PI	Zaine	34.5				
4	SeaTac	Logan	44.3		BMX Racer	Min of Time (s)	
5	Sumner	Zaine	49		Isaac	47.5	
6	PI	Isaac	37.8		Logan	44.3	
7	SeaTac	Isaac	47.5		Zaine	43	
8	SeaTac	Zaine	43				
9	PI	Logan	35.9				
10	Sumner	Zaine	51				
11	Sumner	Logan	53.4				
12	Sumner	Isaac	55.6				
13	PI	Zaine	39				
14							
15							

PivotTable Fields   ▼ ×

Choose fields to add to report:

☑ Track
☑ BMX Racer
☑ Time (s)

Drag fields between areas below:

▼ FILTERS   ⊞ COLUMNS
Track   ▼

⊞ ROWS   Σ VALUES
BMX Racer   ▼   Min of Time (s) ▼

☐ Defer Layout Update   UPDATE

Figure 4.42 *Notice the "not PI" filter on the PivotTable. After you create a PivotTable, use the Filter drop-down item Track to uncheck PI.*

Standard Deviation IF

So far in the chapter you have seen how to make an aggregate calculation like MIN or MAX using the AGGREGATE function, an IF/IF construction, D-functions, or a PivotTable. What if you had to calculate standard deviation (a statistic measure of variation in the data set)? You could use a D-function, a PivotTable, or an IF construction, but you could not use the AGGREGATE function. Why? Because the two standard deviation functions that AGGREGATE provides are function numbers 7 and 8. AGGREGATE's function numbers 1 to 13 cannot handle array operations. In this case, if you wanted to calculate the sample standard deviation with a formula that could be copied down a column, you could choose to use the IF function inside the STDEV.S (Excel 2010) or STDEV (Excel 2007 or earlier) function. Figure 4.43 shows this calculation.

◢	A	B	C	D	E	F	G
1	Calculate Standard Deviation for each city.						
2	City	Calls to Police					
3	Oakland	175			Ave	S.D.	Excel 2010:
4	Richmond	112		Oakland	155.75	42.5157	< Formula {=STDEV.S(IF($A$3:$A$14=D4,$B$3:$B$14))}
5	S.F.	256		Richmond	119.5	12.5565	< Formula {=STDEV.S(IF($A$3:$A$14=D5,$B$3:$B$14))}
6	Oakland	201		S.F.	208.5	64.4903	< Formula {=STDEV.S(IF($A$3:$A$14=D6,$B$3:$B$14))}
7	Richmond	120					
8	S.F.	165			Ave	S.D.	Excel 2007 or earlier:
9	Oakland	102		Oakland	155.75	42.5157	< Formula {=STDEV(IF($A$3:$A$14=D9,$B$3:$B$14))}
10	Richmond	109		Richmond	119.5	12.5565	< Formula {=STDEV(IF($A$3:$A$14=D10,$B$3:$B$14))}
11	S.F.	142		S.F.	208.5	64.4903	< Formula {=STDEV(IF($A$3:$A$14=D11,$B$3:$B$14))}
12	Oakland	145					
13	Richmond	137			#VALUE!	< =AGGREGATE(7,6,$B$3:$B$14/($A$3:$A$14=D9))	
14	S.F.	271			* Function 7 does not perform array calculations.		

Figure 4.43 *Standard deviation is a statistical measure that helps show how reliable an average calculation is; the smaller it is, the more reliable. In this example, Richmond has the most reliable average.*

Filtering Values Inside a Formula

Throughout this chapter you have used the IF function or Boolean math to filter the values inside the formula. This is an important concept to have in your Excel toolbox.

Array Formula Efficiency Rule 15

You can filter values inside a formula with the IF function or with Boolean math.

This is an example of filtering values using the IF function:
=MAX(IF($A$3:$A$12=$F$2,IF($B$3:$B$12=E5,$C$3:$C$12))).

This is an example of filtering values using Boolean math:
=AGGREGATE(15,6,$C$3:$C$13/(($A$3:$A$13<>$F$2)*($B$3:$B$13=E5)),1).

Comparing Aggregate Calculations with Criteria

The following is a summary table of advantages and disadvantages of PivotTables, D-functions, AGGREGATE, and IF/IF:

Aggregate Calculations with Criteria		
Solution	**Advantage**	**Disadvantage**
PivotTables	• Easy to create, especially with multiple criteria. • Easy to change.	• Does not update instantly. • Only 11 functions.
D-functions	• Easy to create. • Fast formula calculation time. • No Ctrl+Shift+Enter.	• Not easily copied down a column or across a row. • Data set must have field names.
AGGREGATE	• Formulas update instantly when data changes. • Easy to copy formula down column or across row. • No Ctrl+Shift+Enter.	• Not easy to create. • Longer calculation time than D-functions. • Can only make array calculations on functions 14–19. For example, it cannot make a standard deviation calculation
IF/IF	• Formulas update instantly when data changes. • Easy to copy formula down column or across row. • Can make more calculations, like STDEV.	• Requires Ctrl+Shift+Enter. • Not easy to create. • Longer calculation time than D-functions.

Timing the Formulas in This Chapter

As discussed in Chapter 2, array formulas pointing to large data sets can increase formula calculation time for a workbook. In general, faster calculation times are more efficient. As you move forward through this book, you will occasionally time the different formulas to determine which formulas are faster. The anecdotal results that I got are listed below. To time your own formulas, look back to Chapter 2 for details. (Timing depends on many factors, and your particular situation may have different timing results.) To see the workbook with the timing results that I got, open the file named 01Time2CriteriaMIN.xlsm in the folder Timing in the zipped folder FilesForCtrl-ShiftEnterBook. The Introduction of this book explains how to get these files. Figure 4.44 shows the timing results (in seconds) that I got for 25,000 rows of data.

Time (s) Single Cell				
	[1] DMIN	[2] DMIN & Data Table	[3] AGGREGATE	[4] MIN/IF/IF
Time 1	0.00619	0.0069	0.01431	0.01442
Time 2	0.00649	0.00692	0.01463	0.01438
Time 3	0.00664	0.00646	0.01371	0.0143
Ave	0.00644	0.00676	0.014216667	0.014366667
% change from [1]	0.0%	5.0%	120.8%	123.1%

Time (s) Whole Column			
	[2] DMIN & Data Table	[3] AGGREGATE	[4] MIN/IF/IF
Time 1	0.00894	0.05715	0.055551
Time 2	0.00894	0.05488	0.059
Time 3	0.00844	0.05707	0.05741
Ave	0.008773333	0.056366667	0.057320333
% change from [2]	0.0%	542.5%	553.3%

Figure 4.44 *The D-function calculates more quickly than MIN/IF or AGGREGATE.*

Throughout the rest of this book, you will see many more examples of comparative array operations.

Chapter Summary

This chapter covers a lot of ground, talking about array calculations that use comparative operators, aggregate calculations with criteria, D-functions, PivotTables, the IF function "trump rule," and even the Excel 2010 function AGGREGATE to help you avoid Ctrl+Shift+Enter. Chapter 5 takes a look at the join array operator and a lot more.

Chapter 5: Join Array Operations

Excel Files

To follow along with the examples in this chapter, you can download the accompanying files, as explained in the Introduction.

Join Operation

So far in the book you have seen math and comparative array operations. This chapter takes a look at an example of a join array operation.

The join operator is the ampersand: &. It allows you to join two items so they can become one. You can join things like numbers, text in double quotes, formula results, and more. You will see how to use the ampersand to make an array operation in the following "two-value lookup" example.

Two Lookup Values for Creating a Cross-Tabulated Report

Figure 5.1 shows the source data in the range A2:C16 and your desired cross-tabulated report in the range E2:G10. The cross-tabulated report must show the Right and Left quantity for each product code. To accomplish this with a formula, you need to create a single formula that you can enter into cell F4 and then copy through the range F4:G10. The problem is that for each cell in the range F4:G10, you have two lookup values! For example, in cell F4, the lookup formula retrieved the quantity 30 based on the lookup value 2A35 2A36 from cell E4 and the second lookup value L in cell F3. Excel's standard lookup functions are programmed to look up only a single value in a single column. This formula has two lookup values in two different columns. One way to accomplish a two-value lookup is to join the two lookup values and the two columns inside the lookup formula. You'll see how to do this next.

	A	B	C	D	E	F	G
1	Create cross tabulated table that looks up quantity sold based on 2 lookup values.						
2	Product Code	L/R?	Qty			Qty	
3	2A45-2A46	R	18		Product Code	L	R
4	2A39-2A40	L	36		2A35-2A36	30	35
5	**2A35-2A36**	**L**	**30**		2A38-2A39	30	36
6	2A38-2A39	R	36		2A39-2A40	36	35
7	2A44-2A45	L	18		2A44-2A45	18	28
8	2A48-2A49	L	20		2A45-2A46	24	18
9	2A45-2A46	L	24		2A46-2A47	30	36
10	2A48-2A49	R	24		2A48-2A49	20	24
11	2A44-2A45	R	28				
12	2A46-2A47	L	30				
13	2A38-2A39	L	30				
14	2A35-2A36	R	35				
15	2A39-2A40	R	35				
16	2A46-2A47	R	36				

Figure 5.1 *Formula goal: Create a cross-tabulated table based on two lookup values.*

As shown in Figure 5.2 you can use the INDEX lookup function and enter the quantity column in the array argument. (The array argument contains the values you want to retrieve.) Typing a comma gets you to the row_num argument, which requires the relative position of the item being looked up. Looking back at Figure 5.1, you can see that the two lookup values and the quantity you need to retrieve are in the relative position 3. The lookup function MATCH is perfect for determining the relative position of an item in a list. You can put the MATCH function into the row_num argument of the INDEX.

Figure 5.2 *Start your formula with INDEX.*

Figure 5.3 shows the start of the MATCH function. In the lookup_value argument for MATCH, you put the cell reference with the product code and lock the column references but not the row. Then you type the join symbol, & (ampersand), and then you use the cell reference with the Left/Right letter and lock the row references but not the column. By joining the two values, you create a single value.

Product Code	L	R	
2A35-2A36	=INDEX($C$3:$C$16,MATCH($E4&F$3		
2A38-2A39		MATCH(**lookup_value**, lookup_array, [ma†	
2A39-2A40			

Figure 5.3 *Create a joined lookup_value.*

To prove to yourself that it is one value, highlight the formula element $E4&F$3 and press the F9 key to evaluate. Figure 5.4 shows that you have taken two lookup values and created a single lookup value. Be sure to use Ctrl+Z to undo this evaluation.

$16,MATCH("2A35-2A36L"

MATCH(**lookup_value**, lookup_array, [match_type])

Figure 5.4 *Using the F9 key you can see that the join operation created a single lookup_value.*

You type a comma to get the lookup_array (the array that contains the items you would like to match against lookup_value to determine relative position). Since you have two columns, you join them in the same way that you joined the lookup values. Figure 5.5 shows this join. In the process of joining the two columns, you have made a "join array operation. Because the lookup_array argument is not innately programmed to perform array operations, and so you need to enter this formula with Ctrl+Shift+Enter.

Figure 5.5 *The lookup_array argument of the MATCH contains a join array operation.*

To see that you have taken two columns and joined them to create a single column, as shown in Figure 5.6, you can highlight the join array operation and press the F9 key to evaluate. That is amazing! Right in the formula, you have made two columns into one. Be sure to use Ctrl+Z to undo this evaluation.

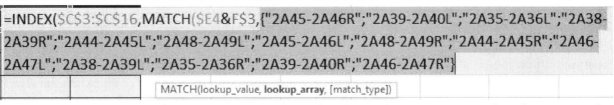

=INDEX($C$3:$C$16,MATCH($E4&F$3,{"2A45-2A46R";"2A39-2A40L";"2A35-2A36L";"2A38-2A39R";"2A44-2A45L";"2A48-2A49L";"2A45-2A46L";"2A48-2A49R";"2A44-2A45R";"2A46-2A47L";"2A38-2A39L";"2A35-2A36R";"2A39-2A40R";"2A46-2A47R"}

MATCH(lookup_value, **lookup_array**, [match_type])

Figure 5.6 *Evaluating the join array operation shows that the resultant array is a single column. Two columns have become one!*

Figure 5.7 shows how you finish the formula by entering a 0 to indicate an exact match for the [match_type] argument because the columns are not sorted.

=INDEX($C$3:$C$16,MATCH($E4&F$3,$A$3:$A$16&$B$3:$B$16,0))

MATCH(lookup_value, lookup_array, **[match_type]**)

Figure 5.7 *Remember to undo the evaluation.*

You enter the formula with Ctrl+Shift+Enter and copy it through the range F4:G10. Figure 5.8 shows the end result. If you need a single-cell formula that can do a two-value lookup, this is a good one.

fx	{=INDEX($C$3:$C$16,MATCH($E4&F$3,$A$3:$A$16&$B$3:$B$16,0))}

	C	D	E	F	G
table that looks up quantity sold based on 2 lookup values.					
	Qty			Qty	
	18		Product Code	L	R
	36		2A35-2A36	30	35
	30		2A38-2A39	30	36
	36		2A39-2A40	36	35
	18		2A44-2A45	18	28
	20		2A45-2A46	24	18
	24		2A46-2A47	30	36
	24		2A48-2A49	20	24

Figure 5.8 *Enter the array formula into cell F4 with Ctrl+Shift+Enter and copy the formula throughout the table.*

An alternative method for joining involves using an extra character between the two joined cells or columns. Figure 5.9 shows this alternative. The idea is that this is a "safe" way to join items so that if you ever create a joined item that is an actual item in the data set, there will be no problem. For example, if you joined 30 and 20 and the item 3020 were in the data set, you might have a problem. In the data set in this example, you did not run this risk, so you did not use an extra character.

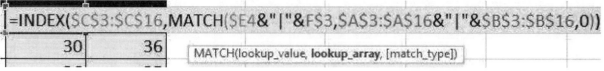

Figure 5.9 *It is safe to add an extra character between the joined items.*

Notes About the Formula
=INDEX($C$3:$C$16,MATCH($E4&F$3,$A$3:$A$16&$B$3:$B$16,0))

The following table presents a summary of the AGGREGATE and Boolean conditional calculation array formula you just learned about.

Impetus for Creating an Array Formula:
You need to retrieve items based on two lookup values, you can't use a helper column, and you need to copy the formula through a range of cells.
Calculation Summary:
1. =INDEX($C$3:$C$16,MATCH($E4&F$3,$A$3:$A$16&$B$3:$B$16,0))
The two arrays are the ranges $A$3:$A$16 and $B$3:$B$16.   You are performing a join operation on two arrays.   This is an array formula because you are performing an operation on an array, and the operation produces a resultant array.   The formula says to look up the quantity based on the lookup values L and 2A35-2A36.
2. =INDEX($C$3:$C$16,MATCH("2A35-2A36L",$A$3:$A$16&$B$3:$B$16,0))
The two lookup values are joined to create single lookup value.   **Array calculation:** $A$3:$A$16&$B$3:$B$16 delivers the resultant array {"2A45-2A46R";"2A39-2A40L";"2A35-2A36L";"2A38-2A39R";"2A44-2A45L";"2A48-2A49L";"2A45-2A46L";"2A48-2A49R";"2A44-2A45R";"2A46-2A47L";"2A38-2A39L";"2A35-2A36R";"2A39-2A40R";"2A46-2A47R"} to the lookup_array argument in MATCH.
3. =INDEX($C$3:$C$16,MATCH("2A35-2A36L",{"2A45-2A46R";"2A39-2A40L";"2A35-2A36L";"2A38-2A39R";"2A44-2A45L";"2A48-2A49L";"2A45-2A46L";"2A48-2A49R";"2A44--2A45R";"2A46-2A47L";"2A38-2A39L";"2A35-2A36R";"2A39-2A40R";"2A46-2A47R"},0))
In essence, the helper column that could sit in the cells but that you did not want in the cells can be created in the formula with this join array operation.
4. =INDEX($C$3:$C$16,3)
MATCH delivers the relative position to the row_num argument in INDEX.
5. The formula delivers the single item 30.
Entering a Formula into a Cell:
The MATCH function lookup_array argument is not innately programmed to handle array operations. You must use Ctrl+Shift+Enter.
Conclusion:
If you cannot use a helper column, you need to copy the formula, and you cannot sort columns, this is a good option.

What if You Have Three Lookup Values? Four?

You can extend this join array operation to include three or more lookup values. If you have three lookup values, simply join the three lookup values in the MATCH lookup_value argument and join the three columns in the lookup_array argument. However, the join operation can require a lot of formula calculation time. Considering other means to do a lookup on two or more values at once is important. Next, you will consider using the DGET function.

Using the DGET Function for a Multiple-Criteria Lookup

DGET is one of the coolest functions ever created. If you have a proper data set (that is, with field names at the top of each column), DGET can do a lookup based on multiple criteria.

> **Note:** D-functions can handle AND criteria (that is, all criteria must be met) or OR criteria (that is, at least one criteria must be met). AND criteria must be in the same row (as shown in Figure 5.10), and OR criteria must be on different rows (see Chapter 11).

Figure 5.10 shows an example. As mentioned earlier in the book, the big drawback to using D-functions is that it is hard to copy them down a column because the criteria argument requires field names with criteria listed below. If you don't need to copy the formula to other cells, you should use the DGET function because it calculates much more quickly and is easier to create than the array formula shown in Figure 5.8 and 5.9. If you need to copy the formula to other cells and you do not want to use the join array operation formula, you could use DGET with the data table trick shown back in Figure 4.16, or you could go a whole new direction and use a helper column. You will see how using a helper column works next.

G4	▼	:	✕	✓	*fx*	=DGET(A2:C16,G3,E3:F4)

◢	A	B	C	D	E	F	G
1	Create cross tabulated table that looks up quantity sold based on 2 lookup values.						
2	Product Code	L/R?	Qty				Qty
3	2A45-2A46	R	18		Product Code	L/R?	Qty
4	2A39-2A40	L	36		2A38-2A39	R	36
5	2A35-2A36	L	30				

Figure 5.10 *DGET is easy to create and calculates more quickly than a join array formula. DGET cannot be easily copied down a column.*

Using a Helper Column to Speed Up Formula Calculation Time for Two Value Lookup

Figure 5.11 shows how you could add a helper column to create a joined key (also called a *concatenated key*) in column A. Cell A3 contains the formula =B3&"|"&C3, which is copied down the column and creates a new column with a single lookup value for each record (row). The lookup formula is a simple VLOOKUP with a joined lookup value: =VLOOKUP($F4&"|"&G$3,$A$3:$D$16,4,0). If you can afford the spreadsheet space for the extra column, this setup is usually easier to create and will calculate more quickly than using an array formula.

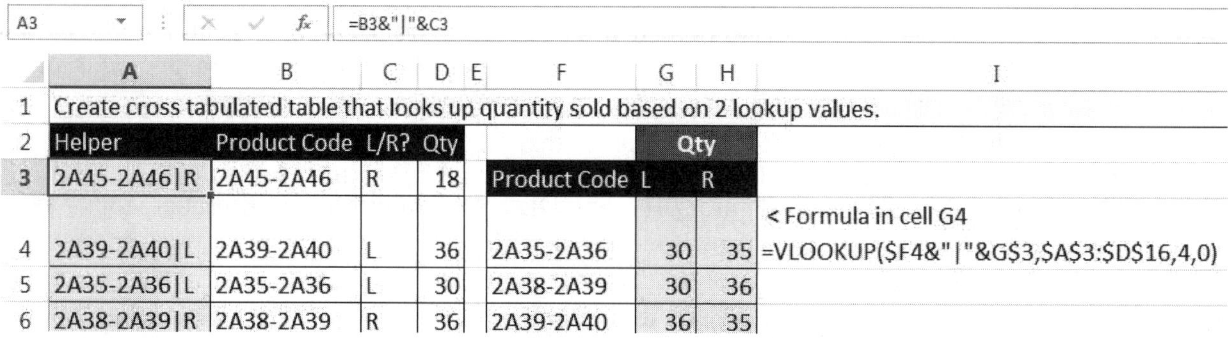

Figure 5.11 *Using a helper column is calculates faster than a join array formula, but it requires extra space in the spreadsheet.*

Using a PivotTable for Two-Value Lookup

Finally, if you do not need the immediate updateability of formulas, you can use a PivotTable to create a cross-tabulated report. Usually a PivotTable is for aggregate calculations with one or more criteria, but because you have no duplicate records in this table, you can use a PivotTable to display the retrieved values. Figure 5.12 shows how you could create this report by using a PivotTable.

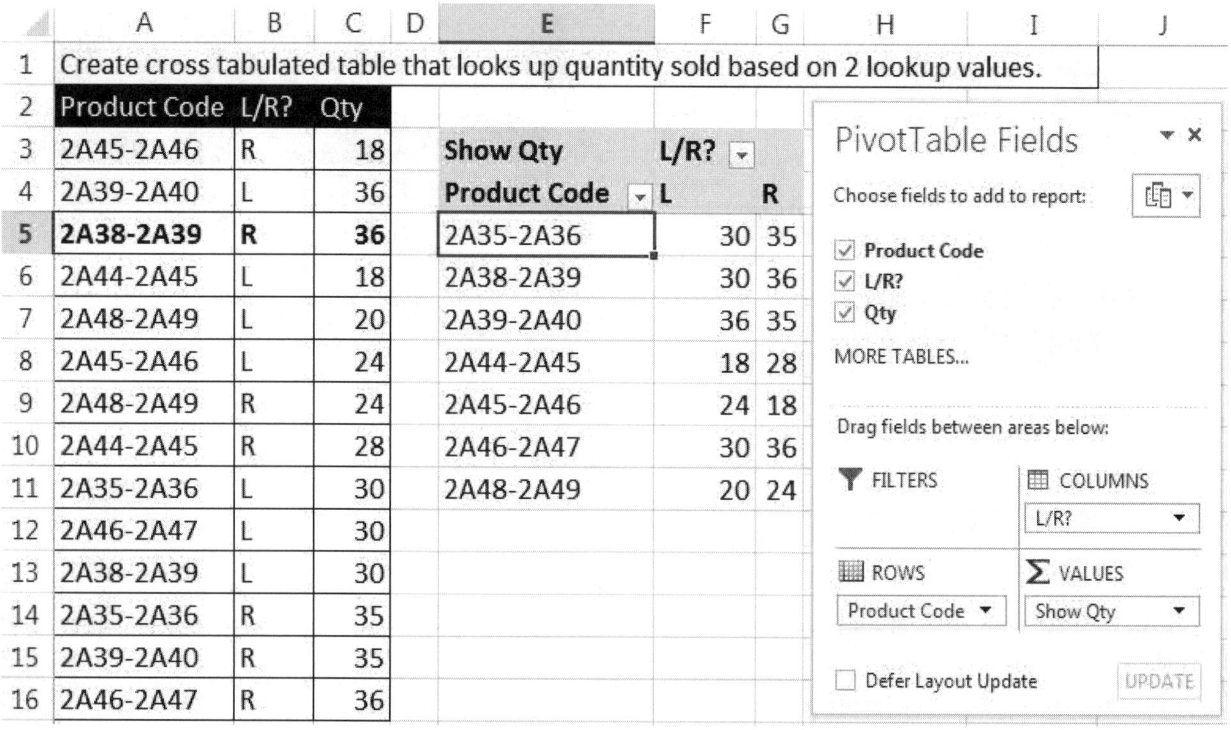

Figure 5.12 *Using a PivotTable is quick and easy, especially if you don't need immediate formula updateability.*

The following section looks at how sorting columns can be helpful for formulas that do a two-value lookup.

Sorting by Two Columns and Using an Approximate Match

When doing a two-value lookup, if you could sort the two columns in the data set, you could use an approximate match lookup rather than exact match for the join array operation formula or a helper column solution. An approximate match calculates much more quickly than an exact match because an exact match looks through the entire column, top to bottom, whereas an approximate match does a binary search, successively dividing the table in half as it searches. As shown in Figure 5.13, the trick is to first sort the L/R? column ascending and then sort the Product Code column ascending; in this way, the combined single joined column will be sorted ascending. Further, notice that the MATCH function [match_type] argument is left empty (omitted) because the default is an approximate match.

	A	B	C	D	E	F	G	H	I	J	K
1	Create cross tabulated table that looks up quantity sold based on 2 lookup values.										
2	Product Code	L/R?	Qty				Qty				
3	2A35-2A36	L	30		Product Code	L	R				
4	2A35-2A36	R	35		2A35-2A36	=INDEX($C$3:$C$16,MATCH($E4&$F$3,$A$3:$A$16&$B$3:$B$16))					
5	2A38-2A39	L	30		2A38-2A39	30	36				
6	2A38-2A39	R	36		2A39-2A40	36	35	MATCH(lookup_value, lookup_array, [match_type])			
7	2A39-2A40	L	36		2A44-2A45	18	28				
8	2A39-2A40	R	35		2A45-2A46	24	18				
9	2A44-2A45	L	18		2A46-2A47	30	36				
10	2A44-2A45	R	28		2A48-2A49	20	24				
11	2A45-2A46	L	24								
12	2A45-2A46	R	18								
13	2A46-2A47	L	30		1) Sort L/R? column, A to Z.						
14	2A46-2A47	R	36		2) Sort Product Code column, A to Z.						
15	2A48-2A49	L	20		3) Leave [match_type] argumnet empty to allow Aproximate Match.						
16	2A48-2A49	R	24								

Figure 5.13 *If you want to speed up the calculation time, sort the two columns and use an approximate match.*

If you are allowed to sort the two columns, you can take the join array formula one step further by switching from the INDEX and MATCH functions to the LOOKUP function. The LOOKUP function can handle array operations without requiring Ctrl+Shift+Enter. You'll see how to use the LOOKUP function next.

LOOKUP Function Arguments: Array Operations Without Ctrl+Shift+Enter

If you can sort two columns ascending, you can use the LOOKUP function. The LOOKUP function does only an approximate match. In addition, this function has separate arguments for the lookup column, called lookup_vector, and for the column that has the values you want to retrieve, called result_vector. But the most amazing thing about the LOOKUP function is that the lookup_vector and result_vector arguments can both handle array operations without requiring Ctrl+Shift+Enter.

As shown in Figure 5.14, you can enter the joined lookup values into the lookup_value argument. Then you put the join array operation into the lookup_vector argument. Finally, you put the Qty column into the result_vector argument. When you enter the formula, you do not need to use Ctrl+-Shift+Enter.

Figure 5.14 *The LOOKUP function does only an approximate match and can innately handle array operations without requiring Ctrl+Shift+Enter.*

The next section looks at what sorting does for the helper column solution shown in Figure 5.11.

A Sorted Helper Column

The sorting methods you've just looked at can also be used on the helper column solution shown in Figure 5.11. If you can sort the columns, you can use an approximate match in the fourth argument of VLOOKUP. Here is what the formula would look like: =VLOOKUP($F4&"|"&G$3,$A$3:$D$16,4). Because an approximate match is the default, you can simply leave the fourth argument empty. For large data sets, switching from an exact match lookup to an approximate match lookup can significantly reduce formula calculation time.

So far in this book, you have seen three functions that can handle array operations without Ctrl+-Shift+Enter: SUMPRODUCT, AGGREGATE, and LOOKUP. The INDEX function is a fourth function that can handle array operations without Ctrl+Shift+Enter.

The INDEX Function Array Argument: Array Operations Without Ctrl+Shift+Enter

Okay, this next example is a bit silly. But it demonstrates how the array argument in the INDEX function can innately handle array operations without requiring the use of Ctrl+Shift+Enter. Figure 5.15 might remind you of the array formula you created for the two-value lookup situation when the columns were not sorted back in Figure 5.7. The reason you had to use Ctrl+Shift+Enter was because the join array operation was located in the lookup_array argument of the MATCH function, which is not programed to handle array operations unless you use Ctrl+Shift+Enter. If there were a way to place that join array operation into a different function that does not require Ctrl+-Shift+Enter and then place that formula element into the MATCH lookup_array argument, you would not have to use Ctrl+Shift+Enter. The INDEX function allows you to do just that.

Figure 5.15 *The join array operation is located in the lookup_array argument.*

> **Note:** For a comprehensive look at how the INDEX and MATCH functions works, refer to the first video on the *Ctrl+Shift+Enter: Mastering Excel Array Formulas* DVD.

The INDEX function normally looks up a single item, either in a two-way array (rows and columns) or in a one-way array (row or column). But INDEX can also look up an entire row or column. In this case, you want to look up an entire column.

The arguments for INDEX looks like this:

INDEX(array,row_num,column_num)

The trick for looking up an entire column is to tell the row_num argument that you want all the rows (remember that an entire column is simply made up of many rows). If you place a zero in the row_num argument or leave it omitted (empty), you tell INDEX to get the entire column—that is, all the rows. This means you can place the join array operation into the array argument of the INDEX function and leave the row_num argument empty, and INDEX will deliver the single-column joined array result to the MATCH lookup_array argument and will not require Ctrl+Shift+Enter. The next four figures show this array formula.

As shown in Figure 5.16, you place the join array operation into the array argument of INDEX. The array argument of INDEX can handle the array operation without the use of Ctrl+Shift+Enter. Because the array operation is in the array argument of INDEX, and it is no longer in the lookup_array argument of MATCH, this formula does not require Ctrl+Shift+Enter.

`=INDEX($C$3:$C$16,MATCH($E4&F$3,INDEX($A$3:$A$16&$B$3:$B$16,),0))`

| 30 | 36 |

INDEX(**array**, row_num, [column_num])

Figure 5.16 *Place the join array operation into the array argument of INDEX and leave the row_num argument empty.*

The close-up in Figure 5.17 shows that the row_num argument for INDEX is left empty to instruct the INDEX function to retrieve the entire column.

`,INDEX($A$3:$A$16&$B$3:$B$16,)`

INDEX(array, **row_num**, [column_num])

Figure 5.17 *The empty row_num argument instructs INDEX to retrieve all the rows in the array.*

As shown in Figure 5.18, to highlight the INDEX function, you click the lookup_value argument in the ScreenTip for the MATCH function.

`=INDEX($C$3:$C$16,MATCH($E4&F$3,INDEX($A$3:$A$16&$B$3:$B$16,),0))`

| 30 | 36 |

MATCH(lookup_value, **lookup_array**, [match_type])

Figure 5.18 *INDEX sits in the lookup_array argument of the MATCH function.*

As shown in Figure 5.19, you press the F9 key (evaluation key) to prove that the INDEX will deliver the entire joined column to the lookup_array argument of MATCH. Be sure to use Ctrl+Z to undo the evaluation.

`=INDEX($C$3:$C$16,MATCH($E4&F$3,{"2A45-2A46R";"2A39-2A40L";"2A35-2A36L";"2A38-2A39R";"2A44-2A45L";"2A48-2A49L";"2A45-2A46L";"2A48-2A49R";"2A44-2A45R";"2A46-2A47L";"2A38-2A39L";"2A35-2A36R";"2A39-2A40R";"2A46-2A47R"},0))`

| 18 | 28 |

MATCH(lookup_value, **lookup_array**, [match_type])

Figure 5.19 *INDEX delivers a single column to the lookup_array argument of the MATCH function.*

As shown in Figure 5.20, you enter the formula in cell F4 and copy it through the range F4:G10. There are no curly braces in the formula bar.

| F4 | ▼ | ⋮ | ✕ ✓ ƒx | =INDEX($C$3:$C$16,MATCH($E4&F$3,INDEX($A$3:$A$16&$B$3:$B$16,),0)) |

	A	B	C	D	E	F	G	H	I	J
1	Create cross tabulated table that looks up quantity sold based on 2 lookup values.									
2	Product Code	L/R?	Qty			Qty				
3	2A45-2A46	R	18		Product Code	L	R			
4	2A39-2A40	L	36		2A35-2A36	30	35			
5	2A35-2A36	L	30		2A38-2A39	30	36			
6	2A38-2A39	R	36		2A39-2A40	36	35			
7	2A44-2A45	L	18		2A44-2A45	18	28			
8	2A48-2A49	L	20		2A45-2A46	24	18			
9	2A45-2A46	L	24		2A46-2A47	30	36			
10	2A48-2A49	R	24		2A48-2A49	20	24			

Figure 5.20 *Ctrl+Shift+Enter is not required because the array argument in the INDEX can handle array operations without using Ctrl+Shift+Enter.*

At the beginning of this section, I said this would be a silly array formula. Well it is because what you have done is add an extra function to the formula to avoid using Ctrl+Shift+Enter. In general, you don't want to make the formula longer or more complicated than necessary. By adding the extra INDEX function, though, you have done just that. Nevertheless, if you *really* wanted to avoid Ctrl+Shift+Enter, this method would work for the unsorted table and two-value lookup.

One last note: Notice here that you added an "extra" function to avoid Ctrl+Shift+Enter. Earlier, you chose to use SUMPRODUCT over SUM, AGGREGATE over MAX/IF/IF, and LOOKUP over INDEX/MATCH; in those cases, you were not adding an extra function but just chose to use one function over the other to avoid using Ctrl+Shift+Enter. Choosing to use one function over the other to avoid Ctrl+Shift+Enter is usually efficient. Adding an extra function to avoid using Ctrl+-Shift+Enter is probably not efficient.

Array Formula Efficiency Rule 16

The following five function arguments can handle arrays without requiring you to enter the array formula with Ctrl+Shift+Enter:

- The array_1, array_2, etc. arguments in SUMPRODUCT
- The lookup_vector argument in the LOOKUP function
- The result_vector argument in the LOOKUP function
- The array argument in INDEX
- The array argument in AGGREGATE for functions 14 to 19

Comparing Two-Value Lookup Solutions: Join Array Formula, DGET, Helper Column, and PivotTable

The following table presents a summary of the advantages and disadvantages of each of the two-value lookup solutions described in this chapter.

Lookups with Two or More Lookup Values		
Solution	**Advantages**	**Disadvantages**
INDEX and MATCH join array formula	• Formula is contained in a single cell.	• Formula calculation time is longer than any of the other options (but could speed up with sorted columns and an approximate match). • Requires Ctrl+Shift+Enter.
LOOKUP join array formula	• Formula is contained in a single cell. • Does not require Ctrl+Shift+Enter.	• Formula can be used only if the two columns can be sorted ascending.
DGET	• Easy to create. • Fast formula calculation time. • Does not require Ctrl+Shift+Enter.	• Not easily copied down a column or across a row (but could use a data table). • Data set must have field names.
Helper column	• Easy to create. • Fast formula calculation time. • Does not require Ctrl+Shift+Enter.	• Takes up spreadsheet space.
PivotTable	• Easy to create.	• Does not update instantly.

Timing the Formulas in This Chapter

As discussed in Chapter 2, pointing array formulas to large data sets can increase formula calculation time for a workbook. In general, faster calculation times are more efficient. This section shows the anecdotal results I got. To time your own formulas, look back to Chapter 2 for details. (Timing depends on many factors, and your particular situation may have different timing results.) To see the workbook with the timing results that I got, open the file named 02Time2ValueLookup.xlsm.xlsm in the folder Timing in the zipped folder FilesForCtrlShiftEnterBook. The Introduction to this book explains how to get these files. Figure 5.21 shows the timing results (in seconds) I got for a small data set with 1,680 rows of data.

Time (s) Single Cell

	[1] DGET	[2] Helper Column	[3] INDEX & MATCH Join Array Formula	
Time 1	0.0039	0.00413	0.00419	
Time 2	0.00389	0.00413	0.00446	
Time 3	0.00364	0.0041	0.00461	
Ave	0.00381	0.00412	0.00442	
% change from [1]	0.0%	8.1%	16.0%	

Time (s) Whole Column

	[4] INDEX & MATCH Join Array Formula w sorted columns	[2] Helper Column	[5] LOOKUP Join Array Formula w sorted columns	[3] INDEX & MATCH Join Array Formula
Time 1	0.01268	0.01488	0.0209	0.02015
Time 2	0.01674	0.01489	0.01862	0.0191
Time 3	0.01346	0.01478	0.02103	0.02314
Ave	0.014293333	0.01485	0.020183333	0.020796667
% change from [4]	0.0%	3.9%	41.2%	45.5%

Figure 5.21 *Timing results for two-value lookup formulas.*

Throughout the rest of this book, you will see a few more examples of join array operations.

Chapter Summary

This chapter discusses using join array operations, two-value lookups, the DGET function, Pivot-Tables, helper columns, and sorted columns to speed up formula calculation time. It also discusses using the functions LOOKUP and INDEX, which do not require the use of Ctrl+Shift+Enter. Chapter 6 covers function argument array operations.

Chapter 6: Function Argument Array Operations

Excel Files

To follow along with the examples in this chapter, you can download the accompanying files, as explained in the Introduction.

Function Argument Operation

So far in this book, you have seen the array operations: math, comparative, and join. This chapter takes a look at a function argument array operation. Before you can see how a function argument array operation works, you need to think about how a function argument that is expecting a single item operates.

Figure 6.1 shows the LEN function. This function counts how many characters are in a cell. The text argument for the LEN function expects a single item. Because of this, the LEN function delivers a single answer. Figure 6.2 shows the answer 15: There are 15 characters in cell A3.

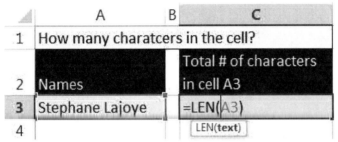

Figure 6.1 *The text in cell A3 is the single item that is given to the text argument.*

| 3 | Stephane Lajoye | | 15 | < Formula =LEN(A3) |

Figure 6.2 *Because the text argument in LEN is given a single item, LEN delivers a single answer.*

Remember this rule for function arguments that expect a single item: If you use a single item with a function argument that expects a single item, the function will deliver a single answer.

But what would happen if you gave the text argument in the LEN function more than one item? The next example illustrates this.

Counting All Characters in a Column with a Function Argument Array Operation

Figure 6.3 shows a column of names. Your goal here is to count how many total characters are in the entire column; that is, you want to count how many characters are in the first name, the second name, and so on. You can start the formula by entering the entire range A2:A6 into the text argument of the LEN function.

	A	B	C
1	Names		Total # of characters in range A2:A69
2	Stephane Lajoye		=LEN(A2:A6)
			LEN(**text**)
3	Jae Klafehn		
4	Broderick Hartjen		
5	Anjanette Orion		
6	Warner Hobb		

Figure 6.3

Figure 6.4 shows that if you evaluate the range A2:A6 (by highlighting it and pressing F9), you see that the text argument for LEN is being given five different text strings. (Be sure to undo the evaluation by pressing Ctrl+Z before moving on.)

> **Note:** A text string just means a sequence of characters (zero or more characters; later you will learn about null text strings) that Excel considers text and not a number or logical.

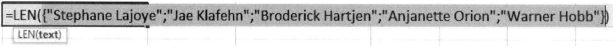
LEN(text)

Figure 6.4 *The text argument is given five text strings to count.*

Figure 6.5 shows that if you evaluate the LEN function (by highlighting it and pressing F9), the function delivers five answers. This means that if you give the LEN function text argument more than one item, it will give you more than one answer. More specifically, when you give the text argument five items, the LEN function gives you a resultant array with five answers. (Be sure to undo the evaluation by pressing Ctrl+Z before moving on.)

=\{15;11;17;15;11\}

Figure 6.5 *If you give the text argument five items, it will deliver a resultant array with five answers.*

Array Formula Efficiency Rule 17

Remember the following about function argument array operations:

- If you use a single item with a function argument that expects a single item, the function will deliver a single answer.
- If you use more than one item with a function argument that expects a single item, the function will deliver more than one answer. Specifically, if you give the function argument *n* items, the function will deliver a resultant array with *n* answers.
- When a function argument is expecting a single item and you give it more than one item, you create a function argument array operation.

If the LEN function is delivering an array of numbers, what are you going to do with the numbers? In this case your goal is to add, so you can place the formula element LEN(A2:A6) into the SUM-PRODUCT function (see Figure 6.6). When you enter the formula, you do not have to use Ctrl+-Shift+Enter because the array argument in SUMPRODUCT can handle array operations without using Ctrl+Shift+Enter.

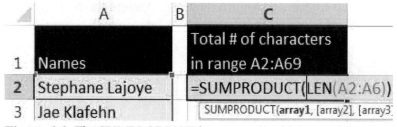

Figure 6.6 *The SUMPRODUCT function will add the resultant array of numbers that is created by the LEN function argument array operation.*

Figure 6.7 shows the final answer. You can see that there are no curly braces in the formula bar.

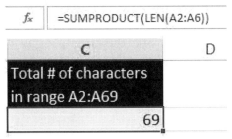

C	D
Total # of characters in range A2:A69	
69	

Figure 6.7 *The array formula does not require Ctrl+Shift+Enter.*

Lookup Addition: Using SUMPRODUCT and SUMIF When a Lookup Table Is Not Sorted

Figure 6.9 shows a transaction data set in the range A3:C7 that lists the sales for each product sold; it does not list the costs. If your goal is to calculate gross profit (sales – costs), calculating total costs is easy, but how do you calculate total costs, given only a lookup table with a single occurrence for each product's cost? One way to solve the problem is to add a helper column with a VLOOKUP formula and then simply sum the column of costs. Figure 6.8 shows this helper column approach.

	A	B	C	D	E	F	G
1	Calculate total sales, costs and gross profit.						
2	Date	Product	Sales	Helper		Lookup Table:	
3	10/17/2012	Quad	36	18		Product	Cost
4	10/17/2012	Tri Fly	9	4		Quad	18
5	10/17/2012	Quad	30	18		Tri Fly	4
6	10/17/2012	Tri Fly	8	4		Fun Fly	2
7	10/17/2012	Fun Fly	6	2			
9	Total Sales		89	< Formula =SUM(C3:C7)			
10	Total Costs		46	< Formula =SUM(D3:D7)			
11	Gross Profit		43	< Formula =B9-B10			
12							

Figure 6.8 *VLOOKUP helper column solution.*

What if you cannot afford the spreadsheet space or you don't care about seeing the individual detail? Is there a single-cell formula you can create that will look up the costs for each transaction and then add them? You might be tempted to try to make a function argument array calculation by placing more than one value into the lookup_value argument of VLOOKUP, as shown in Figure 6.9. However, the lookup_value argument of VLOOKUP is not programmed to make a function argument array calculation. (The HLOOKUP function also exhibits this characteristic.) You therefore have to look at this problem from a different angle.

`=VLOOKUP(B3:B7,F4:G6,2,0)`

VLOOKUP(**lookup_value**, table_array, col_index_num, [range_lookup])

Figure 6.9 *The lookup_value argument cannot handle an array of values.*

One possibility is to use the SUMIF function rather than the VLOOKUP function to do the lookup addition. Figure 6.10 shows how you start the formula. Normally the criteria argument in the SUMIF function is given a single item. Here you give it five separate items. By placing five items in the criteria argument, you make a function argument array operation, and as a result, the SUMIF function will deliver a resultant array with five answers. As shown in Figure 6.11, if you evaluate

SUMIF (by highlight it and pressing F9), you can see that SUMIF delivers the correct five costs. One important reason that SUMIF works as a sort of lookup function is because there are no duplicates in the range F4:F6. If there were duplicates, this formula would not work (the criteria argument can have duplicates, but not the range argument cannot). (Be sure to undo the evaluation by pressing Ctrl+Z before moving on.)

	A	B	C	D	E	F	G
1	Calculate total sales, costs and gross profit						
2	Date	Product	Sales			Lookup Table:	
3	10/17/2012	Quad	36			Product	Cost
4	10/17/2012	Tri Fly	9			Quad	18
5	10/17/2012	Quad	30			Tri Fly	4
6	10/17/2012	Tri Fly	8			Fun Fly	2
7	10/17/2012	Fun Fly	6			* Lookup Table is not sorted.	
9	Total Sales	89					
10	Total Costs	=SUMIF(F4:F6,B3:B7,G4:G6)					
11	Gross Profit	SUMIF(range, **criteria**, [sum_range])					

Figure 6.10 *The criteria argument in the SUMIF is give an array of values.*

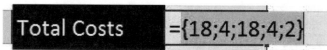

Figure 6.11 *The criteria argument is given five items and so the SUMIF makes a function argument array operation and delivers a resultant array that contains five answers.*

Because you need to add the results of the function argument array operation, you can finish the formula by placing the SUMIF formula element into the SUMPRODUCT function. Figure 6.12 shows the finished formula. Notice that you do not need to use Ctrl+Shift+Enter because the array argument in SUMPRODUCT can handle arrays without it.

Using the SUMIF function inside SUMPRODUCT is a great way to do lookup addition when the cell range in the range argument is not sorted. However, if the cell range in the range argument is sorted ascending, you can use a slightly easier and faster-calculating formula. You'll look at that next.

| B10 | ▼ : × ✓ ƒx | =SUMPRODUCT(SUMIF(F4:F6,B3:B7,G4:G6)) |

	A	B	C	D	E	F	G	H
1	Calculate total sales, costs and gross profit							
2	Date	Product	Sales			Lookup Table:		
3	10/17/2012	Quad	36			Product	Cost	
4	10/17/2012	Tri Fly	9			Quad	18	
5	10/17/2012	Quad	30			Tri Fly	4	
6	10/17/2012	Tri Fly	8			Fun Fly	2	
7	10/17/2012	Fun Fly	6			* Lookup Table is not sorted.		
9	Total Sales	89	< Formula =SUM(C3:C7)					
10	Total Costs	46	< Formula =SUMPRODUCT(SUMIF(F4:F6,B3:B7,G4:G6))					
11	Gross Profit	43	< Formula =B9-B10					

Figure 6.12 *SUMPRODUCT and SUMIF to do lookup addition when the cell range in the range argument is not sorted.*

Lookup Addition: Using SUMPRODUCT and LOOKUP When the Lookup Table Is Sorted

If you need to do lookup addition and the first column in your table is sorted ascending, you can substitute the LOOKUP function for the SUMIF function. The first column of the table must be sorted because LOOKUP can only do an approximate match lookup. In Figure 6.13 notice that the lookup_value argument is making the function argument array operation. Also, notice that you are using the second line in the ScreenTip because you are using the two arguments lookup_value and array, where the array argument always retrieves items from last column. (You'll learn more about the array argument later in this chapter.)

	A	B	C	D	E	F	G	H
1	Calculate total sales, costs and gross profit							
2	Date	Product	Sales			Lookup Table:		
3	10/17/2012	Quad	36			Product	Cost	
4	10/17/2012	Tri Fly	9			Fun Fly	2	
5	10/17/2012	Quad	30			Quad	18	
6	10/17/2012	Tri Fly	8			Tri Fly	4	
7	10/17/2012	Fun Fly	6			* Lookup Table IS sorted A to Z.		
9	Total Sales	89	< Formula =SUM(C3:C7)					
10	Total Costs	=SUMPRODUCT(LOOKUP(B3:B7,F4:G6))						
11	Gross Profit	43	LOOKUP(lookup_value, lookup_vector, [result_vector]) LOOKUP(lookup_value, array)					

Figure 6.13 *If the lookup table is sorted ascending, it is more efficient to use the LOOKUP function inside SUMPRODUCT.*

Notes About the Formula =SUMPRODUCT(SUMIF(F4:F6,B3:B7,G4:G6))

The following table presents a summary of the SUMPRODUCT and SUMIF lookup addition formula.

Impetus for Creating an Array Formula:
There is no built-in formula for lookup addition.
In this example, you did not need to see all the detail, and you did not want to use the space in the spreadsheet for a helper column.
You wanted a single-cell formula to do lookup addition to calculate total costs.
You used SUMIF rather than LOOKUP because the cell range in the range argument is not sorted ascending.
Calculation Summary:
1. =SUMPRODUCT(SUMIF(F4:F6,B3:B7,G4:G6))
The array is the range B3:B7.
You are performing a function argument array operation in the criteria argument of the SUMIF function.
This is an array formula because you are performing a function argumnet operation on an array, and the operation produces a resultant array.
2. =SUMPRODUCT(SUMIF(F4:F6,{"Quad";"Tri Fly";"Quad";"Tri Fly";"Fun Fly"},G4:G6))
• You give the criteria argument five items.
3. =SUMPRODUCT(SUMIF({"Quad";"Tri Fly";"Fun Fly"},{"Quad";"Tri Fly";"Quad";"Tri Fly";"Fun Fly"},{18;4;2}))
There are no duplicates in the range argument of SUMIF. If there were duplicates, the formula would not work.
4. =SUMPRODUCT({18;4;18;4;2})
SUMIF delivers a resultant array that contains the five cost values, one for each item you put into the criteria argument.
Array calculation: SUMIF(F4:F6,B3:B7,G4:G6) delivers the resultant array {18;4;18;4;2} to the array1 argument in SUMPRODUCT.
5. The formula delivers the single item 46.
Entering a Formula into a Cell:
The array1 argument in SUMPRODUCT can handle array operations without Ctrl+Shift+Enter.
Conclusion:
If the cell range in the range argument is not sorted and you cannot use a helper column, this is a good option.
Note:
In Chapter 11, you will learn that although the criteria argument in SUMIF can handle an array, the range and sum_range arguments in SUMIF cannot handle array operations.

Notes About the Formula =SUMPRODUCT(LOOKUP(B3:B7,F4:G6))

The following table presents a summary of the SUMPRODUCT and LOOKUP lookup addition formula.

Impetus for Creating an Array Formula:
There is no built-in formula for lookup addition.
In this case, you did not need to see all the detail, and you did not want to use the space in the spreadsheet for a helper column.
You wanted a single-cell formula to do lookup addition to calculate total costs.
You used LOOKUP rather than SUMIF because the first column in the table is sorted ascending.
Calculation Summary:
1. =SUMPRODUCT(LOOKUP(B3:B7,F4:G6))
The array is the range B3:B7.   You are performing a function argument array operation in the lookup_value argument of the LOOKUP function.   This is an array formula because you are performing a function argument operation on an array, and the operation produces a resultant array.
2. =SUMPRODUCT(LOOKUP({"Quad";"Tri Fly";"Quad";"Tri Fly";"Fun Fly-"},F4:G6))
You give the LOOKUP function five items to look up.
3. =SUMPRODUCT(LOOKUP({"Quad";"Tri Fly";"Quad";"Tri Fly";"Fun Fly-"},F4:G6))
You put a table of values into the array argument of the LOOKUP function.   When using the array argument in LOOKUP, you must remember the rules for how this argument behaves: • With a table that is taller than it is wide or has equal height and width, the argument does vertical lookup.   • The argument retrieves the value from the last column if the table is taller than it is wide or is the same width and height.   • If the table is wider than it is tall, this argument does horizontal lookup.   • The argument retrieves the value from the last row if the table is wider than it is tall.
4. =SUMPRODUCT({18;4;18;4;2})
LOOKUP delivers the five cost values, one for each item you put into the criteria argument.   **Array calculation:** LOOKUP(B3:B7,F4:G6) delivers the resultant array {18;4;18;4;2} to the array1 argument in SUMPRODUCT.
5. The formula delivers the single item 46.
Entering a Formula into a Cell:
The array1 argument in SUMPRODUCT can handle array operations without Ctrl+Shift+Enter.
Conclusion:
If the cell range in the range argument is sorted ascending and you cannot use a helper column, this is a good option.   The SUMPRODUCT and LOOKUP formula calculates significantly faster than the SUMPRODUCT and SUMIF formula.

Timing the Formulas in This Chapter

As discussed in Chapter 2, pointing array formulas to large data sets can increase formula calculation time for a workbook. In general, faster calculation times are more efficient. This section shows the anecdotal results I got. To time your own formulas, look back to Chapter 2 for details. (Timing depends on many factors, and your particular situation may have different timing results.) To see the workbook with the timing results I got, open the file named 04AddTop5.xlsm in the folder Timing in the zipped folder FilesForCtrlShiftEnterBook. The Introduction to this book explains how to get these files. Figure 6.14 shows the timing results (in seconds) I got for 50,000 rows of data.

	[1] SUMPRODUCT & LOOKUP	[2] SUMPRODUCT & SUMIF
Time 1	0.02918	0.09166
Time 2	0.02814	0.096
Time 3	0.0283	0.09184
Ave.	0.02854	0.093166667
% change from [1]	0%	226%

Figure 6.14 *If you can sort, LOOKUP is significantly faster than SUMIF.*

Comparing SUMIF and LOOKUP for Lookup Addition

If you need a single-cell formula to do lookup addition and the first column of the lookup table is sorted, use SUMPRODUCT and LOOKUP because this formula is slight easier to create and much faster to calculate than SUMPRODUCT and SUMIF.

Throughout the rest of this book, you will see many more examples of function argument array operations.

Chapter Summary

This chapter discusses using function argument array operations to create a formula that can count all the characters in a column and two different formulas for doing lookup addition. In Chapter 7 you will learn about array constants.

Chapter 7: Array Constants

Excel Files

To follow along with the examples in this chapter, you can download the accompanying files, as explained in the Introduction.

Array Constants to Hard Code Values into Formulas

So far in this book you have seen many examples of array constants. In fact, every time you have evaluated a formula element by using the F9 key, you have seen an example of an array constant. For example, in the first array formula you created in Chapter 2 (shown again in Figure 7.1), you highlighted the array operation D2:D5-C2:C5, pressed the F9 key, and revealed the resultant array {3;-8;7;6} (see Figure 7.2). But all you did back in Chapter 2 (and in many subsequent examples) was to look at the resultant array to make sure the formula was calculating correctly. You immediately undid the evaluation by using Ctrl+Z so that you did not hard code the values into the formula. If you had not used undo you would have created an array constant that hard codes the values into the formula. In this chapter, you will learn about situations where there is an advantage to keeping a hard-coded array constant in a formula.

	A	B	C	D
1	Stock	Date	Open	Close
2	GOOG	10/1/12	759	762
3	GOOG	10/2/12	765	757
4	GOOG	10/3/12	756	763
5	GOOG	10/4/12	762	768
6				
7	MAX	=MAX(D2:D5-C2:C5)		
		MAX(**number1**, [number2], ...)		

Figure 7.1 *Array operation.*

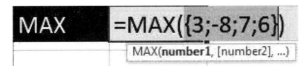

MAX	=MAX({3;-8;7;6})
	MAX(**number1**, [number2], ...)

Figure 7.2 *If the resultant array was left in the formula the values would have been hard coded in using an array constant.*

To begin the discussions about array constants, let's look at three examples that illustrate the three types of array constants you can encounter in Excel and the syntax used to create array constants.

Column Array Constants (Vertical Array Constants)

Figures 7.3 and 7.4 illustrate that if you were to highlight a column of items and evaluate it by pressing F9, you would see the following: The array of items is housed in curly braces; the text is always shown in double quotes; the semicolon means to go down a row; and the column of items uses semicolons.

	A	B
1	Product	Price
2	Majestic Beaut	37
3	Quad	33
4	Sunshine	18
5		
6	=A2:A4	

Figure 7.3 *Cell range: A column filled with rows.*

6	={"Majestic Beaut";"Quad";"Sunshine"}

Figure 7.4 *Array constant: A column filled with rows. Semicolon = rows.*

Row Array Constants (Horizontal Array Constants)

Figures 7.5 and 7.6 illustrate that if you were to highlight a row of items and evaluate it (by pressing F9), you would see the following: The array of items is housed in curly braces; the text is shown in double quotes, and numbers are just numbers; a comma means to go over a column; and the row of items uses commas.

	A	B
1	Product	Price
2	Majestic Beaut	37
3	Quad	33
4	Sunshine	18
5		
6	=A2:B2	

Figure 7.5 *Cell range: A row filled with columns.*

6	={"Majestic Beaut",37}

Figure 7.6 *Array constant: A row filled with columns. Comma = columns.*

Table Array Constants (Two-Way Array Constants)

Figures 7.7 and 7.8 illustrate that if you were to highlight a table (rows and columns) of items and evaluate it (by pressing F9) you would see the following: The array of items is housed in curly braces; the text is shown in double quotes, and numbers are just numbers; and the table of items uses semicolons to mean go down a row and commas to mean go over a column.

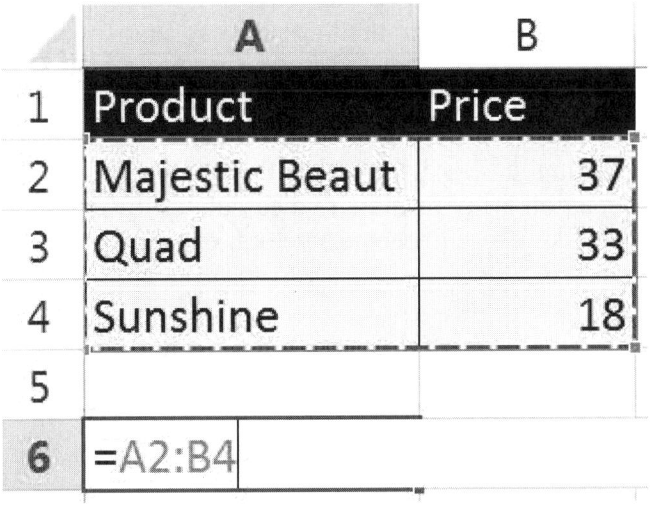

Figure 7.7 *Cell range: A table filled with columns and rows.*

Figure 7.8 *Array constant: A table filled with columns and rows.*

Array Syntax Rules

From the preceding text, you can glean the following array syntax rules:

- Curly braces house the array: one at the beginning and one at the end.
- A semicolon means to go down a row.
- A comma mean to go over a column.
- A text item is contained in two double quotes.
- Numbers, logical values, and error values are not contained in two double quotes.
- The three types of array constants are column (vertical), row (horizontal), and table (two-way).

   Note: The way I remember the difference between semicolon and comma is that *column* starts with the letter *c*, and so does *comma*. In this way, I always remember that column goes with comma, so row goes with semicolon.

Why would you want to hard code an array constant into a formula, especially given Excel's Golden Rule:

   If formula input data can change, put it in a cell and refer to it with cell references. If data will not change, you can hard code it into formula.

The reason is that, for many functions, if you use an array constant rather than a range of cells as your array in an array operation, the array formula will not require Ctrl+Shift+Enter. This means if you have an array in an array calculation that contains items that will not change, you should try to use an array constant and avoid having to use Ctrl+Shift+Enter. The next example looks at a situation where you need to add the three smallest values. It will be the first illustration of using an array constant to avoid Ctrl+Shift+Enter.

Using SUM and SMALL to Add the Three Lowest Scores, Excluding Ties

Figure 7.9 shows a column with golf scores. The goal here is to add the three lowest scores without including any extra values if there is a tie for third (which there is, in this example). The SMALL function is a great function to use to solve this problem because with the k argument you can specify which small value you want. k = 1 finds the minimum value, k = 2 finds the second smallest, and so on. In Figure 7.9 you can see that if you run the SMALL function three times and add the result from each SMALL function, you will get a non-array formula that calculates the correct answer. The problem with this formula is that it can take a bit of time to type out, especially if you want the 10 lowest values.

	A	B	C	D	E	F
1	Must exclude extra values if tie at 3rd					
2	Golfer	Strokes				
3	Verda Duhamel	84				
4	Randolph Sizelove	70				
5	Rudolph Gliem	69				
6	Shiela Hynum	87				
7	Dorris Farah	70				
8	Suzan Serfass	68				
9	Sum 3 lowest scores	=SMALL(B3:B8,1)+SMALL(B3:B8,2)+SMALL(B3:B8,3)				
10		SMALL(array, k)				

Figure 7.9 *The k argument in SMALL allows you to get the kth smallest values.*

To create a more compact formula you can make a function argument array calculation. Figure 7.10 shows how you can enter the array constant {1,2,3}. You can use an array constant to hard code the values into the formula because the values will not change. Because the k argument is given three values, SMALL will deliver three values to the SUM function. As shown in Figure 7.11, if you evaluate the SMALL function (by highlighting it and pressing F9), you can see that SMALL delivers the three correct answers. (Be sure to undo the evaluation by pressing Ctrl+Z before moving on.)

Figure 7.10 *The array constant in the k argument.*

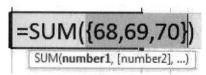

Figure 7.11 *SMALL delivers the three smallest values, excluding the extra 70.*

As shown in Figure 7.12, when you enter the formula, you do not need to use Ctrl+Shift+Enter, and there are no curly braces in the formula bar. Using an array constant in the k argument of SMALL rather than using a cell references allows you to make a function argument array operation without having to use Ctrl+Shift+Enter.

> **Note:** The Excel function help for the SMALL function does not state that array constants can be listed in the k argument or that if you use an array constant rather than a range of cells, you can avoid Ctrl+Shift+Enter. This is evidence of the lack of documentation about how array formulas work that I mentioned in the book's Introduction. I learned about it from the MrExcel Message Board and many years of trial and error.

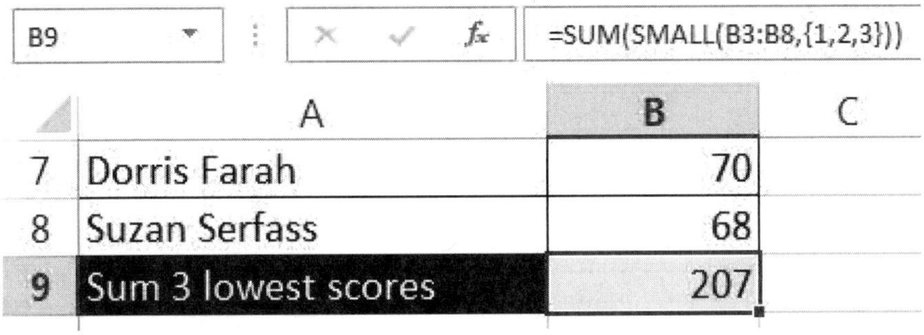

| B9 | ▼ | : | × | ✓ | *fx* | =SUM(SMALL(B3:B8,{1,2,3})) |

⬢	A	B	C
7	Dorris Farah	70	
8	Suzan Serfass	68	
9	Sum 3 lowest scores	207	

Figure 7.12 *Array constant helps you avoid using Ctrl+Shift+Enter.*

> **Note:** It does not matter whether you give the k argument a row array or a column array because in either case, SMALL simply delivers three numbers to the SUM function. SMALL(B3:B8,{1,2,3}) yields {68,69,70}, and SMALL(B3:B8,{1;2;3}) yields {68;69;70}. Either one accomplishes the goal.

As shown in Figure 7.13, if you were to use cell references rather than an array constant, you would have to use Ctrl+Shift+Enter. If you had to use cell references, you could use SUMPRODUCT in place of SUM and avoid Ctrl+Shift+Enter by using a formula like this: =SUMPRODUCT(SMALL(B3:B8,D7:D9)).

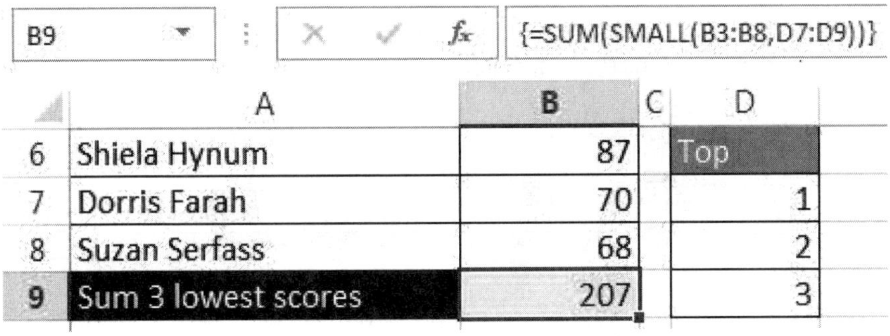

| B9 | ▼ | : | × | ✓ | *fx* | {=SUM(SMALL(B3:B8,D7:D9))} |

⬢	A	B	C	D
6	Shiela Hynum	87		Top
7	Dorris Farah	70		1
8	Suzan Serfass	68		2
9	Sum 3 lowest scores	207		3

Figure 7.13 *Using cell references and SUM requires Ctrl+Shift+Enter.*

Notes About the Formula =SUM(SMALL(B3:B8,{1,2,3}))

The following table presents a summary of the array constant formula.

Impetus for Creating an Array Formula:
You need a formula to add the three smallest values, excluding extra values if there is a tie for third.
You use SMALL because it finds the kth smallest value.
Calculation Summary:
1. =SUM(SMALL(B3:B8,{1,2,3}))
The array is the array constant {1,2,3}.
You are performing a function argument array operation in the k argument of the SMALL function.
This is an array formula because you are performing a function argument operation on an array, and the operation produces a resultant array.
2. =SUM({68,69,70})
Array calculation: SMALL(B3:B8,{1,2,3}) delivers the resultant array {68,69,70} to the number1 argument in the SUM function.
3. The formula delivers the single item 207.
Entering a Formula into a Cell:
Because you use an array constant rather than a range of cells, you do not need to enter the formula with Ctrl+Shift+Enter.
Conclusion:
If you need a formula to add the three smallest values and exclude extra values when there's a tie, this is a good option.
If you need to include ties, use a formula like this: =SUMIF(range,"<="&SMALL(range,3)).

Using SUMIF and SMALL to Add the Three Smallest Scores, Including Ties

In some circumstances, you might want to include the tie values in a summation. Figure 7.14 shows a non-array formula that can calculate the correct answer of 7 (2+1+2+2).

	A	B	C
1	Calls		Add 3 smallest including all ties
2	3		=SUMIF(A2:A6,"<="&SMALL(A2:A6,3))
			SUMIF(range, **criteria**, [sum_range])
3	2		
4	1		
5	2		
6	2		

Figure 7.14 *This formula adds the three smallest scores, including any ties.*

Using SUM and LARGE to Add the Three Largest Scores, Excluding Ties

All the examples you have seen so far are concerned with the SMALL function. The parallel to the SMALL function on the upper end of the scale is the LARGE function. Given a k value, LARGE will find the kth largest value.

Figure 7.15 shows a data set that contains flight times from the Maximum Time Aloft event at a boomerang tournament. In this event, you get five throws, and the three longest times are added to get your final score. The formulas, as shown in Figure 7.15, add the three longest times without including any ties for third.

G3		f_x	=SUM(LARGE(B3:F3,{1;2;3}))

	A	B	C	D	E	F	G
1	Boomerang Tournament Event: Maximum Time Aloft: Add 3 Longest Flights						
2	Thrower	Throw 1	Throw 2	Throw 3	Throw 4	Throw 5	Total of Best 3
3	Dan	34.81	58.13	43.00	25.97	57.57	158.70
4	Rich	69.43	37.30	26.19	37.30	54.08	160.81
5	Vino	35.36	69.00	39.88	33.73	46.38	155.26
6	Gel	45.14	26.63	43.43	39.37	29.48	127.94

Figure 7.15 *The array constant in the k argument instructs LARGE to get the top three scores*

In the last few examples you added the top three or lowest three values. What if you wanted the formula to add the top three but other times you wanted to add the top two or five? Is it possible to create a variable-length array constant?

A Formula for Dynamically Adding the Top *n* Values

In Figure 7.16 you can see two formulas that add the top three values. Formula [1] excludes ties, and formula [2] includes ties. The difference between these formulas and the earlier formulas is that the number of values to add will not be hard coded into the formula, but rather, you want to refer to a cell for this information. If you change the numbers in cells D3 or D6, the total amount will change. Figure 7.17 shows the totals if instead the goal is to add the top two customer sales.

	A	B	C	D	E	F
1	Customer	Sales				
2	QFD	1,465		Top	Add Top 3	Formula [1]: Excludes ties
3	PCV	733		3	4,491	< Formula =SUMPRODUCT(LARGE(B2:B8,ROW(INDIRECT("1:"&D3))))
4	GIGI	1,065				
5	WFMM	1,528		Top	Add Top 3	Formula [2]: Includes ties
6	DDB	1,498		3	5,956	< Formula =SUMIF(B2:B8,">="&LARGE(B2:B8,D6))
7	SLD	1,465				
8	MML	695				

Figure 7.16 *If the numbers in cells D3 or D6 change, the formula should update. You do not want to hard code values into the formulas*

Top	Add Top 2	Formula [1]: Excludes ties
2	3,026	< Formula =SUMPRODUCT(LARGE(B2:B8,ROW(INDIRECT("1:"&D3))))

Top	Add Top 2	Formula [2]: Includes ties
2	3,026	< Formula =SUMIF(B2:B8,">="&LARGE(B2:B8,D6))

Figure 7.17 *The two totals are the same because there is no tie for second.*

Formula [2] is easy enough to understand, but the k argument for the LARGE function in formula [1] contains a formula element that you have not seen before. The next section takes a look this formula element.

Using ROW and INDIRECT for a Dynamic Variable-Length Array of Sequential Numbers

For the formula that excludes ties, you need a variable-length array of sequential numbers. If you are adding the top three, you need the array {1;2;3} in the k argument of LARGE, but if you are adding the top two, you need the array {1;2}. You can create a variable-length array of sequential numbers using the INDIRECT and ROW functions.

You can start the formula with the INDIRECT function, as shown in Figure 7.18. The INDIRECT function is programmed to convert a text string that represents a reference to a reference. The joined formula element "1:"&D3 represents a row reference. If you evaluate the formula element "1:"&D3 (by pressing F9), as shown in Figure 7.19, you can see that this is a text string.

Figure 7.18 *Join "1:" and D3.*

Figure 7.19 *Evaluating shows a row reference as text.*

Making sure that you undo the evaluation with Ctrl+Z, if you now try to evaluate the INDIRECT function to convert the text string "1:3" to a row reference, you get an error that reads "The formula is too long. Formulas should be no longer than 8192 characters." The reason you got the error when you did the Evaluate Formula Element trick in Chapter 2 is because you evaluated it in Edit mode, and the row reference 1:3 contains all the cells in rows 1 to 3. The formula itself has no problem with the reference created by the INDIRECT function. Next, you rap the ROW function around INDIRECT, as shown in Figure 7.20. INDIRECT is sitting in the reference argument of the ROW function. This argument is expecting a single value, and because you are giving it many values, this is a function argument array operation. If you evaluate the ROW function (by pressing F9), you see that the ROW function delivers the array of row numbers, as shown in Figure 7.21. Notice that because these are rows, the array syntax shows semicolons. As noted earlier in this chapter, the array of sequential numbers used for adding the top *n* values or the smallest *n* values can be either a row or column array. Make sure you undo the evaluation by pressing Ctrl+Z.

Figure 7.20 *ROW reports how many rows are in a reference.*

Figure 7.21 *The reference argument in the ROW function expects a single value. You gave it a reference with three rows; therefore the ROW function creates a resultant array with three answers.*

Figure 7.22 shows how you can use the ROW/INDIRECT formula element in the k argument of the LARGE function. This formula element is dynamic and will change. If you put a 2 in cell D3, the array will evaluate to {1;2}. If you put a 5 in cell D3, the array will evaluate to {1;2;3;4;5}.

=LARGE(B2:B8,ROW(INDIRECT("1:"&D3)))

LARGE(array, **k**)

Figure 7.22 *The k argument of LARGE receives the resultant array created by the ROW function reference argument array operation.*

As shown in Figure 7.23 you can finish the formula by placing LARGE into SUMPRODUCT. You are using SUMPRODUCT rather than SUM here because the array1 argument can handle the array operation inside the reference argument of the ROW function without having to use Ctrl+-Shift+Enter. Notice that even though the ROW/INDIRECT formula element delivers what looks like an array constant (refer to Figure 7.21), because the array of sequential numbers was created from a function argument array operation, it would require Ctrl+Shift+Enter if you used the SUM function.

=SUMPRODUCT(LARGE(B2:B8,ROW(INDIRECT("1:"&D3))))

SUMPRODUCT(**array1**, [array2], [array3], ...)

Figure 7.23 *To add the resultant array created by LARGE, place the LARGE formula element into the array 1 argument of the SUMPRODUCT function.*

This ROW/INDIRECT formula element (which could be called a "dynamic variable-length array of sequential numbers") is a useful trick to have in your Excel formula tool box and shows up in a number of types of array formulas. You will see another example of this useful formula element in Chapter 23.

Figure 7.24 shows the finished text and calculating formulas for adding the top five customer sales.

	A	B	C	D	E	F
	✓	fx	=SUMPRODUCT(LARGE(B2:B8,ROW(INDIRECT("1:"&D3))))			
1	Customer	Sales				
2	QFD	1,465		Top	Add Top 5	< Formula ="Add Top "&D3
3	PCV	733		5	7,021	< Formula =SUMPRODUCT(LARGE(B2:B8,ROW(INDIRECT("1:"&D3))))
4	GIGI	1,065				
5	WFMM	1,528				
6	DDB	1,498				
7	SLD	1,465				
8	MML	695				

Figure 7.24 *The formula will add the top n values from the data set.*

Note: The INDIRECT function is a volatile function—that is, it recalculates every time Excel recalculate the spreadsheet, even if the precedents (formula inputs) have not changed. Recalculation can be triggered by simple actions such as entering an item into a cell or inserting a new row. Volatile functions therefore increase formula calculation time. You'll learn more about recalculation in Chapter 13.

Notes About the Formula
=SUMPRODUCT(LARGE(B2:B8,ROW(INDIRECT("1:"&D3))))

The following table presents a summary for a formula that adds the top *n* values.

Impetus for Creating an Array Formula:
You want a formula to add the *n* smallest values, excluding extra values if there is a tie for the *n*th position, and you want the formula input for n to be linked to a cell.
Calculation Summary:
1. =SUMPRODUCT(LARGE(B2:B8,ROW(INDIRECT("1:"&D3))))
2. =SUMPRODUCT(LARGE(B2:B8,ROW(INDIRECT("1:3"))))
INDIRECT converts a row reference listed as text to a reference.
3. =SUMPRODUCT(LARGE(B2:B8,ROW(1:3)))
4. =SUMPRODUCT(LARGE(B2:B8,{1;2;3}))
Array calculation: ROW(1:3) delivers the resultant array {1;2;3} to the k argument in the LARGE function.
5. =SUMPRODUCT({1528;1498;1465})
Array calculation: LARGE(B2:B8,{1;2;3}) delivers the resultant array {1528;1498;1465} to the array1 argument in the SUMPRODUCT function.
6. For the top three scores, the formula delivers the single item 4,491.
Entering a Formula into a Cell:
The array1 argument of SUMPRODUCT can handle array operations, and you can enter the formula without Ctrl+Shift+Enter.
Conclusion:
This is a good options for a dynamic formula for adding the top *n* values where you want formula input n to be a variable in a cell.

Excel Table Feature for Adding the Top Three Values

Before you move on to the next array formula, you need to take a look at the Excel table feature for adding the top three values. If you convert a proper data set to an Excel table (by pressing Ctrl+T), you can add a total row and then use a top-three filter. However, it will include duplicates if there is a tie.

Customer	Sales
QFD	1,465
WFMM	1,528
DDB	1,498
SLD	1,465
Total	**5,956**

Figure 7.25 *Total row in an Excel Table for adding top three values, including ties.*

Calculating Net Cost from Four Series Discounts in a Single Cell

This section looks at another example of how you can use an array constant in an array formula to avoid using Ctrl+Shift+Enter. Back in Chapter 3 you saw a formula to calculate the net cost for a product, given a series discount. The example in Chapter 3 shows the four separate discounts in four separate cells. As shown in Figure 7.26, in this chapter, you need the formula to calculate the net cost, given that the four series discounts are all listed in a single cell.

	A	B	C	D
1	Extract numbers from text string & calculate net cost			
2	Product	Retail Price	Series Discount	Net cost
3	Majestic Beaut	$37	20/05/10/20	
4	Quad	$33	10/10/08/18	
5	Sunshine	$18	15/10/16/16	

Figure 7.26 *Series Discounts are give in a single cell as a text string.*

Here are the calculations that the single-cell formula needs to make:

Description	Calculation
Extract numbers from the text string:	{"20","05","10","20"}
Divide by 100:	{0.20,0.95,0.90,0.80}
Net cost equivalent:	(1-0.20)*(1-0.05)*(1-0.10)*(1-0.20)
Net cost equivalent:	0.80*0.95*0.90*0.80
Net cost equivalent:	0.5472
Net cost:	$37 * 0.5472 = $20.25

The part of the formula that involves an array operation is the part where you simultaneously extract four separate numbers at one time. In order to extract four numbers simultaneously, you use an array constant in the start_num argument of the MID function.

As shown in Figure 7.27, you can start the formula in cell D4 by using the MID function. The MID function extracts text from a text string, given a starting character position in the text string and the number of characters you would like to extract. Normally, the start_num argument gets a single number. For example, if you gave the start_num argument a 1 and the num_chars argument a 2, MID would extract 20. However, in this example, you are putting an array constant filled with four staring positions into the start_num argument. This function argument array operation will therefore force the MID function to deliver four extracted answers. If you evaluate the MID function by pressing F9, you can see that MID does in fact deliver a resultant array with the four extracted discounts (see Figure 7.28). Notice that the MID function delivers text items. This is not a problem because the next step involves a math operation, and any math operation performed on numbers stored as text converts them back to numbers.

Series Discount	Net cost
20/05/10/20	=MID(C3,{1,4,7,10},2)
10/10/08/18	MID(text, **start_num**, num_chars)

Figure 7.27 *Array constant in start_num argument forces MID to make function argument array operation.*

Series Discount	Net cost
20/05/10/20	={"20","05","10","20"}

Figure 7.28 *Resultant array created by MID.*

After undoing the evaluation, the next step is to divide the numbers by 100 and then subtract the results from the number 1, as shown in Figure 7.29. Remember that the division will be performed before the subtraction, so you do not need to isolate the division with unnecessary parentheses. If you evaluate the whole formula by pressing F9, you can see that it delivers the complements of each discount (see Figure 7.30). After you undo the evaluation, the next step is to multiply the complements to get the net cost equivalent and finish the formula.

=1-MID(C3,{1,4,7,10},2)/100

Figure 7.29 *Dividing by 100 converts the text numbers to numbers and creates the decimal numbers you need to subtract from 1.*

={0.8,0.95,0.9,0.8}

Figure 7.30 *Resultant array contains complements*

As shown in Figure 7.31, you finish the formula by putting the formula element 1-MID(C3,{1,4,7,10},2)/100 into the PRODUCT function, multiply the PRODUCT function by the retail price in cell B3, and then make sure to use the ROUND function to round to the penny.

=ROUND(B3*PRODUCT(1-MID(C3,{1,4,7,10},2)/100),2)

PRODUCT(**number1**, [number2], ...)

Figure 7.31 *Formula to calculate Net cost.*

Because you used an array constant as the array in the function argument array calculation, you do not have to enter the formula with Ctrl+Shift+Enter (see Figure 7.32).

| D3 | ▼ | : | × | ✓ | *fx* | =ROUND(B3*PRODUCT(1-MID(C3,{1,4,7,10},2)/100),2) |

◢	A	B	C	D	E
1	Extract numbers from text string & calculate net cost				
2	Product	Retail Price	Series Discount	Net cost	
3	Majestic Beaut	$37	20/05/10/20	20.25	
4	Quad	$33	10/10/08/18	20.17	
5	Sunshine	$18	15/10/16/16	9.72	

Figure 7.32 *Formula does not require Ctrl+Shift+Enter.*

Notes About the Formula
=ROUND(B3*PRODUCT(1-MID(C3,{1,4,7,10},2)/100),2)

The following table presents a summary for the formula that calculates the net cost from a series discount.

Impetus for Creating an Array Formula:
You need a single-cell formula to calculate net cost. You do not want intermediate calculations steps to be housed in helper cells.
Calculation Summary:
1. =ROUND(B3*PRODUCT(1-MID(C3,{1,4,7,10},2)/100),2)
2. =ROUND(B3*PRODUCT(1-{"20","05","10","20"}/100),2)
Array calculation: MID(C3,{1,4,7,10},2) delivers the resultant array {"20","05","10","20"} to the division math operation.
3. =ROUND(B3*PRODUCT(1-{0.2,0.05,0.1,0.2}),2)
Array calculation: {"20","05","10","20"}/100 delivers the resultant array {0.2,0.05,0.1,0.2} to the subtraction math operation.
4. =ROUND(B3*PRODUCT({0.8,0.95,0.9,0.8}),2)
Array calculation: 1-{0.2,0.05,0.1,0.2} delivers the resultant array {0.8,0.95,0.9,0.8} to the number1 argument in the PRODUCT function.
5. =ROUND(B3*0.5472,2)
PRODUCT multiplies the values: {0.8,0.95,0.9,0.8}
6. The formula delivers the single item 20.25.
Entering a Formula into a Cell:
Because you use an array constant rather than a range of cells, you do not need to enter the formula with Ctrl+Shift+Enter.
Conclusion:
This single-cell array formula is a great option for avoiding many intermediate steps.
Note: In Chapter 23 will see a net cost formula that can handle series discounts, regardless of whether a single cell contains one, two, three, or more series discounts.

Hard Coding Array Constants into VLOOKUP to Save Space

Figure 7.33 shows a typical VLOOKUP non-array formula. (The first column is sorted, and VLOOKUP is doing an approximate match.) If you do not want the table to sit in the cells and the data is not going to change, you could hard code the table into the formula. The problem with hard coding an array constant into the formula is that you would have to type the curly braces, semicolons, and commas and be sure to put the text items inside a pair of double quotes. Luckily, there is a great trick that allows you to instantly create an array constant if you already have the table in the cells. As shown in Figure 7.33, the first step is to highlight the table_array range of cells, and the second step is to press the F9 key to convert the range to an array constant (see Figure 7.34. You can then copy the formula down the column and delete the lookup table. Another option is to save the array constant as a defined name. You'll take a look at this next.

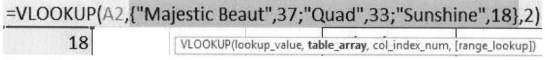

	A	B	C	D	E	F	G
1	Product	A.C.				Lookup Table:	
2	Quad	=VLOOKUP(A2,$F$3:$G$5,2)				Product	Price
3	Sunshine	VLOOKUP(lookup_value, **table_array**, col_index_num, [range_lookup])				Majestic Beaut	37
4	Quad	33				Quad	33
5	Majestic Beaut	37				Sunshine	18

Figure 7.33 *Using VLOOKUP with cell references is a good choice when data might change.*

=VLOOKUP(A2,{"Majestic Beaut",37;"Quad",33;"Sunshine",18},2)
18
VLOOKUP(lookup_value, **table_array**, col_index_num, [range_lookup])

Figure 7.34 *The F9 key can convert the range to an array constant.*

Using Defined Names to Store Array Constants

If you want to save space by using an array constant in a formula, you can save the array constant as a defined name and then use the defined name in your formula. To create a defined name, go to the Formula Ribbon tab, click the Name Manager button in the Defined Names group, and click the New button (or press Ctrl+F3). Figure 7.35 shows the Edit Name dialog box that appears. You use this dialog to create the defined name for the array constant. Figure 7.36 shows how you can use the defined name in the VLOOKUP function.

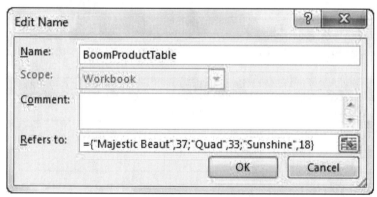

Figure 7.35 *Creating an array constant as a defined name.*

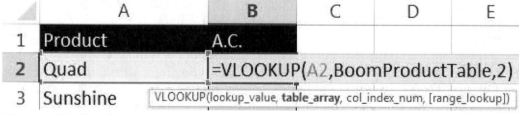

	A	B	C	D	E
1	Product	A.C.			
2	Quad	=VLOOKUP(A2,BoomProductTable,2)			
3	Sunshine	VLOOKUP(lookup_value, **table_array**, col_index_num, [range_lookup])			

Figure 7.36 *The defined name contains an array constant.*

In Figure 7.36, note that you have not created an array formula. You have just used an array constant and a defined name for the lookup table in the table_array argument. But what about the other arguments in VLOOKUP? Could they contain array constants and/or array operations? As you saw in Chapter 6, the lookup_value argument in VLOOKUP cannot handle arrays. But what about the col_index_num argument? Can it handle an array? Read on.

VLOOKUP col_index_num with an Array Constant

Figure 7.37 shows a lookup table with product names in the first column (sorted) and component costs in columns 2 to 8. The goal of the formula is to simultaneously look up columns 2, 4, 5, 7, and 8 to retrieve the costs and then add them. The easiest solution would be to add an extra column at the end of the table and sum only the costs of interest and then do a VLOOKUP to retrieve column 9. If that is not possible, you can make a function argument array operation in the col_index_num argument to retrieve the five columns of costs simultaneously. In Figure 7.37 you can see that the array constant contains five column numbers. This tells VLOOKUP to retrieve the five values (1.35, 2.15, 3, 2, 4) for the Quad product. Using what you have learned so far about array constants not requiring Ctrl+Shift+Enter, you might think that you can just put VLOOKUP into the SUM function and press Enter. Figure 7.38 shows that you would get the incorrect answer if you did this. This is because the col_index_num for VLOOKUP requires Ctrl+Shift+Enter, regardless of whether the array is an array constant or a range of cells. Figure 7.39 shows that you can get the correct answer if you use Ctrl+Shift+Enter. Figure 7.40 shows that you can place VLOOKUP in the SUMPRODUCT function, and because the array1 argument can handle array calculations without Ctrl+Shift+Enter, you can enter the formula with just Enter.

	A	B	C	D	E	F	G	H
1	Product	Overhead	Adm	Pack	Wood	Trace	Paint	Labor
2	Bellen	0.95	0.55	2	1.75	1	1.5	2.5
3	Quad	1.35	0.75	2.15	3	1.45	2	4
4	Sunshine	0.4	0.35	2	1.4	0.75	1.3	1.75
6	Product	COGS						
7	Quad	=SUM(VLOOKUP(A7,A2:H4,{2,4,5,7,8}))						

VLOOKUP(lookup_value, table_array, **col_index_num**, [range_lookup])

Figure 7.37 *An array constant of column numbers in the col_index_num argument.*

6	Product	COGS
7	Quad	1.35

< Formula =SUM(VLOOKUP(A7,A2:H4,{2,4,5,7,8}))

Figure 7.38 *If you do not use Ctrl+Shift+Enter, you get the wrong answer.*

6	Product	COGS
7	Quad	12.5

< Formula {=SUM(VLOOKUP(A7,A2:H4,{2,4,5,7,8}))}

Figure 7.39 *If the col_index_num argument in VLOOKUP contains an array constant or a cell range, it requires Ctrl+Shift+Enter.*

6	Product	COGS
7	Quad	12.5

< Formula =SUMPRODUCT(VLOOKUP(A7,A2:H4,{2,4,5,7,8}))

Figure 7.40 *When you put VLOOKUP in SUMPRODUCT, you do not need Ctrl+Shift+Enter. This is a good formula for looking up and adding multiple columns for a single lookup value.*

Some function arguments can contain array constants without having to use Ctrl+Shift+Enter (for example, an array in SMALL, an array in LARGE, a logical in OR, text in LEN), and some require Ctrl+Shift+Enter (for example, col_index_num in VLOOKUP).

As you go through this book, you would collect a list and keep track of which arguments can handle array constants without requiring you to use Ctrl+Shift+Enter. Even though it may be a bit confusing, it is worth having this information because a formula that does not require Ctrl+Shift+Enter is more robust than one that does.

> **Note**: Efficiency rule 18 will give you a starting list of these arguments.

> **Note:** Notice that how array formulas work is largely based on how the individual function arguments are programmed to work. As you have seen in this book already, some function can handle array operations without Ctrl+Shift+Enter and some cannot. Here you have seen that some function arguments can perform array calculations on array constants without Ctrl+Shift+Enter and some cannot. Because there is no rule for how 100% of Excel function arguments work, the best you can do in formulating guidelines for how array formulas work is to state a guideline and then list the known exceptions.

Math and Comparative Array Operations Using Array Constants

So far in this chapter, you have used array constants in function argument array operations. Figures 7.41 to 7.44 show examples of array constants being used in math and comparative array operations. The following is a general rule to follow for whether a formula will require Ctrl+Shift+Enter: If the array operation contains arrays that are array constants, the formula should not require Ctrl+Shift+Enter. As shown in Figures 7.41, 7.42, and 7.43, if you have an array constant and no other arrays (such as a range of cells), the formula does not require Ctrl+Shift+Enter. The formula in Figure 7.44 requires Ctrl+Shift+Enter because the array operation involves an array other than an array constant—namely, a range of cells.

f_x	=OR(B2={"V.P.";"President";"Admin"})

▲	A	B	C
1	Employee	Title	Meeting T/F?
2	Alvaro Ochocki	V.P.	TRUE
3	Quinton Gesick	Manager	FALSE
4	Morriloo Stoigor	Drosidont	TRUE

Figure 7.41 *This array formula asks "Are the contents of the cell equal to V.P. or President or Admin? The comparative array operation involves an array constant in the logical1 argument of the OR function, and it does not require Ctrl+Shift+Enter.*

f_x	=PRODUCT(1-{0.155,0.1,0.05,0.1525})

▲	A	B	C
1	Net Cost Eqivalent		
2	0.61229756		

Figure 7.42 *This array formula calculates the next cost equivalent for a retail product by multiplying the complements of the discount rates. The math array operation involves an array constant in the number1 argument of the PRODUCT function, and it does not require Ctrl+Shift+Enter.*

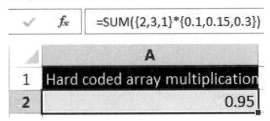

Figure 7.43 *This array formula multiplies two array constants and then adds the results. (I am not sure where you would use a formula like this, but I include it to illustrate the parameters of how array constants work.) The math array operation involves two array constants in the number1 argument of the SUM function, and it does not require Ctrl+Shift+Enter.*

	fx	{=SUM(A2:C2*{0.01,0.015,0.03})}	
	A	B	C	D
1	Day 1	Day 2	Day 3	Commission
2	10000	26000	40000	1690
3	10000	27000	34000	1525

Figure 7.44 *This array formula multiplies a range of cells and an array constant and then adds the results. (It would be better to use SUMPRODUCT here, but I include it to illustrate the parameters of how array constants work.) The math array operation involves a range of cells, and it requires Ctrl+Shift+Enter*

Array Formula Efficiency Rule 18

Rules for array constants:

- Array constants can be used in array formulas and non-array formulas.
- The following array syntax rules apply:
    - Curly braces house the array: one at the beginning and one at the end.
    - A semicolon means go down a row.
    - A comma means go over a column.
    - Text items are contained in double quotes.
    - Numbers, logical values, and error values are not contained in a pair of double quotes.
    - The three types of array constants are column (vertical), row (horizontal), and table (two-way).
- Array constants are limited by the number of characters allowed in a formula (8,192).
- For array formulas:
    - If the array operation contains arrays that are array constants and no other type of array (for example, a range of cells), the formula should not require Ctrl+Shift+Enter.
    - Some function arguments can contain array constants as part of an array operation and do not require Ctrl+Shift+Enter—for example, the array argument in SMALL, the array argument in LARGE, the start_num argument in MID, the logical1 argument in OR, the number1 argument in PRODUCT, and the number1 argument in SUM.
    - Some function arguments DO require Ctrl+Shift+Enter if they contain an array constant—for example, the col_index_num argument in VLOOKUP.

- The following rules apply to array formulas and non-array formulas:
    - If the data in an array will not change and you want to save spreadsheet space, an array constant can be useful.
    - You can save an array constant as a defined name and use the defined name in formulas.

Comparing Solutions for Adding the Smallest or Largest *n* Values

The following table presents a summary of advantages and disadvantages of the solutions for adding the smallest or largest *n* values.

Advantages and Disadvantages in Adding the Smallest or Largest n Values.		
Solution	**Advantage**	**Disadvantage**
=SMALL(B3:B8,1)+SMALL(B3:B8,2)+SMALL(B3:B8,3) **(refer to Figure 7.9)**	I can't think of an advantage.	Formula is unnecessarily long.
=SUM(SMALL(B3:B8,{1,2,3})) **(refer to Figure 7.12)**	Does not require Ctrl+Shift+Enter because of the array constant. Shorter than using multiple SMALLs. Excluded ties.	Excluded ties.
=SUM(SMALL(B3:B8,D7:D9)) **(refer to Figure 7.13)**	Shorter than using multiple SMALLs. Links to cells. Excluded ties.	Requires Ctrl+Shift+Enter. Excluded ties.
=SUMPRODUCT(SMALL(B3:B8,D7:D9)) **(refer to Figure 7.14)**	Links to cells. Excluded ties. Uses SUMPRODUCT to avoid Ctrl+Shift+Enter.	Excluded ties.
=SUMIF(A2:A6,"<="&SMALL(A2:A6,3)) **(refer to Figure 7.14)**	Included ties Links to cells.	Included ties
=SUMPRODUCT(LARGE(B2:B8,ROW(INDIRECT("1:"&D3)))) **(refer to Figure 7.17)**	Creates a dynamic array of sequential values. Excluded ties.	Excluded ties.
Table with Totals row **(refer to Figure 7.25)**	Easy to create and change with a filter.	Not automatic like formulas – must re-fliter if you want to change n.

Timing the Formulas in This Chapter

As discussed in Chapter 2, pointing array formulas to large data sets can increase formula calculation time for a workbook. In general, faster calculation times are more efficient. This section shows the anecdotal results I got. To time your own formulas, look back to Chapter 2 for details. (Timing depends on many factors, and your particular situation may have different timing results.) To see the workbook with the timing results I got, open the file named 04AddTop5.xlsm in the folder Timing in the zipped folder FilesForCtrlShiftEnterBook. The Introduction to this book explains how to get these files. Figure 7.41 shows the timing results (in seconds) I got for 50,000 rows of data for a formula that adds the top five sales numbers. Because there is little timing difference between the formulas, I might consider using formula [4] because it helps avoid the use of Ctrl+Shift+Enter.

	[1] {=SUM(LARGE($A$2: $A$50001,E1:E5))}	[2] =LARGE($A$2:$A$50001,1)+LARGE($A$2:$A$50001,2)+LARGE($A$2:$A$50001,3)+LARGE($A$2:$A$50001,4)+LARGE(A	[3] =SUMPRODUCT(LARGE($A$2:$A$50001,E1:E5))	[4] =SUM(LARGE($A$2:$A$50001,{1,2,3,4,5}))
	Add Top 5	Add Top 5	Add Top 5	Add Top 5
	24998997	24998997	24998997	24998997
Time 1	0.04578	0.04554	0.04565	0.04591
Time 2	0.04587	0.04565	0.04581	0.04549
Time 3	0.04635	0.0457	0.04566	0.04588
Ave	0.046	0.04563	0.045706667	0.04576
% Change from [1]	0.00%	-0.80%	-0.64%	-0.52%

Figure 7.45 *Timing formulas that add the top five sales.*

Throughout the rest of this book you will see a few more examples of array constants in formulas.

Chapter Summary

In this chapter you saw that array constants can sometimes help you avoid the use of Ctrl+Shift+Enter in array formulas and that array constants can save spreadsheet space. In Chapter 8 you will learn about a special kind of array formula that can simultaneously deliver multiple values.

Chapter 8: Array Formulas That Deliver More Than One Value

Excel Files

To follow along with the examples in this chapter, you can download the accompanying files, as explained in the Introduction.

Delivering a Single Result or an Array of Results with an Array Formula

So far in this book, all the array operations have delivered a resultant array to a larger formula which then delivered a single array formula result to a single cell. In this chapter you will learn how to create array operations that deliver a resultant array as the final array formula result. Because cells can only display a single result, if the resultant array is delivering more than one item, you must highlight more than one cell before you create and then enter the array formula using Ctrl+Shift+Enter.

Two types of array formulas can simultaneously deliver more than one value to more than one cell with the use of Ctrl+Shift+Enter:

- Array formulas that you create with various formula elements and put together yourself (You will learn about them in this chapter.)
- Built-in Excel array functions (You will learn about them in Chapter 9.)

Array Formulas That Deliver More Than One Item to More Than One Cell

In Figure 8.1, the goal is to show the sequential numbers 1 to 5 in the range A2:A6 and make it difficult for people to delete an individual cell in the range. Instead of just typing the numbers 1 to 5, you can create an array formula that will deliver the numbers {1;2;3;4;5} and that will also deter cell deletion in the range A2:A6. You will see how to create this array formula next.

	A	B
1	Order	Names
2	=ROW(A2:A6)-ROW(A2)+1	
3		Jude Gunzenhauser
4		Chad Malcome
5		Patricia Glowski
6		Manual Inbody

Figure 8.1 *Array Formula to create sequential numbers. You must highlight five cells, create formula in active cell, and then enter the formula with Ctrl+Shift+Enter.*

Creating an Array of Sequential Numbers: ROW(range)-ROW(FirstCellInRange)+1

Using Figure 8.1 as your guide, here are the steps for creating this array formula:

1. Because you have five items (the numbers 1 to 5), you highlight five cells, the range A2:A6, before you start creating the array formula.

2. You create the formula in the active cell (the light colored cell, in this example A2).

3. You use the ROW function because ROW can look at a range and report the row number for each cell in the range.

4. You start the formula with ROW(A2:A6). The range, A2:A6, in the ROW function creates a function argument array operation, which creates the resultant array {2;3;4;5;6}.

101

5. If you subtract ROW(A2), you get ROW(A2:A6)-ROW(A2), which yields the resultant array {0;1;2;3;4}.

6. Now you add 1 to get ROW(A2:A6)-ROW(A2)+1, which yields the resultant array {1;2;3;4;5}.

7. To enter the array formula and the resultant array with sequential numbers into the cells, you use Ctrl+Shift+Enter.

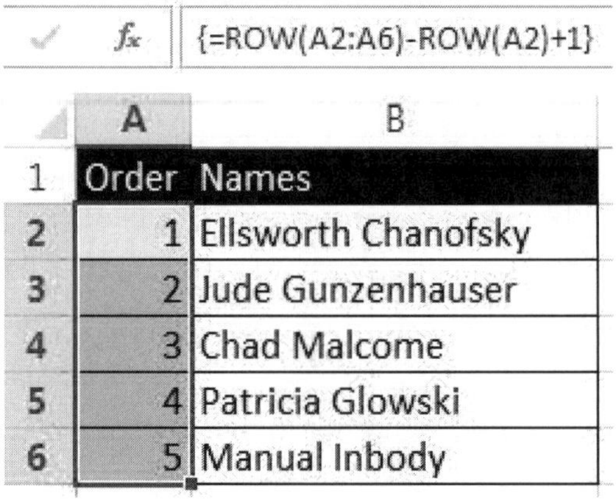

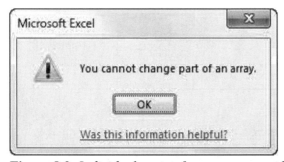

Figure 8.2 *Ctrl+Shift+Enter to deliver the resultant array with the five sequential numbers to five cells.*

As shown in Figure 8.2 the array formula was simultaneously entered into five cells, each cell displays a sequential number, and the formula bar shows the curly braces. With the formula complete, notice a few unique aspects of this type of array formula:

1. If you try to delete a cell in the range A2:A6 or insert a row between 2 and 6, you get the error message shown in Figure 8.3. This is because when you enter an array formula or a function into a block of cells, the array formula becomes a single unit that disallows structural changes such as deleting cells, inserting rows, or deleting individual cell content.

Figure 8.3 *Individual parts of an array cannot be changed.*

2. The keyboard shortcut for highlighting the current array (all the cells that are part of the array formula) is Ctrl+/ (forward slash).

3. It is possible to delete the array formula from all the cells by highlighting the entire array formula and then pressing Delete. Another method for deleting array formula is to select any one cell, press Backspace, and then press Ctrl+Shift+Enter.

4. If you need to edit the array formula, edit any one particular cell in the array and then reenter the array formula with Ctrl+Shift+Enter.

5. If you select any one of the cells in the range that contains the array formula and look in the formula bar, you will see the same formula in each cell. Note that when you created the formula, you did not lock (make absolute) the references A2:A6 or A2. However,

when you used Ctrl+Shift+Enter to put the formula into the cells, the references did not change, as a normal relative cell reference would have changed in a non-array formula. In Figure 8.4 you see that the formula in cell A3 is the same as the formula in cell A2 (refer to Figure 8.2).

Figure 8.4 *Regardless of whether the cell references were entered as absolute or relative, they remain the same in each cell.*

Array Formula Efficiency Rule 19

Two types of array formulas can simultaneously deliver more than one value to more than one cell through the use of Ctrl+Shift+Enter:

- Array formulas that you create with various formula elements and put together yourself
- Built-in Excel array functions

Rules for array formulas that deliver more than one item to more than one cell:

- Select a range of cells, create the formula or function, and then enter it with Ctrl+-Shift+Enter.
- The array formula/function is considered a single unit, and structural changes such as deleting individual cells, deleting individual cell content, or inserting rows in disallowed.
- The keyboard shortcut for highlighting the current array (all the cells that are part of the array formula) is Ctrl+/ (forward slash).
- If you want to delete the array formula/function, you can highlight the entire array formula (by pressing Ctrl+/) and then press Delete. Another method for deleting an array formula is to select any one cell, press Backspace, and then press Ctrl+Shift+Enter.
- If you need to edit your array formula, edit any one particular cell in the array and then reenter the array formula with Ctrl+Shift+Enter.
- When you enter an array formula or a function into more than one cell by using Ctrl+-Shift+Enter, the cell references will be the same in each cell, regardless of whether the cell references in the active cell are locked or not locked (that is, absolute or relative).
- Array functions (except for the TRANSPOSE function) can be placed in other functions that expect a range of values (for example, COUNT, MIN, MAX), and the formula will not require Ctrl+Shift+Enter.
- A formula like ={1;2;3;4;5} or =43 or ="Love" entered into the range A1:A5 with Ctrl+-Shift+Enter is an array formula with no direct array operation. It will show curly braces and will act as a single unit.

Why ROW(range)-ROW(FirstCellInRange)+1 Is Useful

This section takes a closer look at the array formula ROW(A2:A6)-ROW(A2)+1. In particular, it looks at why this formula is efficient and robust. This is important because this formula will show up as a formula element in more advanced array formulas. This formula element has five aspects:

1. Figure 8.5 shows an alternative array formula that can create a sequential array of numbers. The drawback to this formula is that if you insert a row above the table or move the table, the sequential numbers will change and deliver the incorrect numbers. Figure 8.6 shows what would happen if you inserted a row. The formula ROW(A2:A6)-ROW(A2)+1 does not suffer from this deficiency.

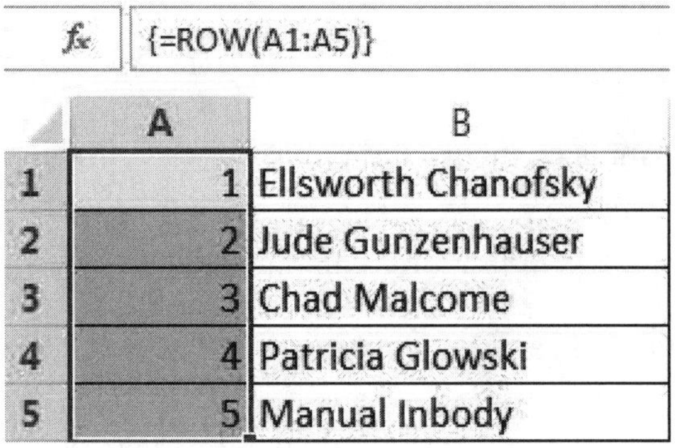

Figure 8.5 *A seemingly less complicated formula to create sequential numbers.*

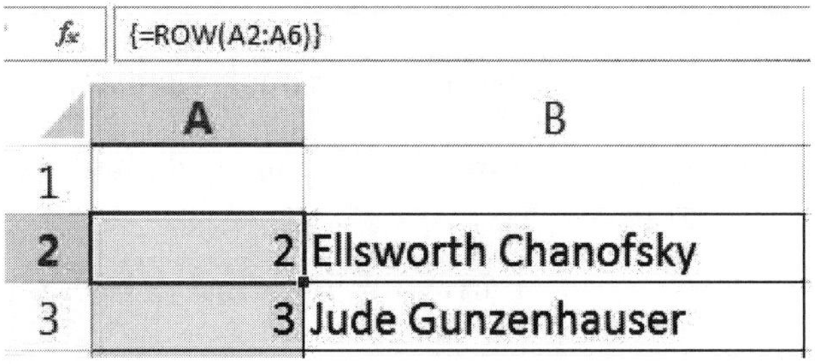

Figure 8.6 *This formula reports the incorrect numbering if a row is inserted above the table.*

As shown in Figure 8.7, using an array constant could work. The problem is that if you have many rows, typing out the array constant takes a long time. The formula ROW(A2:A6)-ROW(A2)+1 can be extended to many rows and does not take a long time to create, and it does not exceed the upper limit of characters for a formula (8,192).

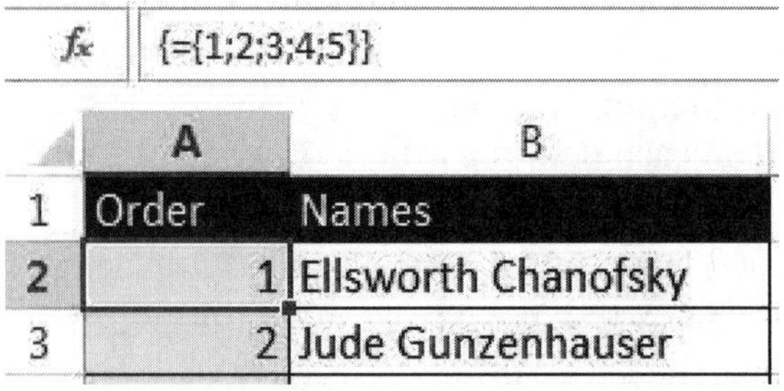

Figure 8.7 *For a large data set, an array constant is inconvenient.*

2. The formula shown in Figure 8.8 maybe easy to create, but if you move the table or insert a row above, the numbers are incorrect. The formula ROW(A2:A6)-ROW(A2)+1 does not have this deficiency.

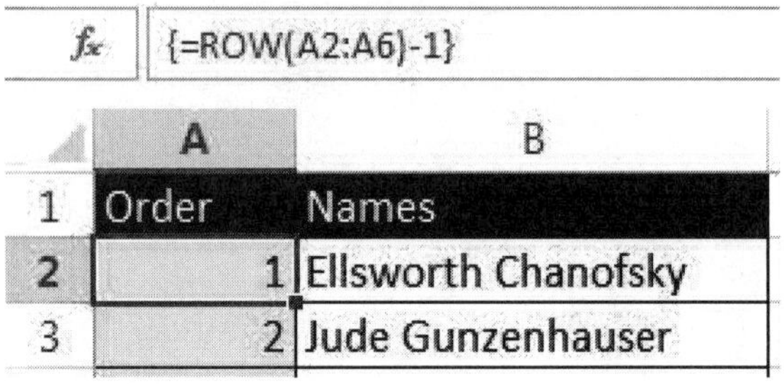

Figure 8.8 *This formula shows the wrong numbers if the table is moved.*

3. Look at the formula ROW(A2:A6)-ROW(A2)+1 in cell A2 (Figure 8.2)and notice that the formula refers to the cell the formula is housed in; that is, the formula sits in cell A2 and has the cell reference A2 in the formula. Most formulas that refer to the cell the formula is housed in get a circular reference error. Not this formula. This is because the formula is not calculating a math type answer; it is just asking, "What row am I in?"

4. One reason the formula ROW(A2:A6)-ROW(A2)+1 will always deliver the correct array of numbers is that it is self-contained in the range that displays the numbers. This means no matter where you move the formula, it will always calculate the correct array of numbers. This benefit will become more obvious when you use this formula as a formula element in the formulas for extracting records (see Chapter 15).

The formula you have used so far creates sequential numbers for records in rows. What if you wanted to do the same thing in a horizontal range, or across the columns? In that case, you could not use the ROW function. Instead, you would use the COLUMN function, as shown in Figure 8.9.

f_x	{=COLUMN(B1:F1)-COLUMN(B1)+1}

	A	B	C	D	E	F
1	Day	1	2	3	4	5
2	Sales	Project 10	Project 8	Project 9	Project 7	Project 2

Figure 8.9 *The COLUMN function can be used to create a horizontal array.*

So far the formulas in this chapter have had the goal of creating sequential numbers and making it difficult to delete the individual cells in the array. Is that really necessary, especially when you could highlight the entire array and delete it? Probably not. If you are not concerned about the cells with the sequential numbers being deleted, there are a few other excellent methods for creating sequential numbering. The following sections look at five of them.

Establishing a Pattern

After typing any two numbers into two cells, you can grab the fill handle (the tiny box in the lower-right corner of a selected cell) with your cursor (the crosshairs cursor, also known as the angry rabbit cursor) and drag down (or to the side, if the numbers are listed horizontally). When you do this, you increment the numbers the based on the difference between the two numbers. If the numbers are 1 and 4, because the difference is 3, the next numbers in the sequence would be 7, 10, and so on (see Figure 8.10).

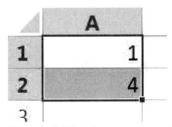

Figure 8.10 *The increment here is "add 3." Grab the fill handle with your cursor and pull as far as you want.*

Holding Down Ctrl While Moving the Cursor

If you type a single number in a cell and then point to the fill handle with your cursor while holding the Ctrl key, you see a small plus symbol above and to the right of the crosshairs; when you see the plus symbol, click and drag down. This will increment numbers by 1.

Highlighting a Number and a Blank Cell

If you highlight a number and the blank cell next to it and then grab the fill handle with your cursor and drag down, you will increment the number by 1 (see Figure 8.11). This trick also works if you highlight a blank cell below the number and drag to the side.

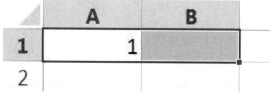

Figure 8.11 *When you select a blank cell also, Excel knows to increment by 1.*

Using Fill Series

Say that you want the numbers 0 to 360 in a column. Highlighting the numbers 0 and 1 and then dragging down 360 rows would take a long time. As an alternative, you can use the Fill Series feature. After typing a 0 in cell A1 and selecting cell A1, go to the Editing group in the Home Ribbon tab and from the Fill drop-down, select Series. When the Series dialog box appears, select the Columns option button and set Step Value to 1 and Stop Value to 360. Figure 8.12 shows these settings. This method is fast!

> **Note:** Alternatively, you could open the Series dialog box by right-clicking the fill handle and dragging down one cell and then back up one cell, releasing the right-click, and selecting Series from context menu.

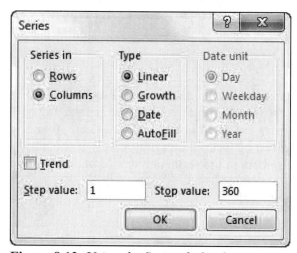

Figure 8.12 *Using the Series dialog box to increment numbers is fast!*

Formula Number Incrementors: Non-Array Formulas to Increment Sequential Numbers Vertically or Horizontally

Figures 8.13 and 8.14 show two useful formulas for incrementing by 1. These formulas use an expandable range, where the first cell reference in the range is locked but the second one is not locked. Like the earlier formulas, this formula is one of the few formulas in Excel that can refer to the cell reference that the formula is housed in without getting a circular reference. These two formula number incrementors show up in many of the array formulas to extract records or data in Chapter 15.

A2		⋮	×	✓	*fx*		=ROWS(A$2:A2)

	A	B	C	D
1	Order	Names		
2	1	Ellsworth Chanofsky		
3	2	Jude Gunzenhauser		
4	3	Chad Malcome		
5	4	Patricia Glowski		
6	5	Manual Inbody		

Figure 8.13 *Incrementing numbers in a column, or vertically. The ROWS function counts how many total rows there are in a range. Because you use an expandable range, as you copy the formula, Excel increments the numbers by 1.*

F1		⋮	×	✓	*fx*		=COLUMNS($B1:F1)

	A	B	C	D	E	F
1	Day	1	2	3	4	5
2	Sales	Project 10	Project 8	Project 9	Project 7	Project 2

Figure 8.14 *Incrementing numbers in a row, or horizontally. The COLUMNS function counts how many total columns there are in a range. Because you use an expandable range, as you copy the formula, Excel increments the numbers by 1.*

When you create sequential numbers in a large range of cells, an important difference between the array formula ROW(range)-ROW(FirstCellInRange)+1 and the non-array formula ROWS(A$1:A1) is that the array formula will have a significantly faster formula calculation time. (The timing results are at the end of this chapter.) That said, for some array formulas in later chapters, formula elements such as ROW(A$2:A2) are indispensable for incrementing numbers.

Using Formula Number Incrementors and INDEX to Display a Table in a Single Column

In this section, we stray off course a bit (but it is okay to stray a bit if you will learn cool formula stuff). Figures 8.15 to 8.19 show other types of formula number incrementors. Figures 8.15 and 8.17 show the formulas; Figures 8.16 and 8.18 show the logic of the formulas with pictures; and Figure 8.19 shows a practical use for these types of formula incrementors. (In Chapter 22 you will see a good use for these number incrementors when you learn about the LINEST array function.)

fx		=INT((ROWS(A1:A$1)-1)/3)+1

	A	B	C
1	1		
2	1		
3	1		
4	2		
5	2		
6	2		

Figure 8.15 *A formula number incrementor to get {1;1;1;2;2;2}.*

=ROWS(A$1:A1)-1	=(ROWS(A$1:A1)-1)/3	=INT((ROWS(A$1:A1)-1)/3)	=INT((ROWS(A$1:A1)-1)/3)+1
0	0	0	1
1	0.333333333	0	1
2	0.666666667	0	1
3	1	1	2
4	1.333333333	1	2
5	1.666666667	1	2

Figure 8.16 *The logic of how INT((ROWS(A1:A$1)-1)/3)+1 works.*

| fx | =MOD(ROWS(A$1:A1)-1,3)+1 |

	A	B	C
1	1		
2	2		
3	3		
4	1		
5	2		
6	3		

Figure 8.17 *A formula number incrementor to get {1;2;3;1;2;3}.*

=ROWS(A$1:A1)-1	=MOD(ROWS(A$1:A1)-1,3)	=MOD(ROWS(A$1:A1)-1,3)+1
0	0	1
1	1	2
2	2	3
3	0	1
4	1	2
5	2	3

Figure 8.18 *The logic of how MOD(ROWS(A$1:A1)-1,3)+1 works. The MOD function reports the remainder after dividing each number by 3. For example, 3/3 has a remainder of zero, whereas 4/3 has a remainder of 1.*

| fx | =INDEX($C$2:$E$4,INT((ROWS(A$1:A1)-1)/3)+1,MOD((ROWS(A$1:A1)-1),3)+1) |

	A	B	C	D	E	F	G	H
1	697		Sales	Rep	Product			
2	Jo		697	Jo	Pro 1			
3	Pro 1		568	Mo	Pro 1			
4	568		510	Jo	Pro 3			
5	Mo							
6	Pro 1							

Figure 8.19 *INDEX is doing a two-way lookup to extract data from a table and orient it vertically, in a single column. The row_num argument in INDEX uses INT((ROWS(A1:A$1)-1)/3)+1, and column_num uses MOD((ROWS(A$1:A1)-1),3)+1.*

Figures 8.20 to 8.23 show a second example of an array formula that can deliver multiple values and also be a deterrent for deleting individual cells. Figure 8.20 shows a typical non-array formula that calculates the quarter from each serial number date. If you want to convert this formula to an array formula that delivers multiple values and help deter cell deletion, you can simply change the single cell in the MONTH function to a range of cells. As shown in Figure 8.21, you highlight all the cells, create the formula, and then enter it with Ctrl+Shift+Enter. Figure 8.22 shows the finished formula, and Figure 8.23 shows the logic of the formula with pictures.

C2	▾	⋮	✕	✓	*fx*	=CEILING(MONTH(A2),3)/3

	A	B	C
1	Date	Sales	Quarter
2	1/5/2015	110859	1
3	12/7/2015	110258	4
4	7/18/2015	70423	3

Figure 8.20 *A non-array formula that you copy down the column.*

	A	B	C	D
1	Date	Sales	Quarter	
2	1/5/2015	110859	=CEILING(MONTH(A2:A4),3)/3	
3	12/7/2015	110258	CEILING(number, **significance**)	
4	7/18/2015	70423	3	

Figure 8.21 *Changing a single cell to a range in the MONTH argument.*

C2	▾	⋮	✕	✓	*fx*	{=CEILING(MONTH(A2:A4),3)/3}

	A	B	C
1	Date	Sales	Quarter
2	1/5/2015	110859	1
3	12/7/2015	110258	4
4	7/18/2015	70423	3

Figure 8.22 *Using Ctrl+Shift+Enter to enter a formula to calculate the quarter.*

{=MONTH(A2:A4)}	{=CEILING(MONTH(A2:A4),3)}	{=CEILING(MONTH(A2:A4),3)/3}
1	3	1
12	12	4
7	9	3

Figure 8.23 *MONTH delivers a number 1 to 12. The CEILING function rounds up to a multiple of 3. Division by 3 yields the quarter.*

Array Constants in Cells for a VLOOKUP Table

This section provides an example of an array formula that can deliver multiple values using a VLOOKUP formula. Figure 8.24 shows a typical VLOOKUP situation. If the goal is to create a lookup table that deters cell deletion, you can create an array constant and enter it into the range A2:B4 by using Ctrl+Shift+Enter. You'll see how to do this next.

| E2 | ▼ | ⋮ | × | ✓ | *fx* | =VLOOKUP(D2,A2:B4,2) |

	A	B	C	D	E
1	Product	Price		Product	Price
2	Majestic Beaut	37		Sunshine	18
3	Quad	33			
4	Sunshine	18			

Figure 8.24 *A typical VLOOKUP.*

Using Figures 8.25 to 8.28 as a visual guide and the following steps, you can enter the lookup table as an array constant:

1. As shown in Figure 8.25, select any cell and create a formula that highlights the table.

2. As shown in Figure 8.26, highlight the range and convert it to an array constant by pressing F9. Immediately (with the array constant still highlighted) use Ctrl+C to copy the array constant and then press the Esc key to revert to the empty cell. (The array constant is copied onto the Clipboard.)

3. As shown in Figure 8.27, highlight (no need to delete the contents first) the table range A2:B4, type an equal sign, and then press Ctrl+V to paste the array constant.

4. Enter the array constant into the range by pressing Ctrl+Shift+Enter. You're done.

	A	B	C	D	E	F	G
1	Product	Price		Product	Price		
2	Majestic Beaut	37		Sunshine	18		
3	Quad	33					
4	Sunshine	18		=A2:B4			

Figure 8.25 *Type equal sign and then select table.*

	A	B	C	D	E	F	G
1	Product	Price		Product	Price		
2	Majestic Beaut	37		Sunshine	18		
3	Quad	33					
4	Sunshine	18		={"Majestic Beaut",37;"Quad",33;"Sunshine",18}			

Figure 8.26 *Evaluate (F9 key) to create array constant. Ctrl+C to copy array constant.*

	A	B	C	D	E	F	G
1	Product	Price		Product	Price		
2	={"Majestic Beaut",37;"Quad",33;"Sunshine",18}						
3	Quad	33					
4	Sunshine	18					

Figure 8.27 *Highlight cells. Ctrl+V to paste array constant into active cell.*

A2			f_x	{={"Majestic Beaut",37;"Quad",33;"Sunshine",18}}

	A	B	C	D	E	F	G
1	Product	Price		Product	Price		
2	Majestic Beaut	37		Sunshine	18		
3	Quad	33					
4	Sunshine	18					

Figure 8.28 *Ctrl+Shift+Enter to enter array constant into cells.*

As shown in Figure 8.28, you now have a lookup table that was created with an array constant entered using Ctrl+Shift+Enter. As a result, this table deters cell deletion.

Using Ctrl+Shift+Enter on a Formula That Does Not Contain a Direct Array Operation

If you highlight the range A1:A5 and type a formula in the active cell (for example, ={1;2;3;4;5}, or =43, or ="Love") and then press Ctrl+Shift+Enter, you will create a "sort of array formula." The range A1:A5 will contain a formula with curly braces that will act as a single unit and disallow any one part to be deleted. However, the formula contains no direct array operation (for example, multiplying, joining, or function argument operation); its only "array" operation is to use Ctrl+-Shift+Enter to enter the formula into multiple cells.

Timing the Formulas in This Chapter

As discussed in Chapter 2, pointing array formulas to large data sets can increase formula calculation time for a workbook. In general, faster calculation times are more efficient. This section shows the anecdotal results I got. To time your own formulas, look back to Chapter 2 for details. (Timing depends on many factors, and your particular situation may have different timing results.) To see the workbook with the timing results I got, open the file named 06SeqNumbers.xlsm in the folder Timing in the zipped folder FilesForCtrlShiftEnterBook. The Introduction to this book explains how to get these files. Figure 8.29 shows the timing results (in seconds) I got. In this particular application of these two formulas, creating sequential numbers in a column, the array formula has a calculating speed advantage.

500 rows

	=ROW(A2:A501)-ROW(A2)+1	=ROWS(C$2:C2)
Time 1	0.0026	0.00363
Time 2	0.00296	0.00379
Time 3	0.00292	0.00328
Ave	0.002826667	0.003566667
% change	0.0%	26.2%

10,000 rows

	=ROW(A2:A10001)-ROW(A2)+1	=ROWS(C$2:C2)
Time 1	0.00486	0.1407
Time 2	0.00485	0.14683
Time 3	0.00498	0.1414
Ave	0.004896667	0.142976667
% change	0.0%	2819.9%

Figure 8.29 *For 10,000 rows, the array formula is significantly faster.*

In Chapter 15, when you learn about formulas to extract data, you will see the formula elements ROW(Range)-ROW(FirstCellInRange)+1 and ROWS(A$2:A2). However, unlike in this chapter, where they are alternatives for the same formula goal, in Chapter 15, they will accomplish entirely different goals within a single array formula. Stay tuned.

Chapter Summary

In this chapter you have learn about array formulas that can deliver more than one value to more than one cell and how to create formula number incrementors. In Chapter 9 you will learn about a group of functions called array functions.

Chapter 9: A First Look at Array Functions: TRANSPOSE, MODE.MULT, and TREND

Excel Files

To follow along with the examples in this chapter, you can download the accompanying files, as explained in the Introduction.

Array Formulas That Deliver an Array of Results

Two types of array formulas can simultaneously deliver more than one value to more than one cell with the use of Ctrl+Shift+Enter:

- Array formulas that you create with various formula elements and put together yourself (You learned about them in Chapter 8.)

- Built-in Excel array functions (You will learn about them in this chapter.)

Both types of array formulas that deliver multiple items have the same rules and guidelines as shown in Chapter 8 (see Array Formula Efficiency Rule 17). As you learned there, you use these steps to enter this type of array formula into multiple cells:

1. If the array formula will yield *n* items and you want to display the *n* items in *n* cells, you must select *n* cells before starting your formula. In addition, you must consider whether the array is a one-way or two-way array when entering the formula.

2. Create your array formula in the active cell.

3. To enter the array formula into the selected cells, press Ctrl+Shift+Enter.

Array Functions

Array functions are built-in functions that are specifically designed to deliver more than one item to more than one cell using Ctrl+Shift+Enter. The following table lists the eight Excel array functions. This chapter looks at three of them: TRANSPOSE, MODE.MULT, and TREND functions. Subsequent chapters look at FREQUENCY, LINEST, MMULT, MINVERSE and MUNIT.

Excel Array Functions		
Function	**Function Category**	**What It Does**
TRANSPOSE	Any	Converts a vertical array or range into a horizontal array or range or vice versa. Works on one-way or two-way arrays or ranges.
MODE.MULT (new in Excel 2010)	Statistics	Calculates mode (statistics). Finds the number that occurs most frequently when there are multiple such values (multiple modes).
TREND	Statistics	Using the least-squares method for best-fitting data to a straight line, returns an array of y values, given these formula inputs: known y values, known x values, and an array of x values used to estimate the array of y values. TREND is different from FORECAST in that it can return an array of x values.
FREQUENCY	Statistics	Counts how many values are in each category, given the upper values for each category.
LINEST	Statistics	An amazing function that simultaneously returns two or more statistics for single or multiple regression, using the least-squares method for best-fitting data to a straight line.
MMULT	Matrix Algebra	Returns the matrix product of two arrays.
MUNIT (new in Excel 2013)	Matrix Algebra	Returns the unit matrix, given a single number.
MINVERSE	Matrix Algebra	Returns the inverse matrix, given a matrix.

The TRANSPOSE Array Function

The TRANSPOSE function does something quite simple: It converts a vertical array into a horizontal array while retaining a link to the source data. And it can do this for a one-way or two-way array table. Figure 9.1 shows a two-way table of source data in the range A2:D4. If the goal is to transpose the data (that is, flip it 90 degrees), you can accomplish this in four steps:

1. Count the number of columns (4) and rows (3) in the source data set.

2. Highlight 3 columns and 4 rows (switching the counts for rows and columns from original data)—in the case, A7:C10.

3. In the active cell, create your TRANSPOSE function with the source data highlighted.

4. Enter the formula with Ctrl+Shift+Enter (see Figure 9.2).

	A	B	C	D
1	**Source data:**			
2	Product 1	Product 2	Product 3	Product 4
3	151	83	168	116
4	140	68	118	49
5				
6	**Linked and transposed:**			
7	=TRANSPOSE(A2:D4			
8	TRANSPOSE(**array**)			
9				
10				

Figure 9.1 *Before you create the formula, highlight a range that has the same number of rows and columns, respectively, as the source data has columns and rows.*

A7 f_x {=TRANSPOSE(A2:D4)}

	A	B	C	D
6	**Linked and transposed:**			
7	Product 1	151	140	
8	Product 2	83	68	
9	Product 3	168	118	
10	Product 4	116	49	

Figure 9.2 *Press Ctrl+Shift+Enter so that the TRANSPOSE function can create a resultant array of transposed data. You see curly braces in formula bar.*

The beauty of the TRANSPOSE function (as opposed to the Paste Special Transpose feature) is that if the data changes, the transposed data will change also. Figure 9.3 shows that the source data has changed, and the TRANSPOSE function reflects the change.

	A	B	C	D
1	**Source Data 1:**			
2	Product 1	Product 2	Product 3	Product 4
3	214	164	57	383
4	392	46	127	297
5				
6	**Linked and transposed:**			
7	Product 1	214	392	
8	Product 2	164	46	
9	Product 3	57	127	
10	Product 4	383	297	

Figure 9.3 *If the source data changes, TRANSPOSE immediately updates.*

Avoiding Zeros from Empty Cells When Using TRANSPOSE, IF, and ISBLANK

As shown in Figure 9.4, sometimes source data has empty cells. This causes the TRANSPOSE function to show a zero.

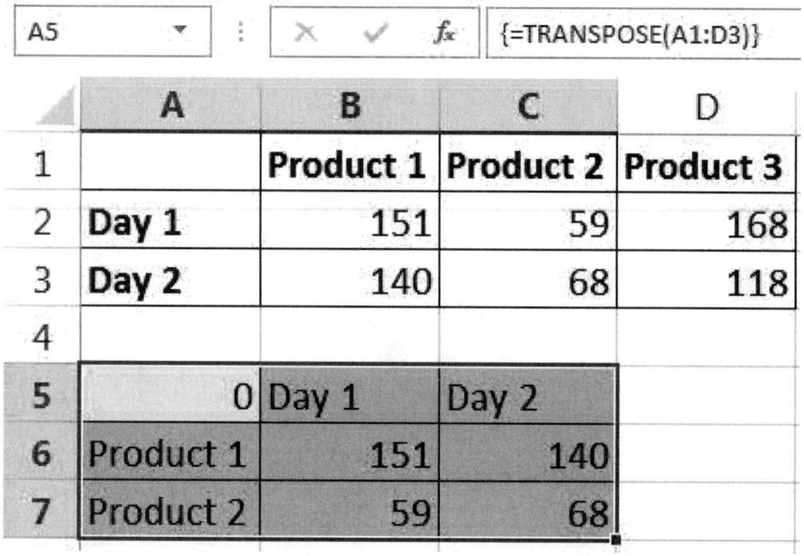

Figure 9.4 *TRANSPOSE treats an empty cell as a zero.*

> **Note:** Some functions, such as TRANSPOSE, VLOOKUP, INDEX, and a few others, treat an empty cell as a zero. Others, such as MIN, MAX, and AVERAGE, do not treat empty cells as zeros. As with so many other things that go on in Excel functions, it comes down to how the individual function argument is programmed to behave. It pays to read Excel function help.

Back in Chapter 4, you learned how to use the IF function to filter an array of items within a formula. In this example, you want to use the IF function, but rather than filtering, you want to use the IF function to substitute a null text string (a way to show "nothing" in a formula) for the zero that Excel sees when it looks at an empty cell. The IF function can then dump the resultant array into the TRANSPOSE function. Figures 9.5 to 9.11 show how to create the formula.

As shown in Figure 9.5 you first enter the TRANSPOSE function. If you entered the range A1:D3, you would get a zero from cell A1. Therefore, you put the IF function into the TRANSPOSE functions to create the array of items.

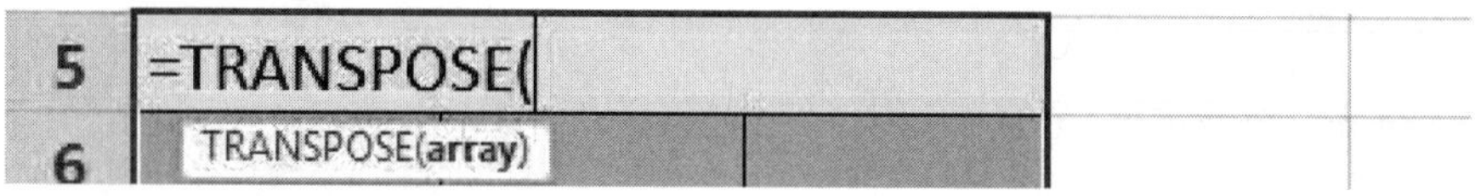

Figure 9.5 *Type "=TRANSPOSE(".*

As shown in Figure 9.6, in the logical_test argument for the IF function, you can use the IS-BLANK function on the range A1:D3. ISBLANK will perform a function argument array operation and return an array of TRUEs and FALSEs. A TRUE means that the cell is empty, and a FALSE means that the cell is not empty.

> **Note:** The ISBLANK function should have been named ISEMPTY. The word *blank* is often misused in Excel. For this reason, I always refer to empty cells as *empty cells* and null text strings as *null text strings* and avoid using the word *blank* altogether.

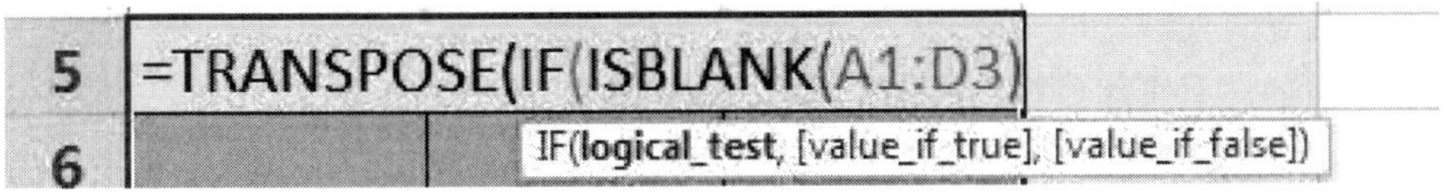

Figure 9.6 *Enter IF and ISNUMBER formula element.*

If you evaluate (by pressing F9) the ISBLANK function, Figure 9.7 shows the resultant array of TRUEs and FALSEs. Notice that because the range A1:D3 contains columns and rows, the array syntax contains commas and semicolons. Be sure to use Ctrl+Z to undo the evaluation before you move forward.

Figure 9.7 *Evaluating (F9 key) shows the resultant array that the ISBLANK function creates.*

As shown in Figure 9.8, in the value_if_true argument, you place a single null text string, which is two double quotes and has zero length. This single null text string is substituted at any location that contains an empty cell.

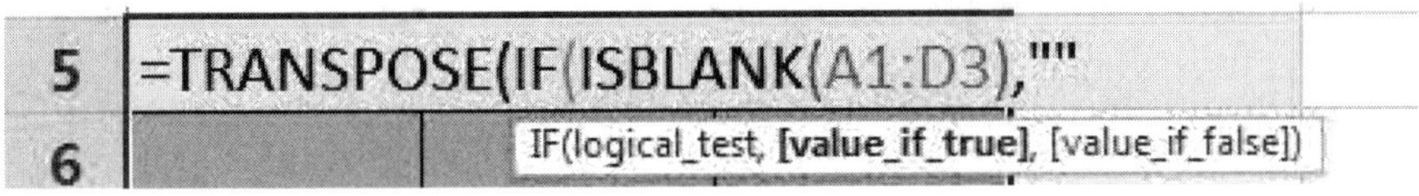

Figure 9.8 *Enter null text string in value_if_true argument.*

Null Text Strings

A null text string is a text string that has zero length. To create a null text string, you type two double quotes, one after the other, with no space between the first double quote and the second double quote. When you use a null text string in a formula, it shows in the cell as nothing (no text at all), even though it is considered a text string with zero length and is no longer considered an empty cell.

As shown in Figure 9.9, in the value_if_false argument you place the range A1:D3. Anytime there is a corresponding FALSE in the logical_test array of TRUEs and FALSEs, the value from the corresponding cell will be in the IF function's resultant array.

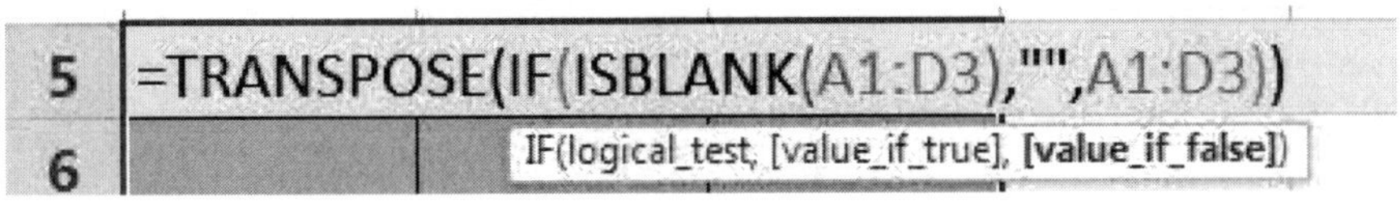

Figure 9.9 *Enter range into value_if_true argument and close with two parentheses*

As shown in Figure 9.10, if you evaluate the IF function (by pressing F9), you can see that the IF function delivers an resultant array of items to the array argument of the TRANSPOSE function that includes a null text string instead of a zero for cell A1. Be sure to use Ctrl+Z to undo the evaluation before you move forward.

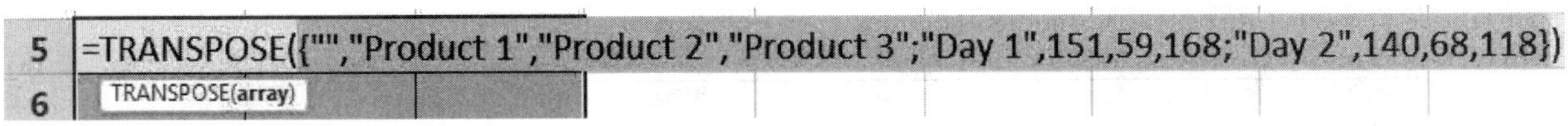

Figure 9.10 *Evaluating (F9 key) shows the resultant array that the IF function creates.*

Figure 9.11 shows the end result after you enter the array formula into the range A5:C7 with Ctrl+Shift+Enter. The finished transposed data set shows nothing in cell A1 instead of a zero, even though there is a null text string in cell A1.

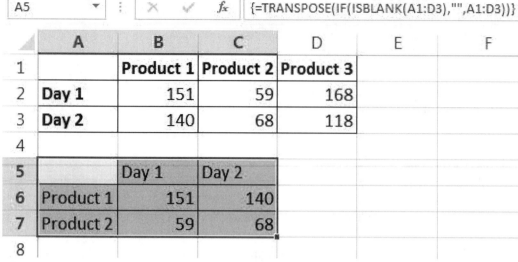

Figure 9.11 *Enter formula with Ctrl+Shift+Enter.*

Notes About the Formula =TRANSPOSE(IF(ISBLANK(A1:D3),"",A1:D3))

The following table presents a summary of the formula for transposing a table without getting zeros in empty cells.

Impetus for Creating an Array Formula:
You need to transpose a table and not show zeros where there are empty cells.
Calculation Summary:
1. =TRANSPOSE(IF(ISBLANK(A1:D3),"",A1:D3))
2. =TRANSPOSE(IF({TRUE,FALSE,FALSE,FALSE;FALSE,FALSE,FALSE,FALSE;FALSE,-FALSE,FALSE,FALSE},"",A1:D3))
Array calculation: ISBLANK(A1:D3) delivers the resultant array {TRUE,FALSE,FALSE,FALSE;-FALSE,FALSE,FALSE,FALSE;FALSE,FALSE,FALSE,FALSE} to the logical_test argument of the IF function.
3. =TRANSPOSE({"","Product 1","Product 2","Product 3";"Day 1",151,59,168;"Day 2",140,68,118})
Array calculation: IF({TRUE,FALSE,FALSE,FALSE;FALSE,FALSE,FALSE,FALSE;FALSE,FALSE,-FALSE,FALSE},"",A1:D3) delivers the resultant array {"","Product 1","Product 2","Product 3";"Day 1",151,59,168;"Day 2",140,68,118} to the array argument of the TRANSPOSE function.
4. =TRANSPOSE({"","Product 1","Product 2","Product 3";"Day 1",151,59,168;"Day 2",140,68,118})
Array calculation: TRANSPOSE({"","Product 1","Product 2","Product 3";"Day 1",151,59,168;"Day 2",140,68,118}) delivers the resultant array {"","Day 1","Day 2";"Product 1",151,140;"Product 2",59,68;"Product 3",168,118} to the range A5:C7.
5. The formula delivers an array of values to the range A5:C7
Entering a Formula into a Cell:
Array functions that deliver multiple values to multiple cells require Ctrl+Shift+Enter.
Conclusion:
If you need to transpose a table and link to the source data, and you want to show nothing (that is, a null text string) rather than zeros, this is a great option. (It is better than just formatting zeros to not show because a zero in the source data should show in the result.)

MODE Calculations

In this section you will learn about the mode calculation. The mode calculation simply determines which number occurs most frequently in a list of numbers.

> **Note:** The mode calculation is usually used on nominal data (that is, data that is not a number and has no inherent order) as a type of average. However, it can also be used on number data (quantitative data), as you will see here.

Figure 9.12 shows a list of times from a race. The goal is to figure out which time occurred most frequently. If you have Excel 2007 or earlier, you can use the MODE function; if you have Excel 2010 or later, you can use the MODE.SNGL function (SNGL stands for single mode). They both calculate exactly the same correct answer; they are duplicate functions, and you can use either one. In Figure 9.12 the value 24 occurred the most frequently because it occurred three times, and no other value occurred more than one time. Therefore, 24 is the mode.

	A	B	C	D
1	Times (mins)		1 Mode	**2007 or earlier**
2	24		24	< Formula =MODE(A2:A8)
3	22.7			
4	24		1 Mode	**2010 or later**
5	19.9		24	< Formula =MODE.SNGL(A2:A8)
6	27.4			
7	21.2			
8	24			

Figure 9.12 *The MODE and MODE.SNGL functions both calculate a single mode.*

> **Note:** When you type =MODE, you see a drop-down like the one shown in Figure 9.13. The MODE function in the drop-down has a yellow triangle icon next to it to indicate that this is a "compatibility function" that exists so that spreadsheets built in earlier versions will work in later versions. However, MODE and MODE.SNGL calculate the same answer. Why the new MODE.SNGL? Function names followed by a "dot" with a function suffix is new convention for the new Excel 2010 statistical functions. Another example of a compatibility function is the STDEV.S function, which is supposed to replace the old STDEV function.

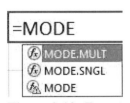

Figure 9.13 *Functions that use dots are the new Excel 2010 statistical functions. The yellow triangle indicates that the function is a "compatibility function".*

The MODE.MULT Array Function

With mode calculations, it is not always the case that there is just one mode. Sometimes there are multiple modes. Figure 9.14 shows a data set with two modes. The time 23.7 and 25.3 both occur three times. Notice that both MODE and MODE.SNGL report only the first one that is encountered in the list and totally ignore the fact that there is more than one mode. When there are multiple modes, you can use the MODE.MULT array function. It makes perfect sense that this is an array function because if there are multiple modes, the function will be delivering multiple values. This means that you must highlight multiple cells and then enter the function with Ctrl+Shift+Enter. Because you know that there are exactly two modes, as shown in Figure 9.14, you highlight exactly two cells (the range C7:C8) and then create the array formula. But what if you did not know how many modes there were? Or what if the data were continually changing, with sometimes one mode and other times multiple modes? In either case, you would not know how many cells to highlight before creating the formula. No problem. You can put on your thinking cap and create a robust formula that will work regardless of how many modes there are.

	A	B	C	D
1	Times (mins)		1 Mode	2007 or earlier
2	24		23.7	< Formula =MODE(A2:A15)
3	23.7			2010 or later
4	25.3		23.7	< Formula =MODE.SNGL(A2:A15)
5	19.9			
6	27.4		> 1 Mode	2010 or later
7	23.7		23.7	< Formula {=MODE.MULT(A2:A15)}
8	26.1		25.3	< Formula {=MODE.MULT(A2:A15)}
9	18.2			
10	18.2			
11	23.7			
12	27.6			
13	25.3			
14	30.4			
15	25.3			

Figure 9.14 *The array function MODE.MULT can find all the modes.*

Figure 9.15 shows a first attempt at a solution. You simply highlight a bunch of cells and enter the MODE.MULT function using Ctrl+Shift+Enter. If you are in a hurry and don't mind the #N/A errors, this "blind" method works okay.

> 1 Mode	
23.7	< Formula {=MODE.MULT(A2:A15)}
25.3	< Formula {=MODE.MULT(A2:A15)}
#N/A	< Formula {=MODE.MULT(A2:A15)}
#N/A	< Formula {=MODE.MULT(A2:A15)}
#N/A	< Formula {=MODE.MULT(A2:A15)}

Figure 9.15 *If you don't know how many modes, just highlight a bunch of cells and press Ctrl+Shift+Enter. The #N/A is a slight bother.*

The reason you are getting the #N/A errors is because you highlighted too many cells. Figure 9.16 shows that if you were to evaluate the formula, you would see that the MODE.MULT is delivering a resultant array of only two values.

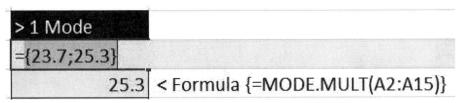

> 1 Mode	
={23.7;25.3}	
25.3	< Formula {=MODE.MULT(A2:A15)}

Figure 9.16 *MODE.MULT returns a vertical array of numbers.*

Another drawback to the "blind" method is that if the data were changing and you were to get a single mode, MODE.MULT would simply repeat the single mode many times, as shown in Figure 9.17.

	A	B	C	D
1	Times (mins)		> 1 Mode	
2	24		23.7	< Formula {=MODE.MULT(A2:A15)}
3	23.7		23.7	< Formula {=MODE.MULT(A2:A15)}
4	23.7		23.7	< Formula {=MODE.MULT(A2:A15)}
5	19.9		23.7	< Formula {=MODE.MULT(A2:A15)}
6	27.4		23.7	< Formula {=MODE.MULT(A2:A15)}
7	23.7			
8	26.1			
9	18.2			
10	18.2			
11	23.7			

Figure 9.17 *If there is a single mode, MODE.MULT will repeat it.*

A much better solution would be to have a formula that counts how many modes there are and then a second formula that displays the modes as you copy the formula down a column.

Extracting Modes, One at a Time: COUNT, IF, ROWS, INDEX, and MODE.MULT

Figure 9.18 shows the beginnings of the solution. In cell C2 you wrap the COUNT function around the MODE.MULT function to count how many modes there are with the formula =COUNT(-MODE.MULT(A2:A15)).

> **Note:** Notice that you do not have to enter this formula with Ctrl+Shift+Enter. Although the MODE.MULT function requires Ctrl+Shift+Enter when you enter it alone into multiple cells, when you house it in a function that can handle a range of values (except for COUNTIF, SUMIF, and the like), it does not require Ctrl+Shift+Enter. All the array functions display this behavior except for the TRANSPOSE function. This observation is reflected in Array Formula Efficiency Rule 17 in Chapter 14.

	A	B	C	D
1	Times (mins)		Count Modes	
2	24		3	< Formula =COUNT(MODE.MULT(A2:A10))
3	19		> 1 Mode	
4	**23.7**			
5	25.3			
6	24			
7	**23.7**			
8	21.4			
9	25.3			
10	18.2			

Figure 9.18 *MODE.MULT delivers a resultant array of numbers to COUNT, and the COUNT function counts the numbers in the array.*

As shown in Figure 9.19, you start the formula to show the modes in cell C4 by putting MODE.MULT into the array argument of INDEX. Figure 9.20 shows that MODE.MULT is simply delivering a vertical array of modes to the array argument of INDEX (notice the semicolons).

=INDEX(MODE.MULT($A$2:$A$10)
INDEX(**array**, row_num, [column_num])

Figure 9.19 *Enter MODE.MULT into array argument of INDEX.*

=INDEX({24;23.7;25.3}
INDEX(**array**, row_num, [column_num])

Figure 9.20 *Evaluating the MODE.MULT reveals a vertical resultant array.*

Because you need to extract items from a vertical array as you copy the formula down across the rows, you need a formula number incrementor that will give you the sequential numbers 1, 2, 3, and so on. As you saw in Chapter 8, you can use the ROWS function for this. As shown in Figure 9.21, you add the formula element ROWS(C$4:C4) to the row_num argument of INDEX. This formula number incrementor instructs INDEX to extract the first mode (row 1), then the second mode (row 2), and so on as the formula is copied down the column. The INDEX, MODE.MULT, and ROWS combination creates the data extraction formula element.

=INDEX(MODE.MULT($A$2:$A$10),ROWS(C$4:C4))

INDEX(array, **row_num**, [column_num])

Figure 9.21 *The ROWS(C$4:C4) formula element is our formula number incrementor that sits in the row_ num argument of INDEX.*

As shown in Figure 9.22, after you enter the formula (you do not need to use Ctrl+Shift+Enter) and copy it down the column, you get some errors.

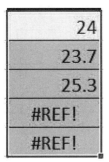

| 24 |
| 23.7 |
| 25.3 |
| #REF! |
| #REF! |

Figure 9.22 *#REF! error in the fourth cell because ROWS(C$4:C7) yields a 4 and INDEX cannot find a fourth number in the vertical resultant array that the MODE.MULT has created.*

You can amend the formula to show a null text string when you copy the formula down past the row with the last mode.

Figure 9.23 shows the formula in cell C4. The logical_test argument of the IF function is asking "Is the formula past the last mode?" The formula number incrementor, ROWS(C$4:C4), creates the sequential numbers 1, 2, 3, and so on. When ROWS(C$4:C4) shows a number bigger than 3, the logical_test argument contains TRUE, and therefore the null text string in the value_if_true argument is delivered to the cell, and the data extraction formula element is not evaluated. You can enter the formula into cell C4 (you do not need to use Ctrl+Shift+Enter) and copy the formula down. Figure 9.24 shows the finished result. The beauty of this formula is that if the data changes, the formula will accurately reflect whether there are no modes, one mode, two modes, or some other number of modes. In the example here, you only copied the formula down five rows. If you might expect more than five modes, then you could copy the formula down as far as you need.

=IF(ROWS(C$4:C4)>$C$2,"",INDEX(MODE.MULT($A$2:$A$10),ROWS(C$4:C4)))

IF(**logical_test**, [value_if_true], [value_if_false])

Figure 9.23 *The logical_test tests whether the formula has been copied down past the third relative position.*

	A	B	C	D
1	Times (mins)		Count Modes	
2	24		3	< Formula =COUNT(MODE.MULT(A2:A10))
3	19		> 1 Mode	
4	**23.7**		24	< Formula =IF(ROWS(C$4:C4)>$C$2,"",INDEX(MODE.MULT($A$2:$A$10),ROWS(C$4:C4)))
5	25.3		23.7	
6	24		25.3	
7	**23.7**			
8	21.4			
9	25.3			
10	18.2			

Figure 9.24 *Completed formula for extracting all modes from a number set.*

Notes About the Formula
=IF(ROWS(C$4:C4)>$C$2,"",INDEX(MODEMULT($A$2:$A$10),ROWS(C$4:C4)))

The following table presents a summary of the formula for extracting modes.

Impetus for Creating an Array Formula:
You need a formula that will automatically update when the data changes and show all the modes and no errors, whether there are zero, one, two, or some other number of modes.
Calculation Summary:
1. =IF(ROWS(C$4:C4)>$C$2,"",INDEX(MODE.MULT($A$2:$A$10),ROWS(C$4:C4)))
2. =IF(1>3,"",INDEX(MODE.MULT($A$2:$A$10),ROWS(C$4:C4)))
3. =IF(FALSE,"",INDEX(MODE.MULT($A$2:$A$10),ROWS(C$4:C4)))
4. =INDEX(MODE.MULT($A$2:$A$10),ROWS(C$4:C4))
5. =INDEX({24;23.7;25.3},ROWS(C$4:C4))
Array calculation: MODE.MULT($A$2:$A$10) delivers the resultant array {24;23.7;25.3} to the array argument of the INDEX function.
6. =INDEX({24;23.7;25.3},1)
7. The formula delivers the single item 24
Entering a Formula into a Cell:
The array function MODE.MULT is housed in a function that can handle an array or a range of values, and it does not require Ctrl+Shift+Enter.
Conclusion:
If you need a formula that can report all the modes anytime the source data changes, this is a great option.
Using the COUNT, IF, and ROWS functions instead of the IFERROR function can reduce calculation time for formulas that point to large data sets.

Extracting Modes, One at a Time: IFERROR, ROWS, INDEX, and MODE.MULT

As an alternative to extracting the modes, you could use the formula shown in Figure 9.25. The IF-ERROR function was a new function introduced in Excel 2007. All you have to do is (1) place the data extraction formula element into the value argument and (2) place a null text string in the value_if_error argument. This function is not as complicated to create as the previous formula, but it has the drawback that all the cells that contain the formula will have to evaluate the data extraction formula element. For large data sets, this can significantly increase formula calculation time.

	A	B	C	D
1	Times (mins)		> 1 Mode	
2	24		=IFERROR(INDEX(MODE.MULT($A$2:$A$10),ROWS(C$2:C2)),"")	
3	19		23.7	IFERROR(**value**, value_if_error)
4	**23.7**		25.3	
5	25.3			

Figure 9.25 *For data extraction formulas, IFERROR may increase formula calculation time.*

Using IF Instead of IFERROR to Reduce Formula Calculation Time for Data Extraction Formulas

Looking back at Figure 9.23, notice that the data extraction formula element INDEX(MODE.MULT($A$2:$A$10),ROWS(C$4:C4)) sits in the value_if_false argument of the IF function and will not be evaluated—and thus not add to any formula calculation time—when the logical_test argument contains TRUE (that is, when the formula is past the row with the last mode). In stark contrast, with the alternative formula shown in Figure 9.25, because the IFERROR function depends on the contents of the value argument to deliver a valid item or an error, the IFERROR function must run the data extraction formula element in all cells. This significantly increases formula calculation time for large data sets (see the end of this chapter for timing results). This means that for large data sets, you should not be using IFERROR in this situation. In Chapter 15, you will see numerous data extraction formulas, and you will need to remember this important formula efficiency fact.

Efficient Use of the IFERROR Function

Given what this chapter has shown so far, are there efficient uses for the IFERROR function? Yes, there are. Although they are not directly related to the discussion, it is worth showing an example of when to use the IFERROR function rather than the IF function.

Figure 9.26 shows a VLOOKUP situation where you must run the VLOOKUP in order to determine whether an error occurs. The logical_test is always "is the lookup_value in the table?" Looking at Figure 9.26, you can see that before Excel 2007 (before IFERROR was available), you had to use the IF function and the ISERROR function and run the VLOOKUP twice. In Excel 2007 or later, IFERROR makes the formula less complicated to create and faster to calculate (because you run the VLOOKUP only one time in each cell). In this case, IFERROR is great, and it is being used efficiently. With the formula shown in Figure 9.25, the IFERROR function was not being used efficiently because you had an alternative logical test to determine when to show a null text string and when not to.

	A	B	C
1	We have to run only 1 VLOOKUP.		
2	Employee	Comm Rate	
3	Jo	0.015	< Formula =IFERROR(VLOOKUP(A3,$A$10:$B$12,2),"")
5	Before 2007, had to run 2 VLOOKUPs.		
6	Employee	Comm Rate	
7	dfsghfd	Not In Table	< Formula =IF(ISERROR(VLOOKUP(A7,$A$10:$B$12,2)), "Not In Table",VLOOKUP(A7,$A$10:$B$12,2))
9	Employee	Comm Rate	
10	Jo	0.015	
11	Phil	0.0175	
12	Sioux	0.019	

Figure 9.26 *IFERROR is great for VLOOKUP! The formula runs VLOOKUP only one time.*

Array Formula Efficiency Rule 20

Keep in mind the following general rules about IFERROR:

- If the formula element in the value argument of the IFERROR function must be run in every cell to determine whether there is an error, using the IFERROR function is efficient. This is an example of an efficient use of IFERROR: =IFERROR(VLOOKUP(A3,$A$10:$B$12,2),"").

- If the formula element in the value argument of the IFERROR function does *not* need to be run in every cell to determine whether there is an error, using the IFERROR function may *not* be efficient. If there is an alternative logical test, then it may be more efficient to use the IF function instead of the IFERROR function. This can be particularly true for large data-extracting array formulas. Here's an example of an inefficient IFERROR use: =IFERROR(INDEX(MODE.MULT($A$2:$A$10),ROWS(C$2:C2)),""). Here's an example of a more efficient alternative: =IF(ROWS(C$4:C4)>$C$2,"",INDEX(MODE.MULT($A$2:$A$10),ROWS(C$4:C4))).

Using PivotTable to find modes.

If you have a lot of data and you want a quick and easy method for "eyeing the mode," using a PivotTable is a great alternative. Figure 9.27 shows a finished PivotTable that allows you to look through the Count of Values PivotTable column and find the modes. You follow these steps to create this PivotTable:

1. Click a cell in the source data column.

2. On the Insert Ribbon tab, click the PivotTable button in the Tables group and then click OK.

3. Drag the Values field to Rows.

4. Drag the Values field to Values.

5. Change the function from Sum to Count (by right-clicking a value and then selecting Summarize Values By followed by Count).

	A	B	C	D
1	Value		Value	Count of Value
2	18		16	2
3	23		18	1
4	16		19	1
5	23		22	1
6	22		23	3
7	25		24	1
8	24		25	2
9	28		28	3
10	16		31	2
11	28		36	1
12	28		Grand Total	17
13	31			
14	23			
15	31			
16	25			
17	19			
18	36			

Figure 9.27 *Using a PivotTable is an easy way to "eyeball" the modes.*

Comparing Calculating Modes Solutions

The following table provides a summary of the advantages and disadvantages of the various solutions for calculating modes.

Calculating Modes		
Solution	**Advantages**	**Disadvantages**
MODE	• Works in any version of Excel.	• Cannot calculate multiple modes. • When there is more than one mode, it does not signal that there is more than one mode.
MODE.SNGL	• Matches the dot+suffix convention of other Excel 2010 statistical functions.	• Only works in Excel 2010 or later. • Cannot calculate multiple modes. • When there is more than one mode, it does not signal that there is more than one mode.
MODE.MULT	• Calculates multiple modes.	• Only works in Excel 2010 or later. • Shows #N/A error in cells highlighted past the last mode. • Repeats single mode if there is only one mode.
COUNT, IF, ROWS, INDEX, and MODE. MULT functions	• Can handle any number of modes and not show #N/A errors or repeated single modes. • Calculates more quickly than IFERROR.	• Only works in Excel 2010 or later.
IFERROR, ROWS, INDEX, and MODE. MULT functions	• Can handle any number of modes and not show #N/A errors or repeated single modes.	• Only works in Excel 2010 or later. • Must run the formula in the values argument of IFERROR in all cells and therefore will increase formula calculation time.
PivotTable	• Fast and easy.	• Does not update immediately when data changes. • You must manually look at the PivotTable data to find mode.

Using the TREND Array Function to Estimate Many *y* Values in Linear Model

In statistics it is common to use past data to calculate the slope and *y*-intercept in order to build a linear model to help predict the future. In math class you probably saw the linear equation model $y = f(x) = mx+b$. In Excel there are a number of different ways to calculate the slope (m = for 1 unit of change in *x*, how far does *y* move?) and the *y*-intercept (b = the point at which the estimated line crosses the *y* axis).

Figures 9.28 to 9.30 show three formula methods for estimating future student test scores, based on the number of hours they claimed they studied for a test. All four functions (SLOPE, INTERCEPT, FORECAST, and TREND) ask for the known *y* values and known *x* values (data from the past). If you are using the SLOPE and INTERCEPT functions, you build a separate $mx+b$ formula (as shown in Figure 9.28). If you are using the FORECAST or TREND functions instead of building a separate $mx+b$ formula, you simply add the *x* value used for the estimation into the function (as shown in Figures 9.29 and 9.30, respectively). If you are estimating many *y* values, you can use the

TREND array function, not the FORECAST function, because when you enter the TREND function (see the range E3:E13 in Figure 9.30) with Ctrl+Shift+Enter, the *m* and *b* values have to be calculated only once, and as a result, the formula calculates significantly faster when you're dealing with large data sets. (See the timing results at the end of this chapter.)

	A	B	C	D	E	F
1	Data From Past Class			Currect Class	Estimation based on past data	
2	X = hours studying for test	Y = score on test		x = hours studying for test	f(x) = Estimation of score they will get on test	
3	2	75		3	74.57329031	< =$E$12*D3+$E$13
4	15	91		10	80.76269083	< =$E$12*D4+$E$13
5	5	79		9	79.87849075	< =$E$12*D5+$E$13
6	1	70		17	86.95209135	< =$E$12*D6+$E$13
7	6	65		23	92.2572918	< =$E$12*D7+$E$13
8	9	98		2	73.68909023	< =$E$12*D8+$E$13
9	25	100		0	71.92069008	< =$E$12*D9+$E$13
10	41	100		8	78.99429068	< =$E$12*D10+$E$13
11	10	82				
12	6	79		SLOPE	0.884200074	< =SLOPE(B3:B13,A3:A13)
13	2	60		INTERCEPT	71.92069008	< =INTERCEPT(B3:B13,A3:A13)

Figure 9.28 *SLOPE and INTERCEPT functions calculate the* m *and* b *values, and then a separate formula calculates the estimate for test score.*

	A	B	C	D	E	F
1	Data From Past Class			Currect Class	Estimation based on past data	
2	X = hours studying for test	Y = score on test		x = hours studying for test	f(x) = Estimation of score they will get on test	
3	2	75		3	74.57329031	< =FORECAST(D3,$B$3:$B$13,$A$3:$A$13)
4	15	91		10	80.76269083	< =FORECAST(D4,$B$3:$B$13,$A$3:$A$13)
5	5	79		9	79.87849075	< =FORECAST(D5,$B$3:$B$13,$A$3:$A$13)
6	1	70		17	86.95209135	< =FORECAST(D6,$B$3:$B$13,$A$3:$A$13)
7	6	65		23	92.2572918	< =FORECAST(D7,$B$3:$B$13,$A$3:$A$13)
8	9	98		2	73.68909023	< =FORECAST(D8,$B$3:$B$13,$A$3:$A$13)
9	25	100		0	71.92069008	< =FORECAST(D9,$B$3:$B$13,$A$3:$A$13)
10	41	100		8	78.99429068	< =FORECAST(D10,$B$3:$B$13,$A$3:$A$13)
11	10	82				
12	6	79				
13	2	60				

Figure 9.29 *When you're calculating many estimates, the problem with the FORECAST function is that it must recalculate the* m *and* b *values in each cell.*

| *fx* | {=TREND(B3:B13,A3:A13,D3:D10)} |

	A	B	C	D	E	F
1	Data From Past Class			Currect Class	Estimation based on past data	
2	X = hours studying for test	Y = score on test		x = hours studying for test	f(x) = Estimation of score they will get on test	
3	2	75		3	74.57329031	< {=TREND(B3:B13,A3:A13,D3:D10)}
4	15	91		10	80.76269083	< {=TREND(B3:B13,A3:A13,D3:D10)}
5	5	79		9	79.87849075	< {=TREND(B3:B13,A3:A13,D3:D10)}
6	1	70		17	86.95209135	< {=TREND(B3:B13,A3:A13,D3:D10)}
7	6	65		23	92.2572918	< {=TREND(B3:B13,A3:A13,D3:D10)}
8	9	98		2	73.68909023	< {=TREND(B3:B13,A3:A13,D3:D10)}
9	25	100		0	71.92069008	< {=TREND(B3:B13,A3:A13,D3:D10)}
10	41	100		8	78.99429068	< {=TREND(B3:B13,A3:A13,D3:D10)}
11	10	82				
12	6	79				
13	2	60				

Figure 9.30 *When you're calculating many estimates, the advantage of the TREND function is that you enter it as an array function, and it has to calculate the* m *and* b *values only one time. TREND has a significantly faster formula calculation time than the FORECAST function does.*

Comparing SLOPE and INTERCEPT, FORECAST, and TREND

The following table provides a summary table of the advantages and disadvantages of SLOPE and INTERCEPT, FORECAST, and TREND.

Advantages and Disadvantages of SLOPE and INTERCEPT, FORECAST, and TREND		
Method	**Advantages**	**Disadvantages**
SLOPE and INTERCEPT	• Fastest calculating.	• Have to calculate slope and intercept in a separate cell.
FORECAST	• Calculates an estimate without extra cells. • Does not require Ctrl+Shift+Enter.	• Must recalculate the slope and intercept in each cell and, as a result, has a significantly slower calculation time than TREND.
TREND	• Calculates an estimate without extra cells. • Significantly faster in calculation time than the FORECAST function.	• Must be entered as an array function, using Ctrl+Shift+Enter (which is not much of a disadvantage, considering the timing advantage).

Timing the Formulas in This Chapter

As discussed in Chapter 2, pointing array formulas to large data sets can increase formula calculation time for a workbook. In general, faster calculation times are more efficient. This section shows the anecdotal results I got. To time your own formulas, look back to Chapter 2 for details. (Timing depends on many factors, and your particular situation may have different timing results.) To see the workbook with the timing results I got, open the files named 07MODE.MULT.xlsm and 08TREND.xlsm in the folder Timing in the zipped folder FilesForCtrlShiftEnterBook. The Introduction to this book explains how to get these files. Figure 9.31 shows the timing results for the IF and IFERROR formulas. Figure 9.32 shows the timing results for the SLOPE, INTERCEPT, FORECAST and TREND functions.

10,000 rows of data. Time in seconds.		
	COUNT, IF, ROWS, INDEX and MODE.MULT functions	IFERROR, ROWS, INDEX and MODE.MULT functions
	[1] =IF(ROWS(D$13:D13)>$D$11,"", INDEX(MODE.MULT($A$3:$A$10002), ROWS(D$13:D13)))	[2] =IFERROR(INDEX(MODE. MULT($A$3:$A$10002), ROWS(E$13:E13)),"")
Time 1	2.213	7.683
Time 2	2.2195	7.73
Time 3	2.219	7.718
Ave	2.217166667	7.710333333
% change	0.0%	247.8%

Figure 9.31 *For the formula to extract modes, the IFERROR formula solutions took significantly longer to calculate.*

125 rows of x and y values from past data. 5000 rows of "New x" values. Time in seconds.			
	[1] =TREND(B4:B127,A4:A127, C4:C5002)	[2] =C4*$D$2+$E$2 SLOPE in D2 INTERCEPT in E2	[3] =FORECAST(C4,$B$4:$B$127, $A$4:$A$127)
Time 1	0.00459	0.00896	0.04599
Time 2	0.0046	0.00887	0.04583
Time 3	0.00458	0.00927	0.05115
Ave	0.00459	0.009033333	0.047656667
% Change	0.0%	96.8%	938.3%

Figure 9.32 *For the formula to estimate many y values based on the linear equation* y = mx+b *and a goal of estimating 5,000 y values, the Ctrl+Shift+Enter array function TREND is fastest in calculating.*

Chapter Summary

In this chapter you learned about array functions, null text strings, and the efficient use of the IF and IFERROR functions for dealing with error values. In Chapter 10 you will learn about the many amazing uses for the SUMPRODUCT function.

Chapter 10: The Amazing SUMPRODUCT Function (and SUMIFS, Too)

Excel Files

To follow along with the examples in this chapter, you can download the accompanying files, as explained in the Introduction.

SUMPRODUCT and the SUMIF, SUMIFS, COUNTIF, and COUNTIFS Functions

Since the SUMIFS function was introduced in Excel 2007, it is hard to talk about the SUMPRODUCT function without also talking about the SUMIF, SUMIFS, COUNTIF, and COUNTIFS functions. This chapter discusses when it is efficient to use the SUMPRODUCT function and when it is better to not use the SUMPRODUCT function and instead use a function like SUMIFS.

The Amazing and Versatile SUMPRODUCT Function

The SUMPRODUCT function has so many amazing applications in Excel that it is the focus of this chapter. This should not be surprising because you have already seen seven great uses of SUMPRODUCT in this book. SUMPRODUCT is useful because it performs two major types of array operations without requiring the use of Ctrl+Shift+Enter to enter the formulas:

- It can multiply two or more arrays and add the result.
- It can take a single array operation and add the resultant array (you have already seen several examples of this).

And, of course, SUMPRODUCT can combine these two types of array operations to allow you to make array operations and then multiply and then add two or more arrays. As has been mentioned a number of times already in the book (refer to Array Formula Efficiency Rule 7), if you have a choice between two equally efficient formulas and one requires Ctrl+Shift+Enter and one does not, choose the one that does not. Because of this, for adding the results from an array calculation, SUMPRODUCT is often preferred over SUM.

In this chapter you will first take another look at some examples covered earlier, and then you'll look at how the function works, and finally you will look at a number of SUMPRODUCT function examples.

Here are the examples you have already seen for SUMPRODUCT in this book:

- In Figure 2.14 you saw the array1 argument in SUMPRODUCT add the differences between two columns: **=SUMPRODUCT(D3:D6-C3:C6)**
- In Figure 3.4 you saw the array1 argument in SUMPRODUCT add the product of a column and a discount rate: **=SUMPRODUCT(B2:B5*(1-B7))**
- In Figure 6.6 you saw the array1 argument in SUMPRODUCT add the resultant array produced by the LEN function for adding up the total number of characters from a column: **=SUMPRODUCT(LEN(A2:A6))**
- In Figure 6.12 you saw the array1 argument in SUMPRODUCT add the resultant array produced by the SUMIF function for a "lookup adding" situation when the data was not sorted: **=SUMPRODUCT(SUMIF(F4:F6,B3:B7,G4:G6))**
- In Figure 6.13 you saw the array1 argument in SUMPRODUCT add the resultant array produced by the LOOKUP function for a lookup addition situation when the data was sorted: **=SUMPRODUCT(LOOKUP(B3:B7,F4:G6))**
- In Figure 7.23 you saw the array1 argument in SUMPRODUCT add the resultant array produced by the LARGE, ROW, and INDIRECT functions for adding the *n* largest val-

ues, where the *n* value was a variable in cell D3:
=SUMPRODUCT(LARGE(B2:B8,ROW(INDIRECT("1:"&D3))))

- In Figure 7.40 you saw the array1 argument in SUMPRODUCT add the resultant array produced by VLOOKUP function and an array constant for a lookup and addition of multiple columns for a single lookup value:
=SUMPRODUCT(VLOOKUP(A7,A2:H4,{2,4,5,7,8}))

That is a huge list of array formulas that use the SUMPRODUCT function! The fact that you have seen this many uses for the SUMPRODUCT function *before* even getting to the chapter specifically about SUMPRODUCT is evidence of just how useful this function is!

Parameters for Using the SUMPRODUCT Function

Here are some important notes and the parameters for how to use the SUMPRODUCT function:

1. SUMPRODUCT takes two or more arrays that are the same dimensions and first multiplies the arrays and then adds the results.

2. You can have 1 to 255 array arguments. The arguments are named array1, array2, and so on. The arrays must be the same dimensions (for example, 1×3 and 1×3, 4×1 and 4×1, 2×4 and 2×4, and so on).

3. SUMPRODUCT treats non-numeric data as zeros.

4. The array arguments can handle array operations and the resultant array produced by the array operation without requiring the use of Ctrl+Shift+Enter.

5. When arrays are not the same dimensions and you need to multiply them, you can use the multiplication operator and place multiplied arrays in a single array argument. If you multiply the arrays directly with the multiplication operator, and there are text values in the cells, the #VALUE error generated by multiplying numbers and text will override SUMPRODUCT's ability to treat non-numeric data as zeros. One method for dealing with this is to use the MMULT function, as demonstrated in Chapter 18.

6. You can house a single array operation in the array1 argument when you need to add the result of an array operation. With this use, you are only using the SUM part of SUM-PRODUCT.

7. SUMPRODUCT can be used for multiple-criteria addition and counting in Excel 2003 or earlier.

8. Because SUMPRODUCT treats non-numeric data as zeros, if you have TRUE and FALSE values that you would like to use in an array calculation, you must convert them to ones and zeros. Any math operation will convert them, but using the double negative is generally the fastest-calculating method. (Timing examples are given later in this chapter.)

9. If you have Excel 2007 or later and you are counting or adding with multiple criteria, consider whether you can use SUMIFS or COUNTIFS because they have faster formula calculation times.

10. SUMPRODUCT can be used to deal with workbook references as a substitute for SUM-IF, COUNTIF, SUMIFS, and COUNTIFS (see the examples later in this chapter).

11. SUMPRODUCT can be used to deal with array calculations that the range arguments of SUMIF, COUNTIF, SUMIFS, and COUNTIFS cannot deal with (see the examples later in this chapter).

Now let's look at a bunch of examples for SUMPRODUCT.

Multiplying Two or More Arrays with the Same Dimensions and Then Adding

The base use for SUMPRODUCT is to enter ranges of cells with the same dimensions into the SUMPRODUCT function, separated by commas. SUMPRODUCT multiplies the corresponding ranges and then adds the results.

Figure 10.1 shows a row of monetary units and a row of quantities. The goal of the formula is to calculate the total bank deposit. In longhand, you would have to create a formula that multiplies each unit and quantity and then add then all up, like this:

$100 * 22+$50 * 0+$20 * 50+$10 * 22+$5 * 25+$1 * 38+$0.50 * 0+$0.25 * 40+$0.10 * 50+$0.05 * 0+$0.01 * 50 = $3,598.50

Luckily, the SUMPRODUCT function can simplify this formula to =SUMPRODUCT(B1:L1,B2:L2). Figure 10.1 shows the formula for total bank deposit.

	A	B	C	D	E	F	G	H	I	J	K	L
1	Monetary Unit	$100	$50	$20	$10	$5	$1	$0.50	$0.25	$0.10	$0.05	$0.01
2	Quantity	22		50	22	25	38		40	50		50
3												
4	Total Bank Deposit	$3,598.50	< Formula =SUMPRODUCT(B1:L1,B2:L2)									

Figure 10.1 *Multiplying two ranges with the same dimensions and then adding.*

Figure 10.2 shows an advantage of SUMPRODUCT over SUM with a direct multiplication math operator. SUMPRODUCT does not require Ctrl+Shift+Enter, and it treats zeros, empty cells, and text entries as zero values. The SUM function array formula creates a #VALUE! error because numbers and text items cannot be directly multiplied.

	A	B	C	D	E	F	G	H	I	J	K	L
1	Monetary Unit	$100	$50	$20	$10	$5	$1	$0.50	$0.25	$0.10	$0.05	$0.01
2	Quantity	22	0	50	22	25	38		40	50	None	50
3												
4	Total Bank Deposit	$3,598.50	< Formula =SUMPRODUCT(B1:L1,B2:L2)									
5	Total Bank Deposit	#VALUE!	< Formula {=SUM(B1:L1*B2:L2)}									

Figure 10.2 *SUMPRODUCT does not require Ctrl+Shift+Enter and treats non-numeric data as zeros.*

Figures 10.3 through 10.5 show three more examples of how to multiply and then add arrays with the same dimensions.

	A	B	C	D	E	F	G
1	Weight	15%	20%	20%	45%		
2							
3	Student	Test 1	Test 2	Test 3	Test 4	Class Total	
4	Tom	60	78	90	91	83.55	< Formula =SUMPRODUCT(B4:E4,$B$1:$E$1)
5	Chin	79	34	85	89	75.7	< Formula =SUMPRODUCT(B5:E5,$B$1:$E$1)
6	Shelia	92	91	89	78	84.9	< Formula =SUMPRODUCT(B6:E6,$B$1:$E$1)

Figure 10.3 *Using SUMPRODUCT to calculate weighted grades.*

	A	B	C
1	From past accounting records:		
2	Units Purchased	Probability	
3	700	0.1	
4	800	0.2	
5	900	0.3	
6	1000	0.25	
7	1100	0.15	
8	Budgeted Monthly Order Quantity	915	< Formula =SUMPRODUCT(A3:A7,B3:B7)

Figure 10.4 *Using SUMPRODUCT to calculate weighted averages for budgets.*

	A	B	C	D	E
1	Gas	Moles	Temperature (Kelvin)	Inverse of Volume (1/Liter)	R = (L*Atmosphere)/ (Moles*Kelvin)
2	Neon	4.73	273	0.040	0.08206
3	Argon	10.21	298	0.067	0.08206
4	Nitrogen	11.64	286	0.100	0.08206
5					
6	Total Pressure	48.20	< Formula =SUMPRODUCT(B2:B4,C2:C4,D2:D4,E2:E4)		

Figure 10.5 *SUMPRODUCT can multiply up to 255 ranges. Here, four columns are multiplied and then added to get total pressure.*

One caveat for SUMPRODUCT is that if you have a formula like =SUMPRODUCT(A10,B10), where both cells are empty, the function will yield an error. If the two cells have numbers or zeros, there will be no error.

Multiplying Three Ranges with Different Dimensions and Then Adding

Figure 10.6 shows a finance example for SUMPRODUCT. In this case, you are estimating the expected return for a portfolio of stocks, based on the probability of economic states (B3:B5), weight for each stock (C1:D1), and estimated individual stock returns (C3:D5). You don't have to worry so much about the finance part, but rather look at the single-cell formula goal: You need to multiply and then add the ranges B3:B5 and C1:D1 and C3:D5. If you did this longhand, it would be difficult:

0.15 * 0.6 * 0+0.7 * 0.6 * 0.06+0.15 * 0.6 * 0.1+0.15 * 0.4 * -0.15+0.7 * 0.4 * 0.05+0.15 * 0.4 * 0.2 = 0.0512

You can get around the requirement that the ranges must all have the same dimensions by directly multiplying the ranges, as shown in Figure 10.6. By multiplying the ranges directly, you create an array operation. Figures 10.5 shows the calculation process that the direct array multiplication operation uses to create the numbers that SUMPRODUCT can then add. Because the array1 argument of SUMPRODUCT can handle arrays, the formula works without using Ctrl+Shift+Enter. The caveat for this sort of calculation is that, unlike SUMPRODUCT, which treats text as a zero, the multiplication operator is incapable of dealing with text and will cause a #VALUE! error. Chapter 18 shows a workaround for this problem.

	A	B	C	D	E
1		**Weight**	0.6	0.4	
2	**Probability of Economic State**		**Stock A Estimated Return**	**Stock B Estimated Return**	
3	Bad	0.15	0	-0.15	
4	OK	0.7	0.06	0.05	
5	Great	0.15	0.1	0.2	
6		E(R)=Expected Return		0.0512	< Formula =SUMPRODUCT(B3:B5*C1:D1*C3:D5)

Figure 10.6 *Multiplication helps you to deal with different-sized arrays.*

B3:B5*C1:D1*C3:D5	➜	B3*C3*C1	B3*D3*D1	➜	0.15*0*0.6	0.15*-0.15*0.4	➜	0	-0.009
		B4*C4*C1	B4*D4*D1		0.7*0.06*0.6	0.7*0.05*0.4		0.0252	0.014
		B5*C5*C1	B5*D5*D1		0.15*0.1*0.6	0.15*0.2*0.4		0.009	0.012

Figure 10.7 *The calculation process that the different-sized arrays go through.*

Adding an Array Operation's Resultant Array: Just the SUM Part

You have already seen a number of examples of how the array argument in the SUMPRODUCT function can handle array operations, without requiring the use of Ctrl+Shift+Enter. Figure 10.8 shows how you can make an array calculation inside the ROUND function and then add the resultant array with SUMPRODUCT to calculate total sales, rounded to the penny. Using SUMPRODUCT rather than SUM is easier.

	A	B	C	D
1	Calculate Rounded Total			
2	**Units**	**Price**		
3	100	0.225		
4	150	0.1275		
5	110	0.09		
6	60	0.0875		
7	270	0.655		
9	**Total Sales**			
10	233.63	< Formula =SUMPRODUCT(ROUND(A3:A7*B3:B7,2))		
11	233.63	< Formula {=SUM(ROUND(A3:A7*B3:B7,2))}		

Figure 10.8 *Multiplying units and price columns and rounding to the penny.*

When to Use SUMPRODUCT to Count or Add with Multiple Criteria

I am writing this book in the year 2013. Since Excel 2007, Excel has offered the COUNTIFS and SUMIFS functions, which can count and add with multiple criteria. In addition, for many years, Excel has also had DCOUNT and DSUM, which can also make multiple-condition calculations. Using COUNTIFS, SUMIFS, DCOUNT, and DSUM can be more efficient than using SUM-

PRODUCT. So why do you need to look at how to use SUMPRODUCT to count or add with multiple criteria? These are some of the reasons:

1. Many people still use versions of Excel from 2003 or earlier and do not have the COUNTIFS and SUMIFS functions.

2. In versions of Excel from 2003 or earlier, it is not always possible to use D-functions because they require a proper data set and are difficult formulas to copy to other cells.

3. Using Excel 2007 or later, you may encounter a spreadsheet with SUMPRODUCT formulas that were created before Excel 2007 was released.

4. SUMPRODUCT can make some multiple-condition calculations that COUNTIFS and SUMIFS cannot make.

Before looking at a SUMPRODUCT solution for multiple criteria counting and adding, let's look at two important alternative formula solutions to help put the SUMPRODUCT solution in the correct context. This discussion assumes that you want a formula solution and not a PivotTable solution.

Figures 10.9 through 10.12 consider a data set with the field names Employee, Project, and Time. The goal of the formula is to count and add the times that the employee Kip spent on Project 2. (This is AND criteria because both conditions must be met for you to include an item in the count or summation.)

As shown in Figure 10.9, the first set of formulas uses COUNTIFS and SUMIFS. The reason it is important to start off with these is because many Excel users who have Excel 2007 or later are still using SUMPRODUCT solutions (and D-functions, too) rather than the more efficient COUNTIFS and SUMIFS solutions.

If you have Excel 2007 or later, COUNTIFS and SUMIFS offer these major advantages:

1. They have a significantly faster formula calculation time than SUMPRODUCT or the equivalent D-functions. For large data sets, they can dramatically reduce calculation time. (You'll learn more about calculation time later in this chapter.)

2. They do not require field names in the data set or in the criteria area, as the D-functions do.

3. They can be easily copied to other cells (using the correct cell references), unlike D-functions. (For more about copying problems, see chapter 4 and chapter 21.)

	A	B	C	D	E	F	G
1	Employee	Project	Time		Criteria:		
2	Kip	Project 2	15.7		Kip	Project 2	
3	Marc	Project 1	19.4				
4	Jo	Project 2	11.9		Count Time		
5	Kip	Project 2	15.2			2	< Formula =COUNTIFS(A2:A7,E2,B2:B7,F2)
6	Jo	Project 2	22.5		Add Time		
7	Kip	Project 1	28.1			30.9	< Formula =SUMIFS(C2:C7,A2:A7,E2,B2:B7,F2)

Figure 10.9 *Excel 2007 or later: COUNTIFS and SUMIFS.*

Figure 10.10 shows examples of the DCOUNT and DSUM functions. If you are using Excel 2003 or earlier and you have a proper data set with field names in the data set and in the criteria area, and you do not need to copy the formula to other cells, using D-functions is efficient because the formula calculation time is significantly faster than with a SUMPRODUCT solution. In addition, the D-function formulas are less complicated to create than the SUMPRODUCT equivalent, especially if you have many conditions.

> **Note:** You can copy D-functions to other cells if you use them in combination with a data table. See Chapter 4 for details.

	A	B	C	D	E	F	G
1	Employee	Project	Time		Employee	Project	
2	Kip	Project 2	15.7		Kip	Project 2	
3	Marc	Project 1	19.4				
4	Jo	Project 2	11.9		Count Time		
5	Kip	Project 2	15.2			2	< Formula =DCOUNT(A1:C7,"Time",E1:F2)
6	Jo	Project 2	22.5		Add Time		
7	Kip	Project 1	28.1			30.9	< Formula =DSUM(A1:C7,"Time",E1:F2)

Figure 10.10 *Excel 2003 and before: DCOUNT and DSUM.*

Figure 10.11 shows examples of counting and adding using the SUMPRODUCT function. If you are using Excel 2003 or earlier and you do not have field names in the data set or in the criteria area, SUMPRODUCT can make the calculation, but the D-functions cannot. (You will learn the details of how to create this SUMPRODUCT solution and why you use the double negatives in just a bit.)

	A	B	C	D	E	F	G
1					Criteria:		
2	Kip	Project 2	15.7		Kip	Project 2	
3	Marc	Project 1	19.4				
4	Jo	Project 2	11.9		Count Time		
5	Kip	Project 2	15.2			2	< Formula =SUMPRODUCT(--(A2:A7=E2),--(B2:B7=F2))
6	Jo	Project 2	22.5		Add Time		
7	Kip	Project 1	28.1			30.9	< Formula =SUMPRODUCT(--(A2:A7=E2),--(B2:B7=F2),C2:C7)

Figure 10.11 *Excel 2003 and before: SUMPRODUCT.*

When running Excel 2003 or earlier, Figure 10.12 shows another advantage that SUMPRODUCT has over the D-functions: You can copy the formulas. In this example, you are adding with two criteria and creating a cross-tabulated table, based on employee name and project. You created a single formula in cell F3 and copied it through the range F3:G5. Take a closer look at the formula in cell F3. Why in the world are there double negatives? The following section answers this question.

| F3 | ▼ | : | × ✓ *fx* | =SUMPRODUCT(--($A$2:$A$8=$E3),--($B$2:$B$8=F$2),$C$2:$C$8) |

	A	B	C	D	E	F	G	H
1	Employee	Project	Time		Total Times			
2	Kip	Project 2	15.7		Employee/Project	Project 1	Project 2	
3	Marc	Project 1	19.4		Kip	28.1	30.9	
4	Jo	Project 2	11.9		Marc	19.4	0	
5	Kip	Project 2	15.2		Jo	0	34.4	
6	Jo	Project 2	22.5					
7	Kip	Project 1	28.1					

Figure 10.12 *Excel 2003 and before: using SUMPRODUCT rather than DSUM to allow copying.*

Converting TRUEs and FALSEs to Ones and Zeros, Usually with Double Negatives

In order to understand why you are using double negatives in the SUMPRODUCT multiple-condition calculations, you need to consider two issues:

1. SUMPRODUCT cannot "see" TRUEs and FALSEs. Remember: SUMPRODUCT treats non-numeric data as zeros.

2. Any math operation converts TRUEs and FALSEs to ones and zeros.

Let's look at a simple example of counting how many "Kip" entries there are in a column. As shown in Figure 10.13, you can create a comparative array operation in the array1 argument of SUMPRODUCT. If you evaluate the comparative array operation (by highlighting it and pressing F9), you can see that you get a resultant array filled with TRUEs and FALSEs, as shown in Figure 10.14. (Be sure to undo the evaluation by pressing Ctrl+Z before moving on.)

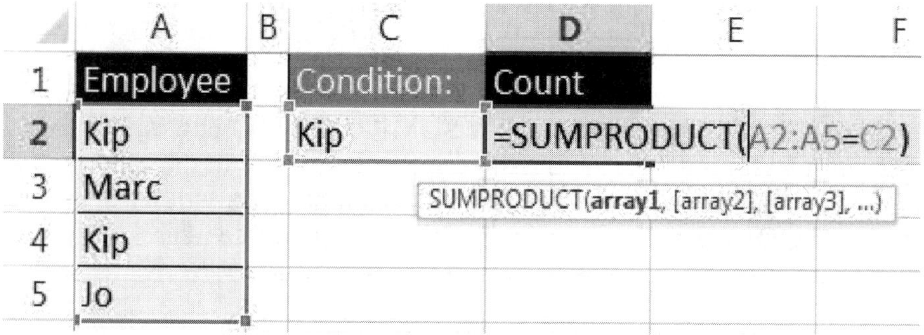

Figure 10.13 *Array operation which asks: "Are any equal to "Kip"?*

Figure 10.14 *Resultant array filled with TRUEs and FALSEs. SUMPRODUCT cannot "see" the logical values.*

As shown in Figure 10.15, if you enter the formula, you get a count of zero because SUMPRODUCT treats the logical values as zeros. However, if you could convert the TRUEs and FALSEs to ones and zeros, SUMPRODUCT could "see" the numbers and then add them.

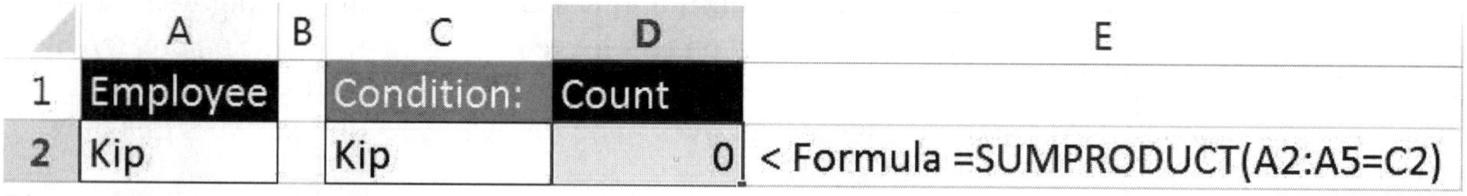

Figure 10.15 *SUMPRODUCT treats non-numeric data as zeros and therefore the TRUE values are not counted. As a result you get a count of zero.*

Converting TRUEs and FALSEs to ones and zeros can be accomplished by performing any math operation on the logical values. Figure 10.16 shows various ways you can accomplish this. TRUE gets converted to a one, and FALSE gets converted to a zero.

	A	B	C	D	E	F	G
1	Operation	TRUE	Convert	Formula	FALSE	Convert	Formula
2	--	TRUE	1	< Formula =--B2	FALSE	0	< Formula =--E2
3	+0	TRUE	1	< Formula =B3+0	FALSE	0	< Formula =E3+0
4	*1	TRUE	1	< Formula =B4*1	FALSE	0	< Formula =E4*1
5	/1	TRUE	1	< Formula =B5/1	FALSE	0	< Formula =E5/1
6	^1	TRUE	1	< Formula =B6^1	FALSE	0	< Formula =E6^1

Figure 10.16 *Any math operation will convert TRUE to 1 and FALSE to 0.*

Figure 10.17 shows how you can use the different math operations (or the N function) in the SUM-PRODUCT array formula to count how many Kips are in column A.

	A	B	C	D	E
1	Employee		Condition:	Count	
2	Kip		Kip	2	< Formula [1]=SUMPRODUCT(--(A2:A5=C2))
3	Marc			2	< Formula [2]=SUMPRODUCT((A2:A5=C2)+0)
4	Kip			2	< Formula [3]=SUMPRODUCT((A2:A5=C2)/1)
5	Jo			2	< Formula [4]=SUMPRODUCT((A2:A5=C2)*1)
6				2	< Formula [5]=SUMPRODUCT((A2:A5=C2)^1)
7				2	< Formula [6]=SUMPRODUCT(N(A2:A5=C2))

Figure 10.17 *Six different methods to convert the TRUEs and FALSEs to ones and zeros so that the SUM-PRODUCT function can get a count of two.*

But how does SUMPRODUCT do the conversion? Figure 10.18 shows Excel's calculation process for Formula [1], the formula that uses the double negative to convert the TRUEs and FALSEs to ones and zeros.

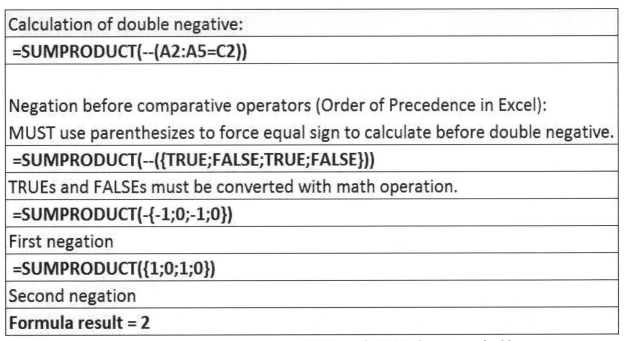

Calculation of double negative:
=SUMPRODUCT(--(A2:A5=C2))
Negation before comparative operators (Order of Precedence in Excel):
MUST use parenthesizes to force equal sign to calculate before double negative.
=SUMPRODUCT(--({TRUE;FALSE;TRUE;FALSE}))
TRUEs and FALSEs must be converted with math operation.
=SUMPRODUCT(-{-1;0;-1;0})
First negation
=SUMPRODUCT({1;0;1;0})
Second negation
Formula result = 2

Figure 10.18 *Getting SUMPRODUCT to interpret TRUEs and FALSEs by using a double negative.*

Timing the Conversion of TRUEs and FALSEs to Ones and Zeros

When you need to convert TRUEs and FALSEs to ones and zeros, which operator should you use? Most of the time, any of them are okay. And, in fact, by the end of this book, you will see good uses for all the math operators. One way you can decide which operator to use for the SUMPRODUCT is to time the formula and see which calculates most quickly. Numerous timing tests have been done throughout Excel history. Excel masters Aladin Akyurek and Charles Williams have written online about the use of double negatives at the following links:

- http://www.mrexcel.com/forum/excel-questions/339081-how-can-i-sum-values-one-column-based-criteria-two-corisponding-columns.html#post1671486
- http://www.mrexcel.com/forum/excel-questions/70547-count-function.html
- http://msdn.microsoft.com/en-you/library/aa730921.aspx

I have done numerous tests over the years and have found that using a double negative usually is a bit faster than using the other methods. Figure 10.19 shows the latest anecdotal test results I got for 100,000 rows of data, when I timed each formula nine times and then took an average. (You can see these results in the workbook 09ConvertingTRUEandFALSE.xlsm, which is in the Timing folder in the zipped files that accompany the book. See Chapter 2 for details about how to time your own formulas.)

	A	B	C	D	E	F
1	Name		Name			
2	Marc		Kip			
3	Kip					
4	Jo		100,000 rows of data. Times in seconds.			
5	Kip		Count	Formula	Average Time	% Change From [1]
6	Marc		11214	< Formula [1]=SUMPRODUCT(--(A2:A100001=N2))	0.0234989	0.00%
7	Kip		11214	< Formula [4]=SUMPRODUCT((A2:A100001=N2)*1)	0.0260167	10.71%
8	Marc		11214	< Formula [3]=SUMPRODUCT((A2:A100001=N2)/1)	0.0261256	11.18%
9	Jo		11214	< Formula [2]=SUMPRODUCT((A2:A100001=N2)+0)	0.0274333	16.74%
10	Marc		11214	< Formula [6]=SUMPRODUCT(N(A2:A100001=N2))	0.0299078	27.27%
11	Marc		11214	< Formula [5]=SUMPRODUCT((A2:A100001=N2)^1)	0.0327833	39.51%

Figure 10.19 *Timing results for different methods of converting TRUEs and FALSEs to ones and zeros. Double Negative tends to be fastest.*

The fact that the double negative usually has a faster calculating time and the fact that the unary negation operator occurs near the top of the Excel's order of formula precedence are the main reasons it is common to see double negatives used to convert TRUEs and FALSEs to ones and zeros.

Array Formula Efficiency Rule 21

Using a double negative is an efficient way to convert TRUEs and FALSEs to ones and zeros when you're using SUMPRODUCT. The fact that the double negative usually has a faster calculating time and the fact that the unary negation operator occurs near the top of the Excel's order of formula precedence are the main reasons it is common to see it used to convert TRUEs and FALSEs to ones and zeros.

Now that you have seen that the double negative is an efficient means to convert TRUEs and FALSEs to ones and zeros when using SUMPRODUCT, let's go back to the formula for adding with two criteria (refer to Figure 10.11) and step through how the formula calculates.

Notes About the Formula =SUMPRODUCT(--(A2:A7=E2),--(B2:B7=F2),C2:C7)

The following table presents a summary of the formula for adding with two criteria from Figure 10.11.

Calculation Summary:
1. =SUMPRODUCT(--(A2:A7=E2),--(B2:B7=F2),C2:C7)
Array calculations 1 and 2: --(A2:A7=E2) delivers the resultant array {1;0;0;1;0;1} to the array1 argument in SUMPRODUCT.
2. =SUMPRODUCT({1;0;0;1;0;1},--(B2:B7=F2),C2:C7)
Array calculations 3 and 4: --(B2:B7=F2) delivers the resultant array {1;0;1;1;1;0} to the array2 argument in SUMPRODUCT.
3. =SUMPRODUCT({1;0;0;1;0;1},{1;0;1;1;1;0},C2:C7)
Array calculation 5: {1;0;0;1;0;1}*{1;0;1;1;1;0} delivers the resultant array {1;0;0;1;0;0} to the SUMPRODUCT.
4. =SUMPRODUCT({1;0;0;1;0;0},{15.7;19.4;11.9;15.2;22.5;28.1})
Array calculation 6: {1;0;0;1;0;0}*{15.7;19.4;11.9;15.2;22.5;28.1} delivers the resultant array {15.7;0;0;15.2;0;0} to the SUMPRODUCT.
5. The formula delivers the single item 30.9.

And Criteria (Boolean Multiplication) and SUMPRODUCT

Conditional calculations using the AGGREGATE function (refer to Chapter 4) and all the conditional calculations that you have made so far in this chapter all use AND criteria: All conditions must be met in order to include the item in the count or summation. If you have the formula =SUMPRODUCT(--(A2:A7=E2),--(B2:B7=F2),C2:C7), it is only when you get a TRUE in the first array and a TRUE in the second array that you are allowed to use the corresponding number in the third array for the summation. When the SUMPRODUCT multiplies the first two arrays filled with ones and zeros by the third array that is filled with numbers, it is called **Boolean multiplication**. In Chapter 11 you will learn more about Boolean math.

Adding with Three Criteria: SUMIFS Instead of DSUM or SUMPRODUCT

This section and the next section look at the speed advantage that SUMIFS has over the SUMPRODUCT function when you're making multiple-condition calculations. Figure 10.20 shows a data set with three fields. This data set has 50,000 rows of data. (Because the data set is so big, it is in a separate Excel file from the file with most of the figures in this book. The file name is 10-ThreeCriteria.xlsm, and it can be found in the Timing folder in the zipped files that accompany the book.) The goal of the formulas in Figure 10.21 is to add with three criteria. The next section looks at the timing results for each of these formulas.

	A	B	C	D
1	Date	Rep	Calls	
2	3/10/13	Sioux	18.2	
3	6/17/14	Chin	19.0	
4	12/1/13	Fin	47.0	
5	10/13/13	Fin	17.9	
6	1/29/14	Sioux	40.5	
7	3/3/13	Fin	26.0	
8	7/16/14	Chin	12.1	

Figure 10.20 *Data set with 50,000 rows of data.*

	E	F	G	H	I	J	K	L	M	N
1		**D Function criteria:**								
2		Date	Date	Rep						
3		>=10/7/2013	<=10/13/2013	Sioux						
4										
5		Date	Date	Rep						
6		10/7/2013	10/13/2013	Sioux						
7										
8	SUM	Formula								
9	3907	Formula [1]: =SUMIFS(C2:C50001,A2:A50001,">="&F6,A2:A50001,"<="&G6,B2:B50001,H6)								
10	3907	Formula [2]: =DSUM(A1:C50001,"Calls",F2:H3)								
11	3907	Formula [3]: =SUMPRODUCT(--(A2:A50001>=F6),--(A2:A50001<=G6),--(B2:B50001=H6),C2:C50001)								

Figure 10.21 *Formulas for adding with three criteria.*

Timing the SUMIFS, DSUM, and SUMPRODUCT Functions

Figure 10.22 shows the anecdotal timing results I got for these formulas running over 50,000 rows of data. The SUMIFS formula is significantly faster-calculating than the SUMPRODUCT formula. In addition, the SUMIFS formula is easier to copy to other cells than the DSUM formula. For these reasons, it is often more efficient to use the SUMIFS function for adding with multiple criteria if you have Excel 2007 or later. (Similar results are found if you compare COUNTIFS and AVER-AGEIFS to the corresponding D-functions or SUMPRODUCT formulas. See Chapter 2 for details about how to time your own formulas.)

Formula	Time 1	Time 2	Time 3	Ave	% Change
[1] SUMIFS	0.01897	0.01835	0.0187	0.01867	0.00%
[2] DSUM	0.02027	0.01751	0.02112	0.01963	5.14%
[3] SUMPRODUCT	0.02996	0.03773	0.02975	0.03248	73.94%

Figure 10.22 *Timing results for the formulas from Figure 10.21. SUMIFS is fast.*

Comparative Operator Syntax Differences for SUMIFS, DSUM, and SUMPRODUCT

The functions SUMIFS, DSUM, and SUMPRODUCT have different requirements when using comparative operators. Figures 10.23 to 10.26 highlight the differences between them. (These examples are in the file with most of the figures in this book, in the file named CtrlShiftEnterBookFinishedFile.xlsm.)

	A	B	C	D
1	Date	Date	Rep	
2	>=10/7/2013	<=10/13/2013	Sioux	
3				
4	SUM	Formula		
5	58.70	< Formula =SUMIFS(C8:C19,A8:A19,A2,A8:A19,B2,B8:B19,C2)		
6				
7	Date	Rep	Calls	
8	10/13/13	Sioux	18.2	
9	10/15/13	Chin	19.0	

Figure 10.23 *SUMIFS will accept criteria from a cell that contains both the comparative operator and the hurdle value. In this example, you have a "between two dates" criteria, where A2 contains the criteria "greater than or equal to the lower date" and B2 contains the criteria "less than or equal to the upper date".*

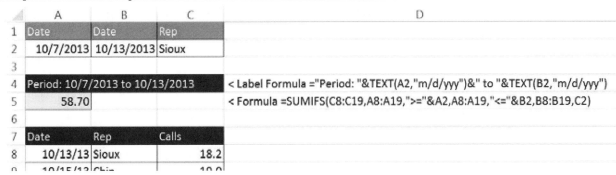

Figure 10.24 *SUMIFS will accept criteria that are joined together in the formula, where the hurdle value is from a cell and the comparative operators (in a pair of double quotes) is directly in the formula. This is a useful technique if the cell formula input (the hurdle value) is also being used by other formulas.*

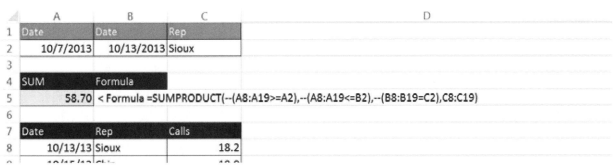

Figure 10.25 *DSUM requires that the comparative operator be placed in the cell. DSUM does not have the same flexibility as SUMIFS.*

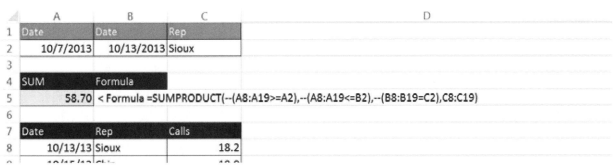

Figure 10.26 *SUMPRODUCT requires that the comparative operator be placed directly between the array and criteria to create an array operation. The direct array operation is part of the reason that SUMPRODUCT takes longer to calculate than SUMIFS.*

The following table lists the key differences in how comparative operators are used in SUMIFS, DSUM, and SUMPRODUCT. (Guidelines for SUMIFS are the same as for SUMIF, COUNTIF, COUNTIFS, AVERAGEIF, and AVERAGEIFS. Guidelines for DSUM are same as for other D-functions.)

Key Differences in Comparative Operators in SUMIFS, DSUM, and SUMPRODUCT:		
SUMIFS, SUMIF, COUNTIFS, etc.	**DSUM and Other D-functions**	**SUMPRODUCT**
• Comparative operator can be placed in a cell with a hurdle. • Comparative operator can be joined to a hurdle that sits in a cell.	• Comparative operator must be placed in a cell with a hurdle.	• Comparative operator is placed directly between the array and criteria to create an array operation.

In the last few sections, SUMIFS, SUMIF, COUNTIFS, and the like are looking like the *only* functions to use for calculations with multiple criteria if you have Excel 2007 or later. Next, however, you will look at a few situations where SUMPRODUCT can be better than SUMIFS and the like in any version.

Workbook References: SUMIFS and the Like Can't, but SUMPRODUCT Can

SUMIFS, SUMIF, COUNTIFS, and the like all contain a range argument or a criteria_range argument that holds the range of values with the criteria. The range and criteria_range arguments cannot handle arrays under any circumstances. When you use a workbook reference and then close the workbook with the external data, the workbook reference converts to an array and causes the function to show a #VALUE! error. As shown in Figure 10.27, when you have both the workbook with the formula and the workbook with the external data open at the same time, there is no problem: The SUMIFS function calculates the correct total of 41. However, as shown in Figure 10.28, when the workbook with the external data is closed, SUMIFS yields an error. The same error occurs if you use workbook references with the other functions related to SUMIFS, such as COUNTIF. As shown in Figures 10.27 and 10.28, the SUMPRODUCT function does not have this problem. SUMPRODUCT is a better choice in this example.

	A	B
1	Condition3/2/2013	
2	Roger	
3		
4	Add with SUMIFS	
5	41.00	
6	=SUMIFS([ExternalData.xlsm]Names!$B$2:$B$6,[ExternalData.xlsm]Names!$A$2:$A$6,A2)	
7	Add with SUMPRODUCT	
8	41.00	
9	=SUMPRODUCT(--([ExternalData.xlsm]Names!$A$2:$A$6=A2),[ExternalData.xlsm]Names!$B$2:$B$6)	

Figure 10.27 *Because the workbook with the external data is open, there is no error.*

	A	B
1	Condition3/2/2013	
2	Roger	
3		
4	Add with SUMIFS	
5	#VALUE!	
6	=SUMIFS('H:\[ExternalData.xlsm]Names'!$B$2:$B$6,'H:\[ExternalData.xlsm]Names'!$A$2:$A$6,A2)	
7	Add with SUMPRODUCT	
8	41.00	
9	=SUMPRODUCT(--('H:\[ExternalData.xlsm]Names'!$A$2:$A$6=A2),'H:\[ExternalData.xlsm]Names'!$B$2:$B$6)	

Figure 10.28 *With a workbook with the formula open and a workbook with the external data closed, SUMIFS causes #VALUE! error, but SUMPRODUCT doesn't.*

> **Note:** Creating workbook references in formulas is similar to adding a regular cell reference to a formula. The only difference is that while your formula is in Edit mode, you can click the workbook in the taskbar (or press Ctrl+Tab) to jump to the external workbook and then select your range in the external workbook sheet. Also, when the external workbook is open, the workbook reference shows the workbook name and sheet reference. When it is closed, it shows the entire file path name.

An alternative to using SUMPRODUCT to deal with the fact that SUMIF and the like cannot handle external references is to build the conditional adding/counting/averaging formula in the external workbook and then simply use a workbook reference that points from the workbook with the formula to the workbook with the external data. In this way, your workbook reference will not have to be placed inside the range or criteria_range argument. If your project requirements allow such a calculation, this is a great trick.

Counting How Many Friday the 13ths Fall Between Two Dates

What if you had to add all the Friday the 13ths between a start date and an end date?

> **Note:** The publisher of this book, Bill MrExcel Jelen, specifically requested that this formula be included in the book because it is one of his favorite array formulas! Not only that, but MrExcel learned this formula from Bob Umlas, in his book *This Isn't Excel, It's Magic!*

As shown in Figure 10.29, the goal of the formula is to find a single-cell formula that will look at the start date and end date and figure out how many Friday the 13ths there are. This seems like a nearly impossible task for a single-cell formula! What makes it particularly daunting is that you do not have the full list of dates to look through.

	A	B
1	**How Many Friday 13th?**	
2	Start	12/9/2012
3	End	11/9/2014
4	How Many Friday 13th?	

Figure 10.29 *Our goal is to count how many Friday the 13ths fall between two dates.*

Luckily, there is a formula element that you can construct that will create an array of sequential dates, given a start date and an end date. In fact, in Chapter 7 you already saw a formula element that will create an array of sequential numbers. Chapter 7 calls the formula element a "dynamic variable-length array of sequential numbers." Figure 10.30 shows how you can use a similar formula element to create an array of sequential dates in cell B4. (Chapter 7 explains the hows and whys of this formula element.) If you were to evaluate this formula element, you would see that this formula element creates an array of the serial number dates from 41252 to 41952.

	A	B	C	D
1	**How Many Friday 13th?**			
2	Start	12/9/2012		
3	End	11/9/2014		
4	How Many Friday 13th?	=ROW(INDIRECT(B2&":"&B3))		

Figure 10.30 *"Dynamic variable-length array of sequential numbers (first shown back in chapter 7)."*

Figure 10.31 shows a small part of the evaluated array that the ROW function delivers, which contains 701 serial number dates.

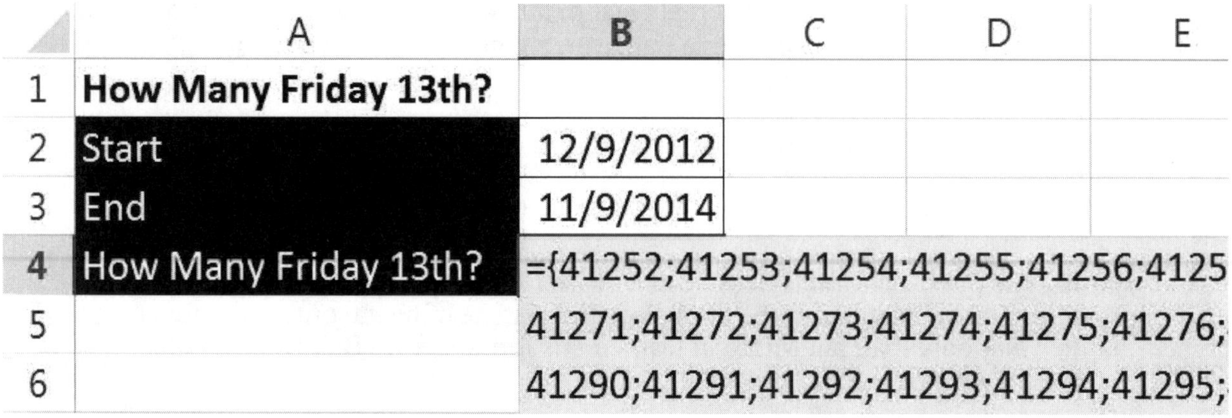

	A	B	C	D	E
1	**How Many Friday 13th?**				
2	Start	12/9/2012			
3	End	11/9/2014			
4	How Many Friday 13th?	={41252;41253;41254;41255;41256;4125			
5		41271;41272;41273;41274;41275;41276;			
6		41290;41291;41292;41293;41294;41295;			

Figure 10.31 *Array operation creates a resultant array filled with serial number dates.*

Because you cannot find Friday the 13ths from serial numbers, you need to use the TEXT function to format the array of numbers so that they show the names of the day and the numbers—for example, "Fri 13". As shown in Figure 10.32, by placing the ROW/INDIRECT array calculation in the value argument of TEXT, you make a function argument array operation.

```
=TEXT(ROW(INDIRECT(B2&":"&B3))
  TEXT(value, format_text)
```

Figure 10.32 *TEXT function will allow you to format the serial number dates as text so that you can count the Friday the 13ths.*

To get the TEXT function to show the serial number dates in the text format you want, you must enter a custom number format to display the numbers with a three-letter abbreviation for the name of the day and the number of the day. As shown in Figure 10.33, you type the custom number format "ddd d" into the format_text argument of the TEXT function.

```
=TEXT(ROW(INDIRECT(B2&":"&B3)),"ddd d")
  TEXT(value, format_text)
```

Figure 10.33 *Format_text argument gets the custom number format "ddd d".*

Figure 10.34 shows a small part of the evaluated array that the TEXT function delivers, which contains 701 text strings.

```
';"Tue 27";"Wed 28";"Thu 29";"Fri 30";"
/ed 11";"Thu 12";"Fri 13";"Sat 14";"Sun 1
25";"Thu 26";"Fri 27";"Sat 28";"Sun 29";'
```

Figure 10.34 *The resultant array shows text strings that contain the day as a three letter abbreviation and the day number.*

As shown in Figure 10.35, next you must convert the array of text strings to an array of logical values by equating the array to the text string "Fri 13".

=TEXT(ROW(INDIRECT(B2&":"&B3)),"ddd d")="Fri 13"

Figure 10.35 *Create the array operation that asks the question: Is the day equal to "Fri 13"?*

Figure 10.36 shows a small part of the evaluated array that the comparative operator array operation delivers. The array contains 701 logical values. TRUE means the serial number date is a Friday the 13th!

:;FALSE;FALSE;FALSE;FALSE;I
:;FALSE;TRUE;FALSE;FALSE;F
:;FALSE;FALSE;FALSE;FALSE;I

Figure 10.36 *TRUE means the day is "Fri 13".*

Figure 10.37 shows a common mistake that many Excel people (including me) have made throughout the years. You have created the formula element TEXT(ROW(INDIRECT(B2&":"&B3)),"ddd d")="Fri 13", and now you try to place it into the range argument of the COUNTIF function. This makes logical sense, especially since most of the function arguments in Excel can handle array operations. (The only one you have seen so far that cannot is lookup_value in VLOOKUP.) I mean, all you need to do is count how many TRUEs there are in the array of logical values, right?

=COUNTIF(TEXT(ROW(INDIRECT(B2&":"&B3)),"ddd d")="Fri 13"
COUNTIF(**range**, criteria)

Figure 10.37 *Array operations will not work in the range argument of COUNTIF.*

You finish the COUNTIF function by typing TRUE as the criteria in the criteria argument, as shown in Figure 10.38.

=COUNTIF(TEXT(ROW(INDIRECT(B2&":"&B3)),"ddd d")="Fri 13",TRUE)
COUNTIF(range, **criteria**)

Figure 10.38 *This formula will not work.*

But as soon as you enter the formula into the cell, you get the error message as shown in Figure 10.39. Figure 10.39 shows the error that displays in Excel 2013; in other versions you may get a slightly different message. In any version, the message does not provide helpful information. It should say something like this: "The range argument in the COUNTIF function is not programmed to handle arrays or array operations" because that is exactly what is going on here. In COUNTIF, SUMIF, AVERAGEIF, SUMIFS, COUNTIFS, and AVERAGEIFS, the range and criteria_range arguments cannot handle an array. No problem, though; SUMPRODUCT will come to the rescue.

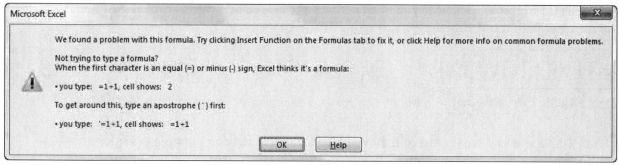

Figure 10.39 *The error message that you get when you place an array operation into the range argument is not very helpful.*

As shown in Figure 10.40 and 10.41, you can place the comparative operator array operation in parentheses, place a double negative in front, and place all that in SUMPRODUCT.

Figure 10.40 *SUMPRODUCT can handle array operations.*

f_x	=SUMPRODUCT(--(TEXT(ROW(INDIRECT(B2&":"&B3)),"ddd d")="Fri 13"))			
	A	B	C	D
1	**How Many Friday 13th?**			
2	Start	12/9/2012		
3	End	11/9/2014		
4	How Many Friday 13th?	3		

Figure 10.41 *There are three Friday the 13ths between the start and End date.*

SUMPRODUCT has come to the rescue a few times when you could not use SUMIF, COUNTIF, and similar functions.

Array Formula Efficiency Rule 22

A number of function arguments cannot handle arrays (array operations, array constants, and arrays created by workbook references):

- lookup_value argument in VLOOKUP
- lookup_value argument in HLOOKUP
- range argument in SUMIF
- range argument in COUNTIF
- range argument in COUNTIF
- criteria_range argument in SUMIFS
- criteria_range argument in COUNTIFS
- criteria_range argument in AVEARGEIFS

Comparing Methods for Counting or Adding with Criteria

The following table provides a summary of the advantages and disadvantages of the various methods for counting or adding with criteria.

Counting or Adding with Criteria		
Method	**Advantage**	**Disadvantage**
COUNTIFS SUMIFS	• Calculates more quickly than D-functions or SUMPRODUCT. • Doesn't require field names in the data set or criteria area. • Easy to copy a formula to other cells.	• Works only in Excel 2007 or later versions. • The range argument cannot handle arrays at all. • The range argument cannot handle workbook references when the workbook is closed (closing the workbook converts the workbook reference to an array that SUMIFS and the like cannot handle.).
DCOUNT DSUM	• Calculates more quickly than SUMPRODUCT. • Usually less complicated to create than a SUMPRODUCT formula.	• Calculates more slowly than COUNTIFS and SUMIFS. • Requires field names in the data set and criteria area. • Difficult to copy formulas without using a data table.
SUM-PRODUCT	• Array arguments can handle array operations without Ctrl+-Shift+Enter. • Doesn't require field names in the data set or criteria area. • Easy to copy a formula to other cells. • Handles workbook references when a workbook is closed.	• Calculates more slowly than D-functions and COUNTIFS and SUMIFS. • Can be complicated to create a formula.

IF Inside SUMPRODUCT

Chapter 4 discusses the IF function Ctrl+Shift+Enter trump rule, which became Array Formula Efficiency Rule 14: If you have an array operation in the IF function, the formula require Ctrl+Shift+Enter, regardless of where the IF function sits in the larger formula. This means that even if you put an IF function that contains an array operation into a function argument that can handle array operations (like the array arguments in the AGGREGATE or SUMPRODUCT functions), the formula will still require Ctrl+Shift+Enter.

As shown in Figure 10.42, if you use the IF function inside SUMPRODUCT, the formula requires Ctrl+Shift+Enter. The formula in cell A5 was not entered with Ctrl+Shift and therefore shows a #VALUE! error. The formula in cell A6 was entered with Ctrl+Shift and therefore calculates correctly. The problem with using IF inside SUMPRODUCT is that users of the spreadsheet may mistakenly think that the SUMPRODUCT's array argument can handle the array operation inside the IF function. To avoid this potential ambiguity, it may be better to use the formulas shown in A10 and A11.

	A	B	C	D
1	Date	Date	Rep	
2	10/7/2013	10/13/2013	Sioux	
3				
4	SUM	Formula		
5	#VALUE!	< Formula =SUMPRODUCT(IF(A14:A25>=A2,IF(A14:A25<=B2,IF(B14:B25=C2,C14:C25))))		
6	58.70	< Formula {=SUMPRODUCT(IF(A14:A25>=A2,IF(A14:A25<=B2,IF(B14:B25=C2,C14:C25)))))}		
7				
8	Less ambiguity if you use these:			
9	SUM	Formula		
10	58.70	< Formula =SUMPRODUCT(--(A14:A25>=A2),--(A14:A25<=B2),--(B14:B25=C2),C14:C25)		
11	58.70	< Formula {=SUM(IF(A14:A25>=A2,IF(A14:A25<=B2,IF(B14:B25=C2,C14:C25))))}		
12				
13	Date	Rep	Calls	
14	10/13/13	Sioux	18.2	
15	10/15/13	Chip	19.0	

Figure 10.42 *Using the IF function inside the SUMPRODUCT function may cause ambiguity.*

Array Formula Efficiency Rule 23

Important aspects of the SUMPRODUCT function:

- It can multiply and then add arrays with the same dimensions.

- It can add the results from an array operation with Ctrl+Shift+Enter. (With arrays of different dimensions, you can use the multiplication operator and a single array argument to get an answer.)

- It can handle workbook references, whereas functions such as COUNTIF and COUNTIFS cannot.

- It can handle arrays, whereas the range and criteria_range arguments in functions such as COUNTIF and COUNTIFS cannot.

- If you have Excel 2007 or later, many multiple-condition calculations can be more efficiently completed by using COUNTIF, COUNTIFS, and other similar functions.

- If you are making multiple-condition calculations and you do not need to copy the formula, it might be more efficient to use D-functions.

- To use the IF function inside the SUMPRODUCT function, you have to use Ctrl+Shift+Enter. To be less ambiguous, consider using an alternative formula.

Chapter Summary

In this chapter you learned about the amazing SUMPRODUCT function. Chapter 11 discusses Boolean logic.

Chapter 11: Boolean Logic: AND Criteria and OR Criteria

Excel Files

To follow along with the examples in this chapter, you can download the accompanying files, as explained in the Introduction.

Reminder of the AND Criteria You Have Already Seen

So far in this book, you have used AND criteria numerous times. As a reminder, here are four formulas that you have already created using AND criteria:

- In Figure 10.24 you saw this formula for adding with two criteria:
  =SUMIFS(C8:C19,A8:A19,">="&A2,A8:A19,"<="&B2,B8:B19,C2)
- In Figure 10.25 you saw this formula for adding with two criteria:
  =DSUM(A7:C19,"Calls",A1:C2)
- In Figure 4.39 you saw this minimum with two criteria array formula that uses Boolean math AND criteria:
  =AGGREGATE(15,6,$C$3:$C$13/(($A$3:$A$13<>$F$2)*($B$3:$B$13=E5)),1)
- In Figure 10.26 you saw this adding with three criteria array formula that uses Boolean math AND criteria:
  =SUMPRODUCT(--(A8:A19>=A2),--(A8:A19<=B2),--(B8:B19=C2),C8:C19)

In all four formulas, AND criteria means that all conditions or logical tests must be met in order for the corresponding number to be included in the calculation. This chapter expands the discussion to also include OR criteria.

Boolean Data

The word *Boolean* comes from the 19th century mathematician George Boole, who introduced Boolean algebra in 1854. Boolean is a data type that has only two possibilities—either TRUE or FALSE or 1 or 0:

$$TRUE = 1 \qquad\qquad FALSE = 0$$

Boolean Math: AND Criteria and OR Criteria

For Boolean logic, this section looks at the AND calculation and the OR calculation. I use the terms *AND criteria* and *OR criteria* because in Excel you often use these calculations to create reports, extract data, or make calculations based on a set of criteria. In addition, I tend to use the synonym *Boolean math* for *Boolean logic* because you use multiplication for AND criteria and addition for OR criteria.

> **Note:** Here are some synonyms you may encounter for AND and OR:
>
> - AND = conjunction = concurrent = intersection = joint = both = all conditions = multiplication
> - OR = inclusive = disjunction = alternation = union = at least one = one or more = adding

The following are some of the different possibilities you can have for AND criteria and OR criteria when you run two logical tests:

AND Criteria = All Logical Tests Are TRUE = Multiplication
TRUE*TRUE = 1*1 = 1 = TRUE
TRUE*FALSE = 1*0 = 0 = FALSE
FALSE*TRUE = 0*1 = 0 = FALSE
FALSE*FALSE = 0*0 = 0 = FALSE
OR Criteria = At Least One Logical Test Is TRUE = Addition
TRUE+TRUE = 1+1– 2 – 2 – TRUE
TRUE+FALSE = 1+0= 1 = 1 = TRUE
FALSE+TRUE = 0+1= 1 = 1 = TRUE
FALSE+FALSE = 0+0= 0 = 0 = FALSE

These logical calculations can be extended to any number of logical tests. The following are the results for three logical tests:

AND Criteria = All Logical Tests Are TRUE = Multiplication
TRUE*TRUE*TRUE = 1*1*1 = 1 = TRUE
FALSE*TRUE*TRUE = 0*1*1 = 0 = FALSE
TRUE*FALSE*TRUE = 1*0*1 = 0 = FALSE
TRUE*TRUE*FALSE = 1*1*0 = 0 = FALSE
TRUE*FALSE*FALSE = 1*0*0 = 0 = FALSE
FALSE*TRUE*FALSE = 0*1*0 = 0 = FALSE
FALSE*FALSE*TRUE = 0*0*1 = 0 = FALSE
FALSE*FALSE*FALSE = 0*0*0 = 0 = FALSE
OR Criteria = At Least One Logical Test Is TRUE = Addition
TRUE+TRUE+TRUE = 1+1+1 = 3 = TRUE
FALSE+TRUE+TRUE = 0+1+1 = 2 = TRUE
TRUE+FALSE+TRUE = 1+0+1 = 2 = TRUE
TRUE+TRUE+FALSE = 1+1+0 = 2 = TRUE
TRUE+FALSE+FALSE = 1+0+0 = 1 = TRUE
FALSE+TRUE+FALSE = 0+1+0 = 1 = TRUE
FALSE+FALSE+TRUE = 0+0+1 = 1 = TRUE
FALSE+FALSE+FALSE = 0+0+0 = 0 = FALSE

For Boolean math AND criteria, you use multiplication so that any time a 0 (FALSE) shows up, the end result will be 0, or FALSE. The only time an AND logical test can result in a TRUE is when all the logical tests are TRUE, or 1.

For Boolean math OR criteria, you use addition so that any time a nonzero number (TRUE) shows up, the end result will be the nonzero number, or TRUE. The only time an OR logical test can result in a FALSE is when all the logical tests are FALSE, or 0.

The key concept that you should have in your head as you go on to build bigger array formulas is that AND criteria and OR criteria are filters you put on the data set before creating the end product. Now let's look at some examples.

AND Criteria

When you run an AND logical test, all tests must evaluate to TRUE in order for the AND logical test to report a TRUE. If any one test reports a FALSE, the AND logical test reports a FALSE.

As a reminder of how pervasive AND criteria is in Excel, Figures 11.1 to 11.7 show examples of Excel formulas and features that use AND criteria. For these examples, there are four criteria. This means you must get four TRUEs in order for a number to be included in the calculation.

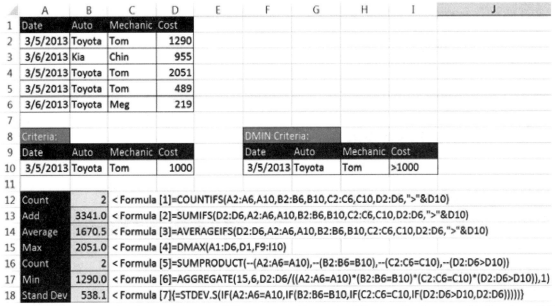

Figure 11.1 *Formulas [1] to [4] use AND criteria. Formula [5] uses Boolean multiplication AND criteria. Formula [6] uses Boolean multiplication and division AND criteria. Formula [7] uses the IF function and Boolean AND criteria.*

Notes: For a reminder of how Formulas [1], [2], [3], and [5] work, see Chapter 10. For a reminder of how Formulas [4], [6], and [7] work, see Chapter 4.

	A	B	C	D	E	F	G
1	Date	Auto	Mechanic	Cost		Date	3/5/2013
2	3/5/2013	Toyota	Tom	1290		Mechanic	Tom
3	3/6/2013	Kia	Chin	955		Auto	Toyota
4	3/5/2013	Toyota	Tom	2051			
5	3/5/2013	Toyota	Tom	489		Cost	Sum of Cost
6	3/6/2013	Toyota	Meg	219		1290	1290
7						2051	2051
8						Grand Total	3341

Figure 11.2 *A PivotTable with filters can make a sum calculation with AND criteria.*

	A	B	C	D	E	F
1	Date	Auto	Mechanic	Cost		
2	3/5/2013	Toyota	Tom	1290		
4	3/5/2013	Toyota	Tom	2051		
7				1670.5		< Formula =SUBTOTAL(101,[Cost])
8						function_num argument for
9						SUBTOTAL function: 101 = Average

Figure 11.3 *The Table feature with applied filters and a totals row can make an average calculation with AND criteria.*

	A	B	C	D
1	Date ⛛	Auto ▾	Mechanic ▾	Cost ⛛
2	3/5/2013	Toyota	Tom	1290
4	3/5/2013	Toyota	Tom	2051

Figure 11.4 *The Filter feature can filter a table using AND criteria.*

	A	B	C	D	E	F	G	H	I
1	Criteria:								
2	Date	Auto	Mechanic	Cost					
3	3/5/2013	Toyota	Tom	>1000					
4									
5	Date	Auto	Mechanic	Cost		Extract Area:			
6	3/5/2013	Toyota	Tom	1290		Date	Auto	Mechanic	Cost
7	3/6/2013	Kia	Chin	955		3/5/2013	Toyota	Tom	1290
8	3/5/2013	Toyota	Tom	2051		3/5/2013	Toyota	Tom	2051
9	3/5/2013	Toyota	Tom	489					
10	3/6/2013	Toyota	Meg	219					

Figure 11.5 *Advanced Filter can extract records using AND criteria.*

	A	B	C	D	E	F
1	Date	Auto	Mechanic	Cost	Helper:	
2	3/5/2013	Toyota	Tom	1290	TRUE	< Formula =AND(A2=$A$10,B2=$B$10,C2=$C$10,D2>=$D$10)
3	3/6/2013	Kia	Chin	955	FALSE	< Formula =AND(A3=$A$10,B3=$B$10,C3=$C$10,D3>=$D$10)
4	3/5/2013	Toyota	Tom	2051	TRUE	< Formula =AND(A4=$A$10,B4=$B$10,C4=$C$10,D4>=$D$10)
5	3/5/2013	Toyota	Tom	489	FALSE	< Formula =AND(A5=$A$10,B5=$B$10,C5=$C$10,D5>=$D$10)
6	3/6/2013	Toyota	Meg	219	FALSE	< Formula =AND(A6=$A$10,B6=$B$10,C6=$C$10,D6>=$D$10)
7						
8	Criteria:					
9	Date	Auto	Mechanic	Cost		
10	3/5/2013	Toyota	Tom	1000		
11						
12	Count		2	< Formula [1] =COUNTIF(E2:E6,TRUE)		

Figure 11.6 *The AND function with four logical tests can be used in a helper column. Although there is no need for an AND formula helper column in this particular example (because COUNTIFS would probably be better), in Chapter 15, when you study formulas to extract data, you will see a good use for such a solution.*

	A	B	C	D	E	F
1	Date	Auto	Mechanic	Cost	Helper:	
2	3/5/2013	Toyota	Tom	1290	1	< Formula =(A2=$A$10)*(B2=$B$10)*(C2=$C$10)*(D2>=$D$10)
3	3/6/2013	Kia	Chin	955	0	< Formula =(A3=$A$10)*(B3=$B$10)*(C3=$C$10)*(D3>=$D$10)
4	3/5/2013	Toyota	Tom	2051	1	< Formula =(A4=$A$10)*(B4=$B$10)*(C4=$C$10)*(D4>=$D$10)
5	3/5/2013	Toyota	Tom	489	0	< Formula =(A5=$A$10)*(B5=$B$10)*(C5=$C$10)*(D5>=$D$10)
6	3/6/2013	Toyota	Meg	219	0	< Formula =(A6=$A$10)*(B6=$B$10)*(C6=$C$10)*(D6>=$D$10)
7						
8	Criteria:					
9	Date	Auto	Mechanic	Cost		
10	3/5/2013	Toyota	Tom	1000		
11						
12	Count		2	< Formula [1] =SUM(E2:E6)		

Figure 11.7 *Instead of using Excel's built-in AND function, you can directly multiply the logical tests to create a Boolean helper column.*

As you can see in these examples, Excel functions like SUMIFS, array formulas using Boolean math or IF functions, PivotTables, the Excel Table feature with a filter and totals row, Filter, Advanced Filter, and helper column solutions can all make AND criteria calculations.

Multiplication, Division, and the IF Function for a Boolean Array Formula AND Criteria

Look back at Figure 11.1, and you can see three array formulas (Formulas [5], [6], and [7]). To better understand the different ways that AND criteria can work in formulas, the following pages step through each of these array formulas and show how they calculate.

Notes About the Formula
=SUMPRODUCT(--(A2:A6=A10),--(B2:B6=B10),--(C2:C6=C10),--(D2:D6>D10))

The following table presents a summary of Formula [5] from Figure 11.1.

Formula Goal:
Count records in a data set that meet all four criteria.
Calculation Summary:
1. =SUMPRODUCT(--(A2:A6=A10),--(B2:B6=B10),--(C2:C6=C10),--(D2:D6>D10))
Parentheses force the comparative operator to calculate first.
2. =SUMPRODUCT(--({TRUE;FALSE;TRUE;TRUE;FALSE}), --({TRUE;FALSE;TRUE;TRUE;TRUE}), --({TRUE;FALSE;TRUE;TRUE;FALSE}), --({TRUE;FALSE;TRUE;FALSE;FALSE}))
Because SUMPRODUCT cannot "see" TRUEs and FALSEs, you have to use the math operation double negative to convert the logical to numbers.
3. =SUMPRODUCT({1;0;1;1;0},{1;0;1;1;1},{1;0;1;1;0},{1;0;1;0;0})
4. =PRODUCT({1;0;1;1;0}*{1;0;1;1;1}*{1;0;1;1;0}*{1;0;1;0;0})
Each number will be distributed through to the corresponding position: 1 * 1 * 1 * 1 = 1 0 * 0 * 0 * 0 = 0 1 * 1 * 1 * 1 = 1 1 * 1 * 1 * 0 = 0 0 * 1 * 0 * 0 = 0
5. =SUM({1;0;1;0;0})
Only when the four arrays have a corresponding 1 * 1 * 1 * 1 = 1 do you get a 1 in the resultant array.
6. The formula delivers the single item 2.
Key Concepts:
The resultant array, {1;0;1;0;0}, is filled with ones and zeros. Because you are counting, the zeros do not adversely affect the calculation. The zero values are a way of "filtering" the values in the formula. You use SUMPRODUCT instead of SUM so you don't have to use Ctrl+Shift+Enter.

Notes About the Formula =AGGREGATE(15,6,D2:D6/((A2:A6=A10)*(B2:B6=B10)*(C2:C6 =C10)*(D2:D6>D10)),1)

The following table presents a summary of Formula [6] from Figure 11.1.

Formula Goal:
Find the minimum value, based on four criteria.
Calculation Summary:
1. =AGGREGATE(15,6,D2:D6/((A2:A6=A10)*(B2:B6=B10)*(C2:C6=C10)*(D2:D6>D10)),1)
The 15 in the function_num argument tells AGGREGATE to make the SMALL function calculation. The 6 in the options argument tells AGGREGATE to ignore errors in the array argument. The 1 in the k argument tells the SMALL function to find the first smallest value in the array argument. Parentheses force the comparative operator to calculate first.
2. =AGGREGATE(15,6,D2:D6/({TRUE;FALSE;TRUE;TRUE;FALSE}*{TRUE;-FALSE;TRUE;TRUE;TRUE}*{TRUE;FALSE;TRUE;TRUE;FALSE}*{TRUE;FALSE;TRUE;-FALSE;FALSE}),1)
In the denominator you perform Boolean multiplication of the four arrays of logical values. The direct math operation multiplication will convert the logical values to ones and zeros, like this: TRUE * TRUE * TRUE * TRUE = 1 / FALSE * FALSE * FALSE * FALSE = 0 / TRUE * TRUE * TRUE * TRUE = 1 / TRUE * TRUE * TRUE * FALSE = 0 / FALSE * TRUE * FALSE * FALSE = 0
3. =AGGREGATE(15,6,D2:D6/{1;0;1;0;0},1)
Only when the four arrays have a corresponding TRUE * TRUE * TRUE * TRUE = 1 do you get a 1 in the resultant array.
4. =AGGREGATE(15,6,{1290;955;2051;489;219}/{1;0;1;0;0},1)
You are *not* using multiplication for this last Boolean AND criteria calculation because if you did, the minimum value would be zero, and that would interfere with getting the formula to calculate the correct answer. You use division as the Boolean math operator so that the zeros in the denominator will be converted to #DIV/0! errors, and because AGGREGATE has options = 6, the errors will be ignored. If you did not use division, you would get this: {1290;955;2051;489;219} * {1;0;1;0;0} = {1290;0;2051;0;0} Because you use division, you get this: {1290;955;2051;489;219} / {1;0;1;0;0} = {1290;#DIV/0!;2051;#DIV/0!;#DIV/0!} These are the keys to this calculation: using division, getting errors in the resultant array, and using a 6 in the options argument to filter the values in the formula.
5. =AGGREGATE(15,6,{1290;#DIV/0!;2051;#DIV/0!;#DIV/0!},1)
You filtered the values in the formula using Boolean multiplication and division.
6. The formula delivers the single item: 1290
Key Concepts:
The resultant array, {1290;#DIV/0!;2051;#DIV/0!;#DIV/0!}, is filled with numbers and errors. The errors are the filter that allow you to calculate only on the correct numbers. You use AGGREGATE instead of MIN with four IF functions so you don't have to use Ctrl+Shift+Enter.

Notes About the Formula
=STDEV.S(IF(A2:A6=A10,IF(B2:B6=B10,IF(C2:C6=C10,IF(D2:D6>D10,D2:D6)))))

The following table presents a summary of Formula [7] from Figure 11.1.

Formula Goal:
Calculate the standard deviation, based on four criteria.
Calculation Summary:
1. =STDEV.S(IF(A2:A6=A10,IF(B2:B6=B10,IF(C2:C6=C10,IF(D2:D6>D10,D2:D6)))))
If there are four criteria, use four IF functions. The first IF sits in the number1 argument of the STDEV.S function. Each successive IF sits in the logical_test argument of the previous IF function.
You intentionally leave the value_if_false argument of the IF function empty (that is, nothing in it) so that the IF function will place the logical value FALSE into the resultant array whenever there are *not* four successive TRUE values.
2. =STDEV.S(IF({TRUE;FALSE;TRUE;TRUE;FALSE},IF({TRUE;-FALSE;TRUE;TRUE;TRUE},IF({TRUE;FALSE;TRUE;TRUE;FALSE},IF({TRUE;-FALSE;TRUE;FALSE;FALSE},{1290;955;2051;489;219})))))
The four IF functions select a number from that array of numbers in the value_if_true argument only when there are four TRUE values. For all other cases, the IF places a FALSE in the resultant array. The FALSE vales are a way of "filtering" the values in the formula.
The IF does this:
TRUE and TRUE and TRUE and TRUE = 1290
FALSE and FALSE and FALSE and FALSE = FALSE
TRUE and TRUE and TRUE and TRUE = 2051
TRUE and TRUE and TRUE and FALSE = FALSE
FALSE and TRUE and FALSE and FALSE = FALSE
3. =STDEV.S({1290;FALSE;2051;FALSE;FALSE})
The four IF functions dump the array of numbers and FALSE values into the STDEV.S function. STDEV.S is programmed to ignore FALSE.
4. The formula delivers the single item 538.1
Key Concepts:
The resultant array, {1290;FALSE;2051;FALSE;FALSE}, is filled with numbers and FALSE values. The FALSE values are the filter that allow you to calculate only on the correct numbers.
If you don't mind entering the formula with Ctrl+Shift+Enter, using multiple IF functions is conceptually straightforward.

Comparing Multiplication, Division, and the IF Function for Boolean Array Formula AND Criteria

There are a few key differences between the various methods for performing Boolean array formula AND criteria calculations:

- **Multiplication**: Zeros filter out the items that do not meet all criteria. The resultant array contains zeros. If zeros do not adversely affect the calculation, this method is great.
- **Division**: #DIV/0 errors filter out the items that do not meet all criteria. The resultant array contains #DIV/0 errors. If #DIV/0 errors do not adversely affect the calculation, this method is great.
- **IF function**: FALSE values filter out the items that do not meet all criteria. The resultant array contains FALSE values. If FALSE values do not adversely affect the calculation, this method is great.

OR Criteria: Be Careful Not to Double Count!

When you run an OR logical test, only one test needs to evaluate to TRUE in order for the OR logical test to report a TRUE. The only circumstance when a FALSE is reported is when all logical tests come out to be FALSE. Two of the phrases you may hear to describe an OR logical test are "at least one" (logical test) and "one or more" (logical test).

This section shows two examples that illustrate how Boolean OR criteria addition works. The first example is shown in Figure 11.8. You have a list of managers' names in column A and a Boolean OR criteria formula in column B. This is the OR logical test: "Is the name in the cell Gidget OR Rodger?" Notice that because the OR logical test (two separate questions) is being asked of a single cell, you *cannot* get two TRUE values. For example, the contents of cell A2 cannot be both Gidget and Rodger.

	A	B	C	D	E
1	Managers	Gidget or Rodger?			Managers
2	Gidget	1	< Formula =(A2=$E$2)+(A2=$E$3) = TRUE+FALSE = TRUE = 1		Gidget
3	Rodger	1	< Formula =(A3=$E$2)+(A3=$E$3) = FALSE+TRUE = TRUE = 1		Rodger
4	Davis	0	< Formula =(A4=$E$2)+(A4=$E$3) = FALSE+FALSE = FALSE = 0		
5	Rodger	1	< Formula =(A5=$E$2)+(A5=$E$3) = FALSE+TRUE = TRUE = 1		
6	Bernardina	0	< Formula =(A6=$E$2)+(A6=$E$3) = FALSE+FALSE = FALSE = 0		

Figure 11.8 *The answer to the question "Gidget OR Rodger?" can never have two TRUEs. The OR criteria is being applied to a single cell.*

The second example, as you can see in Figure 11.9, shows a slightly different construction for the OR logical test. Instead of the OR question being pointed at a single cell, the two separate questions are pointing at two separate cells. In this example, the Boolean OR criteria formula is testing whether a customer's net assets are greater than $100,000 OR the credit rating is greater than or equal to 3.5. Because the two questions are being asked of two different cells, you *can* get two TRUE values.

	A	B	C	D	E	F	G
1	Customer	Net Assets	Credit Rating	Extend Credit?			OR Criteria:
2	J.K. LLC	85,024	4	1	< Formula =(B2>$G$3)+(C2>=$G$5) = FALSE+TRUE = TRUE = 1		Net Assets
3	Fruits Inc.	111,104	3.5	2	< Formula =(B3>$G$3)+(C3>=$G$5) = TRUE+TRUE = TRUE = 2		100,000
4	SW	89,236	2.4	0	< Formula =(B4>$G$3)+(C4>=$G$5) = FALSE+FALSE = FALSE = 0		Credit Rating
5	PCC	113,212	3	1	< Formula =(B5>$G$3)+(C5>=$G$5) = TRUE+FALSE = TRUE = 1		3.5
6	Gigi's Inc.	100,000	1.4	0	< Formula =(B6>$G$3)+(C6>=$G$5) = FALSE+FALSE = FALSE = 0		

Figure 11.9 *The answer to the question "NA>100000 OR CR>=3.5?" may have two TRUEs. The OR criteria is being applied to two different cells.*

So why is it important to make the distinction between an OR question that *cannot* get more than one TRUE and an OR question that *can* get more than one TRUE? It is important for formula building. For OR questions that can get more than one TRUE, you have to be careful when building formulas! This means you have to learn about two types of OR logical test formulas. I think of the two formulas types in these terms:

OR logical test that *cannot* get more than one TRUE:
- OR questions are usually pointing at a single cell.
- Usually this means the OR questions are looking through a single column.

OR logical test that *can* get more than one TRUE:

- OR questions are usually pointing at different cells.
- Usually this means the OR questions are looking through a multiple columns.

To learn about the two different types of formulas, you will next look at formulas that count using OR criteria.

Counting with an OR Logical Test That *Cannot* Get More Than One TRUE

Figure 11.10 shows a small data set and five formulas that can count with OR criteria when you *cannot* get more than one TRUE.

	A	B	C	D
1	Managers		Managers	
2	Gidget		Gidget	
3	Rodger		Rodger	
4	Davis			
5	Rodger			
6	Bernardina			
8	Count	3	< Formula [1] =COUNTIF(A2:A6,C2)+COUNTIF(A2:A6,C3)	
9	Count	3	< Formula [2] =DCOUNTA(A1:A6,A1,C1:C3)	
10	Count	3	< Formula [3] =SUMPRODUCT((A2:A6=C2)+(A2:A6=C3))	
11	Count	3	< Formula [4] {=SUM(IF((A2:A6=C2)+(A2:A6=C3),1))}	
12	Count	3	< Formula [5] =SUMPRODUCT(--ISNUMBER(MATCH(A2:A6,C2:C3,0)))	

Figure 11.10 *You can never get a cell that contains both Gidget and Rodger. The OR criteria counting formula is looking at a single column.*

Notes About the Formulas to Count with an OR Logical Test That *Cannot* Get >1 TRUE

The following table discusses how each formula from Figure 11.10 calculates.

Formula [1]: =COUNTIF(A2:A6,C2)+COUNTIF(A2:A6,C3)
• Because both COUNTIF functions are looking at the same column, and each cell can never have both Gidget and Rodger, it will count correctly.

Formula [2]: =DCOUNTA(A1:A6,A1,C1:C3)
• Use DCOUNTA because you are counting text, not numbers.
• OR criteria for D-functions must be set up in different rows (unlike AND criteria, which must be in the same row).
• DCOUNTA will include null text strings in the count. This means if you have null text strings delivered by formulas, they will be counted.

Formula [3]: =SUMPRODUCT((A2:A6=C2)+(A2:A6=C3))
• (A2:A6=C2)+(A2:A6=C3) ➜ {T;F;F;F;F}+{F;T;F;T;F} ➜ {1;1;0;1;0}
• There is no need for a double negative because the addition is a math operator that converts the logical values to ones and zeros.

Formula [4]: {=SUM(IF((A2:A6=C2)+(A2:A6=C3),1))}

- =SUM(IF((A2:A6=C2)+(A2:A6=C3),1)) ➔ =SUM(IF({1;1;0;1;0},1)) ➔ =SUM({1;1;FALSE;1;FALSE})
- The logical_test argument in IF contains an array of numbers. This works perfectly because the logical_test argument interprets any nonzero number as TRUE and interprets zero as FALSE.

Formula [5]: =SUMPRODUCT(--ISNUMBER(MATCH(A2:A6,C2:C3,0)))

- =SUMPRODUCT(--ISNUMBER(MATCH(A2:A6,C2:C3,0))) ➔ =SUMPRODUCT(--ISNUMBER({1;2;#N/A;2;#N/A})) ➔ =SUMPRODUCT(--{TRUE;TRUE;FALSE;TRUE;FALSE}) ➔ =SUMPRODUCT({1;1;0;1;0})
- The important things to remember for the MATCH function are that you need to put the list of OR criteria into the lookup_array argument and you need to put the entire column of items into the lookup_value argument. The MATCH function returns the relative position of an item in a list (a number), and then the ISNUMBER function "sees" the number while ignoring the #N/A errors.
- Remember from Chapter 6 that this is a function argument array operation, and because you give the lookup_value argument the entire column of items, the MATCH function will return a position or an error for each item in the list. In the example, you gave the lookup_value argument five items, and so the MATCH delivers an array of five items: numbers mean "count," and #N/A means "don't count."
- The #N/A errors are "filtering" out the items that should not be included in the count.
- If you have many OR criteria tests on a single column, this formula is usually easiest to create and fastest to calculate.
- **Note:** I learned this use of the MATCH function to enact OR criteria from hamy72 at YouTube. Thanks, hamy72!!!

These five formulas are pretty amazing! But to fully compare and contrast the formulas, you must look at how all five formulas operate on a large data set. Figure 11.11 shows the same basic formulas, but here they run six OR criteria over 500 rows.

	A	B	C	D	E
1	Count total calls for group 1				
2	Count		68		[1] =COUNTIF(B9:B518,D11)+COUNTIF(B9:B518,D12)+COUNTIF(B9:B518,D13)+ COUNTIF(B9:B518,D14)+COUNTIF(B9:B518,D15)+COUNTIF(B9:B518,D16)
3	Count		68		[2] =DCOUNTA(B8:B518,B8,D10:D16)
4	Count		68		[3] =SUMPRODUCT(--((B9:B518=D11)+(B9:B518=D12)+(B9:B518=D13)+ (B9:B518=D14)+(B9:B518=D15)+(B9:B518=D16)))
5	Count		68		[4] {=SUM(IF((B9:B518=D11)+(B9:B518=D12)+(B9:B518=D13) +(B9:B518=D14)+(B9:B518=D15)+(B9:B518=D16),1))}
6	Count		68		[5] =SUMPRODUCT(--ISNUMBER(MATCH(B9:B518,D11:D16,0)))
7					
8	Date of Call	Managers		OR Criteria	
9	10/18/13	Davis Wolford		Group 1	
10	10/6/13	Bernardina Free		Managers	
11	10/19/13	Bernardina Free		Gidget Marlow	
12	10/20/13	Celesta Granger		Rodger Riddle	
13	10/13/13	Nana Hathaway		Kym Handy	
14	10/18/13	Nana Hathaway		Zulma Farrell	
15	11/20/13	Yulanda Casillas		Edgardo Dalton	
16	10/26/13	Gema Tapia		Jama Monk	

Figure 11.11 *Each OR criteria counting formula is looking at a single column. The six-criteria OR logical test is pointing to a single cell.*

The most immediate observation is that Formulas [1], [3], and [4] look like really long formulas, whereas Formulas [2] and [5] look much shorter. In terms of typing out the formulas, Formulas [2] and [5] have the advantage.

The following section examines the formula calculation time aspect of these formulas.

Timing Counting Formulas for an OR Logical Test That *Cannot* Get More Than One TRUE

The file for these timing results is named 11-OR-CriteriaSingleColumn.xlsm, and it can be found in the Timing folder in the zipped files that accompany the book. To time your own formulas, see Chapter 2 for details. (Timing depends many factors, and your particular situation may have different timing results.)

Figure 11.12 shows the anecdotal results I got from OR criteria counting formulas with six criteria that looked at 10,000 rows of data. If you are counting with OR criteria and the logical test will never result in more than one TRUE, Formula [1] is fastest, but it will take you a while to type the formula out. Formulas [2] and [5] may be the best bets because they are easy to create and relatively fast.

10,000 rows of data. Time in seconds					
	[1] COUNTIF +	[2] DCOUNTA	[3] SP, Boolean +	[4] SUM(IF Boolean +	[5] SP, ISNUMBER, MATCH
Time 1	0.00488	0.00659	0.01231	0.01157	0.0079
Time 2	0.00486	0.00603	0.01198	0.01112	0.0076
Time 3	0.00493	0.00665	0.0105	0.01174	0.00765
Ave	0.00489	0.006423333	0.01159667	0.011476667	0.007716667
% Change	0.00%	31.36%	137.15%	134.70%	57.81%

Figure 11.12 *An OR logical test that looks at a single column. A particular test* cannot *get more than one* TRUE.

Comparing Formulas to Count with an OR Logical Test That *Cannot* Get More Than One TRUE

The following table provides a summary of formulas to count with an OR logical test that *cannot* get more than one TRUE.

Counting with an OR Logical Test That CANNOT Get More Than One TRUE		
Formula	**Advantage**	**Disadvantage**
[1] COUNTIF	• Calculates the fastest. • Easy to copy the formula.	• With many criteria, the formula is long.
[2] DCOUNTA	• Calculates the second fastest. • Easy to create. • Even with many criteria, this formula remains short. • Counts null text strings.	• Requires field names in the data set and in the criteria area. • Formula is difficult to copy. • Counts null text strings.
[3] SUMPRODUCT with Boolean addition	• Easy to copy the formula.	• With many criteria, the formula is long.
[5] SUM and IF and Boolean addition	• Easy to copy the formula. • The logical_test argument of IF interprets any nonzero number as TRUE.	• With many criteria, the formula is long. • Requires Ctrl+Shift+Enter.
[6] SUMPRODUCT and ISNUMBER and MATCH	• Even with many criteria, this formula remains short. • Easy to copy the formula. • For formulas that require many OR array calculations, this formula is easy to create and usually faster than Boolean addition.	• May be a bit slower in calculating than Boolean OR criteria addition for two criteria.

Using a Formula to Count with an OR Logical Test That *Can* Get More Than One TRUE

As shown in Figure 11.13, if you are not careful about building OR criteria formulas, you may double count. In this example, the OR logical test is testing whether a customer's net assets are greater than $100,000 OR the credit rating is greater than or equal to 3.5. Because the two questions are being asked of two different columns, you have the potential of getting an answer for a particular customer that reports two TRUE values. Two TRUE values will cause a double count for that customer. For example, Fruits Inc. has assets greater than $100,000 and a credit rating of greater than or equal to 3.5. Formulas [4] and [5] double count Fruits Inc. Formulas [1], [2], and [3] do not double count Fruits Inc.

	A	B	C	D	E	F	G	H
1	Customer	Net Assets	Credit Rating		OR Criteria:		OR Criteria for DCOUNT:	
2	J.K. LLC	85,024	4		Net Assets		Net Assets	Credit Rating
3	Fruits Inc.	111,104	3.5		100,000		>100000	
4	SW	89,236	2.4		Credit Rating			>=3.5
5	PCC	113,212	3		3.5			
6	Gigi's Inc.	100,000	1.4					
7								
8	Count		3	< Formula [1] {=SUM(IF((B2:B6>E3)+(C2:C6>=E5),1))}				
9	Count		3	< Formula [2] =DCOUNT(B1:C6,,G2:H4)				
10	Count		3	< Formula [3] =SUMPRODUCT(--((B2:B6>E3)+(C2:C6>=E5)>0))				
11	Count		4	< Incorrect Formula [4] =COUNTIF(B2:B6,">"&E3)+COUNTIF(C2:C6,">="&E5)				
12	Count		4	< Incorrect Formula [5] =SUMPRODUCT((B2:B6>E3)+(C2:C6>=E5))				

Figure 11.13 *The individual OR logical test is pointing to two different cells and therefore may get two TRUE values for its answer. The OR criteria counting formula is looking at two columns.*

> **Note:** I posted a question at the MrExcel Message Board, and Barry Houdini helped me learn this important point about not double counting with OR criteria. Thanks, Barry!

Here is an important point: Formula [1] has two fewer array operations to perform than does Formula [3], which helps Formula [1] calculate more quickly than Formula [3]. It makes sense that fewer array operations leads to faster formula calculation times.

Notes About the Formulas to Count with an OR Logical Test That *Can* Get More Than One TRUE

The following table discusses the details of the formulas from Figure 11.13.

Formula [1]: {=SUM(IF((B2:B6>E3)+(C2:C6>=E5),1))}
• =SUM(IF((B2:B6>E3)+(C2:C6>=E5),1)) ➔ =SUM(IF({1;2;0;1;0},1)) ➔ =SUM({1;1;-FALSE;1;FALSE})
• The beauty of this formula is that you can place a Boolean OR logical test addition calculation in the logical_test argument of the IF function, and because the logical_test argument interprets any nonzero number as a TRUE and zero as a FALSE, this works perfectly.
• Key concept: For the IF function logical_test argument, {1;2;0;1;0} = ({TRUE;TRUE;-FALSE;TRUE;FALSE},
• Even though there is an array operation that delivers an array of numbers in the logical_test argument, you are allowed to place the single number 1 in the value_if_true argument, and the resultant IF function array will be filled with ones and FALSEs: {1;1;FALSE;1;FALSE}.
• This formula has two fewer array operations to perform than does Formula [3]. Formula [3] must run these two additional tests: double negative and greater than zero. This helps to make this formula the fastest calculating of the three formulas.
Formula [2]: =DCOUNT(B1:C6,,G2:H4)
• Because OR criteria that is pointing at more than one column, you must use a combination of AND criteria (same row) and OR criteria (different rows).
Formula [3]: =SUMPRODUCT(--((B2:B6>E3)+(C2:C6>=E5)>0))

It is worth going through the calculation steps for this formula:

1. =SUMPRODUCT(--((B2:B6>E3)+(C2:C6>=E5)>0))

The innermost parentheses instruct the formula to calculate the two comparative array operations.

2. =SUMPRODUCT(--({F;T;F;T;F}+{T;T;F;F;F}>0))

The Boolean OR criteria addition calculation comes next because Excel evaluates addition before comparative operators.

3. =SUMPRODUCT(--({1;2;0;1;0}>0))

A number greater than 1 could cause the formula to count incorrectly.

The next set of parentheses instruct the formula to calculate the "greater than zero" comparative array operation.

4. =SUMPRODUCT(--{T;T;F;T;F})

Double negative math converts the logical values to ones and zeros.

5. =SUMPRODUCT({1;1;0;1;0})

You are using just the SUM part of SUMPRODUCT because you only used the array1 argument.

The formula delivers the single item: 3

Note: This formula has two more array operations to perform (double negative and greater than zero) than Formula [1].

Formula [4]: =COUNTIF(B2:B6,">"&E3)+COUNTIF(C2:C6,">="&E5)
• This formula gets a double count because when there are two TRUEs, each COUNTIF counts 1.
Formula [5]: =SUMPRODUCT((B2:B6>E3)+(C2:C6>=E5))
• This formula gets a double count because (B2:B6>E3)+(C2:C6>=E5) ➔ {F;T;F;T;F}+{T;T;F;F;F} ➔ {1;2;0;1;0}

Timing Counting Formulas for an OR Logical Test That *Can* Get More Than One TRUE

The file for these timing results is named 12-OR-CriteriaMultipleColumns.xlsm, and it can be found in the Timing folder in the zipped files that accompany the book. To time your own formulas, see Chapter 2 for details. (Timing depends many factors, and your particular situation may have different timing results.)

Figure 11.14 shows the anecdotal results I got from OR criteria counting where there is a possibility of getting more than one TRUE for a particular OR logical test. This data set had 100,000 rows of data. Formula [1] is a bit faster than the others. Remembering to use Ctrl+Shift+Enter for this SUM and IF and Boolean OR criteria calculation may be worth the extra time savings over Formula [3].

	A	B	C	D	E	F	G	H
1					100,000 rows of data. Time in seconds.			
2	Net Assets	Credit Rating			OR Criteria:		OR Criteria for DCOUNT:	
3	11868	3.8			Net Assets		Net Assets	Credit Rating
4	93414	1.8			100,000		>100000	
5	140766	0			Credit Rating			>=3.5
6	184524	2.7			3.5			
7	180448	1.9						
8	182855	4.6		Count	73435	< [1] {=SUM(IF((A3:A100001>E4)+(B3:B100001>=E6),1))}		
9	239530	1.7		Count	73435	< [2] =DCOUNT(A2:B100001,,G3:H5)		
10	220839	3.7		Count	73435	< [3] =SUMPRODUCT(--((A3:A100001>E4)+(B3:B100001>=E6)>0))		
11	47500	3.5						
12	190266	0.6			[1] {=SUM(IF((A3:A100001>E4)+(B3:B100001>=E6),1))}	[2] =DCOUNT(A2:B100001,,G3:H5)	[3] =SUMPRODUCT(--((A3:A100001>E4)+(B3:B100001>=E6)>0))	
13	102691	4.7		Time 1	0.04343	0.04173	0.053	
14	234009	1.5		Time 2	0.04201	0.04846	0.05503	
15	226333	2.7		Time 3	0.04756	0.05101	0.05855	
16	99931	0.4		Ave	0.044333333	0.047066667	0.055526667	
17	244152	4.7		% Change	0.00%	6.17%	25.25%	

Figure 11.14 *An OR logical test that looks at a multiple columns. A particular test* can *get more than one TRUE. Formula [1] is fastest and easiest to create.*

Comparing Formulas to Count with an OR Logical Test That *Cannot* Get More Than One TRUE

The following table provides a comparison of the three formulas for counting with an OR logical test that *cannot* get more than one TRUE.

Count with an OR Logical Test That *Can* Get More Than One TRUE		
Formula	**Advantage**	**Disadvantage**
[1] SUM and IF and Boolean addition	• Easy to copy the formula. • The logical_test argument of IF interprets any nonzero number as TRUE. • Has two fewer array operations than Formula [3]. • Calculates fastest.	• Requires Ctrl+Shift+Enter.
[2] DCOUNTA	• Calculates second fastest.	• Requires field names in the data set and in the criteria area. • Difficult to copy the formula. • For many OR criteria, the criteria area is tedious to create.
[3] SUMPRODUCT with Boolean addition	• Has the longest calculating time. • Easy to copy the formula.	• Has two more array operations to perform than with Formula [1].

Formula [1] looks good because it calculates fastest and it easiest to create.

OR Criteria for Adding, Averaging, and Finding min or max

The same OR criteria concepts you have learned about in this chapter can be applied to other aggregate calculations. Figures 11.15 to 11.17 show how to do sum, average, minimum, and maximum calculations with different OR criteria.

	A	B	C	D	E	F	G
1	Region	Sales	Customer		OR Criteria:		
2	West	186,343	SWQ		Region		
3	East	293,630	IGG		West		
4	West	77,970	IGG		MidWest		
5	South	27,643	SWQ				
6	MidWest	34,097	IGG				
7	MidWest	159,800	SWQ				
8							
9	OR Criteria from same column (A particular logical test CANNOT result in two TRUEs.						
10	Add	458,210.0	< Formula [1] =SUMIF(A2:A7,E3,B2:B7)+SUMIF(A2:A7,E4,B2:B7)				
11	Average	114,552.5	< Formula [2] {=AVERAGE(IF((A2:A7=E3)+(A2:A7=E4),B2:B7))}				

Figure 11.15 *Sum and average calculations with OR criteria applied to a single column. An individual OR Logical Test cannot produce more than one TRUE.*

	A	B	C	D	E	F	G	H
1	Region	Sales	Customer		OR Criteria:			
2	West	186,343	SWQ		Region			
3	East	293,630	IGG		West			
4	West	77,970	IGG		Customer			
5	South	27,643	SWQ		IGG			
6	MidWest	34,097	IGG					
7	MidWest	159,800	SWQ					
8								
9	OR Criteria from different columns (A particular logical test CAN result in two TRUEs.							
10	Add	592,040	< Formula [1] {=SUM(IF((A2:A7=E3)+(C2:C7=E5),B2:B7))}					
11	Average	148,010	< Formula [2] {=AVERAGE(IF((A2:A7=E3)+(C2:C7=E5),B2:B7))}					
12	Add	592,040	< Formula [3] =SUMPRODUCT(--((A2:A7=E3)+(C2:C7=E5)>0),B2:B7)					2 Extra array opeartions over [1]
13	Add	670,010	< Formula [4] =SUMIF(A2:A7,E3,B2:B7)+SUMIF(C2:C7,E5,B2:B7)					Double counts 3rd entry

Figure 11.16 *Sum and average calculations with OR criteria applied to different columns. An individual OR Logical Test may produce more than one TRUE. Formula [1] calculate the correct sum. Formula [2] calculates the correct average. Formula [3] calculates the correct sum but takes longer to calculate than Formula [1]. Formula [4] does not calculate the correct sum because it does adds the third entry.*

	A	B	C	D	E	F	G
1	Region	Sales	Customer		OR Criteria:		
2	West	186,343	SWQ		Region		
3	East	293,630	IGG		West		
4	West	77,970	IGG		Customer		
5	South	27,643	SWQ		IGG		
6	MidWest	34,097	IGG				
7	MidWest	159,800	SWQ				
8							
9	OR Criteria from different columns (A particular logical test CAN result in two TRUEs.						
10	MIN	34,097	< Formula [1] {=MIN(IF((A2:A7=E3)+(C2:C7=E5),B2:B7))}				
11	MIN	34,097	< Formula [2] =AGGREGATE(15,6,B2:B7/((A2:A7=E3)+(C2:C7=E5)>0),1)				
12	MAX	293,630	< Formula [3] {=MAX(IF((A2:A7=E3)+(C2:C7=E5),B2:B7))}				
13	MAX	293,630	< Formula [4] =AGGREGATE(14,6,B2:B7*((A2:A7=E3)+(C2:C7=E5)>0),1)				

Figure 11.17 *MIN and MAX calculations with OR criteria applied to different columns. An individual OR Logical Test may produce more than one TRUE. Notice that for the Formula [2] AGGREGATE function minimum calculation (function 15), you use division to filter out the zero values, whereas for the formula [4] AGGREGATE function maximum calculation (Function 14) you can use multiplication, and the resulting zeros will not affect the calculation. (Division would work for max also.) The IF function inside the MIN or MAX functions in Formulas [1] and [3] has one fewer array operation than the AGGREGATE formula.*

Using AND Criteria and OR Criteria in the Same Formula: OR Logica.l Test *Cannot* Get More Than One TRUE

When you have a logical test that combines both AND and OR criteria, the same rules you have already learned apply. This means the type of formula you choose depends on whether not the OR logical test can get more than one TRUE value. Figure 11.18 shows an example for when the OR logical test *cannot* get more than one TRUE value, and Figure 11.19 shows an example for when the OR logical test CAN get more than one TRUE value.

Figure 11.18 shows a data set where you have three AND criteria, but the last AND criteria is an OR criteria:

- Date >= 3/18/2013

AND

- Date <=5/12/2013

AND

- Region = West OR Region = Midwest

For any particular OR logical test, there *cannot* be more than one TRUE. The OR logical test is pointing at a single column. Figure 11.18 shows formulas for counting, summing, finding the minimum value, and calculating an average. In general, Formula [1] (COUNTIFS) is the fastest for counting, and Formula [5] (SUMIFS) is the fastest for summing. If you have many OR Criteria, Formula [4] (for counting) and Formula [6] (for summing) may be easier to create.

	A	B	C	D	E	F	G	H
1	Date	Region	Sale		Criteria:			
2	3/11/13	West	340,936		Date	Date	Region	
3	2/15/13	East	226,110		3/18/13	5/12/13	West	
4	4/16/13	Midwest	295,977				Midwest	
5	5/22/13	East	433,524					
6	3/22/13	West	374,854					
7	2/25/13	Midwest	251,871					
8								
9	OR Criteria comes from 1 column. A particular OR logical test CANNOT get two TRUEs.							
10	Criteria: Between 3/18 and 5/12 for West or Midwest							
11	Count		2	[1] =COUNTIFS(A2:A7,">="&E3,A2:A7,"<="&F3,B2:B7,G3)+				
12				COUNTIFS(A2:A7,">="&E3,A2:A7,"<="&F3,B2:B7,G4)				
13	Count		2	[2] =SUMPRODUCT(--(A2:A7>=E3),--(A2:A7<=F3),--((B2:B7=G3)+(B2:B7=G4)))				
14	Count		2	[3] {=SUM(IF((A2:A7>=E3)*(A2:A7<=F3)*((B2:B7=G3)+(B2:B7=G4)),1))}				
15	Count		2	[4] =SUMPRODUCT(--(A2:A7>=E3),--(A2:A7<=F3),--ISNUMBER(MATCH(B2:B7,G3:G4,0)))				
16								
17	Sum Sales	670,831		[5] =SUMIFS(C2:C7,A2:A7,">="&E3,A2:A7,"<="&F3,B2:B7,G3)+				
18				SUMIFS(C2:C7,A2:A7,">="&E3,A2:A7,"<="&F3,B2:B7,G4)				
19	Sum Sales	670,831		[6] =SUMPRODUCT(--(A2:A7>=E3),--(A2:A7<=F3),--ISNUMBER(MATCH(B2:B7,G3:G4,0)),C2:C7)				
20	Min Sales	295,977		[7] =AGGREGATE(15,6,C2:C7/((A2:A7>=E3)*(A2:A7<=F3)*((B2:B7=G3)+(B2:B7=G4))),1)				
21	Ave Sales	335,416		8 {=AVERAGE(IF((A2:A7>=E3)*(A2:A7<=F3)*((B2:B7=G3)+(B2:B7=G4)),C2:C7))}				

Figure 11.18 *AND and OR criteria when an OR logical test is pointing at a single column.*

Using AND Criteria and OR Criteria in the Same Formula: OR Logical Test *Can* Get More Than One TRUE

Figure 11.19 shows a data set where you have three AND criteria, but the last AND criteria is an OR criteria:

- Net Assets > 100,000

AND

- Net Income >= 37,500

AND

- Rating 1 >= 3.5 OR Rating 2 >= 6

For any particular OR logical test, there Can be more than one TRUE. The OR logical test is pointing at multiple columns. Figure 11.19 shows formulas for counting, finding the maximum value, and calculating an average.

	A	B	C	D	E	F	G
1	Customer	Net Assets	Credit Rating 1	Credit Rating 2	Net Income	Helper	
2	J.K. LLC	85,024	4	6	31,267	FALSE	=AND(B2>$B$10,E2>$D$10,OR(C2>=$C$10,D2>=$C$12))
3	Fruits Inc.	111,104	3.5	9	73,346	TRUE	=AND(B3>$B$10,E3>$D$10,OR(C3>=$C$10,D3>=$C$12))
4	SW	89,236	2.4	7	65,334	FALSE	=AND(B4>$B$10,E4>$D$10,OR(C4>=$C$10,D4>=$C$12))
5	PCC	113,212	3	5	45,609	FALSE	=AND(B5>$B$10,E5>$D$10,OR(C5>=$C$10,D5>=$C$12))
6	Gigi's Inc.	100,000	1.4	1	34,550	FALSE	=AND(B6>$B$10,E6>$D$10,OR(C6>=$C$10,D6>=$C$12))
7	Fabulous Figs	159,800	4.3	6	43,500	TRUE	=AND(B7>$B$10,E7>$D$10,OR(C7>=$C$10,D7>=$C$12))
8							
9	Criteria:	Net Assets	Rating 1	Net Income			
10		100,000	3.5	37,500			
11			Rating 2				
12			6				
13	OR Criteria comes from 2 columns. A particular OR logical test CAN get two TRUEs.						
14	Extend Credit if: Net Assets >100,000 AND Net Income > 37,500 AND at least 1 credit rating hurdle equaled or surpassed.						
15	Count	2	[1] =COUNTIF(F2:F7,TRUE)				
16	Count	2	[2] {=SUM(IF(B2:B7>B10,IF(E2:E7>D10,IF((C2:C7>=C10)+(D2:D7>=C12),1)))))}				
17	Count	2	[3] =SUMPRODUCT(--(B2:B7>B10),--(E2:E7>D10),--((C2:C7>=C10)+(D2:D7>=C12)>0))				
18	Count	2	[4] {=SUM(IF((B2:B7>B10)*(E2:E7>D10)*((C2:C7>=C10)+(D2:D7>=C12)),1))}				
19	Max Net Assets	159,800	[5] {=MAX(IF((B2:B7>B10)*(E2:E7>D10)*((C2:C7>=C10)+(D2:D7>=C12)),B2:B7))}				
20	Ave Net Assets	135,452	[6] {=AVERAGE(IF((B2:B7>B10)*(E2:E7>D10)*((C2:C7>=C10)+(D2:D7>=C12)),B2:B7))}				

Figure 11.19 *AND and OR criteria when an OR logical test is pointing at multiple columns.*

As shown in Figure 11.19, this example shows a helper column solution that uses the AND and OR functions together. For counting, the helper column solution is fastest calculating. (In Chapter 15, you'll see that using a helper column with the AND and OR functions is a great option because it helps you significantly reduce formula calculation time.) If you cannot have a helper column, you can use Formulas [2], [3], or [4], which are all efficient for counting. Notice that for both the MAX and AVERAGE functions (Formulas [5] and [6]), you use the IF function to filter the values. Here's a close-up of the Boolean calculation that is in the logical_test argument for both the MAX and AVERAGE functions:

(B2:B7>B10)*(E2:E7>D10)*((C2:C7>=C10)+(D2:D7>=C12))

Notice that there are two multiplication symbols (for the AND criteria operators) and one addition operator (for the OR criteria operator). This sort of Boolean calculation structure for AND and OR criteria is common. You will see it in Chapter 15, when you learn about extracting data with formulas.

Filter, Advanced Filter, and PivotTables Can Handle OR Criteria

Remember that OR criteria can be enforced using Filter, Advanced Filter, and PivotTables. I don't show examples of these options here, but you should keep in mind that if formulas are not needed, you do have these quick-and-easy options. In essence, here is what each can do:

- For Filter, you simply check and uncheck the items you would like from the list of items. In Excel 2010 or later, you can use a slicer on an Excel table for OR criteria by holding down the Ctrl key and clicking the items.
- For Advanced Filter, you use the same rules as with D-functions for the criteria area: AND criteria is in the same row, and OR criteria is in different rows.

- PivotTables can be filtered with OR criteria from either the Filter option in the row and column headers or by dropping a field in the report filter or by using a slicer. You add OR criteria in a slicer by holding down the Ctrl key and clicking the items.

Array Formula Efficiency Rule 24

Boolean calculations that use AND and OR criteria are "filters" you use in formulas:

- **AND criteria:** For Boolean math AND criteria, you use multiplication so that any time a zero (FALSE) shows up, the end result will be zero, or FALSE. The only time an AND logical test can result in a TRUE is when all the logical tests are TRUE, or one.
- Here are the different Boolean filters you can use for AND criteria:
  - **Multiplication**: Zeros filter out the items that do not meet all criteria. The resultant array contains zeros. If zeros do not adversely affect the calculation, this method is great.

  - **Division**: #DIV/0 errors filter out the items that do not meet all criteria. The resultant array contains #DIV/0 errors. If #DIV/0 errors do not adversely affect the calculation, this method is great.

  - **IF function**: FALSE values filter out the items that do not meet all criteria. The resultant array contains FALSE values. If FALSE values do not adversely affect the calculation, this method is great.

- **OR criteria:** For Boolean math OR criteria, you use addition so that any time a nonzero number (TRUE) shows up, the end result will be the nonzero number, or TRUE. The only time an OR logical test can result in a FALSE is when all the logical tests are FALSE, or zero.
- OR logical tests have two situations:
  - For any particular OR logical test, there *cannot* be more than one TRUE. The OR logical test is pointing at a single column.

  - Boolean addition can be used for counting.

    - If you have many OR criteria, you can use the combination of ISNUMBER and MATCH functions.

  - For any particular OR logical test, there *can* be more than one TRUE. The OR logical test is pointing at a multiple columns.

    - For Boolean addition, you may have to amend the array calculation to account for the fact that you can get a count greater than one.

    - The IF function logical_test argument will interpret Boolean addition correctly because it considers any nonzero number to be TRUE.

- AND and OR criteria can be used in the same formula.

Chapter Summary

In this chapter you learned about Boolean calculations that use AND and OR criteria. Chapter 12 discusses the importance of choosing the correct function.

Chapter 12: When Is an Array Formula Really Needed?

Excel Files

To follow along with the examples in this chapter, you can download the accompanying files, as explained in the Introduction.

Selecting the Fastest-Calculating Function or Formula

When you create array formulas, the array operations in the array formulas can sometimes significantly increase formula calculation time. This short chapter looks at two examples of how choosing a non-array formula over an array formula can significantly reduce formula calculation time.

Counting Dates When Criteria Is Text: TEXT and SUMPRODUCT or COUNTIFS?

Figure 12.1 shows a data set with serial number dates shown in. The criteria for counting is given as a year (number) in cell E8 and month (text) in cell F8. The goal is to count how many dates fall within this month. The problem is that you have a data mismatch. The data in column A are serial number dates, and the criteria is a mix of number and text. Figure 12.1 shows five formula options you can use to accomplish the goal.

	A	B	C	D	E	F	G	H	I	J
1	Date	Sales	Helper							
2	10/27/12	$5,012	102012		< Helper Formula =MONTH(A2)&YEAR(A2)					
3	10/5/12	$6,523	102012							
4	12/28/11	$1,589	122011							
5	10/30/12	$2,489	102012							
6	10/25/11	$5,789	102011		Year & month criteria mismatched against serial number dates.					
7	11/26/11	$5,790	112011		Year	Month				
8	11/27/11	$5,791	112011		2012	Oct				
10	Count									
11	3	[1] =COUNTIF(C2:C8,MONTH(F8&1)&E8)								
12	3	[2] =COUNTIFS(A2:A8,">=1"&F8&E8,A2:A8,"<="&EOMONTH(1&F8&E8,0))								
13	3	[3] =COUNTIF(A2:A8,"<="&EOMONTH(1&F8&E8,0))-COUNTIF(A2:A8,"<"&1&F8&E8)								
14	3	[4] =SUMPRODUCT(--(MONTH(A2:A8)&YEAR(A2:A8)=MONTH(1&F8)&E8))								
15	3	[5] =SUMPRODUCT(--(TEXT(A2:A8,"mmmyyy")=F8&E8))								

Figure 12.1 *Counting serial number dates, given year (number) and month (text).*

Notes About the Formulas to Count Dates with Data Mismatch

The following table examines how each of the formulas in Figure 12.1 works.

Formula [1]:
=COUNTIF(C2:C8,MONTH(F8&1)&E8) and helper formula =MONTH(A2)&YEAR(A2)

- If you can afford the space, you can use an easy-to-create helper column formula and COUNTIF.

- The MONTH function takes a serial number and reports a number between 1 and 12.

- The YEAR function takes a serial number and reports the year.

- Date functions such as MONTH and EOMONTH understand a text month like Oct to be Oct 1 if you join the number 1 to it, as in either F8&1 or 1&F8.

- Helper column solutions usually calculate faster than other solutions.

Formula [2]: =COUNTIFS(A2:A8,">=1"&F8&E8,A2:A8,"<="&EOMONTH(1&F8&E8,0))

- If you have Excel 2007 or later, you can use the COUNTIFS and EOMONTH functions.

- You are given a year as a number and a month as text. This means you must create your own upper and lower dates so you can count between them.

- The first of the month always starts with 1, so you can create the lower date with this join operation: ">=1"&F8&E8. Join operations always create text, but this is not a problem for COUNTIFS because it understands dates as text.

- You use the EOMONTH function with a zero so that you get the end of the current month. EOMONTH is dynamic: It gets the 28th or 29th in February and the 30th or 31st in any other month.

- Because you need upper and lower dates, you need to create your own lower and upper dates so you can count the dates between and the lower and upper date values.

- This is usually the fastest calculating of the single-cell solutions.

Formula [3]:
=COUNTIF(A2:A8,"<="&EOMONTH(1&F8&E8,0))-COUNTIF(A2:A8,"<"&1&F8&E8)

- If you do not have Excel 2007 or later, you can use two COUNTIF functions for any BETWEEN criteria. For inclusive upper and lower values, the trick is to count all the values equal to or less than the upper value (using COUNTIF) and then subtract all the values less than the lower value (using COUNTIF).

- In Excel 2003 or earlier, you add EOMONTH by selecting Tools, Add-in, Data Analysis Toolpak.

- This formula is much faster that the two SUMPRODUCT solutions (Formulas [4] and [5]).

Formula [4]: =SUMPRODUCT(--(MONTH(A2:A8)&YEAR(A2:A8)=MONTH(1&F8)&E8))

- The MONTH and YEAR functions can extract year and month number data from serial numbers.

- The amazing thing about this formula is that even though it uses four functions, it is still much faster calculating than the TEXT and SUMPRODUCT combination (two functions).

- For situations where you can't use COUNTIF or COUNTIFS, such as for non-counting array formulas where you need an array of TRUEs and FALSEs or ones and zeros, this is faster calculating than the formula that uses SUMPRODUCT and TEXT.

Formula [5]: =SUMPRODUCT(--(TEXT(A2:A8,"mmmyyy")=F8&E8))

- The TEXT function is programmed to format numbers as text, given a custom number format. You can convert the entire column of serial numbers to text items in the form mmmyyy (which yields a three-letter month and a four-digit year).

- This is the slowest of the five formulas.

Timing Formulas to Count Dates with Data Mismatch

The file for these timing results is named 15-TEXTorCOUNTIF.xlsm, and it can be found in the Timing folder in the zipped files that accompany the book. To time your own formulas, see Chapter 2 for details. (Timing depends many factors, and your particular situation may have different timing results.)

Figure 12.2 and 12.3 show the anecdotal results I got from timing the formulas shown in Figure 12.1. Of particular note is the fact when you copy Formula [5] (which uses SUMPRODUCT and TEXT) to many cells, the timing differences between the fastest and slowest formulas increases significantly. This makes sense because the more cells that have slow formulas, the slower the overall spreadsheet will go.

	A	B	C	D	E	F	G	H
1	Date	Sales	Helper		Y	M	count	
2	3/14/11	$60	32011		2012	Oct	682	[1] =COUNTIF(C2:C25000,MONTH(F2&1)&E2)
3	12/10/11	$35	122011				682	[2] =COUNTIFS(A2:A25000,">=1"&F2&E2,A2:A25000,"<="&EOMONTH(1&F2&E2,0))
4	1/13/11	$31	12011				682	[3] =COUNTIF(A2:A25000,"<="&EOMONTH(1&F2&E2,0))-COUNTIF(A2:A25000,"<"&1&F2&E2)
5	7/7/11	$32	72011				682	[4] =SUMPRODUCT(--(MONTH(A2:A25000)&YEAR(A2:A25000)=MONTH(1&F2)&E2))
6	10/28/11	$12	102011				682	[5] =SUMPRODUCT(--(TEXT(A2:A25000,"mmmyyy")=F2&E2))
7	5/9/13	$77	52013					
8	3/8/12	$63	32012					25,000 rows. Time in seconds. Timing 1 cell.

	H	I	J	K	L	M
9		[1] COUNTIF Helper	[2] COUNTIFS & EOMONTH	[3] 2 COUNTIF & EOMONTH	[4] SP & MONTH & YEAR	[5] SP & TEXT
10	Time 1	0.00895	0.00883	0.01111	0.0371	0.05993
11	Time 2	0.00891	0.00914	0.01104	0.03875	0.04267
12	Time 3	0.00871	0.00868	0.01081	0.0293	0.04466
13	Ave	0.008856667	0.008883333	0.010986667	0.03505	0.049086667
14	% Change	0.00%	0.30%	24.05%	295.75%	454.23%
16	Ave			0.010986667	0.03505	0.049086667
17	% Change			0.00%	219.02%	346.78%

Remaining column A data:
	A	B	C
9	11/19/13	$21	112013
10	3/18/12	$46	32012
11	5/15/12	$64	52012
12	3/31/13	$23	32013
13	7/24/12	$71	72012
14	12/17/11	$65	122011
15	2/19/13	$97	22013
16	8/28/11	$91	82011
17	11/18/12	$17	112012

Figure 12.2 *The TEXT function for a date data mismatch can take a long time to calculate.*

	P	Q	R	S	T	U	V	W	X	Y	Z	AA	AB
10	[1] =COUNTIF($A$2:$A$25000,"<="&EOMONTH(1&Q$11&$P12,0))-COUNTIF($A$2:$A$25000,"<"&1&Q$11&$P12)												
11		Jan	Feb	Mar	Apr	May	Jun	Jul	Aug	Sep	Oct	Nov	Dec
12	2011	667	669	715	662	703	695	732	720	696	698	713	692
13	2012	760	633	744	687	714	677	719	677	690	682	680	676
14	2013	732	587	713	653	695	696	725	700	693	672	715	717
15													
16	[2] =SUMPRODUCT(--(TEXT($A$2:$A$25000,"mmmyyy")=Q$17&$P18))												
17		Jan	Feb	Mar	Apr	May	Jun	Jul	Aug	Sep	Oct	Nov	Dec
18	2011	667	669	715	662	703	695	732	720	696	698	713	692
19	2012	760	633	744	687	714	677	719	677	690	682	680	676
20	2013	732	587	713	653	695	696	725	700	693	672	715	717

22	25,000 rows. Time in seconds. Timing WHOLE TABLE of formulas.		
23		[1]	[2]
24	Time 1	0.15677	1.1271
25	Time 2	0.1562	1.12843
26	Time 3	0.1563	1.12492
27	Ave	0.156423	1.126817
28	% Change	0.00%	620.36%

Figure 12.3 *Many SUMPRODUCT and TEXT formulas = longer calculation time.*

The conclusion is that using a COUNTIF or COUNTIFS non-array formula can be much faster than using an alternative array formula.

> **Note:** If you have to create an array operation (as you might have to do in formulas that extract data), it pays to look at different function options. In the example here, you saw how using a MONTH and YEAR function combination is much faster than using a TEXT function solution.

Adding Yearly Sales with Year Criteria Mismatched Against Serial Dates: SUMPRODUCT, SUMIFS or SUMIF?

Figure 12.4 shows an example of a data mismatch with a year (number) matched against a column of serial number dates. Figure 12.4 shows six formula options that add the sales for the year. The syntax and calculation steps are similar to those in the formulas discussed in the last section. Notice that in Formulas [1] and [2], because the beginning and end days of the year (1/1 and 12/31) are always the same, you can hard code that criteria into the upper and lower dates.

	A	B	C	D	E	F
1	Date	Sales	Helper			
2	10/27/2012	306	2012		< Helper Formula =YEAR(A2)	
3	2/5/2011	530	2011			
4	6/28/2010	167	2010			
5	10/30/2012	639	2012		Criteria	
6	11/25/2010	635	2010		2012	
8	Add					
9	945			[1] =SUMIFS(B2:B6,A2:A6,">=1/1/"&E6,A2:A6,"<=12/31/"&E6)		
10	945			[2] =SUMIF(A2:A6,"<=12/31/"&E6,B2:B6)-SUMIF(A2:A6,"<1/1/"&E6,B2:B6)		
11	945			[3] =SUMIFS(B2:B6,C2:C6,E6)		
12	945			[4] =SUMIF(C2:C6,E6,B2:B6)		
13	945			[5] =SUMPRODUCT(--(YEAR(A2:A6)=E6),B2:B6)		
14	945			[6] {=SUM(IF(YEAR(A2:A6)=E6,B2:B6))}		

Figure 12.4 *Year needs to be matched against serial number dates.*

Timing Formulas to Add Yearly Sales with Year Criteria Mismatched Against Serial Dates

Figure 12.5 shows the anecdotal timing results of these formulas. The file for these timing results is named 16-SUMIForYEAR.xlsm, and it can be found in the Timing folder in the zipped files that accompany the book. The conclusion is that using a SUMIFS or SUMIF non-array formula can be much faster than using an alternative array formula.

	A	B	C	D	E	F	G	H	I	J	K	L
1	Date	Sales	Helper		Criteria	Count						
2	9/21/11	634	2011		2012	2957559	[1] =SUMIFS(B2:B25000,A2:A25000,">=1/1/"&E2,A2:A25000,"<=12/31/"&E2)					
3	12/9/14	838	2014			2957559	[2] =SUMIF(A2:A25000,"<=12/31/"&E2,B2:B25000)-SUMIF(A2:A25000,"<1/1/"&E2,B2:B25000)					
4	6/14/14	307	2014			2957559	[3] =SUMIFS(B2:B25000,C2:C25000,E2)					
5	9/14/13	812	2013			2957559	[4] =SUMIF(C2:C25000,E2,B2:B25000)					
6	6/17/13	704	2013			2957559	[5] =SUMPRODUCT(--(YEAR(A2:A25000)=E2),B2:B25000)					
7	9/1/12	93	2012			2957559	[6] {=SUM(IF(YEAR(A2:A25000)=E2,B2:B25000))}					
8	8/15/12	699	2012									
9	3/2/12	531	2012		25,000 rows. Time in seconds. Timing 1 cell.							
10	11/21/14	796	2014			[1] SUMIFS	[2] 2 SUMIF	[3] SUMIFS Helper	[4] SUMIF Helper	[5] SUMPRODUCT & YEAR	[6] SUM & YEAR	
11	5/7/14	235	2014		Time 1	0.00997	0.01162	0.01371	0.01381	0.02101	0.0216	
12	3/18/11	5	2011		Time 2	0.01025	0.01143	0.0139	0.01386	0.02007	0.02151	
13	8/1/14	202	2014		Time 3	0.01041	0.01153	0.01367	0.01395	0.02009	0.02083	
14	7/19/14	468	2014		Ave	0.01021	0.011526667	0.01376	0.013873333	0.02039	0.021313333	
15	1/22/13	491	2013		% Change	0.00%	12.90%	34.77%	35.88%	99.71%	108.75%	

Figure 12.5 *When adding with a year criteria mismatched against serial number dates, in Excel 2007 use SUMIFS, and in Excel 2003 or before use two SUMIF functions.*

Array Formula Efficiency Rule 25

Sometimes you can substitute non-array formulas for array formulas and significantly reduce formula calculation time. You can substitute COUNTIF or COUNTIFS for a SUMPRODUCT and TEXT function formula. You can also substitute the IF function for the IFERROR function. In both cases, you reduce formula calculation time.

Further, if you have to make an array calculation, selecting a particular function over another function may reduce formula calculation time. You can use the YEAR and MONTH functions over the TEXT function to reduce formula calculation time.

Chapter Summary

In this chapter you learned that sometimes you can substitute non-array formulas for array formulas and significantly reduce formula calculation time. In Chapter 13 you will learn about the INDEX and OFFSET functions, which can create dynamic ranges.

Chapter 13: Dynamic Ranges with the INDEX and OFFSET Functions

Excel Files

To follow along with the examples in this chapter, you can download the accompanying files, as explained in the Introduction.

Dynamic Ranges

An array is a collection of two or more items. A range is one example of an array. In this chapter you will learn about how to create a dynamic range using formulas.

A **dynamic range** is a range you can use in formulas, charts, PivotTables, and other locations that expect a range that can expand or contract when you add or delete source data or change based on some criteria as the formula that contains the range is copied down a column.

Figures 13.1 and 13.2 illustrate an expanding source data set. If you use a dynamic range inside the SUM function, the range A2:A4 will automatically expand to A2:A5 if a new number is added to the source data set.

	A	B	C	D
1	Numbers		Add	
2	2		9	< Formula =SUM(A2:A4)
3	3			
4	4			
5				

Figure 13.1 *SUM is looking at range A2:A4.*

	A	B	C	D
1	Numbers		Add	
2	2		19	< Formula =SUM(A2:A5)
3	3			
4	5			
5	9			

Figure 13.2 *Inside the SUM function, a dynamic range will automatically expand from A2:A4 to A2:A5 if new data is added.*

Figure 13.3 illustrates a second good use for dynamic ranges in formulas. You need the formula range inside the COUNTIF function to look at the numbers for only a given semester. In cell C5, you need the COUNTIF to look at the range B2:B5, but when you copy the formula down to C7, you need COUNTIF to be looking at the range B6:B7.

	A	B	C	D	E	F
1	Semester	Grades	# Greater than 2.5		Hurdle	
2	Fall - 2012	3.8			2.5	
3		3.6				
4		2.3				
5		2.6	3		< Formula =COUNTIF(B2:B5,">"&E$2)	
6	Win. - 201	2.1				
7		2.9	1		< Formula =COUNTIF(B6:B7,">"&E$2)	
8	Ave.	2.88333				

Figure 13.3 *As you copy the formula down the column, the range must change to be pointing only at numbers for the given semester.*

Creating Dynamic Ranges with Formulas

So how do you create dynamic ranges? You can use either the INDEX function or the OFFSET function to create dynamic ranges. I tend to use the INDEX function more often than OFFSET because OFFSET is a volatile function.

Volatile Functions

Volatile functions recalculate every time Excel recalculate the spreadsheet, even if the precedents (formula inputs) have not changed. Recalculation can be triggered by simple actions such as entering an item into a cell or inserting a new row. Volatile functions therefore increase formula calculation time. These are some of the actions that can trigger recalculation:

- Entering new data
- Deleting or inserting a row or column
- Performing certain AutoFilter actions
- Double-clicking a row or column divider
- Renaming a worksheet
- Changing the position of a worksheet in relation to other worksheets

The following are also volatile functions: CELL, INDIRECT, INFO, NOW, OFFSET, RAND, and TODAY.

If recalculation speed is not an issue (because you have small data sets, not many formulas, or don't care), the volatility of OFFSET is not a problem.

Using the Excel Table Feature to Create Dynamic Ranges

If you convert a proper data set to an Excel table, the ranges in the table are dynamic. This amazing feature was added in Excel 2003 and is great if you are going to have an expanding table of data. In Excel 2003 you can convert a proper data set using the keyboard Ctrl + L and in Excel 2007 or later you can use Ctrl + T. A number of limitations to this feature make dynamic ranges created with formulas useful. These are some of the limitations of Excel tables:

- Dynamic ranges like the one illustrated in Figure 13.3 cannot be created using an Excel table.
- Some formulas do not work in Excel tables (for example, =ROWS(A$1:A1)).
- You can't use the Subtotal feature in an Excel table.
- You can't use custom views in an Excel table.

This means it can be useful to learn how to create dynamic ranges with formulas.

INDEX: Formulas to Look Up a Column or Row

The most basic type of formula-created dynamic range is a formula that can look up an entire column or row of values (or items) based on a condition. You can use the INDEX function to do this. The INDEX function has three arguments:

=INDEX(array,row_num,column_num)

Normally, you can perform a two-way lookup by giving INDEX an array with rows and columns in the array argument, a row number in the row_num argument, and a column number in the column_num argument, and INDEX retrieves the intersection value. If your goal is to retrieve an entire column instead of the intersection item, you simply give the INDEX function a column number for the column_num argument and a zero or an empty value for the row_num argument. By leaving the row_num argument empty or zero, you are saying "get all the rows" in the selected column.

If your goal is to retrieve an entire row, you give the INDEX function a row number for the row_num argument and a zero or an empty value for the column_num argument. By leaving the column_num argument empty or zero, you are saying "get all the columns" in the selected row.

Figure 13.4 illustrates these formulas for looking up columns or rows. Since the goal of the formula is to add all the numbers from a column or row, you wrap the SUM function around INDEX.

	A	B	C	D	E	F	G	H	I
1	Lookup entire column. Feb = 1, 5, 3, 2.								
2	Jan	Feb	Mar				Month	Total	
3	2	1	2				Feb	11	< =SUM(INDEX(A3:C6,,MATCH(G3,A2:C2,0)))
4	5	5	2				Feb	11	< =SUM(INDEX(A3:C6,0,MATCH(G3,A2:C2,0)))
5	2	3	5						
6	4	2	4						
7									
8	Lookup the entire row. Feb = 1, 5, 3, 2.								
9	Jan	2	5	2	4		Month	Total	
10	Feb	1	5	3	2		Feb	11	< =SUM(INDEX(B9:E11,MATCH(G10,A9:A11,0),))
11	Mar	2	2	5	4		Feb	11	< =SUM(INDEX(B9:E11,MATCH(G10,A9:A11,0),0))

Figure 13.4 *If the condition is Feb, INDEX retrieves the range B3:B6 for the column lookup and B10:E10 for the row lookup.*

	A	B	C	D	E	F	G	H	I
1	Lookup entire column. Mar = 2, 2, 5, 4.								
2	Jan	Feb	Mar				Month	Total	
3	2	1	2				Mar	13	< =SUM(INDEX(A3:C6,,MATCH(G3,A2:C2,0)))
4	5	5	2				Mar	13	< =SUM(INDEX(A3:C6,0,MATCH(G3,A2:C2,0)))
5	2	3	5						
6	4	2	4						
8	Lookup the entire row. Mar = 2, 2, 5, 4.								
9	Jan	2	5	2	4		Month	Total	
10	Feb	1	5	3	2		Mar	13	< =SUM(INDEX(B9:E11,MATCH(G10,A9:A11,0),))
11	Mar	2	2	5	4		Mar	13	< =SUM(INDEX(B9:E11,MATCH(G10,A9:A11,0),0))

Figure 13.5 *If the condition is Mar, INDEX retrieves the range C3:C6 for the column lookup and B11:E11 for the row lookup.*

INDEX-Delivered Ranges Usually Do Not Require Ctrl+Shift+Enter

The INDEX function delivers a range, which is a type of array. However, most of the time you are not required to use Ctrl+Shift+Enter to enter the formula. If you put the range that is delivered by INDEX into another function, such as the SUM function, the formula does not require Ctrl+Shift+Enter. If you look back at Figures 13.4 and 13.5, you can see that the formulas do not require Ctrl+Shift+Enter because you performed no direct array operation. There are two exceptions:

- If you place a direct array operation that requires Ctrl+Shift+Enter into the formula, then you need to use Ctrl+Shift+Enter.

- If you want to deliver the multiple values to multiple cells, then you must use Ctrl+Shift+Enter.

Formulas for Dynamic Ranges to Handle Expanding and Contracting Ranges

Before you create a dynamic range formula, you must ask these questions about the range:

- Is it a vertical range (a column filled with rows)?
- Is it a horizontal range (a row filled with columns)?
- Is it a two-way range (with rows and columns)?
- Is it number data, text data, or mixed data?
- Are there empty cells?

The answers to these questions determine what sort of formula you might use. In most situations, you will have to use the lookup formula concept "lookup last." The following sections look at various formulas to determine the last row in a data set.

MATCH: Determining the Last Relative Position in a Data Set

Figure 13.6 shows four columns of different data types: The range A5:A10 contains mixed data with no empty cells before the last item; the range A16:A21 contains mixed data with empty cells before the last item; the range C5:C10 contains number data with empty cells before the last item; and the range C16:C21 contains text data with empty cells before the last item. In all four cases, in order to create a dynamic range with a formula that will expand and contract when you add or subtract data, you need to determine the last relative position in the column. (Note that many Excel users say "last row in the data set" imprecisely. To be clear, I say "last relative position" so that, for example, you don't say row 9 when you mean position 5 for the range A5:A10 in Figure 13.6.) Figure 13.6 shows six possible formulas.

The key lookup formula concept for Formulas [2] to [6] is that when you have a lookup value that is bigger than any value in the range and you do an approximate match (that is, leave the third argument in MATCH empty), you will always get the last relative position in the list, even if there are empty cells.

	A	B	C	D
1	Lookup last anything	Count "not empty" cells	Lookup last number	"Big Number" concept
2	5	[1] =COUNTA(A5:A10)	4	[3] =MATCH(9.99999999999999E+307,C5:C10)
3			4	[4] =MATCH(100,C5:C10)
4	No empty cells		Numbers	
5	text		43	
6	#DIV/0!			
7	43		56	
8	TRUE		2	
9	34			
10				
11				
12	Lookup last anything	Array operation "Not empty or Null Text String"	Lookup last text	"Big Text" concept
13	5	[2] {=MATCH(2,1/(A16:A21<>""))}	6	[5] =MATCH("Ω",C16:C21)
14			5	[6] =MATCH(REPT("z",255),C16:C21)
15	Mixed w Empty		Text	
16	#DIV/0!		Word 1	
17	43		Word 2	
18			Word 3	
19	TRUE			
20	Word 4		zzz	
21			Ω	

Figure 13.6 *Looking up the last row for various data types.*

Notes About the Formulas to Find Last Relative Position

The following table explains how the formulas in Figure 13.6 work.

Formula [1]: =COUNTA(A5:A10)
• This formula reports the last relative position for data sets that will *never* have empty cells before the last item in the list. COUNTA functions counts non-empty cells. This formula works on any type of data, even on null text strings that are delivered by formulas.
• If there is an empty cell before the last item in the list, this method will fail to deliver the correct answer.

Formula [2]: {=MATCH(2,1/(A16:A21<>""))}
• For mixed data when there are empty cells before the last item, you can use MATCH and a direct array operation.
• The array operation in the lookup_array argument of MATCH works like this: 1/(A16:A21<>"") ➔ 1/{#DIV/0!;TRUE;FALSE;TRUE;TRUE;FALSE} ➔ {#DIV/0!;1;#DIV/0!;1;1;#DIV/0!}
• Because the number 2 is bigger than any value in the array, the approximate match picks out the last number 1 and reports the 5 position.
• This formula requires Ctrl+Shift+Enter because the lookup_array argument of MATCH is not programmed to handle array operations. If any function argument that holds this MATCH formula element requires Ctrl+Shift+Enter, the formula also requires Ctrl+Shift+Enter.
• This formula works on any type of data, even on null text strings that are delivered by formulas.

Formula [3]: =MATCH(9.99999999999999E+307,C5:C10)
• This formula is for number data. By putting a number bigger than any number in the range and using an approximate match, you can get the position of the last number. The biggest number that Excel can handle is 9.99999999999999E+307 (that is, 15 significant digits). Using this number ensures that you will always get the last relative position in a range of numbers, even if there are empty cells.
• **Note:** I learned this "big number" trick from the Amazing Formula Master Aladin Akyurek, who has helped many times over the years at the MrExcel Message Board.

Formula [4]: =MATCH(100,C5:C10)
• You can use any "big number" that you would like, as long as it is *always* bigger than any number in the range. However, for consistency, it is efficient to use the number 9.99999999999999E+307, or something close, like 9.9E+307.

Formula [5]: =MATCH("Ω",C16:C21)
• This formula is for text data. This is the "big text" concept. If you give MATCH a lookup_value value that is bigger than anything in the range, it will always report that last relative position, even if there are empty cells. The last letter of the Greek alphabet is Ω, omega. Using this as a lookup_value yields the position of the last text item.
• To insert the omega character into the lookup_value argument of MATCH, hold down the Alt key and then press 2, then 3, then 4 on the number pad, in succession.
• This formula works on any type of data, even on null text strings, which are text items with zero length.

Formula [6]: =MATCH(REPT("z",255),C16:C21)
• This formula is for text data. Like Formula [5], it uses the "big text" concept. The REPT function repeats the letter *z* 255 times. Since there are no words with that many z letters, it can always get the last one. Why 255? Because the most characters that a lookup_value (in any lookup function) can handle is 255. This will not pick up the omega character, but it will pick up null text strings.

All the concepts you have just learned about for finding the last relative position in a column will work for finding the last relative position in a row also. Figure 13.7 shows an example of finding the position of the last number in a row.

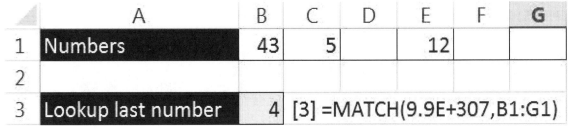

	A	B	C	D	E	F	G
1	Numbers	43	5		12		
2							
3	Lookup last number	4	[3] =MATCH(9.9E+307,B1:G1)				

Figure 13.7 *The last number is in relative position 4.*

INDEX and MATCH Functions: Retrieving the Last Item in a Range

Figures 13.8 and 13.9 show how to use the MATCH and INDEX functions to look up the last item in a range. These two figures show number and text data types in a vertical orientation, but if the data type or orientation were different, any of the MATCH function examples from the last section could be used inside the INDEX function to get the last item in a range.

	A	B	C	D	E	F
1	ID	Length	Cost		Last in column	
2	WI/i-5000	6.50"	$0.12		0.65	< =INDEX($C$2:$C$8,MATCH(9.9E+307,$C$2:$C$8))
3	BA/n-3964	4.25"	$0.09		Last in column	
4	VK/t-6164	7.00"	$0.35		EQ/y-7201	< =INDEX($A$2:$A$8,MATCH("Ω",$A$2:$A$8))
5	EQ/y-7201	3.75"	$0.65			
6						
7						
8						

Figure 13.8 *Using formulas to look up the last item in a range when there are four records.*

	A	B	C	D	E	F
1	ID	Length	Cost		Last in column	
2	WI/i-5000	6.50"	$0.12		$0.22	< =INDEX($C$2:$C$8,MATCH(9.9E+307,$C$2:$C$8))
3	BA/n-3964	4.25"	$0.09		Last in column	
4	VK/t-6164	7.00"	$0.35		IA/e-4588	< =INDEX($A$2:$A$8,MATCH("Ω",$A$2:$A$8))
5	EQ/y-7201	3.75"	$0.65			
6	RR/a-3207	2.00"	$0.45			
7	IA/e-4588	3.10"	$0.22			
8						

Figure 13.9 *Using formulas to look up the last item in a range when there are six records.*

Using INDEX and MATCH to Create Dynamic Ranges That Expand and Contract

As shown in Figure 13.10, you have a data validation drop-down list in cell E2 that is based on the text items in the range $A$2:$A$5 and a VLOOKUP formula in cell F2 that contains the lookup table from the range $A$2:$C$5.

	A	B	C	D	E	F	G
1	ID	Length	Cost		ID	Cost	
2	WI/i-5000	6.50"	$0.12		EQ/y-7201	0.65	< =VLOOKUP(E2,$A$2:$C$5,3,0)
3	BA/n-3964	4.25"	$0.	WI/i-5000			
4	VK/t-6164	7.00"	$0.	BA/n-3964 VK/t-6164			
5	EQ/y-7201	3.75"	$0.	EQ/y-7201			
6							

Figure 13.10 *Drop-down list and VLOOKUP formula.*

The problem with this setup is that if you add more data to the table, the data validation drop-down list and the lookup table in the VLOOKUP will not update. Currently, the last item in the Cost column is in cell $C$5. If you were to add a new record, the new last item in the Cost column would be in cell $C$6. This means the lookup table in the VLOOKUP would have to change from $A$2:$C$5 to $A$2:$C$6. Notice that both ranges start with the same cell reference: $A$2. If only there were a way to get the ending cell reference in a range to update when you added or deleted records. Well, there is a way: You can use the INDEX function to do a cell reference lookup.

You can accomplish a cell reference lookup by placing the INDEX function into the context of a cell reference. *Context* for a cell reference simply means that two cell references have a colon between them, like this: $A$2:$C$5. $A$2 and $C$5 alone are simply single-cell references. However, if you place a colon between them ($A$2:$C$5), they become beginning and ending cell references in a range.

A static range looks like this:

$A$2:$C$5

A dynamic range created with a formula looks like this:

$A$2:INDEX($C$2:$C$8,MATCH(9.99E+307,$C$2:$C$8))

Because the INDEX function sits behind a colon and a beginning cell reference, it will no longer retrieve the last item in the range; rather, it will retrieve the cell address (cell reference) of the last item in the range. To see this formula in action, create the formulas shown in cell E2 in Figure 13.11.

	A	B	C	D	E	F
1	ID	Length	Cost			
2	WI/i-5000	6.50"	$0.12		=$A$2:INDEX($C$2:$C$8,MATCH(9.99E+307,$C$2:$C$8))	
3	BA/n-3964	4.25"	$0.09			
4	VK/t-6164	7.00"	$0.35			
5	EQ/y-7201	3.75"	$0.65			
6						

Figure 13.11 *Context is everything: INDEX knows to retrieve the cell reference because it sits behind a colon and a beginning cell reference.*

To prove to that this formula really does create a dynamic range, you can evaluate different parts of the formula and see what results you get. Using Figures 13.12 to 13.17 as your guide, here is what you want to do:

- Figure 13.12: Highlight the INDEX formula element.
- Figure 13.13: Press F9 to evaluate INDEX to see that it returns just last item. This proves that INDEX normally returns that last item. Undo the evaluation with Ctrl+Z.
- Figure 13.14: Highlight the entire formula and evaluate this. Because INDEX is in the context of a cell reference, now the formula returns the entire table in array syntax. Undo the evaluation with Ctrl+Z.
- Figure 13.15: Enter the formula with Ctrl+Shift+Enter. Remember that this is an array of many items, and a single cell cannot display many items at once. Notice that it displays only the first item in the array. Also note that this is not the end use for the formula, so this is just one convenient way to store the formula until you do something else with it later.
- Figure 13.16 and 13.17: Run the Evaluate Formula feature (by pressing Alt, M, V) to see that, in fact, INDEX does return the cell reference $C$5.

`=$A$2:INDEX($C$2:$C$8,MATCH(9.99E+307,$C$2:$C$8))`

Figure 13.12 *Highlighting only the INDEX formula element.*

`=$A$2:0.65`

Figure 13.13 *INDEX alone retrieves the last item.*

`={"WI/i-5000",6.5,0.12;"BA/n-3964",4.25,0.09;"VK/t-6164",7,0.35;"EQ/y-7201",3.75,0.65}`

Figure 13.14 *The beginning cell reference, colon, and INDEX retrieve the entire range.*

E2	▼	⋮	✕ ✓	*fx*	{=$A$2:INDEX($C$2:$C$8,MATCH(9.99E+307,$C$2:$C$8))}

◢	A	B	C	D	E
1	ID	Length	Cost		
2	WI/i-5000	6.50"	$0.12		WI/i-5000

Figure 13.15 *You use Ctrl+Shift+Enter because there are multiple items.*

Evaluation:
`$A$2:INDEX($C$2:$C$8,4)`

Figure 13.16 *INDEX is in the context of a cell reference.*

Evaluation:
`$A$2:$C$5`

Figure 13.17 *Using INDEX to look up the cell reference.*

As shown in Figures 13.18 to 13.20, the formula accommodates adding or deleting records and even empty cells.

	A	B	C	D	E
1	ID	Length	Cost		
2	WI/i-5000	6.50"	$0.12		={"WI/i-5000",6.5,0.12; "BA/n-3964",4.25,0.09; "VK/t-6164",7,0.35;"EQ/y-7201",3.75,0.65;"RR/a-3207",2,0.45;"IA/e-4588",3.1,0.22}
3	BA/n-3964	4.25"	$0.09		
4	VK/t-6164	7.00"	$0.35		
5	EQ/y-7201	3.75"	$0.65		
6	RR/a-3207	2.00"	$0.45		
7	IA/e-4588	3.10"	$0.22		
8					

Figure 13.18 *The dynamic range formula works if you add records.*

	A	B	C	D	E	F	G
1	ID	Length	Cost				
2	WI/i-5000	6.50"	$0.12		={"WI/i-5000",6.5,0.12; "BA/n-3964",4.25,0.09}		
3	BA/n-3964	4.25"	$0.09				
4							

Figure 13.19 *The dynamic range formula works if you delete records.*

	A	B	C	D	E
1	ID	Length	Cost		
2	WI/i-5000	6.50"	$0.12		={"WI/i-5000",6.5,0.12; "BA/n-3964",4.25,0.09; "VK/t-6164",7,0.35;"EQ/y-7201",3.75,0.65;"RR/a-3207",2,0;"IA/e-4588",3.1,0.22}
3	BA/n-3964	4.25"	$0.09		
4	VK/t-6164	7.00"	$0.35		
5	EQ/y-7201	3.75"	$0.65		
6	RR/a-3207	2.00"			
7	IA/e-4588	3.10"	$0.22		
8					

Figure 13.20 *The dynamic range formula works if you have empty cells.*

Important Points to Consider for Dynamic Range Formulas

The following are some important points to consider when creating dynamic range formulas:

- Highlight enough rows to accommodate all potential records.
  - If your data set has numbers in the C column and will *never* have more than 50 records, use something like this:
    =$A$2:INDEX($C$2:$C$60,MATCH(9.99E+307,$C$2:$C$60)).

  - If your data set has numbers in the C column and will *never* have more than 500 records, use something like this:
    =$A$2:INDEX($C$2:$C$500,MATCH(9.99E+307,$C$2:$C$500)).

  - If your data set has numbers in the C column and you are not sure how many records there will be, you could use something like this:
    =$A$2:INDEX($C:$C,MATCH(9.99E+307,$C:$C)).

- Do not type extraneous data below your table in the ranges that your formulas are using because doing so can cause the formulas to create the incorrect range. For example, if your formula is using the potential range $C$2:$C$50, and the last bit of data that is part of the table is in cell C25, do not type a number in cell C49 because your formulas will then consider it the last number in the column.

Defined Name Dynamic Range Formulas

The formula you created for the dynamic range cannot be used directly to create a data validation drop-down list. If you try to use it, you get the error message "You may not use reference operators (such as unions, intersections, and ranges) or array constants for Data Validation criteria." This is not a problem because you can store the formula in a defined name and then use that defined name for the data validation drop-down list.

A few other aspects make defined names useful:

- Using defined names is helpful any time you have a dynamic range formula because a defined name can be used in many Excel locations, such as formulas, charts, PivotTables, VBA code, and other locations that expect a range or formula.

- If you create a defined name that contains a formula that requires Ctrl+Shift+Enter and then place that defined name in a cell formula, the formula will not require Ctrl+Shift+Enter (see Chapter 23).

The approach that I take in using formulas in defined names is to first create the formulas in the cells and then copy and paste the formulas into the defined name dialog box. I do it this way because it is much easier to create formulas in cells than it is to create formulas in the defined name dialog box. Figure 13.21 shows how you can create the formulas for the drop-down list and the lookup table in the cells.

	A	B	C	D	E	F	G	H
1	ID	Length	Cost		Table			
2	WI/i-5000	6.50"	$0.12		WI/i-5000	< {=$A$2:INDEX($C$2:$C$8,MATCH(9.99E+307,$C$2:$C$8))}		
3	BA/n-3964	4.25"	$0.09		Drop-down			
4	VK/t-6164	7.00"	$0.35		WI/i-5000	< {=$A$2:INDEX($A$2:$A$8,MATCH("Ω",$A$2:$A$8))}		
5	EQ/y-7201	3.75"	$0.65					
6					Select ID	Length	Cost	
7								
8								

Figure 13.21 *Creating dynamic range formulas in cells first.*

Once you have created the name for the drop-down list (cell E4), you can copy the formula in the cell in Edit mode. Now you are ready to paste it into the New Name dialog box.

You can open the New Name dialog box by pressing Ctrl+F3 and then click on the New button or by going to the Formulas Ribbon Tab, Defined Names group, click Name Manager button, click New button. In the New Name dialog box, shown in Figure 13.22, follow these steps:

1. Type a name without spaces in the Name text box.

2. Type a comment in the Comment text box.

3. Paste your formula into the Refers To text box.

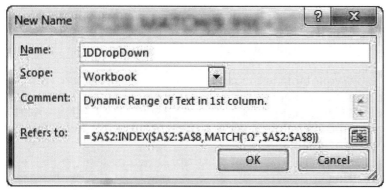

Figure 13.22 *A defined name dynamic range formula.*

Next you need to enter the defined name in the Data Validation dialog box (see Figure 13.23) by following these steps:

1. Select cell E7.

2. Open the Data Validation dialog box by pressing Alt, D, L.

3. Select List in the Allow text box.

4. Type an equal sign and the defined name into the Source text box.

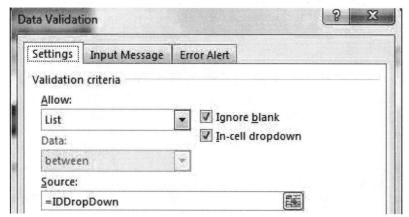

Figure 13.23 *Entering a defined name in the Data Validation dialog box.*

Now that you have a dynamic drop-down in cell E7, you need to create the dynamic VLOOK-UP formula in cell F7. You can either use the formula for the dynamic lookup table, as shown in Figure 13.24, or you can create a defined name for the dynamic lookup table and use that defined name in the formula. After you enter the formula in cell F7, you can copy it to cell G7.

	A	B	C	D	E	F	G	H
1	ID	Length	Cost		Table			
2	WI/i-5000	6.50"	$0.12		WI/i-5000	< {=$A$2:INDEX($C$2:$C$8,MATCH(9.99E+307,$C$2:$C$8))}		
3	BA/n-3964	4.25"	$0.09		Drop-down			
4	VK/t-6164	7.00"	$0.35		WI/i-5000	< {=$A$2:INDEX($A$2:$A$8,MATCH("Ω",$A$2:$A$8))}		
5	EQ/y-7201	3.75"	$0.65					
6					Select ID	Length	Cost	
7					WI/i-5000	=VLOOKUP($E7,$A$2:INDEX($C$2:$C$8,MATCH(9.99E+307,		
8						$C$2:$C$8)),COLUMNS($F$7:F7)+1,0)		
9						VLOOKUP(lookup_value, **table_array**, col_index_num, [range_lookup])		

Figure 13.24 *The table_array argument contains the dynamic range formula.*

With both of the dynamic range formulas in place for the drop-down list and VLOOKUP formula, you can test it. Figure 13.25 shows that if you add data, the drop-down list and VLOOKUP formula update perfectly. They also work if you delete data.

	A	B	C	D	E	F	G
1	ID	Length	Cost				
2	WI/i-5000	6.50"	$0.12				
3	BA/n-3964	4.25"	$0.09				
4	VK/t-6164	7.00"	$0.35				
5	EQ/y-7201	3.75"	$0.65				
6	RR/a-3207	2.00"			Select ID	Length	Cost
7	IA/e-4588	3.10"	$0.22		IA/e-4588	3.10"	$0.22
8					WI/i-5000		
9					BA/n-3964		
10					VK/t-6164		
					EQ/y-7201		
					RR/a-3207		
11					IA/e-4588		

Figure 13.25 *If you add or delete data, the dynamic formulas work perfectly!*

A Formula for a Dynamic Table When There Are Data Inconsistencies

In some cases you may have a data set that has an empty row or that has missing data in one or more of the columns, and you would still like to define a dynamic range with a formula that includes the last row of data. Figure 13.26 shows a data set that has missing data, and Figures 13.27 and 13.28 show two formulas that define the range $A$2:$C$6 despite the empty row and missing data.

	A	B	C
1	Date	Sales	Rep
2	3/14/2013	$259.00	JR
3	3/14/2013	$458.00	Quin
4	3/15/2013	$159.00	JR
5			
6		$513.00	
7			

Figure 13.26 *Missing data is not optimal. You need a formula to define the range $A$2:$C$6.*

`=$A$2:INDEX($C$2:$C$7,MAX((ROW($A$2:$C$7)-ROW($A$2)+1)*($A$2:$C$7<>"")))`

Figure 13.27 *This formula defines the range $A$2:$C$6. This dynamic range formula requires Ctrl+Shift+Enter if used in a cell formula. However, if you create a defined name that uses this formula and then use that defined name in a formula, the formula does not require Ctrl+Shift+Enter.*

`=$A$2:INDEX($C$2:$C$7,AGGREGATE(14,4,(ROW($A$2:$C$7)-ROW($A$2)+1)*($A$2:$C$7<>""),1))`

Figure 13.28 *This formula defines the range $A$2:$C$6. When you use AGGREGATE instead of MAX, any cell formula you use that accepts ranges does not require Ctrl+Shift+Enter.*

Let's consider an even more unusual situation. What if you had a rogue space in some cells below the data set? If you were concerned about this, you could add the TRIM function (which removes all spaces except for single spaces between words), as shown in Figure 13.29.

`=$A$2:INDEX($C$2:$C$7,MAX((ROW($A$2:$C$7)-ROW($A$2)+1)*(TRIM($A$2:$C$7)<>"")))`

Figure 13.29 *This formula defines a range even if there are rogue spaces below the data set.*

Notes About the Formula
=$A$2:INDEX($C$2:$C$7,MAX((ROW($A$2:$C$7)-ROW($A$2)+1)*(TRIM($A$2:$C$7)<>"")))

The following table steps through the calculation process used in the formula
=$A$2:INDEX($C$2:$C$7,MAX((ROW($A$2:$C$7)-ROW($A$2)+1)*(TRIM($A$2:$C$7)<>""))).

Impetus for Creating an Array Formula:
This formula creates a dynamic range even if there are empty cells, empty rows, or even spaces below the data set.
Calculation Notes:
1. =$A$2:INDEX($C$2:$C$7,MAX((ROW($A$2:$C$7)-ROW($A$2)+1)*(TRIM($A$2: $C$7)<>"")))
TRIM gets rid of any rogue spaces. It removes any spaces except single spaces between words.
2. =$A$2:INDEX($C$2:$C$7,MAX((ROW($A$2:$C$7)-ROW($A$2)+1)*({"41347","259","-JR";"41347","458","Quin";"41348","159","JR";"","345","";"","","";"","",""}<>"")))
The trimmed range is now asked the question "Are you not an empty cell or null text string?"
3. =$A$2:INDEX($C$2:$C$7,MAX((ROW($A$2:$C$7)-ROW($A$2)+1)*{TRUE,TRUE,TRUE;TRUE,TRUE,TRUE;TRUE,TRUE,TRUE;FALSE,TRUE,FALSE;FALSE,FALSE,FALSE;FALSE,-FALSE,FALSE}))
The formula element now calculates ((ROW($A$2:$C$7)-ROW($A$2)+1)). You have seen this before (in Chapter 8). This is an array formula element that creates an array of sequential numbers or relative positions.
4. =$A$2:INDEX($C$2:$C$7,MAX({1;2;3;4;5;6}*{TRUE,TRUE,TRUE;TRUE,TRUE,TRUE;TRUE,TRUE,TRUE;FALSE,TRUE,FALSE;FALSE,FALSE,FALSE;FALSE,FALSE,FALSE}))
Next you perform Boolean AND criteria. Notice that the first array is a vertical, or column, array filled with numbers in different rows (rows = semicolon), and the second array is a table array with both rows (semicolon) and columns (commas). When you multiply these, the numbers from the first array are distributed across the columns or in a row such as this: MAX({1;2;3;4;5;6}*{TRUE,TRUE,TRUE;TRUE,TRUE,TRUE;TRUE,TRUE,TRUE;FALSE,TRUE,-FALSE;FALSE,FALSE,FALSE;FALSE,FALSE,FALSE}) ➔ MAX({1,1,1;2,2,2;3,3,3;0,4,0;0,0,0;0,0,0 }+ ➔ 4
6. =$A$2:INDEX($C$2:$C$7,4) ➔ $A$2:$C$5

Using OFFSET to Create Dynamic Ranges

The OFFSET function can define a dynamic range. This function has five arguments:

=OFFSET(reference, rows, cols, height, width)

The following table describes these arguments:

Argument	Description
reference	Starting point: the cell or range in the upper-left corner of a range.
rows	How many rows up (minus number) or down (positive number) to move from the reference. Empty or 0 means to not move.
cols	How many columns left (minus number) or right (positive number) to move from the reference. Empty or 0 means to not move.
height	The height of the data set. When this argument is omitted, the data set is assumed to be the same height as a reference.
width	The width of the data set. When this argument is omitted, the data set is assumed to be same width as a reference.

Using the OFFSET function is quite straightforward: You tell OFFSET the starting point of the dynamic range (reference), how many cells you want to move away from the start position (rows and cols), and the height and width (height and width). Then OFFSET defines the range.

Figure 13.30 shows an OFFSET example which assumes that only numbers will be entered. There will be no empty cells before the last number, and you will not enter numbers past cell A10.

The dynamic range starts in cell $A$2 (the reference argument), it moves no rows up or down (the rows argument is empty), it moves no columns left or right (the cols argument is empty), the height is 2 (the height argument), and the width is 1 because the width argument is left empty and so it assumes the width of the reference.

	A	B	C	D	E
1	Weight		Dynamic Range		
2	174		=OFFSET($A$2,,,COUNT($A$2:$A$10))		
3	171		OFFSET(reference, rows, cols, [height], [width])		
4					

Figure 13.30 *OFFSET defines the range $A$2:$A$3.*

Using a Dynamic Range to Define a Table Within a Table: OFFSET or INDEX?

As shown in Figures 13.31, you have a data set with cities in the first column. Some cities are repeated because you have more than one representative in each city. You would like to create a dynamic range of rep names based on the city name in cell E2. If you have Seattle in cell E2, you need the formula to define the range $B$4:$B$6. If you have SF in cell E2, you need the formula to define the range $B$2:$B$3. This sort of formula could be used for a data validation drop-down list where you want the list of names to be based on a city name. Figures 13.31, 13.32, and 13.33 show three formulas that can accomplish this.

	A	B	C	D	E	F	G	H	I
1	Cities	Reps	Phone		Cities				
2	SF	K.C.	555-9912		Seattle	=OFFSET($B$1,MATCH($E$2,$A$2:$A$6,0),,			
3	SF	J.P.	555-6535			COUNTIF($A$2:$A$6,$E$2))			
4	Seattle	D.D.	555-1888			OFFSET(reference, rows, cols, [height], [width])			
5	Seattle	S.O.	555-7429						
6	Seattle	E.K.	555-8744						

Figure 13.31 *OFFSET, MATCH, and COUNTIF define the range $B$4:$B$6.*

```
=INDEX($B$2:$B$6,MATCH($E$2,$A$2:$A$6,0)):
INDEX($B$2:$B$6,MATCH(2,1/($A$2:$A$6=$E$2)))
INDEX(array, row_num, [column_num])
INDEX(reference, row_num, [column_num], [area_num])
```

Figure 13.32 *Two INDEX functions, two MATCH functions, and COUNTIF define the range $B$4:$B$6.*

```
=INDEX($B$2:$B$6,MATCH($E$2,$A$2:$A$6,0)):
INDEX($B$2:$B$6,MATCH($E$2,$A$2:$A$6,0)+
COUNTIF($A$2:$A$6,$E$2)-1)
INDEX(array, row_num, [column_num])
INDEX(reference, row_num, [column_num], [area_num])
```

Figure 13.33 *Two INDEX functions, two MATCH functions, and an array operation define the range $B$4:$B$6. The array operation will cause this formula to calculate more slowly than the one in Figure 13.32.*

Notes About the Formulas to Create a Dynamic Range for a Table Within a Table

The following table explains the formulas to create a dynamic range for a table within a table.

Formula [1]: =OFFSET($B$1,MATCH($E$2,$A$2:$A$6,0),,COUNTIF($A$2:$A$6,$E$2))
• The reference argument means the range starts at cell $B$1.
• MATCH finds the relative position of Seattle in the range A2:A6, which is 3. Because 3 sits in the rows argument, you add 3 rows to the start cell $B$1 to get $B$4. The new start cell for the range is cell $B$4.
• The cols argument is empty, so you neither add nor subtract columns from cell $B$4.
• COUNTIF counts 3 Seattle items in the range A2:A6. Because 3 sits in the height argument, the height of the dynamic range will be 3.
• The width argument is empty, and so the dynamic range will be the same width as the range in the reference argument, which is 1 column.
• The dynamic range defined is $B$4:$B$6 when cell E2 contains Seattle and $B$2:$B$3 when it is SF.

Formula [2]: =INDEX($B$2:$B$6,MATCH($E$2,$A$2:$A$6,0)):INDEX($B$2:$B$6,-MATCH($E$2,$A$2:$A$6,0)+COUNTIF($A$2:$A$6,$E$2)-1)
• This dynamic range formula uses INDEX to find the start and ending cell references for the range.
• The formula element **INDEX($B$2:$B$6,MATCH($E$2,$A$2:$A$6,0))** gets the cell reference **$B$4**.
• The formula becomes **=$B$4:INDEX($B$2:$B$6,MATCH($E$2,$A$2:$A$6,0)+COUNTIF($A$2:$A$6,$E$2)-1)**.
• Here is how the formula element **MATCH($E$2,$A$2:$A$6,0)+COUNTIF($A$2:$A$6,$E$2)-1** calculates: MATCH($E$2,$A$2:$A$6,0)+COUNTIF($A$2:$A$6,$E$2)-1 ➜ =3+COUNTIF($A$2:$A$6,$E$2)-1 ➜ 3+3-1 = 5.
• The formula becomes **=$B$4:INDEX($B$2:$B$6,5)**.
• The formula becomes **$B$4:$B$6**.

Formula [3]: =INDEX($B$2:$B$6,MATCH($E$2,$A$2:$A$6,0)):INDEX($B$2:$B$6,MATCH(2,1/($A$2:$A$6=$E$2)))
• This formula is similar to the last formula except that instead of using the combination of MATCH and COUNTIF to determine the last position of the word Seattle, this formula uses an array operation to determine the last position of the word Seattle.
• This formula element has an array operation in it: **INDEX($B$2:$B$6,MATCH(2,1/($A$2:$A$6=$E$2)))**.
• MATCH and the array operation are calculated this way: MATCH(2,1/($A$2:$A$6="Seattle")) ➜ MATCH(2,1/{FALSE;FALSE;TRUE;TRUE;TRUE}) ➜ MATCH(2,{#DIV/0!;#DIV/0!;1;1;1}) ➜ 5
• The formula becomes **=$B$4:INDEX($B$2:$B$6,5)**.
• The formula becomes **$B$4:$B$6**.

Comparing OFFSET and INDEX for Creating Dynamic Ranges

OFFSET is a volatile function, and INDEX is not. If volatility is not important in a particular case, which one you use really is a matter of preference. Whereas the OFFSET function creates the dynamic range with inputs that define the staring position and the size of the range, INDEX creates the dynamic range by looking up cell references or row and column reference.

Charts with Defined Name Dynamic Range Formulas

A great use for dynamic range formulas is making charts. For example, if you have a data set where data is being added, it might be convenient to have the new data automatically added to the chart. Another example would be to plot a different set of numbers, based on criteria from a cell. In both of these cases, these are the steps to create a dynamic range for the chart:

1. Create the dynamic range formula.

2. Create a defined name that uses the dynamic range formula.

3. Create the chart.

4. Insert the defined names into the chart.

You'll see how to do this next.

Figure 13.34 shows the data set. The goal is to plot the sales numbers and sales rep names on a column chart based in the city name in cell F1. If cell F1 contains Seattle, you want just the names and numbers for Seattle, and if cell F1 contains SF, you want just the names and numbers for SF. Cell A8 contains the dynamic range formulas for the sales range, and cell A9 contains the dynamic range formulas for the reps range. (I created one with OFFSET and one with INDEX just for illustration purposes. You can choose whichever you prefer.) You will use the dynamic formula for the rep range for the horizontal axis, and you will use the sales range for the column heights.

Next, you need to create two defined names. Figures 13.35 shows one of the defined names being created in the Edit Name dialog box.

	A	B	C	D	E	F	G	H	I	J	K
1	Cities	Reps	Sales		Cities	Seattle					
2	SF	K.C.	$5,735.00								
3	SF	J.P.	$5,662.00								
4	Seattle	D.D.	$1,798.00								
5	Seattle	S.O.	$2,447.00								
6	Seattle	E.K.	$1,795.00								
8	1798	Sales Range: {=OFFSET($C$1,MATCH($F$1,$A$2:$A$6,0),,COUNTIF($A$2:$A$6,$F$1))}									
9	D.D.	Reps Range {=INDEX($B$2:$B$6,MATCH($F$1,$A$2:$A$6,0)):INDEX($B$2:$B$6,									
10						MATCH($F$1,$A$2:$A$6,0)+COUNTIF($A$2:$A$6,$F$1)-1)}					

Figure 13.34 *Creating dynamic range formulas.*

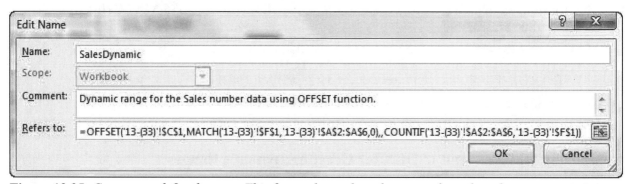

Figure 13.35 *Create two defined names. This figure shows the sales range formula only.*

After you create the first name, create the second defined name and call it RepsDynamic.

Before you can use the two defined names, you must make a chart that is based on the cell values. Figure 13.36 shows a basic column chart created from the values in B1:C6.

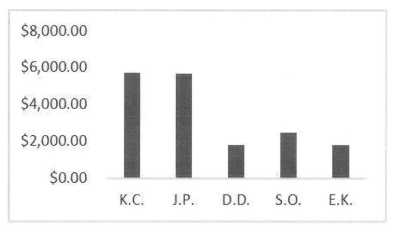

Figure 13.36 *Creating a chart based on values in cells.*

Next, you need to replace the cell ranges in the chart with the dynamic range defined name formulas. To do this, click the chart and then in the Chart Tools section of the Design Ribbon tab, click the Select Data button. Next, select the Sales series on the left and click the Edit button, as shown in Figure 13.37.

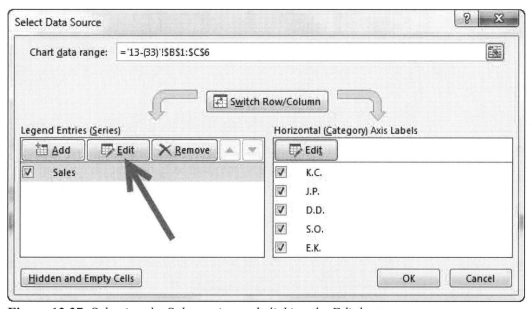

Figure 13.37 *Selecting the Sales series and clicking the Edit button.*

The next step in the process is the most important. As shown in Figure 13.38, you must highlight only the cell range in the Series Values text box. Do not highlight the sheet reference. This means that if you see this:

='13-(33)'!$C$2:$C$6

You must highlight only this part (**bold part**):

='13-(33)'!**$C$2:$C$6**

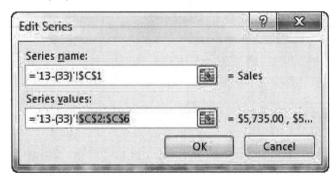

Figure 13.38 *Highlighting only the cell range in the Series Values text box.*

After you highlight only the cell range in the Series Values text box, press the Delete key to delete the cell range and then type the defined name as, shown in Figure 13.39. Make sure to *not* delete the exclamation point. Then click OK.

Figure 13.39 *After deleting the cell range, type the defined name.*

After you click OK, a strange thing happens. The sheet reference and defined name convert into a workbook reference and a defined name (unless you have set the scope to workbook for your defined name). This is supposed to happen, so don't worry. Click the Edit button to see that this conversion has occurred.

Edit Series

=CtrlShiftEnterBookFinishedFile.xlsm!SalesDynamic

Figure 13.40 *After you create a sheet reference and defined name, it converts to a workbook reference and defined name.*

Next, using the same steps you just used in Figures 13.38 to 13.40, insert the second defined name, RepsDynamic, into the chart. Here is how you do it:

1. Open the Select Data Source dialog box.

2. On the right, click the Edit button for the horizontal (category) axis labels.

3. Highlight the cell range in the Axis Label Range text box. Do not highlight the sheet reference. Do not highlight the exclamation point. Then press Delete.

4. Insert the defined name RepsDynamic after the sheet reference and click OK.

As shown in Figures 13.40 and 13.42, you can test the chart by changing the city name in cell F1.

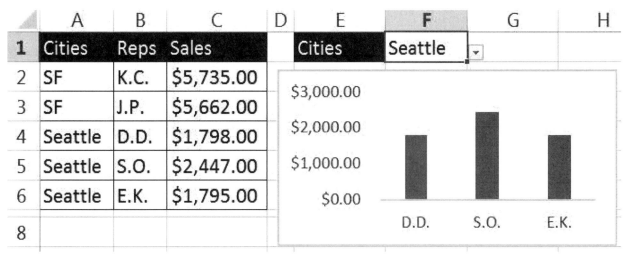

Figure 13.41 *When you select Seattle, only the names and numbers for Seattle show.*

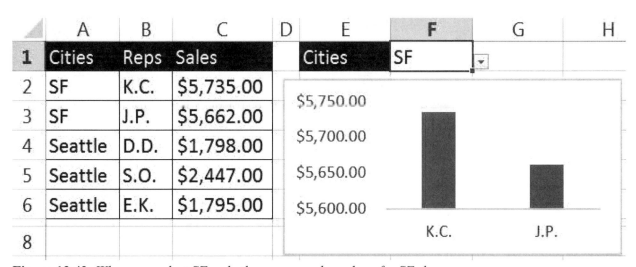

Figure 13.42 *When you select SF, only the names and numbers for SF show.*

Using a PivotTable to Create a Dynamic Chart

Using a PivotTable with a slicer and a chart is a great alternative for a dynamic chart. Here are the basic steps in using this solution:

1. Create a PivotTable.

2. Insert a slicer. (In Excel 2010 use the PivotTable Tools Option Ribbon tab; in Excel 2013 use the PivotTable Tools Analyze Ribbon tab).

3. Click in a single cell in the PivotTable and press Alt+F1 to create default chart.

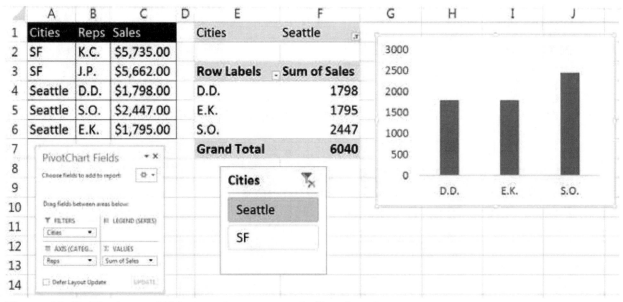

Figure 13.43 *The Report Filter or a slicer can easily filter this chart.*

Using a Dynamic Range to Always Get the Last Five Numbers in a Column

Figure 13.44 shows a column with numbers. In this section, you want to create a formula that will always add the last five entries. As you have previously learned how to do, you can create a dynamic range that uses the INDEX and MATCH functions to look up the last cell reference in a column that contains a number. Look at Figure 13.44. You can see that Formula [1] uses this tactic to look up the ending cell reference.

For the staring cell reference, all you have to do is subtract 4 from the relative position of the last number, and the formula is done. However, Formula [1] will treat cell A6 (empty) as part of the last five numbers. If this is not what you want, then you can use Formula [2] rather than Formula [1].

Formula [2] requires Ctrl+Shift+Enter because the IF function in the formula has an array operation that requires Ctrl+Shift+Enter, no matter what other functions is housing it. If you want to create a formula that does not require Ctrl+Shift+Enter, you can create a defined name to store the formula and then use the defined name in the formula rather than using the actual formula. When you do this, the formula does not require Ctrl+Shift+Enter. If you create the defined name LastFive for Formula [2], as shown in Figure 13.45, the formula does not require Ctrl+Shift+Enter.

	A	B	C	D	E
1	Numbers	Last?			
2	1		5		
3	2				
4	2	Include empty			
5	1		5	[1]	=SUM(INDEX($A$2:$A$10,MATCH(9.99E+307,$A$2:$A$10)-$C$2+1)
6		Exclude empty			:INDEX($A$2:$A$10,MATCH(9.99E+307,$A$2:$A$10)))
7	1		7	[2]	{=SUM(INDEX($A$2:$A$10,
8	1				LARGE(IF(ISNUMBER($A$2:$A$10),ROW($A$2:$A$10)-ROW($A$2)+1),$C$2))
9					:INDEX($A$2:$A$10,MATCH(9.99E+307,$A$2:$A$10))))}

Figure 13.44 *Formulas to add the last five numbers in a column.*

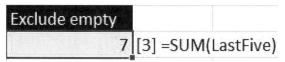

Figure 13.45 *A formula to add the last five numbers in a column.*

Notes About the Formula
LARGE(IF(ISNUMBER($A$2:$A$10),ROW($A$2:$A$10)-ROW($A$2)+1),$C$2)

The following table explains the LARGE function formula element for Formula [2].

Impetus for Creating an Array Formula:
This formula element has to pick up the relative position of the fifth-to-last number in the list and not be influenced by empty cells.
Calculation Notes:
LARGE(IF(ISNUMBER($A$2:$A$10),ROW($A$2:$A$10)-ROW($A$2)+1),$C$2)
Inside the LARGE function you need to create an array of all the relative positions that are associated with cells that have numbers. To accomplish this, you use the IF and ISNUMBER functions and the formula element that creates an array of all the relative positions: LARGE(IF(ISNUMBER($A$2:$A$10),ROW($A$2:$A$10)-ROW($A$2)+1),$C$2) ➔ LARGE(IF({TRUE;TRUE;TRUE;TRUE;FALSE;TRUE;TRUE;FALSE;FALSE},ROW($A$2:$A$10)-ROW($A$2)+1),$C$2) ➔ LARGE({1;2;3;4;FALSE;6;7;FALSE;FALSE},5) ➔ 2 INDEX then uses this 2 to look up the start cell reference for the dynamic range.

Using a Dynamic Range to Pick Up Only Values Entered Since the Last Text Entry in the First Column

Figure 13.46 shows a data set with quarters and grade. In cell C4 you want a single formula that you can copy down to count the number of grades for the quarter that are greater than 2.5. You can use the COUNTIF function for this, but the range that the COUNTIF will be pointing to will be changing as you copy the formula down. Looking at the Quarter column (column A), you can see that you need the range to change every time the new quarter comes up. If you combine the "lookup last text item" trick with an expandable range, you can create the dynamic range you need. Figure 13.46 shows the formula you can enter in cell C4 and copy down the column.

> **Note:** The range argument in COUNTIF cannot handle array operations (see Chapter 10). Because the INDEX formula creates a range and does not contain a direct array operation, the range argument in COUNTIF can handle the IN-DEX-produced range.

⊿	A	B	C	D
1		Hurdle	2.5	
3	Quarter	Grades	Count of Grades > 2.5	
4	Fall-12	3.8		=IF(A5<>"",COUNTIF(INDEX($B$3:B4,MATCH("Ω",$A$3:A4)):B4,">"&$C$1),"")
5		3.6		
6		2.3		
7		2.6	3	
8	Win-12	2.1		
9		2.9	1	
10	Spr-12	3		
11		2.9		
12		2.1	2	
13	Sum-12	2.4		
14		1.4		
15		3.8	1	
16	Ave.	2.742		

Figure 13.46 *Using a dynamic range to pick up only values entered since the last text entry in the first column.*

Notes for the Formula from Cell C9:
=IF(A10<>"",COUNTIF(INDEX($B$3:B9,MATCH("Ω",$A$3:A9)):B9,">"&$C$1),"")

The following table explains how this formula calculates.

Impetus for Creating an Array Formula:
You need a dynamic range that will pick up only values entered since the last text entry in column A.
Calculation Notes for the Formula from Cell C9:
1. =IF(A10<>"",COUNTIF(INDEX($B$3:B9,MATCH("Ω",$A$3:A9)):B9,">"&$C$1),"")
Notice the expandable ranges in this formula: $B$3:B9 and $A$3:A9. The formula element MATCH("Ω",$A$3:A9) delivers the relative position 6, which is the relative position of the text Win-12 in the range $A$3:A9.
2. =IF(A10<>"",COUNTIF(INDEX($B$3:B9,6):B9,">"&$C$1),"")
The formula element INDEX($B$3:B9,6) retrieves the cell reference B8.
3. =IF(A10<>"",COUNTIF(B8:B9,">"&$C$1),"")
4. =IF(A10<>"",COUNTIF(B8:B9,">2.5"),"")
5. =IF(A10<>"",1,"")
Because A10 is *not* empty, IF delivers a 1 to the cell.
The formula result in cell C9 is 1.

Array Formula Efficiency Rule 26

Consider the following about dynamic range formulas:

- A dynamic range is a range that you can use in a formula, chart, PivotTable, and so on that can expand or contract or change based on a set of criteria.

- You can use the INDEX function to create dynamic ranges:
    - INDEX can look up a row or column.

        - A zero or an omitted value in the row_num argument of INDEX tells the function to look up all the rows of a column.

        - A zero or an omitted value in the column_num argument of INDEX tells the function to look up all the columns of a row.

    - INDEX can be used to look up a cell reference. If you place the INDEX function in the context of a range of cells (before or after a colon), INDEX will look up a cell reference rather than the cell content.

    - The output from INDEX is a range, so even though evaluating it will show array syntax, it is a range that can be used in functions that expect a range, without requiring Ctrl+Shift+Enter.

- You can use the OFFSET function to create dynamic ranges:
    - OFFSET has five arguments:

        - Reference: This is the starting point for the cell or range (usually the upper-left corner of the range).

        - Rows: How many rows up (minus number) or down (positive number) you want to move from the reference. Empty or 0 means to not move.

        - Cols: How many columns left (minus number) or right (positive number) you want to move from the reference. Empty or 0 means to not move.

        - Height: The height of the data set. When this argument is omitted, the data set is assumed to be the same height as a reference.

        - Width: The width of the data set. When this argument is omitted, the data set is assumed to be same width as a reference

    - OFFSET is a volatile function that recalculates at each recalculation (like using the Enter key or inserting a row).

- Defined names are useful for storing dynamic range formulas:
    - Defined names are useful any time you have a dynamic range formula because they can be used in many Excel locations, such as formulas, charts, PivotTables, VBA code, and other locations that expect a range.

    - If you create a defined name that contains a formula that requires Ctrl+Shift+Enter and then place that defined name in a cell formula, the formula will not require Ctrl+-Shift+Enter.

Chapter Summary

In this chapter you learned about creating dynamic range formulas. Chapter 14 summarizes all the Array Formula Efficiency Rules that you have learned through the first 13 chapters.

Chapter 14: Array Formula Efficiency Rules

Excel Files

To follow along with the examples in this chapter, you can download the accompanying files, as explained in the Introduction.

Where You Have Been and Where You Are Going

This chapter presents the first 26 Array Formula Efficiency Rules that you have learned about through the first 13 chapters. Rules 27, 28 and 29 will be presented later in the book. However, it will be helpful at this point in the book to review what you have learned so far before moving on to the advanced topics in chapters 15 through 23. These Array Formula Efficiency Rules are guidelines for building array formulas and will serve as the nuts and bolts of what you need to know to make most any array formula that you can dream up.

Array Formula Efficiency Rule 1

In order to be proficient with creating formulas solutions, you must know the following:

- Excel's Golden Rule (if a formula input can change put it into a cell and refer to it with a cell reference)
- The formula elements
- The math and comparative operators
- The types of formulas
- Excel's order of precedence for calculating formulas
- Number formatting principles
- Excel's default alignment for data

See Chapter 1 or Video 1 on the *Ctrl+Shift+Enter: Mastering Excel Array Formulas* DVD.

Array Formula Efficiency Rule 2

An *array* is a collection of two or more items. See Chapter 2.

Array Formula Efficiency Rule 3

There are three types of arrays in Excel:

- A **reference array** contains more than one cell. Examples include a range of cells, a worksheet reference, and a defined name.
- An **array created by a formula element**, also called a *resultant array*, is an array of items created by the array operation.
- An **array constant** is an array of values hard coded into a formula.

See Chapter 2.

Array Formula Efficiency Rule 4

An *array formula* is a formula that contains an operation (math, comparative, join, or function argument) on an array of items rather than on single items, and, the operation delivers a resultant array of items rather than a single item. This operation is called an *array operation* and is distinguish from an *aggregate operation*, which delivers a single item. The resultant array of items (also called an array created by a formula element) can be used as a formula element in a larger formula, or it can be the final answer that the array formula delivers to a range of cells. The final answer from an array formula can either be a single item or an array of items.

See Chapter 2 and Chapter 8.

Array Formula Efficiency Rule 5

You can use the Evaluate Formula Element trick to see what a formula element evaluates to before you enter the formula into the cell by following these steps:

1. Select the formula element.

2. Press F9.

3. Look at the resultant array and check to see if the formula creation is on the right track, and.

4. Press Ctrl+Z to undo the evaluation.

See Chapter 2.

Array Formula Efficiency Rule 6

Whenever you have a column of calculations and you either don't care about all the individual calculations or you can't afford the spreadsheet real estate, it is almost certainly possible to just do away with the column of calculations and instead create an array calculation in a single cell. The caveat is that you must also consider formula calculation time for single-cell calculations. See Chapter 2.

Array Formula Efficiency Rule 7

If you have a choice between two equally efficient array formulas and one requires Ctrl+-Shift+Enter and one does not, you should choose the one that does not require Ctrl+Shift+Enter. A formula that does not require Ctrl+Shift+Enter does not run the risk of getting a #VALUE! or implicit intersection error. See Chapter 2.

Array Formula Efficiency Rule 8

We can formalize the rules for entering an array formula into a cell like this:

*   If the function argument does not innately handle array operations and you give it an array operation, you must enter the formula with Ctrl+Shift+Enter. The MAX function number1 argument is an example of an argument that does not innately handle array operations, and therefore you need to press Ctrl+Shift+Enter when you place an array operation in the number1 argument. The SUMPRODUCT array1 argument is an example of a function that *does* innately handle array operations and therefore does *not* require you to press Ctrl+Shift+Enter when you place an array operation into the array1 argument. (See Chapter 2.)

*   After you enter a formula with Ctrl+Shift+Enter, Excel places curly braces at the beginning and end of the formula. If you try to type in these curly braces, they will appear as text, not as part of an array formula. (See Chapter 2.)

- If you don't use Ctrl+Shift+Enter for a formula that requires it, you will get a #VALUE! error or a potentially incorrect answer from implicit intersection. (See Chapter 2.)
- Several caveats are discussed in later chapters:

Array constants usually do not require Ctrl+Shift+Enter (see Chapter 7).

IF function array calculations always require Ctrl+Shift+Enter (see Chapters 4 and 10).

Defined names that contain array operations do not require Ctrl+Shift+Enter (see Chapters 13 and 23).

Array Formula Efficiency Rule 9

Points to think about if you are trying to decide between a single-cell formula or a helper column that contains a multistep solution:

- Use a helper column or a multistep solution when you want to see all the detail and can afford the real estate.
- Use a single-cell formula to save spreadsheet real estate and when you don't care about all the detail.
- Sometimes helper column solutions calculate more quickly than single-cell array formulas.

See Chapters 2 and 15.

Array Formula Efficiency Rule 10

After you have created a multistep solution with different formulas in different cells, a useful trick for creating your own single-cell array formulas is to start in the final result cell and move backward through the multistep solution. You can also do this in the opposite direction, starting in the first cell and working your way forward though the multistep solution. See Chapters 3 and 18.

Array Formula Efficiency Rule 11

An array calculation that uses an operator can be structured in three possible ways:

Array, operator, array
Array, operator, single item
Single item, operator, array

See Chapter 3.

Array Formula Efficiency Rule 12

Consider using D-functions as an alternative to array formulas if you have a proper data set with field names and you do not need to copy your formula down a column or across a row. The advantage of using D-functions is that they are easy to create and calculate formulas more quickly than most comparable array formulas. Using a D-function in combination with a data table is a workaround if you want a formula that you can copy down a column or across a row.

See Chapters 4 and 11 and 21.

Array Formula Efficiency Rule 13

Consider using PivotTables as an alternative to array formulas. Think about the following advantages and disadvantages:

- Advantages of PivotTables: Easy to create, especially if there are multiple criteria, and easy to change.
- Disadvantages of PivotTables: Do not update instantly (refreshing is easy, though), only 11 functions, and formatting is limited.
- Advantages of array formulas: Instantly update when data changes and give you access to hundreds of functions.

See Chapters 4 and 13.

Array Formula Efficiency Rule 14

IF Function Ctrl+Shift+Enter Trump Rule:

If you have an array operation in the IF function, the formula requires Ctrl+Shift+Enter, regardless of where the IF function sits in the larger formula. This means that even if you put an IF function that contains an array operation into a function argument that can handle array operations (like the array arguments in the AGGREGATE or SUMPRODUCT functions), the formula will still require Ctrl+Shift+Enter. In some cases, rather than use the IF function with an array operation in a function argument that does not require Ctrl+Shift+Enter, it may be less ambiguous to not use the IF function and instead find an alternative formula.

See Chapters 4, 10, 17.

Array Formula Efficiency Rule 15

You can filter values inside a formula with the IF function or with Boolean math:

- From Chapter 4, this is an example of filtering values using the IF function: =MAX(IF($A$3:$A$12=$F$2,IF($B$3:$B$12=E5,$C$3:$C$12))).
- From Chapter 4, this is an example of filtering values using Boolean math: =AGGREGATE(15,6,$C$3:$C$13/(($A$3:$A$13<>$F$2)*($B$3:$B$13=E5)),1).

See Chapters 4, 9, 10, 11, and 15.

Array Formula Efficiency Rule 16

The following five function arguments can handle arrays without requiring you to enter the array formula with Ctrl+Shift+Enter:

- The array_1, array_2, etc. arguments in SUMPRODUCT
- The lookup_vector argument in the LOOKUP function
- The result_vector argument in the LOOKUP function
- The array argument in INDEX
- The array argument in AGGREGATE for functions 14 to 19

See Chapters 2, 3, 4, 5, 10, and 15.

Array Formula Efficiency Rule 17

Remember the following about function argument array operations:

- If you use a single item with a function argument that expects a single item, the function will deliver a single answer.

- If you use more than one item with a function argument that expects a single item, the function will deliver more than one answer. Specifically, if you give the function argument *n* items, the function will deliver *n* answers.

- When a function argument is expecting a single item and you give it more than one item, you create a function argument array operation.

Array Formula Efficiency Rule 18

Rules for array constants:

- Array constants can be used in array formulas and non-array formulas.

- The following array syntax rules apply:

  - Curly braces house the array: one at the beginning and one at the end.

  - A semicolon means go down a row.

  - A comma means go over a column.

  - Text items are contained in double quotes.

  - Numbers, logical values, and error values are not contained in a pair of double quotes.

  - The three types of array constants are column (vertical), row (horizontal), and table (two-way).

- Array constants are limited by the number of characters allowed in a formula (8,192).

- For array formulas:

  - If the array operation contains arrays that are array constants and no other type of array (for example, a range of cells), the formula should not require Ctrl+Shift+Enter.

  - Some function arguments can contain array constants as part of an array operation and do not require Ctrl+Shift+Enter—for example, the array argument in SMALL, the array argument in LARGE, the start_num argument in MID, the logical1 argument in OR, the number1 argument in PRODUCT, and the number1 argument in SUM.

  - Some function arguments *do* require Ctrl+Shift+Enter if they contain an array constant—for example, the col_index_num argument in VLOOKUP.

- The following rules apply to array formulas and non-array formulas:

  - If the data in an array will not change and you want to save spreadsheet space, an array constant can be useful.

  - You can save an array constant as a defined name and use the defined name in formulas.

See Chapter 7.

Array Formula Efficiency Rule 19

Two types of array formulas can simultaneously deliver more than one value to more than one cell through the use of Ctrl+Shift+Enter:

- Array formulas that you create with various formula elements and put together yourself
- Built-in Excel array functions

Rules for array formulas that deliver more than one item to more than one cell:

- Select a range of cells, create the formula or function, and then enter it with Ctrl+-Shift+Enter.
- The array formula/function is considered a single unit, and structural changes such as deleting individual cells, deleting individual cell content, or inserting rows in disallowed.
- The keyboard shortcut for highlighting the current array (all the cells that are part of the array formula) is Ctrl+/ (forward slash).
- If you want to delete the array formula/function, you can highlight the entire array formula (by pressing Ctrl+/) and then press Delete. Another method for deleting an array formula is to select any one cell, press Backspace, and then press Ctrl+Shift+Enter.
- If you need to edit your array formula, edit any one particular cell in the array and then reenter the array formula with Ctrl+Shift+Enter.
- When you enter an array formula or a function into more than one cell by using Ctrl+-Shift+Enter, the cell references will be the same in each cell, regardless of whether the cell references in the active cell are locked or not locked (that is, absolute or relative).
- Array functions (except for the TRANSPOSE function) can be placed in other functions that expect a range of values (for example, COUNT, MIN, MAX), and the formula will not require Ctrl+Shift+Enter.
- A formula like ={1;2;3;4;5} or =43 or ="Love" entered into the range A1:A5 with Ctrl+-Shift+Enter is an array formula with no direct array operation. It will show curly braces and will act as a single unit.

See Chapters 8, 9, 16, 17, 18, 22, and 23.

Array Formula Efficiency Rule 20

Keep in mind the following general rules about IFERROR:

- If the formula element in the value argument of the IFERROR function must be run in every cell to determine whether there is an error, using the IFERROR function is efficient. This is an example of an efficient use of IFERROR: =IFERROR(VLOOKUP(A3,$A$10:$B$12,2),"").
- If the formula element in the value argument of the IFERROR function does *not* need to be run in every cell to determine whether there is an error, using the IFERROR function may *not* be efficient. If there is an alternative logical test, then it may be more efficient to use the IF function instead of the IFERROR function. This can be particularly true for large data-extracting array formulas. Here's an example of an inefficient IFERROR use: =IFERROR(INDEX(MODE.MULT($A$2:$A$10),ROWS(C$2:C2)),""). Here's an example of a more efficient alternative: =IF(ROWS(C$4:C4)>$C$2,"",INDEX(MODE.MULT($A$2:$A$10),ROWS(C$4:C4))).

See Chapter 9 and 15.

Array Formula Efficiency Rule 21

Using a double negative is an efficient way to convert TRUEs and FALSEs to ones and zeros when you're using SUMPRODUCT. The fact that the double negative usually has a faster calculating time and the fact that the unary negation operator occurs near the top of the Excel's order of formula precedence are the main reasons it is common to see it used to convert TRUEs and FALSEs to ones and zeros.

See Chapter 10.

Array Formula Efficiency Rule 22

A number of function arguments cannot handle arrays (array operations, array constants, and arrays created by workbook references):

1. lookup_value argument in VLOOKUP

2. lookup_value argument in HLOOKUP

3. range argument in SUMIF

4. range argument in COUNTIF

5. range argument in COUNTIF

6. criteria_range argument in SUMIFS

7. criteria_range argument in COUNTIFS

8. criteria_range argument in AVEARGEIFS

See Chapters 6 and 10.

Array Formula Efficiency Rule 23

Important aspects of the SUMPRODUCT function:

- It can multiply and then add arrays with the same dimensions.
- It can add the results from an array operation with Ctrl+Shift+Enter. (With arrays of different dimensions, you can use the multiplication operator and a single array argument to get an answer.)
- It can handle workbook references, whereas functions such as COUNTIF and COUNTIFS cannot.
- It can handle arrays, whereas the range and criteria_range arguments in functions such as COUNTIF and COUNTIFS cannot.
- If you have Excel 2007 or later, many multiple-condition calculations can be more efficiently completed by using COUNTIF, COUNTIFS, and other similar functions.
- If you are making multiple-condition calculations and you do not need to copy the formula, it might be more efficient to use D-functions.
- To use the IF function inside the SUMPRODUCT function, you have to use Ctrl+Shift+Enter. To be less ambiguous, consider using an alternative formula.

See Chapter 10.

Array Formula Efficiency Rule 24

Boolean calculations that use AND and OR criteria are "filters" you use in formulas:

- **AND criteria:** For Boolean math AND criteria, you use multiplication so that any time a zero (FALSE) shows up, the end result will be zero, or FALSE. The only time an AND logical test can result in a TRUE is when all the logical tests are TRUE, or one.
- Here are the different Boolean filters you can use for AND criteria:
  - **Multiplication**: Zeros filter out the items that do not meet all criteria. The resultant array contains zeros. If zeros do not adversely affect the calculation, this method is great.
  - **Division**: #DIV/0 errors filter out the items that do not meet all criteria. The resultant array contains #DIV/0 errors. If #DIV/0 errors do not adversely affect the calculation, this method is great.
  - **IF function**: FALSE values filter out the items that do not meet all criteria. The resultant array contains FALSE values. If FALSE values do not adversely affect the calculation, this method is great.
- **OR criteria:** For Boolean math OR criteria, you use addition so that any time a nonzero number (TRUE) shows up, the end result will be the nonzero number, or TRUE. The only time an OR logical test can result in a FALSE is when all the logical tests are FALSE, or zero.
- OR logical tests have two situations:
  - For any particular OR logical test, there *cannot* be more than one TRUE. The OR logical test is pointing at a single column.
    - Boolean addition can be used for counting.
    - If you have many OR criteria, you can use the combination of ISNUMBER and MATCH functions.
  - For any particular OR logical test, there *can* be more than one TRUE. The OR logical test is pointing at a multiple columns.
    - For Boolean addition, you may have to amend the array calculation to account for the fact that you can get a count greater than one.
    - The IF function logical_test argument will interpret Boolean addition correctly because it considers any nonzero number to be TRUE.
- AND and OR criteria can be used in the same formula.

See Chapters 11 and 15.

Array Formula Efficiency Rule 25

Sometimes you can substitute non-array formulas for array formulas and significantly reduce formula calculation time. In Chapter 12 you saw how you can substitute COUNTIF or COUNTIFS for a SUMPRODUCT and TEXT function formula, and in Chapter 9 you saw how you can substitute the IF function for the IFERROR function. In both cases, you reduced formula calculation time.

Further, if you have to make an array calculation, selecting a particular function over another function may reduce formula calculation time. In Chapter 12 you saw how using the YEAR and MONTH functions over the TEXT function can reduce formula calculation time.

Helper cells can also help to reduce formula calculation time (chapter 15).

Helper columns can also help to reduce formula calculation time. (Chapters 4 and 15)

See Chapters 4 and 9 and 12 and 15.

Array Formula Efficiency Rule 26

Consider the following about dynamic range formulas:

- A dynamic range is a range that you can use in a formula, chart, PivotTable, and so on that can expand or contract or change based on a set of criteria.
- You can use the INDEX function to create dynamic ranges:
  - INDEX can look up a row or column.

    - A zero or an omitted value in the row_num argument of INDEX tells the function to look up all the rows of a column.

    - A zero or an omitted value in the column_num argument of INDEX tells the function to look up all the columns of a row.

  - INDEX can be used to look up a cell reference. If you place the INDEX function in the context of a range of cells (before or after a colon), INDEX will look up a cell reference rather than the cell content.

  - The output from INDEX is a range, so even though evaluating it will show array syntax, it is a range that can be used in functions that expect a range, without requiring Ctrl+Shift+Enter.

- You can use the OFFSET function to create dynamic ranges:
  - OFFSET has five arguments:

    - Reference: This is the starting point for the cell or range (usually the upper-left corner of the range).

    - Rows: How many rows up (minus number) or down (positive number) you want to move from the reference. Empty or 0 means to not move.

    - Cols: How many columns left (minus number) or right (positive number) you want to move from the reference. Empty or 0 means to not move.

    - Height: The height of the data set. When this argument is omitted, the data set is assumed to be the same height as a reference.

    - Width: The width of the data set. When this argument is omitted, the data set is assumed to be same width as a reference

  - OFFSET is a volatile function that recalculates at each recalculation (like using the Enter key or inserting a row).

- Defined names are useful for storing dynamic range formulas:
  - Defined names are useful any time you have a dynamic range formula because they can be used in many Excel locations, such as formulas, charts, PivotTables, VBA code, and other locations that expect a range.

  - If you create a defined name that contains a formula that requires Ctrl+Shift+Enter and then place that defined name in a cell formula, the formula will not require Ctrl+-Shift+Enter.

Array Formula Efficiency Rule 27

There are three different ways you can multiply arrays in Excel: direct array multiplication using the multiplication symbol, the SUMPRODUCT function and the MMULT function. Here is a description of the basic process for each:

- Directly multiplying column header numbers times a table of numbers will carry the respective column header number throughout the respective column to create a resultant array having the same dimensions as the table of numbers. A similar process can be used when there are row headers times a table, with the respective row numbers being carried through the respective row to create a resultant array having the same size as the table. Finally, direct multiplication can be performed on same-sized arrays, where each corresponding element in each array is multiplied to create a resultant array having the same size as the arrays being multiplied.

- You can use the SUMPRODUCT function on arrays that have the same dimensions where each corresponding element in each array is multiplied. Although there is a resultant array after the PRODUCT part of SUMPRODUCT performs the multiplication, the final answer of the multiplying is summed by the SUM part of the SUMPRODUCT to create a single number answer.

- You can use the MMULT array function on arrays where the number of columns of the first array is equal to the number of rows of the second array, and your goal is to perform matrix multiplication. The resultant array created by the MMULT has the dimensions rows of the first array by columns of the second array.

See Chapters 10 and 18.

Array Formula Efficiency Rule 28

Tips for figuring out the logic of how a particular array formula is working:

- Break the formula into the smallest possible pieces and place each piece is a separate cell. This allows you to see how each part is working. It gives you a different perspective than looking at the whole formula in a single cell. This is especially true when the formula element changes as the formula is copied. If you place a formula element like this in a cell and copy it, you can explicitly see what the part is doing.

- While the formula is in a single cell, run the Evaluate Formula feature (by pressing Alt, M, V or selecting Evaluate Formula from the Formula Auditing group of the Formula Ribbon tab). The Evaluator Formula feature is great for seeing the steps that Excel goes through when calculating a formula. There are two drawbacks to this feature: (1) Sometimes the evaluated formula element is too big for the Evaluate Formula dialog box; and (2) sometimes this dialog does not show all the steps or it shows a different result from using the F9 key when the formula is in Edit mode.

- Use the Evaluate Formula Element trick (see Array Formula Efficiency Rule 5). Press the F9 key to evaluate each separate part of the formula while the formula is in Edit mode in the cell. You can see this trick throughout the book. This is an invaluable trick for learning how a formula does what it does. After you evaluate the formula element with the F9 key, immediately undo it with Ctrl+Z. If you do not undo and you evaluate two or more times in a row, you will not be able to undo it all back to the beginning. This is because there is only one undo while in Edit mode. If the formula elements evaluates to more than 8,192 characters, you will get an error message. 8,192 is the maximum number of characters that a cell can display. One advantage that the F9 key has over the Evaluate Formula feature is that the F9 method sometimes shows what a formula element evaluates to, whereas the Evaluate Formula feature does not.

- Read Microsoft's function help. The function help articles reveal many of the hidden powers of functions.

- Watch the ScreenTips to see which argument is highlighted in bold to help you understand where a particular formula element is sitting in the larger formula. To highlight a particular formula element, you can click the argument name in the ScreenTip; this high-lights the complete formula element that sits in the function argument.

- Use the combination of the Evaluate Formula Element trick (by pressing F9) and read-ing the function argument name in the ScreenTip to "see" what each formula element is delivering to the given function argument.

- After entering the completed formula and then putting the cell in Edit mode, you can press the F9 key to evaluate each part of the formula. When you are done looking at what each formula element evaluates to, press the Esc key to revert to the formula you had in the cell before you put the cell into Edit mode. Be careful: If you press Enter after using the F9 key, the evaluated values will be hard coded into the formula. (You can use Ctrl+Z to undo it, though.)

- Don't give up if you don't figure it out right away. Over the years, a few formulas have taken me days to figure out. It is worth the fight when you get it.

See Chapter 23.

Array Formula Efficiency Rule 29

If you create a defined name that contains a formula that requires Ctrl+Shift+Enter and then place that defined name in a cell formula, the formula does not require Ctrl+Shift+Enter.

See Chapters 13 and 23.

The Remaining Chapters

Armed with this set of guidelines, you're ready to move through Chapters 15 to 24, applying these Array Formula Efficiency Rules to solve problems.

Chapter 15: Extracting Data, Based on Criteria

Excel Files

To follow along with the examples in this chapter, you can download the accompanying files, as explained in the Introduction.

Mega-Array-Formulas

Now that you have a set of Array Formula Efficiency Rules, you can start to create some larger and more amazing array formulas that will do seemingly impossible jobs for you. In this chapter, you will start with a mega-array-formula that can extract data from a data set, given a set of criteria.

Extracting Data (Records) from a Table, List, or Database

Extracting data from a data set based on AND or OR criteria is a common task in Excel. You can accomplish this task by using any of these methods:

- Filter
- Advanced Filter
- A non-array formula with a helper column
- An array formula that uses the SMALL function and the INDEX function
- An array formula that uses the AGGREGATE function and the INDEX function

Consider the following important points about these five methods:

- Filter and Advanced Filter are generally much easier to use than formulas, but they do not instantly update, as formulas do.
- Formulas can instantly update when criteria in cells are changed.
- Non-array formula with helper column solutions can calculate significantly faster than array formulas.
- Array formulas may use many cell references and contain many calculations and therefore may have long formula calculation times. To reduce calculation time, it is important to consider using helper columns, Boolean logic construction, and efficient functions.
- You are not considering VBA solutions here, even though using them is a great way to automate data extraction.

Throughout this chapter (just as you have done throughout the rest of this book), you will use small data sets to make learning easier, and then you will time some large data sets at the end of the chapter.

Using Filter and AutoFilter to Extract Data

The Filter feature (also known as AutoFilter) is flat-out easy to use. Many data extraction tasks do not need formulas and can be quickly accomplished with Filter. If you have a proper data set with field names, you can turn on the Filter feature by pressing Ctrl+Shift+L. You can then use the drop-down arrows at the top of each column to filter the data. Once the data set is filtered, you simply highlight the data, copy the visible cells, and paste them in a new location above or below the data set, on a new worksheet, or in a new workbook.

Figure 15.1 shows a data set with the fields Date, Region, Customer, and Units. You will use this data set for most of the examples in this chapter. Figures 15.2 to 15.4 show the extracted records obtained by applying three different filters that are each copied and pasted to an extract area.

	A	B	C	D
1	Data Set:			
2				
3	Date	Region	Customer	Units
4	7/29/13	West	WFMI	929
5	2/7/12	East	SW	681
6	9/23/12	Midwest	K	1393
7	4/14/12	West	WFMI	530
8	7/26/12	East	WFMI	1058
9	10/12/13	Midwest	SW	1023
10	11/3/12	West	K	436
11	9/3/13	West	K	1311
12	4/23/12	Midwest	K	368
13	7/13/12	West	WFMI	1206
14				
15	Extract Area:			
16				
17				
18				

Figure 15.1 *A proper data set with all the data.*

Figure 15.2 shows the extracted records using the following AND criteria filter: Date >=6/1/2012 AND Date <=5/31/2013 AND Region = West. Here are the steps to accomplish this filter:

1. Click the drop-down for the Date field, click Date Filters, click Between, and enter the upper and lower dates.

2. Click the drop-down for the Region field and check only West.

15	Extract Area:			
16	Date	Region	Customer	Units
17	11/3/12	West	K	436
18	7/13/12	West	WFMI	1206

Figure 15.2 *Filtering with three AND criteria.*

Figure 15.3 shows the extracted records, using the following OR criteria: Region = East OR Region = West. Here is the step to accomplish this filter:

1. Click the drop-down for the Region field and check West and East.

15	Extract Area:			
16	Date	Region	Customer	Units
17	7/29/13	West	WFMI	929
18	2/7/12	East	SW	681
19	4/14/12	West	WFMI	530
20	7/26/12	East	WFMI	1058
21	11/3/12	West	K	436
22	9/3/13	West	K	1311
23	7/13/12	West	WFMI	1206

Figure 15.3 *Filtering with two OR criteria on the same column.*

Figure 15.4 shows the records extracted using the following AND and OR criteria: Date >=6/1/2012 AND Date <=5/31/2013 AND (Region = East OR Region = West). Notice that the OR criteria is operating on a single column. Here are the steps to accomplish this filter:

1. Click the drop-down for the Date field, click Date Filters, click Between, and enter the upper and lower dates.

2. Click the drop-down for the Region field, click the check box for West, and click the check box for East.

15	Extract Area:			
16	Date	Region	Customer	Units
17	7/26/12	East	WFMI	1058
18	11/3/12	West	K	436
19	7/13/12	West	WFMI	1206

Figure 15.4 *Filtering with three AND criteria, where the third AND is an OR criteria on the same column.*

If you have OR criteria that is operating on more than one column, the Filter feature is not much help. However, you can create a helper column with a formula, filter to show only the TRUE values, and copy and paste the records to an extract area, as shown in Figure 15.5.

	A	B	C	D	E	F
1	Filter for extracting records with AND and OR Criteria.					
2	Date	Date	Region	<< = OR Criteria operating on 2 columns.		
3	6/1/2012	5/31/2013	West			
4			Customer			
5			K			
6	Data Set:					
8	Date	Region	Customer	Units	Helper	
9	7/29/13	West	WFMI	929	FALSE	< Formula =AND(A10>=$A$3,A10<=$B$3,OR(B10=$C$3,C10=$C$5))
10	2/7/12	East	SW	681	FALSE	
11	9/23/12	Midwest	K	1393	TRUE	
12	4/14/12	West	WFMI	530	FALSE	
13	7/26/12	East	WFMI	1058	FALSE	
14	10/12/13	Midwest	SW	1023	FALSE	
15	11/3/12	West	K	436	TRUE	
16	9/3/13	West	K	1311	FALSE	
17	4/23/12	Midwest	K	368	FALSE	
18	7/13/12	West	WFMI	1206	TRUE	
19						
20	Extract Area:					
21	Date	Region	Customer	Units		
22	9/23/12	Midwest	K	1393		
23	11/3/12	West	K	436		
24	7/13/12	West	WFMI	1206		

Figure 15.5 *A helper column with a formula can help Filter do things that it does not normally do.*

These examples show how using Filter can be fast and easy. In many situations, you do not need the updateability that formulas bring, and so Filter is the best tool.

Using Advanced Filter for Extracting Records

Like the Filter feature, Advanced Filter is often easier to use than array formulas. Advanced Filter is different from the Filter feature in that you must type your criteria into cells, and you must use a dialog box instead of drop-down arrows at the top of each column to filter the data. Advanced Filter can also accomplish a few filter tasks that the Filter feature cannot (as you'll in just a bit).

These are the general steps for using Advanced Filter:

1. Just as with the D-functions that you used earlier in the book, for Advanced Filter to work, you must have a proper data set with field names, and you must set up a criteria area with field names and criteria, with AND criteria on the same row (line) and OR criteria on different rows (lines).

2. To open the Advanced Filter dialog box, click in a single cell in the data set and press either Alt, D, F, A (in Excel 2003 or earlier) or Alt A, Q (in Excel 2007 or later) or from the Data Ribbon tab, select Advanced Filter from the Sort & Filter group.

3. Complete the Advanced Filter dialog box by doing the following:

- Selecting the Copy to Another Location button.

- Enter cell ranges for a proper data set in the List Range text box.

- Enter cell ranges for the criteria area in the Criteria Range text box.

- Enter the cell address for the upper-left corner of the extract range in the Copy To text box. Use an empty cell because Advanced Filter will extract field names and all the records that match the criteria. Make sure there is nothing below the extract range because Advanced Filter clears everything below the extract range each time you run Advanced Filter.

1. Click OK. The field names and records are extracted, and two defined names appear in the Name Manager dialog (which you open by pressing Ctrl+F3): Criteria and Extract. Because of these names, when you run the Advanced Filter dialog a second or third time, the dialog remembers the ranges you entered previously. Therefore, you can simply change the criteria and rerun Advanced Filter.

2. When you run Advanced Filter more than one time, you can change the cell address in the Copy To text box so it does not interfere with previous extract.

Figures 15.6 through 15.11 show examples of using Advanced Filter to extract data. The captions below each figure give a brief description.

Figure 15.6 shows an example of using Advanced Filter with AND criteria.

	A	B	C	D	E	F	G
1	**Advanced Filter for extracting records with AND Criteria.**						
2	Criteria:	Date	Date	Region			
3		>=6/1/12	<=5/31/13	West			
5	Data Set:						
7	Date	Region	Customer	Units			
8	7/29/13	West	WFMI	929			
9	2/7/12	East	SW	681			
10	9/23/12	Midwest	K	1393			
11	4/14/12	West	WFMI	530			
12	7/26/12	East	WFMI	1058			
13	10/12/13	Midwest	SW	1023			
14	11/3/12	West	K	436			
15	9/3/13	West	K	1311			
16	4/23/12	Midwest	K	368			
17	7/13/12	West	WFMI	1206			
19	Extract Area:						
20	Date	Region	Customer	Units			
21	11/3/12	West	K	436			
22	7/13/12	West	WFMI	1206			

Advanced Filter dialog:

Action
- ○ Filter the list, in-place
- ● Copy to another location

List range: $A$7:$D$17
Criteria range: $B$2:$D$3
Copy to: $A$20

☐ Unique records only

[OK]   [Cancel]

Figure 15.6 *Using Advanced Filter to extract data using three AND criteria.*

Figure 15.7 shows an example of using Advanced Filter with OR criteria.

	A	B	C	D	E	F	G
1	**Advanced Filter for extracting records with OR Criteria.**						
2	Criteria:	Region					
3		West					
4		East					
6	Data Set:						
8	Date	Region	Customer	Units			
9	7/29/13	West	WFMI	929			
10	2/7/12	East	SW	681			
11	9/23/12	Midwest	K	1393			
12	4/14/12	West	WFMI	530			
13	7/26/12	East	WFMI	1058			
14	10/12/13	Midwest	SW	1023			
15	11/3/12	West	K	436			
16	9/3/13	West	K	1311			
17	4/23/12	Midwest	K	368			
18	7/13/12	West	WFMI	1206			
20	Extract Area:						
21	Date	Region	Customer	Units			
22	7/29/13	West	WFMI	929			
23	2/7/12	East	SW	681			
24	4/14/12	West	WFMI	530			
25	7/26/12	East	WFMI	1058			
26	11/3/12	West	K	436			
27	9/3/13	West	K	1311			
28	7/13/12	West	WFMI	1206			

Figure 15.7 *Using Advanced Filter to extract data using two OR criteria.*

Figure 15.8 shows an example of using Advanced Filter with AND and OR criteria (OR operating on one column).

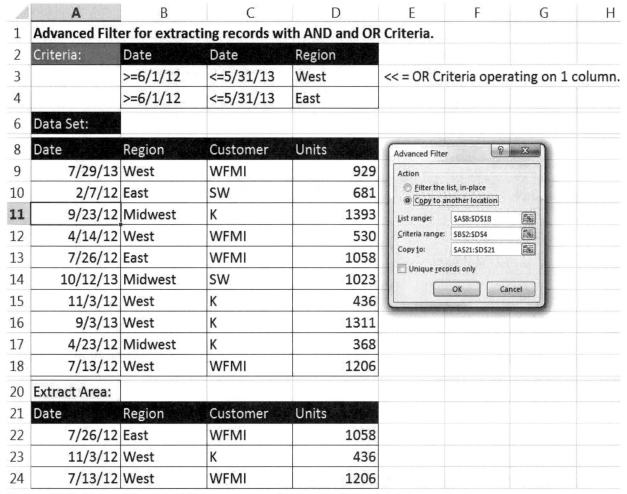

	A	B	C	D	E	F	G	H
1	**Advanced Filter for extracting records with AND and OR Criteria.**							
2	Criteria:	Date	Date	Region				
3		>=6/1/12	<=5/31/13	West	<< = OR Criteria operating on 1 column.			
4		>=6/1/12	<=5/31/13	East				
6	Data Set:							
8	Date	Region	Customer	Units				
9	7/29/13	West	WFMI	929				
10	2/7/12	East	SW	681				
11	9/23/12	Midwest	K	1393				
12	4/14/12	West	WFMI	530				
13	7/26/12	East	WFMI	1058				
14	10/12/13	Midwest	SW	1023				
15	11/3/12	West	K	436				
16	9/3/13	West	K	1311				
17	4/23/12	Midwest	K	368				
18	7/13/12	West	WFMI	1206				
20	Extract Area:							
21	Date	Region	Customer	Units				
22	7/26/12	East	WFMI	1058				
23	11/3/12	West	K	436				
24	7/13/12	West	WFMI	1206				

Advanced Filter dialog box:
- Action
  - ○ Filter the list, in-place
  - ● Copy to another location
- List range: $A$8:$D$18
- Criteria range: $B$2:$D$4
- Copy to: $A$21:$D$21
- ☐ Unique records only
- [OK] [Cancel]

Figure 15.8 *Using Advanced Filter to extract data using AND and OR criteria. Because you are using an OR criteria that operates on a single column, you have to repeat the date AND criteria on each line.*

Figure 15.9 shows an example of using Advanced Filter with AND and OR criteria (OR operating on two columns).

	A	B	C	D	E	F	G
1	**Advanced Filter for extracting records with AND and OR Criteria.**						
2	Criteria:	Date	Date	Region	Customer		
3		>=6/1/12	<=5/31/13	West		<< = OR Criteria	
4		>=6/1/12	<=5/31/13		K	operating on	
5						2 columns.	
6	Data Set:						
8	Date	Region	Customer	Units			
9	7/29/13	West	WFMI	929			
10	2/7/12	East	SW	681			
11	9/23/12	Midwest	K	1393			
12	4/14/12	West	WFMI	530			
13	7/26/12	East	WFMI	1058			
14	10/12/13	Midwest	SW	1023			
15	11/3/12	West	K	436			
16	9/3/13	West	K	1311			
17	4/23/12	Midwest	K	368			
18	7/13/12	West	WFMI	1206			
20	Extract Area:						
21	Date	Region	Customer	Units			
22	9/23/12	Midwest	K	1393			
23	11/3/12	West	K	436			
24	7/13/12	West	WFMI	1206			

Advanced Filter dialog box:

Action
- ○ Filter the list, in-place
- ● Copy to another location

List range: $A$8:$D$18
Criteria range: $B$2:$E$4
Copy to: $A$21:$D$21

☐ Unique records only

[OK] [Cancel]

Figure 15.9 *Using Advanced Filter to extra data using AND and OR criteria. This is a data extract that AutoFilter cannot do unless it has a formula helper column.*

Figure 15.10 shows an example of using Advanced Filter with formula criteria.

	A	B	C	D	E	F	G	H
1		Date	Date	Region				
2		6/1/2012	5/31/2013	West				
3				Customer				
4				K				
5	**Advanced Filter with Formula Criteria**							
6	Criteria:	FormulaBelow	<< = Cell must have text that is NOT a field name or be empty					
7		FALSE	< Formula =AND(A11>=$B$2,A11<=$C$2,OR(B11=$D$2,C11=$D$4))					
8	Data Set:		** Formula as if it where a helper column					
10	Date	Region	Customer	Units				
11	7/29/13	West	WFMI	929				
12	2/7/12	East	SW	681				
13	9/23/12	Midwest	K	1393				
14	4/14/12	West	WFMI	530				
15	7/26/12	East	WFMI	1058				
16	10/12/13	Midwest	SW	1023				
17	11/3/12	West	K	436				
18	9/3/13	West	K	1311				
19	4/23/12	Midwest	K	368				
20	7/13/12	West	WFMI	1206				
22	Extract Area:							
23	Date	Region	Customer	Units				
24	9/23/12	Midwest	K	1393				
25	11/3/12	West	K	436				
26	7/13/12	West	WFMI	1206				

Advanced Filter dialog box:

Action
- ○ Filter the list, in-place
- ◉ Copy to another location

List range: $A$10:$D$20
Criteria range: $B$6:$B$7
Copy to: $A$23:$D$23

☐ Unique records only

[OK] [Cancel]

Figure 15.10 *Advanced Filter can utilize logical formulas as criteria. But you must set up the inputs for the Criteria Range text box so that the cell above the logical formula has text that does not match a field name or is empty. Notice that the Criteria Range text box contains the range B6:B7; normally this range would include a field name from the data set and a criterion. But because you are using a logical formula, cell B6 contains text that is* not *a field, and B7 contains a logical formula. (This is the same data extract example you as in Figures 15.5 and 15.9.)*

Figure 15.11 shows an example of using Advanced Filter with unique records only.

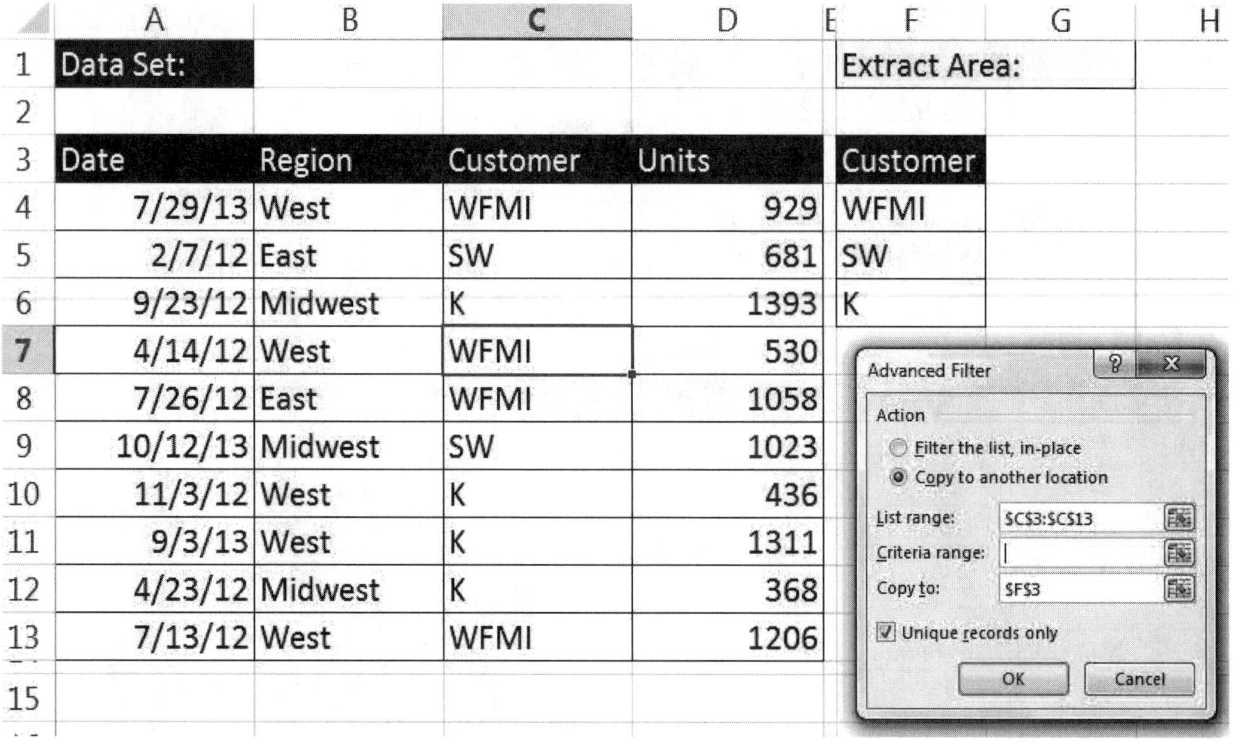

	A	B	C	D	E	F	G	H
1	Data Set:					Extract Area:		
2								
3	Date	Region	Customer	Units		Customer		
4	7/29/13	West	WFMI	929		WFMI		
5	2/7/12	East	SW	681		SW		
6	9/23/12	Midwest	K	1393		K		
7	4/14/12	West	WFMI	530				
8	7/26/12	East	WFMI	1058				
9	10/12/13	Midwest	SW	1023				
10	11/3/12	West	K	436				
11	9/3/13	West	K	1311				
12	4/23/12	Midwest	K	368				
13	7/13/12	West	WFMI	1206				
15								

Advanced Filter dialog box:

Action
○ Filter the list, in-place
● Copy to another location

List range: $C$3:$C$13
Criteria range:
Copy to: $F$3

☑ Unique records only

OK   Cancel

Figure 15.11 *If you want to extract a unique list from a single column, you can easily do so with Advanced Filter. You just check the Unique List check box in the Advanced Filter dialog box. This trick always requires that a field name be included in the List Range text box. If you do not include a field name, you will get a duplicate value for the first entry in the list.*

These Advanced Filter examples show that Advanced Filter gives you more filtering ability than does the Filter feature. Advanced Filter gives you the following extra abilities:

- You can see the criteria in the cells (not hidden behind an AutoFilter drop-down arrow).
- You can handle complicated AND and OR criteria.
- You can use formulas as criteria.
- You can get a unique list.

Both Filter and Advanced Filter have great uses, but sometimes you want the immediate update-ability of formulas. Next you'll see why using formulas can be much more difficult than using Filter and Advanced Filter.

Why Formulas for Extracting Records Are So Complicated

When you extract data from a table, you are really doing a type of lookup. Standard lookup functions in Excel, such as INDEX and MATCH and VLOOKUP, are great, but they have a hard time with duplicates. As shown in Figure 15.12, if the goal is to extract records with three criteria, you get two records that match the criteria. For a vertical table, lookup formulas do not have a hard time extracting data from multiple columns; it is the multiple rows that lookup formulas have a hard time with. If you need formula to extract records, you have two basic choices:

- **Use a standard lookup function based on a helper column.** The helper column contains a formula that gives you sequential numbers like 1, 2, and 3 anytime the formula finds a record that matches the criteria. These sequential numbers solve the duplicate problem because there is a unique identifier for each matched record. The helper column serves as the lookup column that lookup functions needs for looking up and retrieving data.

- **An array formula based on a full data set.** These formulas are self-contained and do not require an extra column. For these formulas, you have to create an array of relative positions for the records that match the criteria inside the formula. When you have many criteria and the data sets are large, the formula elements that create the array of relative positions can have many cell references and calculations and, therefore, dramatically increases formula creation time. Nevertheless, these formulas can extract records with criteria when there are duplicates without a helper column, whereas the standard built-in Excel lookup functions cannot.

	A	B	C	D
2	Criteria:	Date	Date	Region
3		6/1/2012	5/31/2013	West
5	Data Set:			
7	Date	Region	Customer	Units
8	7/29/13	West	WFMI	929
9	2/7/12	East	SW	681
10	9/23/12	Midwest	K	1393
11	4/14/12	West	WFMI	530
12	7/26/12	East	WFMI	1058
13	10/12/13	Midwest	SW	1023
14	11/3/12	West	K	436
15	9/3/13	West	K	1311
16	4/23/12	Midwest	K	368
17	7/13/12	West	WFMI	1206

Figure 15.12 *Two records need to be extracted. Standard lookup functions have a hard time with duplicates.*

The following sections look at these two ways of using a formula to extra records.

Using a Non-Array Formula with a Helper Column

If you want to use a formula to extract records, the best aspect of helper column solutions is that they can calculate dramatically faster than similar array formulas (Array Formula Efficiency Rule 25).

Using a Helper Column with AND Criteria and INDEX and MATCH Lookup

Say that you have three AND criteria that will determine which records to extract. As shown in Figure 15.13, you can use the AND function in a helper column. This helper column will serve as the lookup column for the INDEX function. The problem with using the AND function alone is that you get two TRUE values, which means you are back to the problem of having duplicates in the lookup column. What you would really like is for the lookup column to contain numbers, where the first TRUE in cell E14 would have the number 1, and the second TRUE in E17 would have contain 2. You can accomplish this by amending the formula.

	A	B	C	D	E	F	G	H	I	J	K
1	**Helper Column and INDEX to extract records with AND Criteria**										
2	Criteria:	Date	Date	Region							
3		6/1/2012	5/31/2013	West							
4											
5	Data Set:						Count				
6											
7	Date	Region	Customer	Units	Helper						
8	7/29/13	West	WFMI	929	=AND(A8>=B$3,A8<=C$3,B8=D$3)						
9	2/7/12	East	SW	681	AND(logical1, [logical2], **[logical3]**, [logical4], ...)						
10	9/23/12	Midwest	K	1393	FALSE		Extract Area:				
11	4/14/12	West	WFMI	530	FALSE		No	Date	Region	Customer	Units
12	7/26/12	East	WFMI	1058	FALSE		1				
13	10/12/13	Midwest	SW	1023	FALSE		2				
14	11/3/12	West	K	436	TRUE		3				
15	9/3/13	West	K	1311	FALSE		4				
16	4/23/12	Midwest	K	368	FALSE		5				
17	7/13/12	West	WFMI	1206	TRUE		6				

Figure 15.13 *First part of helper column formula involves the AND function.*

As shown in Figure 15.14, you place the AND function in the number1 argument of the SUM function, and you place the relative cell reference "one cell above" in the number2 argument of the SUM function. Why do this? It seems like a strange formula construction. Here is why this formula works:

- The Boolean (logical) values TRUE and FALSE that the AND function delivers will be converted to ones and zeros, respectively, through the adding action of the SUM function.
- The SUM function is programmed to ignore text and so when the relative cell reference "one cell above" in the number2 argument looks at cell E7 and sees the text "Helper", that text will be ignored.
- When the formula gets down to cell E14, it will be adding the 0 value from one cell above, and the TRUE value delivered by the AND function. This will result in a formula result of 1.
- In cells E15 and E16, the formula will be adding the 1 value from one cell above and the FALSE value delivered by the AND function. This will result in a formula result of 1.

- In cell E17, the formula will be adding the 1 value from one cell above and the TRUE value delivered by the AND function. This will result in a formula result of 2.

- The duplicate values may initially look like a problem, but when you use the standard lookup function, you can do an exact match and, therefore, all duplicate values except for the first one will be ignored. (That is the definition of an exact match when doing a lookup.)

- By doing an exact match, not only are you ignoring duplicates, you also indirectly create a column with unique identifiers (1, 2, and so on) that the LOOKUP function can use to retrieve the data. Only the first 1 and first 2 will be picked up by the lookup function.

	A	B	C	D	E	F G	H	I	J
7	Date	Region	Customer	Units	Helper				
8	7/29/13	West	WFMI		929	=SUM(AND(A8>=B$3,A8<=C$3,B8=D$3),E7)			
9	2/7/12	East	SW		681	SUM(number1, [number2], [number3], ...)			
10	9/23/12	Midwest	K	1393	0	Extract Area:			
11	4/14/12	West	WFMI	530	0	No Date		Region	Custo
12	7/26/12	East	WFMI	1058	0	1			
13	10/12/13	Midwest	SW	1023	0	2			
14	11/3/12	West	K	436	1	3			
15	9/3/13	West	K	1311	1	4			
16	4/23/12	Midwest	K	368	1	5			
17	7/13/12	West	WFMI	1206	2	6			

Figure 15.14 *The final helper column formula uses the SUM function to add the logical value that the AND function delivers to the value one cell above.*

Using Helper Cells

You can add a helper cell that will count the total records that you need to extract. Figure 15.15 shows how you can use the MAX function in cell H6 to count the number of matched records. (Thanks, Peter_SSs, for your post at the MrExcel Message Board that helped me learn to use the MAX function on a helper column!) The idea of a helper cell is similar to the idea of a helper column: It helps reduce formula calculation time. The final lookup formula for extracting data needs to know the number of records to extract. If you place the formula element MAX($E$8:$E$17) in the final formula, every cell that contains that formula has to run the MAX formula element. This means the same calculation has to be repeated many times. In order to remove this repeated formula calculation, if you put the formula element into a separate cell, off to the side, and instead refer to the formula result with a cell reference, the solution calculates more quickly. The MAX formula has to be calculated only one time.

You can use the idea of using a helper cell (or a column or row) to reduce formula calculation time anytime you have a formula element that makes the identical calculation in more than one cell (Array Formula Efficiency Rule 25).

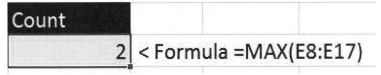

Figure 15.15 *Cell H6 contains the MAX function to calculate the number of matching records. This is an example of a helper cell.*

As shown in Figure 15.16, you can begin the data extraction formula (lookup formula) by using the IF function in cell H12. Because the formula needs to accommodate a variable number of extracted records, logical_test checks to see if the matched record number (1 in cell $G12) is greater than the count of the number of matched records in cell $H$6. If logical_test evaluates to TRUE, a null text string is delivered to the cell. value_if_false will contain the standard lookup function.

> **Note:** As discussed in Chapter 9, when you are copying data extraction formulas to many cells, it is preferable to use the IF function instead of the IFERROR function. Whereas the IFERROR function runs the lookup function in every cell, the IF function chooses between running the lookup function and delivering a null text string. For large data extraction formulas that are copied to many cells, the IF function is a better choice.

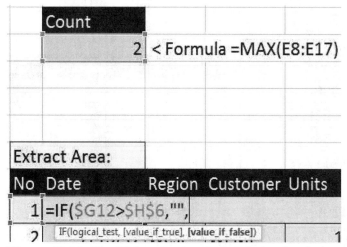

Figure 15.16 *The IF function is a better choice for data extract formulas than the IFERROR function.*

Figure 15.17 shows the finished data extraction formula. Notice these details:

- The range in the array argument of INDEX has mixed cell references with only the row reference locked (absolute) so that as the formula is copied to the side, a different column of data is extracted. However, as it is copied down, it is locked.

- The MATCH lookup_value argument contains the matched record number, 1, in cell $G12. (Only the column reference is locked so that the entire row "sees" the matched record number, but when the formula is copied down, it moves to the next number.)

- MATCH lookup_array is locked in all directions (absolute), and match_type is 0 (zero) so that it performs an exact match lookup.

	A	B	C	D	E	F G	H	I	J	K	L	M
5	Data Set:						Count					
6							2	< Formula =MAX(E8:E17)				
7	Date	Region	Customer	Units	Helper							
8	7/29/13	West	WFMI	929	0							
9	2/7/12	East	SW	681	0							
10	9/23/12	Midwest	K	1393	0		Extract Area:					
11	4/14/12	West	WFMI	530	0		No Date	Region Customer Units				
12	7/26/12	East	WFMI	1058	0	1	=IF($G12>$H$6,"",INDEX(A$8:A$17,MATCH($G12,$F$8:$F$17,0)))					
13	10/12/13	Midwest	SW	1023	0	2	IF(logical_test, [value_if_true], [value_if_false])					
14	11/3/12	West	K	436	1	3						
15	9/3/13	West	K	1311	1	4						
16	4/23/12	Midwest	K	368	1	5						
17	7/13/12	West	WFMI	1206	2	6						

Figure 15.17 *The completed formula can be entered into cell H12.*

After the formula in cell H12 is entered, it is copied through the range H12: K17.

> **Note:** When you copy a cell, the copy action copies the formula and formatting. To avoid copying the date number formatting in this example, either use the smart tag option Fill Without Formatting or adjust formatting after the copy action.

You copied the formula down to row 17. But how far down should you copy the data extraction formula? You should always copy it down as far as or further than the largest number of potential extracted records.

Figure 15.18 shows why you use formulas instead of Filter or Advanced Filter: If you change the data, the formulas update instantly. Figure 5.19 shows how you can amend the formula if you do not want the No column (Number column) with matched record numbers by using the Number Incrementor Formula Element, ROWS(H$12:H12).

	A	B	C	D	E	F	G	H	I	J	K
1	Helper Column and INDEX to extract records with AND Criteria										
2	Criteria:	Date	Date	Region							
3		2/1/2012	10/31/2013	West							
4											
5	Data Set:							Count			
6									5	< Formula =MAX(E8:E17)	
7	Date	Region	Customer	Units	Helper						
8	7/29/13	West	WFMI	929	1						
9	2/7/12	East	SW	681	1						
10	9/23/12	Midwest	K	1393	1			Extract Area:			
11	4/14/12	West	WFMI	530	2			No	Date	Region	Customer	Units
12	7/26/12	East	WFMI	1058	2			1	7/29/13	West	WFMI	929
13	10/12/13	Midwest	SW	1023	2			2	4/14/12	West	WFMI	530
14	11/3/12	West	K	436	3			3	11/3/12	West	K	436
15	9/3/13	West	K	1311	4			4	9/3/13	West	K	1311
16	4/23/12	Midwest	K	368	4			5	7/13/12	West	WFMI	1206
17	7/13/12	West	WFMI	1206	5			6				

Figure 15.18 *Why do you use formulas? When data change, the formulas update.*

```
=IF(ROWS(H$12:H12)>$H$6,"",INDEX(A$8:A$17,MATCH(ROWS(H$12:H12),$E$8:$E$17,0)))
```

Figure 15.19 *This formula would work without the No column.*

The following sections look at a three more examples of how to use helper columns to extract data from data sets.

Using a Helper Column, OR Criteria, and VLOOKUP as a Lookup Function

Figure 15.20 shows an example of a helper column that uses OR criteria placed in the front of the table (the first column) so you can use the VLOOKUP function. Notice the use of the COLUMNS function in the col_index_num argument of VLOOKUP to increment the numbers 2, 3, 4, and 5 as the formula is copied to the side.

	A	B	C	D	E	F	G	H	I	J	K
1	Helper Column and VLOOKUP to extract records with OR Criteria										
2	Criteria:	Customer									
3		K									
4		SW									
5							Count				
6	Data Set:							6	< Formula =MAX(A10:A19)		
7											
8	Formula in A10: =SUM(ISNUMBER(MATCH(D10,$B$3:$B$4,0)),A9)						Extract Area:				
9	Helper	Date	Region	Customer	Units		Date	Region	Customer	Units	
10	0	7/29/13	West	WFMI	929		=IF(ROWS(G$10:G10)>$G$6,"",VLOOKUP(ROWS(G$10:				
11	1	2/7/12	East	SW	681		G10),$A$10:$E$19,COLUMNS($G$10:G10)+1,0))				
12	2	9/23/12	Midwest	K	1393		VLOOKUP(lookup_value, table_array, col_index_num, [range_lookup])			23	
13	2	4/14/12	West	WFMI	530		11/3/12	West	K	436	
14	2	7/26/12	East	WFMI	1058		9/3/13	West	K	1311	
15	3	10/12/13	Midwest	SW	1023		4/23/12	Midwest	K	368	
16	4	11/3/12	West	K	436						
17	5	9/3/13	West	K	1311						
18	6	4/23/12	Midwest	K	368						
19	6	7/13/12	West	WFMI	1206						

Figure 15.20 *Using a helper column, OR criteria, and VLOOKUP.*

> **Note:** When all the OR logical tests point at a single column, you can use one of two formula constructions: ISNUMBER/MATCH functions or an OR function. The ISNUMBER/MATCH combination tends to calculate more quickly and is easier to create when there are many criteria. In this example, because there are only two criteria, you could use either of the following:
>
> - =SUM(ISNUMBER(MATCH(D10,$B$3:$B$4,0)),A9)
> - =SUM(OR(D10=$B$3,D10=$B$4),A9)

Using a Helper Column and AND and OR Criteria to Extract Only Some of the Columns of Data with INDEX and MATCH

Figure 15.21 shows an example of a helper column that uses AND and OR criteria to extract just the data from the Date and Units columns. Notice that INDEX is doing a two-way lookup with a MATCH function in the row_num argument and a second MATCH function in the column_num argument.

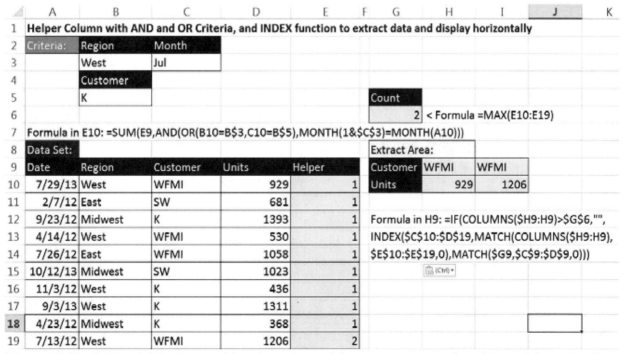

	A	B	C	D	E	F	G	H	I	J	K
1	Helper Column with AND and OR Criteria, and INDEX function to extract data from just some of the columns										
2	Criteria:	Region	Lower Units	Upper Units							
3		West	400	1300							
4		Customer									
5		K					Count				
6								4	< Formula =MAX(E10:E19)		
7	Formula in E10: =SUM(E9,AND(OR(B10=B$3,C10=B$5),D10>=C$3,D10<=D$3))										
8	Data Set:						Extract Area:				
9	Date	Region	Customer	Units	Helper		Date	Units			
10	7/29/13	West	WFMI	929	1		=IF(ROWS(G$10:G10)>$G$6,"",INDEX($A$10:$D$19,				
11	2/7/12	East	SW	681	1		MATCH(ROWS(G$10:G10),$E$10:$E$19,0),MATCH(				
12	9/23/12	Midwest	K	1393	1		G$9,$A$9:$D$9,0)))				
13	4/14/12	West	WFMI	530	2		7/13/12	1206			
14	7/26/12	East	WFMI	1058	2						
15	10/12/13	Midwest	SW	1023	2						
16	11/3/12	West	K	436	3						
17	9/3/13	West	K	1311	3						
18	4/23/12	Midwest	K	368	3						
19	7/13/12	West	WFMI	1206	4						

Figure 15.21 *AND and OR criteria and a two-way lookup to retrieve data from just the Date and Units columns.*

Using a Helper Column with AND and OR Criteria to Extract Data and Display Horizontally

Figure 5.22 shows a data extract solution where a data mismatch exists between the month criteria and the serial number dates in the Date field. In addition, this problem illustrates that data can be extracted from a vertical table and displayed horizontally by using the COLUMNS function in the logical test argument of the IF function and in the lookup_value argument of the MATCH function.

	A	B	C	D	E	F	G	H	I	J	K
1	Helper Column with AND and OR Criteria, and INDEX function to extract data and display horizontally										
2	Criteria:	Region	Month								
3		West	Jul								
4		Customer									
5		K					Count				
6								2	< Formula =MAX(E10:E19)		
7	Formula in E10: =SUM(E9,AND(OR(B10=B$3,C10=B$5),MONTH(1&$C$3)=MONTH(A10)))										
8	Data Set:						Extract Area:				
9	Date	Region	Customer	Units	Helper		Customer	WFMI	WFMI		
10	7/29/13	West	WFMI	929	1		Units	929	1206		
11	2/7/12	East	SW	681	1						
12	9/23/12	Midwest	K	1393	1		Formula in H9: =IF(COLUMNS($H9:H9)>$G$6,"",				
13	4/14/12	West	WFMI	530	1		INDEX($C$10:$D$19,MATCH(COLUMNS($H9:H9),				
14	7/26/12	East	WFMI	1058	1		$E$10:$E$19,0),MATCH($G9,$C$9:$D$9,0)))				
15	10/12/13	Midwest	SW	1023	1						
16	11/3/12	West	K	436	1						
17	9/3/13	West	K	1311	1						
18	4/23/12	Midwest	K	368	1						
19	7/13/12	West	WFMI	1206	2						

Figure 15.22 *AND and OR criteria with a data mismatch between a text month and the serial number dates in the Date field. The data is extracted from a vertical table and displayed horizontally with the use of a two-way lookup and the COLUMNS function.*

You just saw five examples of how you can use helper columns for various data extraction situations. Helper columns are important because they can significantly reduce overall formula calculation time in a workbook. However, if helper columns cannot be used, then you need to switch over to array formulas. Next, you will see how to build an array formula to extract records from a data set.

Creating an Array of "Matched Record" Relative Positions Inside a Formula

The whole trick to getting a data extracting array formula to work is to create an array of "matched record" relative positions inside the formula. In Figure 15.23 you can see that based on the AND criteria, the matched records are in the relative positions 7 and 10. Since you can't use a helper column, you have to create the numbers 7 and 10 inside the formula. The 7 and 10 will then be used by the row_num argument in the INDEX function. Luckily, you have already studied the two formula concepts that you need to create this array of matched record relative positions:

- In Chapters 4 and 11 you learned about using Boolean math and the IF function to filter items inside a formula.
- In Chapter 8 you learned about a formula element that creates an array of sequential numbers, or relative positions: ROW(range)-ROW(FirstCellInRange)+1.

If you are using Excel 2007 or before, you can create this array by using the SMALL and IF functions, which means the formula will require Ctrl+Shift+Enter. If you are using Excel 2010 or later, you can use the AGGREGATE function and Boolean division, which means the formula does *not* require Ctrl+Shift+Enter.

▲	A	B	C	D	E	F	G	H	I
1	**Array Formula with AND Criteria**								
2	Criteria:	Date	Date	Region					
3		6/1/2012	5/31/2013	West					
5	Count								
6									
7									
9	Data Set:								
10	Date	Region	Customer	Units		Extract Area:			
11	7/29/13	West	WFMI	929		Date	Region	Customer	Units
12	2/7/12	East	SW	681					
13	9/23/12	Midwest	K	1393					
14	4/14/12	West	WFMI	530					
15	7/26/12	East	WFMI	1058					
16	10/12/13	Midwest	SW	1023					
17	11/3/12	West	K	436					
18	9/3/13	West	K	1311					
19	4/23/12	Midwest	K	368					
20	7/13/12	West	WFMI	1206					

Figure 15.23 *Matched records are in the relative positions 7 and 10.*

Using an Array Formula for Extracting Data Using SMALL, IF, and INDEX Functions and AND Criteria

As shown in Figure 15.24, you start the formula in cell F12 by nesting three IF functions together in the array argument of the SMALL function. The three IF logical tests will be the AND criteria filter to choose only the relative positions that you want. As shown in Figure 15.25, you place the formula element to create an array of relative positions into the value_if_true argument of the IF function and then close off the three IFs with three close parentheses.

> **Note:** For the formula element to create an array of relative positions, you can use any one of the columns in the data set. This example uses the Date column—ROW($A$11:$A$20)-ROW($A$11)+1—but you could just as easily use the Region, Customer, or Units columns. For example, you could use ROW($B$11:$B$20)-ROW($B$11)+1. As long as the ranges are contained within the data set, it usually does not matter.

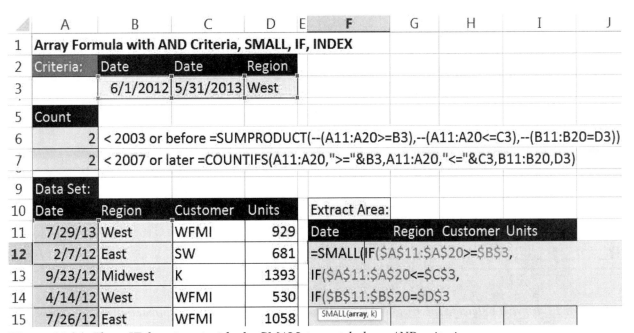

Figure 15.24 provides the following spreadsheet layout:

	A	B	C	D	E	F	G	H	I	J
1	Array Formula with AND Criteria, SMALL, IF, INDEX									
2	Criteria:	Date	Date	Region						
3		6/1/2012	5/31/2013	West						
5	Count									
6		2	< 2003 or before	=SUMPRODUCT(--(A11:A20>=B3),--(A11:A20<=C3),--(B11:B20=D3))						
7		2	< 2007 or later	=COUNTIFS(A11:A20,">="&B3,A11:A20,"<="&C3,B11:B20,D3)						
9	Data Set:									
10	Date	Region	Customer	Units		Extract Area:				
11	7/29/13	West	WFMI	929		Date	Region	Customer	Units	
12	2/7/12	East	SW	681		=SMALL(IF($A$11:$A$20>=$B$3,				
13	9/23/12	Midwest	K	1393		IF($A$11:$A$20<=$C$3,				
14	4/14/12	West	WFMI	530		IF($B$11:$B$20=$D$3				
15	7/26/12	East	WFMI	1058		SMALL(array, k)				

Figure 15.24 *Three IF functions inside the SMALL to match three AND criteria.*

Figure 15.25 *Formula element to create an array of relative positions sits in the value_if_true argument.*

If you evaluate the three IF functions, as shown in Figure 15.26, you can see the array of matched record relative positions that the three IFs deliver to the array argument of the SMALL function. (Be sure to undo the evaluation before you create the result of the formula.)

=SMALL({FALSE;FALSE;FALSE;FALSE;FALSE;
FALSE;7;FALSE;FALSE;10}

SMALL(**array**, k)

Figure 15.26 *Evaluating the three IF functions to see the resultant array filled with the relative position of the matched records and FALSEs.*

Why do you put the array of matched record relative positions into SMALL? You do this because SMALL can extract the 7 and then the 10 as you copy it down the column, and it can deliver those numbers to the row_num argument of the INDEX function. When you put the number incrementor, ROWS(F$12:F12), into the k argument of SMALL (Figure 15.27), SMALL can deliver the correct relative position to the row_num argument of the INDEX function as the formula is copied throughout the range. Figure 15.28 shows what you would get by entering this SMALL formula with Ctrl+Shift+Enter into cell F12 and then copying it through the range F12:I17.

=SMALL(IF($A$11:$A$20>=$B$3,
IF($A$11:$A$20<=$C$3,
IF($B$11:$B$20=$D$3,
ROW($A$11:$A$20)-ROW($A$11)+1))),
ROWS(F$12:F12))

SMALL(array, **k**)

Figure 15.27 *Formula element to create sequential numbers as the formula is copied down sits in the k argument of SMALL.*

Extract Area:			
Date	Region	Customer	Units
7	7	7	7
10	10	10	10
#NUM!	#NUM!	#NUM!	#NUM!
#NUM!	#NUM!	#NUM!	#NUM!

Figure 15.28 *Errors because there are only two records that match.*

As shown in Figure 15.29, the entire SMALL formula element sits in the row_num argument of INDEX and will deliver the relative position to the row_num argument of INDEX.

```
=INDEX(A$11:A$20,SMALL(IF($A$11:$A$20>=$B$3,
IF($A$11:$A$20<=$C$3,
IF($B$11:$B$20=$D$3,
ROW($A$11:$A$20)-ROW($A$11)+1))),
ROWS(F$12:F12)))
```

INDEX(array, **row_num**, [column_num])
INDEX(reference, **row_num**, [column_num], [area_num])

Figure 15.29 *SMALL sits in the row_num argument of INDEX.*

As shown in Figure 15.30, if you enter this INDEX with Ctrl+Shift+Enter in cell F12 and then copy it through the range, you will get the extracted records. The #NUM! error is caused by the number incrementor, ROWS(F$12:F12), which is delivering numbers past row 2 even though there are no matched records. Figure 15.31 shows how you can use the IF function to either run the look-up formula or show a null text string. As mentioned in Chapter 9, you should use the IF function instead of the IFERROR function when you create data extraction formulas. You can see in this formula that the formula has a lot of stuff to calculate through, so by using IF to either evaluate the formula or place a null text string in the cell, you save a lot of calculation time.

Extract Area:			
Date	Region	Customer	Units
11/3/12	West	K	436
7/13/12	West	WFMI	1206
#NUM!	#NUM!	#NUM!	#NUM!
#NUM!	#NUM!	#NUM!	#NUM!

Figure 15.30 *There are no records to extract past row two.*

```
=IF(ROWS(F$12:F12)>$A$7,"",INDEX(A$11:A$20,SMALL(
IF($A$11:$A$20>=$B$3,
IF($A$11:$A$20<=$C$3,
IF($B$11:$B$20=$D$3,
ROW($A$11:$A$20)-ROW($A$11)+1))),
ROWS(F$12:F12))))
```

IF(logical_test, [value_if_true], **[value_if_false]**)

Figure 15.31 *Use IF rather IFERROR for data extracting formulas.*

You can enter the finished formulas, as shown in Figure 5.32, into cell F12 with Ctrl+Shift+Enter and then copy it through the range. (The IF function contains an array calculation and therefore you must use Ctrl+Shift+Enter.) Figure 15.33 shows the beauty of formulas: When the criteria change, the formulas instantly update.

Note: I have to thank Aladin Akyurek and Domenic at the MrExcel Message Board for teaching me these formula techniques for extracting data with formulas. Thanks, Aladin! Thanks, Domenic!

	A	B	C	D	E	F	G	H	I	J
1	Array Formula with AND Criteria, SMALL, IF, INDEX									
2	Criteria:	Date	Date	Region						
3		6/1/2012	5/31/2013	West						
5	Count									
6	2	< 2003 or before	=SUMPRODUCT(--(A11:A20>=B3),--(A11:A20<=C3),--(B11:B20=D3))							
7	2	< 2007 or later	=COUNTIFS(A11:A20,">="&B3,A11:A20,"<="&C3,B11:B20,D3)							
9	Data Set:									
10	Date	Region	Customer	Units		Extract Area:				
11	7/29/13	West	WFMI	929		Date	Region	Customer	Units	
12	2/7/12	East	SW	681		11/3/12	West	K	436	
13	9/23/12	Midwest	K	1393		7/13/12	West	WFMI	1206	
14	4/14/12	West	WFMI	530						
15	7/26/12	East	WFMI	1058						
16	10/12/13	Midwest	SW	1023						
17	11/3/12	West	K	436						
18	9/3/13	West	K	1311						
19	4/23/12	Midwest	K	368						
20	7/13/12	West	WFMI	1206						

Figure 15.32 *Two records are extracted.*

	A	B	C	D	E	F	G	H	I	J
1	**Array Formula with AND Criteria, SMALL, IF, INDEX**									
2	Criteria:	Date	Date	Region						
3		2/15/2012	8/31/2013	West						
5	Count									
6	4	< 2003 or before =SUMPRODUCT(--(A11:A20>=B3),--(A11:A20<=C3),--(B11:B20=D3))								
7	4	< 2007 or later =COUNTIFS(A11:A20,">="&B3,A11:A20,"<="&C3,B11:B20,D3)								
9	Data Set:									
10	Date	Region	Customer	Units		Extract Area:				
11	7/29/13	West	WFMI	929		Date	Region	Customer	Units	
12	2/7/12	East	SW	681		7/29/13	West	WFMI	929	
13	9/23/12	Midwest	K	1393		4/14/12	West	WFMI	530	
14	4/14/12	West	WFMI	530		11/3/12	West	K	436	
15	7/26/12	East	WFMI	1058		7/13/12	West	WFMI	1206	
16	10/12/13	Midwest	SW	1023						
17	11/3/12	West	K	436						
18	9/3/13	West	K	1311						
19	4/23/12	Midwest	K	368						
20	7/13/12	West	WFMI	1206						

Figure 15.33 *When you change the criteria, four records are extracted instantly.*

Next, you will time the difference between using the IF and IFERROR functions, and you will also time the array formula against a helper column solution.

Timing IF and IFERROR for Array Formulas That Extract Data

The file for these timing results is named 18-IForIFERROR.xlsm, and it can be found in the Timing folder in the zipped files that accompany the book. To time your own formulas, see Chapter 2 for details. (Timing depends many factors, and your particular situation may have different timing results.)

Here are the two formulas I timed here:

Formula [1]: =IF(ROWS(F$13:F13)>$J$2,"",INDEX(A$2:A$250000,SMALL(IF($A$2:$A$250000=$F$2,IF($B$2:$B$250000=$G$2,IF($C$2:$C$250000=$H$2,ROW($D$2:$D$250000)-ROW($D$20)+1))),ROWS(F$13:F13))))

Formula [2]: =IFERROR(INDEX(A$2:A$250000,SMALL(IF($A$2:$A$250000=$F$2,IF($B$2:$B$250000=$G$2,IF($C$2:$C$250000=$H$2,ROW($D$2:$D$250000)-ROW($D$20)+1))),ROWS(K$13:K13))),"")

Figure 15.34 show the anecdotal results I got.

250,000 rows. Time in seconds.

Time	Formula [1]	Formula [2]
Time 1	2.998	15.374
Time 2	3.002	15.371
Time 3	3.009	15.383
Ave	3.003	15.376
% Change	0.0%	412.0%

Figure 15.34 *The IF function is much faster than IFERROR. But notice that IF took about 3 seconds, and IFERROR took about 15 seconds.*

Comparing Formula Calculation Time for a Helper Column and the SMALL IF for Array Formulas That Extract Data

The file for these timing results is named 19-HelperOrSMALL.xlsm, and it can be found in the Timing folder in the zipped files that accompany the book. To time your own formulas, see Chapter 2 for details. (Timing depends many factors, and your particular situation may have different timing results.)

Here are the two formulas that I timed here:

Formula set [1]: =SUM(E1,AND(A2=$G$2,B2=$H$2,C2=$I$2)) and =IF-(ROWS(H$16:H16)>$K$2,"",INDEX(D$2:D$250000,MATCH(ROWS(H$16:H16),$E$2:$E$250000,0))))

Formula [2]: =IF(ROWS(H$16:H16)>$K$2,"",INDEX(D$2:D$250000,SMALL(IF($A$2:$A$250000=$G$2,IF($B$2:$B$250000=$H$2,IF($C$2:$C$250000=$I$2,ROW($D$2:$D$250000)-ROW($D$2)+1))),ROWS(H$16:H16))))

Figure 15.35 show the anecdotal results I got.

250,000 rows. Time in seconds.

Time	Formula [1]	Formula [2]
Time 1	0.359	2.818
Time 2	0.35875	2.784
Time 3	0.36	2.79
Ave	0.35925	2.7973333
% Change	0.0%	678.7%

Figure 15.35 *The helper column is much faster than the array formula.*

Using an Array Formula for Extracting Data Using AGGREGATE, Boolean Math and INDEX, and AND Criteria

If you have Excel 2010 or later, you can substitute the AGGREGATE function for the SMALL function so that you can avoid Ctrl+Shift+Enter. As you learned in Chapters 4 and 11, you can use Boolean math to filter the values inside the array argument of AGGREGATE. In this example, the filtered values will be the matched relative positions. As shown in Figure 15.36, you start the formula in the same way you started the formula that uses SMALL and IF.

	A	B	C	D	E	F	G	H	I	J
1	Array Formula with AND Criteria, AGGREGATE, Boolean math, INDEX									
2	Criteria:	Date	Date	Region						
3		6/1/2012	5/31/2013	West						
5										
6	Count									
7		2	< Formula =COUNTIFS(A11:A20,">="&B3,A11:A20,"<="&C3,B11:B20,D3)							
9	Data Set:									
10	Date	Region	Customer	Units		Extract Area:				
11	7/29/13	West	WFMI	929		Date	Region	Customer	Units	
12	2/7/12	East	SW	681		=IF(ROWS(F$12:F12)>$A$7,"",INDEX(A$11:A$20,				
13	9/23/12	Midwest	K	1393			INDEX(array, row_num, [column_num])			
							INDEX(reference, row_num, [column_num], [area_num])			
14	4/14/12	West	WFMI	530						
15	7/26/12	East	WFMI	1058						
16	10/12/13	Midwest	SW	1023						
17	11/3/12	West	K	436						
18	9/3/13	West	K	1311						
19	4/23/12	Midwest	K	368						
20	7/13/12	West	WFMI	1206						

Figure 15.36 *You can use SMALL or AGGREGATE in the row_num argument of INDEX.*

As shown in Figure 15.37, AGGREGATE sits in the row_num argument of INDEX. You use 15 in the function_num argument of AGGREGATE to instruct AGGREGATE to make the SMALL calculation, and you use 6 in the options argument to instruct AGGREGATE to ignore errors. You build the Boolean math array in the array argument of AGGREGATE. Notice that in the numerator, parentheses are around the formula element that creates the array of relative positions to force the subtraction and addition to calculate before the division. Also notice that in the denominator, parentheses are around the conditional Boolean multiplication force the multiplication to calculate before the division.

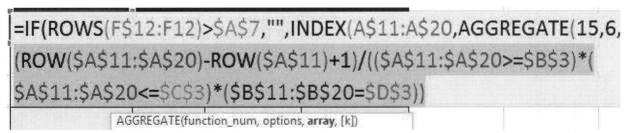

```
=IF(ROWS(F$12:F12)>$A$7,"",INDEX(A$11:A$20,AGGREGATE(15,6,
(ROW($A$11:$A$20)-ROW($A$11)+1)/(($A$11:$A$20>=$B$3)*(
$A$11:$A$20<=$C$3)*($B$11:$B$20=$D$3))
                    AGGREGATE(function_num, options, array, [k])
```

Figure 15.37 *AGGREGATE in the row_num argument of INDEX. Array operations to deliver a resultant array with relative positions in the array argument of AGGREGATE.*

As shown in Figure 15.38, if you evaluate the numerator, you see all the relative positions, and if you evaluate the denominator, you see that you get a one when all conditions have been met and a zero when the AND criteria is not met.

```
=IF(ROWS(F$12:F12)>$A$7,"",INDEX(A$11:A$20,AGGREGATE(15,6,
{1;2;3;4;5;6;7;8;9;10}/{0;0;0;0;0;0;1;0;0;1}
          AGGREGATE(function_num, options, array, [k])
```

Figure 15.38 *Zeros in denominator will cause #DIV/0! Errors.*

As shown in Figure 15.39, if you evaluate the entire Boolean math array operation in the array argument, you get an array of matched record relative positions and #DIV/0! errors. The errors "filter" out the relative positions that do not meet the criteria. The 6 in the options argument tells AGGREGATE to ignore the errors.

```
=IF(ROWS(F$12:F12)>$A$7,"",INDEX(A$11:A$20,AGGREGATE(15,6,
{#DIV/0!;#DIV/0!;#DIV/0!;#DIV/0!;#DIV/0!;#DIV/0!;7;#DIV/0!;#DIV/
0!;10}     AGGREGATE(function_num, options, array, [k])
```

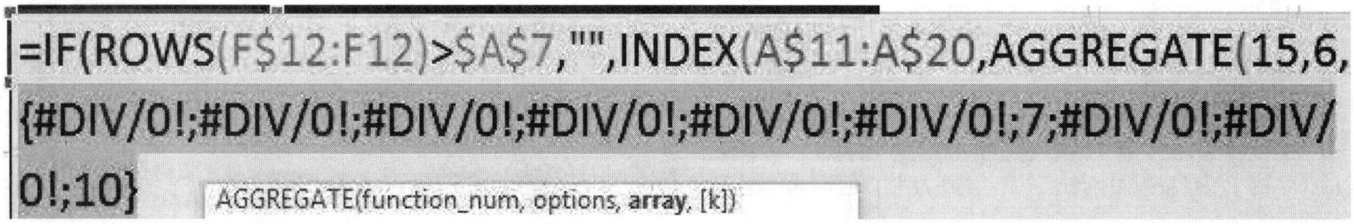

Figure 15.39 *#DIV/0! Errors are the filter. The 6 in the options argument of the AGGREGATE will cause AGGREGATE to ignore the errors.*

As shown in Figure 15.40, you can finish the formula by placing the number incrementor, ROWS(F$12:F12), into the k argument of AGGREGATE, adding the remaining three parentheses, and then entering the formula with just Enter, rather than Ctrl+Shift+Enter. Figures 15.41 and 15.42 show that you can change the criteria, and the formulas update instantly.

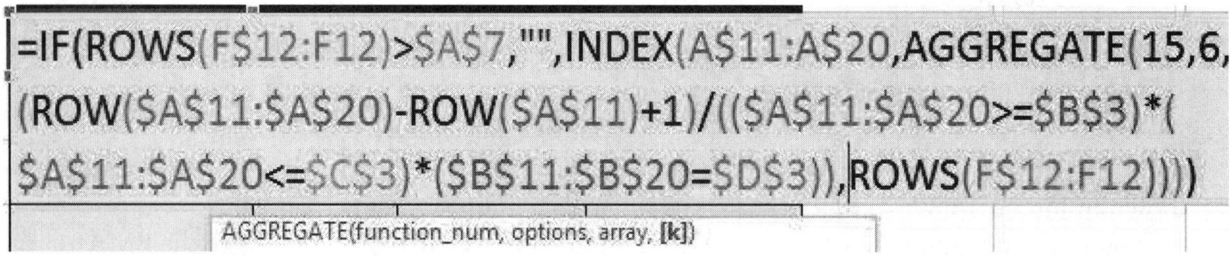

```
=IF(ROWS(F$12:F12)>$A$7,"",INDEX(A$11:A$20,AGGREGATE(15,6,
(ROW($A$11:$A$20)-ROW($A$11)+1)/(($A$11:$A$20>=$B$3)*(
$A$11:$A$20<=$C$3)*($B$11:$B$20=$D$3)),ROWS(F$12:F12))))
          AGGREGATE(function_num, options, array, [k])
```

Figure 15.40 *Finished array formula. No Ctrl+Shift+Enter is necessary.*

	A	B	C	D	E	F	G	H	I
1	**Array Formula with AND Criteria, AGGREGATE, Boolean math, INDEX**								
2	Criteria:	Date	Date	Region					
3		6/1/2012	5/31/2013	West					
5									
6	Count								
7	2	< Formula =COUNTIFS(A11:A20,">="&B3,A11:A20,"<="&C3,B11:B20,D3)							
9	Data Set:								
10	Date	Region	Customer	Units		Extract Area:			
11	7/29/13	West	WFMI	929		Date	Region	Customer	Units
12	2/7/12	East	SW	681		11/3/12	West	K	436
13	9/23/12	Midwest	K	1393		7/13/12	West	WFMI	1206
14	4/14/12	West	WFMI	530					
15	7/26/12	East	WFMI	1058					
16	10/12/13	Midwest	SW	1023					
17	11/3/12	West	K	436					
18	9/3/13	West	K	1311					
19	4/23/12	Midwest	K	368					
20	7/13/12	West	WFMI	1206					

Figure 15.41 *Two records are extracted.*

	A	B	C	D	E	F	G	H	I
1	**Array Formula with AND Criteria, AGGREGATE, Boolean math, INDEX**								
2	Criteria:	Date	Date	Region					
3		2/15/2012	8/31/2013	West					
5									
6	Count								
7	4	< Formula =COUNTIFS(A11:A20,">="&B3,A11:A20,"<="&C3,B11:B20,D3)							
9	Data Set:								
10	Date	Region	Customer	Units		Extract Area:			
11	7/29/13	West	WFMI	929		Date	Region	Customer	Units
12	2/7/12	East	SW	681		7/29/13	West	WFMI	929
13	9/23/12	Midwest	K	1393		4/14/12	West	WFMI	530
14	4/14/12	West	WFMI	530		11/3/12	West	K	436
15	7/26/12	East	WFMI	1058		7/13/12	West	WFMI	1206
16	10/12/13	Midwest	SW	1023					
17	11/3/12	West	K	436					
18	9/3/13	West	K	1311					
19	4/23/12	Midwest	K	368					
20	7/13/12	West	WFMI	1206					

Figure 15.42 *When the criteria changes, the formulas update.*

Timing SMALL and AGGREGATE for Array Formulas That Extract Data

The file for these timing results is named 20-AGGREGATEorSMALL.xlsm, and it can be found in the Timing folder in the zipped files that accompany the book. To time your own formulas, see Chapter 2 for details. (Timing depends many factors, and your particular situation may have different timing results.)

Here are the two formulas I timed:

Formula [1]: =IF(ROWS(G$16:G16)>$J$2,"",INDEX(D$2:D$250000,AGGREGATE(15,6,(ROW($D$2:$D$250000)-ROW($D$2)+1)/(($A$2:$A$250000=$F$2)*($B$2:$B$250000=$G$2)*($C$2:$C$250000=$H$2)),ROWS(G$16:G16))))

Formula [2]: =IF(ROWS(F$13:F13)>$J$2,"",INDEX(A$2:A$250000,SMALL(IF($A$2:$A$250000=$F$2,IF($B$2:$B$250000=$G$2,IF($C$2:$C$250000=$H$2,ROW($D$2:$D$250000)-ROW($D$20)+1))),ROWS(F$13:F13))))

Figure 15.43 show the anecdotal results I got.

250,000 rows. Time in seconds.		
Time	Formula [1]	Formula [2]
Time 1	2.59906	2.8866
Time 2	2.5925	2.7548
Time 3	2.59454	2.7496
Ave	2.5953667	2.797
% Change	0.0%	7.8%

Figure 15.43 *The timing for SMALL and for AGGREGATE to extract relative positions from the filtered array of matched record relative positions is similar.*

Returning Multiple Items from One Lookup Value

The standard lookup functions in Excel—such as VLOOKUP, MATCH, and INDEX—can't return multiple items from one lookup value unless you build an array formula. As shown in Figure 15.44, you need to look up the group name Cascade from cell D3, find all occurrences in the Group field, and return the associated employee names from the Employees field.

You could use either of the following formulas to accomplish this:

No Ctrl+Shift+Enter: =IF(ROWS(D$6:D6)>E$3,"",INDEX($A$3:$A$52,AGGREGATE(15,6,(ROW($A$3:$A$52)-ROW(A$3)+1)/($B$3:$B$52=D$3),ROWS(D$6:D6))))

Requires Ctrl+Shift+Enter: =IF(ROWS(D$6:D6)>E$3,"",INDEX($A$3:$A$52,SMALL(IF($B$3:$B$52=D$3,ROW($A$3:$A$52)-ROW(D$3)+1),ROWS(D$6:D6))))

Figure 15.44 shows an example of the AGGREGATE formula that does not require Ctrl+Shift+Enter.

Figure 15.44 *You can use SMALL or AGGREGATE in the row_num argument of INDEX.*

An alternative to using this array formula is to create a helper column, as shown in Figure 15.45.

	A	B	C	D	E	F	G	H	I
1	Formula in cell A3: =C3&COUNTIF(C$3:C3,C3)								
2	Helper	Employees	Group		Groups	Count			
3	Cascade1	Jules Horowitz	Cascade		Cascade	16	< Formula =COUNTIF($C$3:$C$52,E3)		
4	Kroner1	Aliza Burden	Kroner						
5	Yanaki1	Jessika Hwang	Yanaki		Employees				
6	Yanaki2	Josiah Marroquin	Yanaki		Jules Horowitz	< Formula =IF(ROWS(E$6:E6)>F$3,"",			
7	Cascade2	Stormy Haight	Cascade		Stormy Haight	VLOOKUP(E$3&ROWS(E$6:E6),$A$3:$B$52,2,0))			

Figure 15.45 *Using a helper column with an ampersand (&) for an expandable range inside COUNTIF.*

Extracting Data with OR Criteria from a Single Column: Boolean or MATCH?

This example is an extension of the previous example. After you extract all the employee names for a particular group, you might then want to use all the employee names as OR criteria to extract records from a data set. Note the following in Figure 15.46:

1. The OR criteria names are in the range I6:I21.

2. For each record in the data set, the formula must ask the question "Is the employee name equal to any of the names in the range I6:I21?" This means that there are 16 individual OR logical tests that are all pointing at a single cell.

3. You use the ISNUMBER/MATCH construction instead of stringing together 16 Boolean OR addition array calculations because it is easier to create and it calculates more quickly.

	A	B	C	D	E	F	G	H	I
1		Formula in G5: =SUMPRODUCT(--ISNUMBER(MATCH($B$5:$B$936,$I$6:$I$21,0)))							
2									
3	**Array Formula to extract with Many OR Criteria**								
4	Date	Employee	Contacts Made			<<== Count Employees in this data set.			OR Criteria
5	7/12/14	Delpha Mayers	24				158		Employee
6	11/5/14	Georgianne Walls	3						Jules Horowitz
7	12/15/14	Rosamond Allard	51		No	Employee	Contacts Made		Stormy Haight
8	12/6/14	Kerrie Worrell	49		1	=IF(ROWS(F$8:F8)>$G$5,"",INDEX(B5:B$936,			
9	11/3/14	Franchesca Novak	35		2	SMALL(IF(ISNUMBER(MATCH($B$5:$B$936,$I$6:$I$21,0)),			
10	7/7/14	Eulalia Clement	54		3	ROW($B$5:$B$936)-ROW($B$5)+1),ROWS(F$8:F8))))			
11	12/12/14	Susan Cannon	65		4	Ivelisse Goins	65		Franchesca Novak
12	11/26/14	Josiah Marroquin	5		5	Idalia Osullivan	65		Shandra Rife
13	6/25/14	Lynn Taylor	38		6	Jules Horowitz	5		Rhett Seymore
14	7/18/14	Shandra Rife	12		7	Idalia Osullivan	68		Eulalia Clement
15	8/3/14	Karma Roper	48		8	Rhett Seymore	67		Allena Swenson
16	12/19/14	Delpha Mayers	25		9	Marlana Huang	19		Alyse Hopson
17	7/11/14	Angel Casey	62		10	Allena Swenson	47		Pansy Sam
18	7/2/14	Mickey Bolduc	18		11	Jules Horowitz	9		Marlana Huang
19	10/23/14	Dominick Dunn	39		12	Alyse Hopson	39		Marcelle Raley
20	10/21/14	Arnold Ford	45		13	Stormy Haight	12		Idalia Osullivan
21	9/24/14	Ivelisse Goins	65		14	Franchesca Novak	19		Lupe Donovan
22	8/18/14	Levi Reese	75		15	Alyse Hopson	8		
23	8/28/14	Troy Hicks	25		16	Alyse Hopson	28		

Figure 15.46 *For data extraction formulas with more than two OR criteria applied to a single column, use ISNUMBER/MATCH.*

You could also use this formula in cell F8:

=IF(ROWS(F$8:F8)>$G$5,"",INDEX(B5:B$936,AGGREGATE(15,6,(ROW($B$5:$B$936)-ROW($B$5)+1)/ISNUMBER(MATCH($B$5:$B$936,$I$6:$I$21,0)),ROWS(F$8:F8))))

Timing Boolean OR Addition and ISNUMBER/MATCH for Array Formulas That Extract Data

The data for these timing results are in two files. The names are 22-BooleanOrMATCH-ManyExamples.xlsm and 21-OR-MATCHorBoolean.xlsm, and they can be found in the Timing folder in the zipped files that accompany the book. To time your own formulas, see Chapter 2 for details. (Timing depends many factors, and your particular situation may have different timing results.)

For the first timing example, I used a data set with 1,000 rows of data and 400 rows of formulas. From the 22-BooleanOrMATCH-ManyExamples.xlsm file on the sheet tab named 15-1000-OR (3), here are the two formulas I timed:

Formula [1]: =IF(ROWS(K$19:K19)>$H$16,"",INDEX(C$2:C$1001,SMALL(IF(ISNUMBER(MATCH($B$2:$B$1001,$F$18:$F$32,0)),ROW($C$2:$C$1001)-ROW($C$2)+1),ROWS(K$19:K19))))

Formula [2]: =IF(ROWS(H$19:H19)>$H$16,"",INDEX(C$2:C$1001,SMALL(IF(($B$2:$B$1001=$F$18)+($B$2:$B$1001=$F$19)+($B$2:$B$1001=$F$20)+($B$2:$B$1001=$F$21)+($B$2:$B$1001=$F$22)+($B$2:$B$1001=$F$23)+($B$2:$B$1001=$F$24)+($B$2:$B$1001=$F$25)+($B$2:$B$1001=$F$26)+($B$2:$B$1001=$F$27)+($B$2:$B$1001=$F$28)+($B$2:$B$1001=$F$29)+($B$2:$B$1001=$F$30)+($B$2:$B$1001=$F$31)+($B$2:$B$1001=$F$32), ROW($C$2:$C$1001)-ROW($C$2)+1),ROWS(H$19:H19))))

Figure 15.47 show the anecdotal results I got.

1000 rows of data. 400 rows of formulas. Time in seconds.		
	Formula [1]	Formula [2]
Time 1	0.318	0.7476
Time 2	0.327	0.7571
Time 3	0.321	0.755
Ave	0.322	0.753233333
% Change	0.0%	133.9%

Figure 15.47 *Timing for 1,000 rows of data and 400 rows of formulas.*

For the second timing example, I used a data set with 10,000 rows of data and more than 3,000 rows of formulas. From the 21-OR-MATCHorBoolean.xlsm file on the sheet tab named 16 OR, here are the two formulas I timed:

Formula [1]: =IF(ROWS(G$20:G20)>$F$6,"",INDEX(A$2:A$10000,SMALL(IF(ISNUMBER(MATCH($B$2:$B$10000,$E$6:$E$22,0)),ROW($C$2:$C$10000)-ROW($C$2)+1),ROWS(G$20 :G20))))

Formula [2]: =IF(ROWS(G$20:G20)>$F$6,"",INDEX(A$2:A$10000,SMALL(IF(($B$2:$B$ 10000=$E$6)+($B$2:$B$10000=$E$7)+($B$2:$B$10000=$E$8)+($B$2:$B$10000=$E$9)+($B$2:$B$10000=$E$10)+($B$2:$B$10000=$E$11)+($B$2:$B$10000=$E$12)+($B$2:$B$100 00=$E$13)+($B$2:$B$10000=$E$14)+($B$2:$B$10000=$E$15)+($B$2:$B$10000=$E$16)+($B$2:$B$10000=$E$17)+($B$2:$B$10000=$E$18)+($B$2:$B$10000=$E$19)+($B$2:$B$10 000=$E$20)+($B$2:$B$10000=$E$21)+($B$2:$B$10000=$E$22),ROW($C$2:$C$10000)-RO-W($C$2)+1),ROWS(G$20:G20))))

Figure 15.47 show the anecdotal results I got.

3481 rows of formulas, 10,000 rows of data. Time in seconds.		
	Formula [1]	Formula [2]
Time 1	24.3	49.4
Time 2	24.2	49.2
Time 3	24.2	48.89
Ave	24.23333333	49.16333333
% Change	0.0%	102.9%

Figure 15.48 *When there are many OR criteria (16, in this example), formulas to extract data take a long time. Advanced Filter or Filter may be a better solution. The ISNUMBER/MATCH construction took about 24 seconds, and the 16 Boolean OR calculations took about 49 seconds.*

The following section provides examples of array formulas to extract data in various circumstances. The examples alternate between using SMALL and AGGREGATE.

Extracting Data with OR Criteria Operating on More Than One Column and AND Criteria

Figures 15.49and 15.50 show a data set, criteria, and formulas. The goal of this formula is to extract records that are either West region OR customer K AND the units are between 400 and 1,300. There are two things you should notice in this example: (1) This is a two-way lookup where the SMALL function is delivering a relative row position to the row_num argument of INDEX, and MATCH is delivering the relative column position to the column_num argument of INDEX and (2) the OR logical tests can result in the number 1 or 2, but this will not cause a problem because the logical_test argument of IF interprets any nonzero number as TRUE.

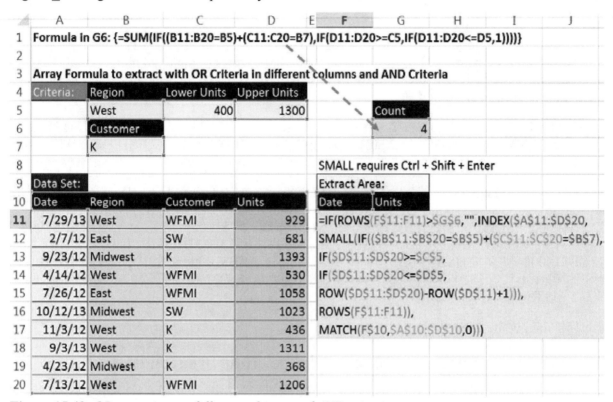

Figure 15.49 *OR operating on different columns and AND criteria.*

Extract Area:	
Date	Units
7/29/13	929
4/14/12	530
11/3/12	436
7/13/12	1206

Figure 15.50 *Four records should be extracted.*

Extracting Data with OR and AND Criteria, Including Numbers Divisible by 5

Figures 15.51 and 15.52 show a data set, criteria, and formulas. The goal of this formula is to extract records that are either West region OR customer K AND the unit number must be divisible by 5. In this example, you should notice two things about the Boolean math: (1) MOD looks through the column of numbers and divides by 5, and when the remainder is zero, you get a TRUE; and 2) the Boolean OR calculation must be set against the logical test "are you greater than zero?" because you run the risk of getting two TRUE values from the two columns.

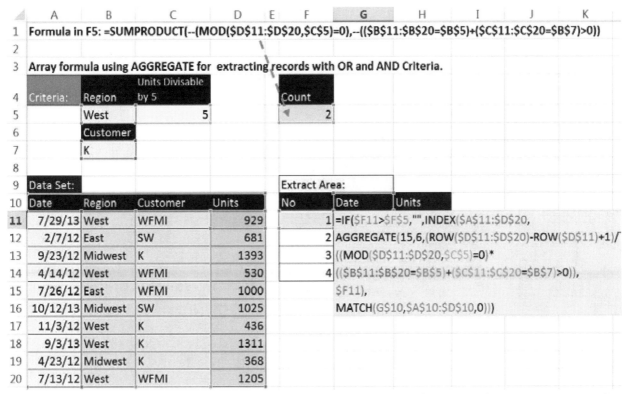

Figure 15.51 *Formula to extract with AND criteria, including the use of the MOD function to extract only numbers divisible by 5.*

Extract Area:		
No	Date	Units
1	4/14/2012	530
2	7/13/2012	1205

Figure 15.52 *Two records should be extracted.*

Extracting Data Items in List 1 That Are Not in List 2: Comparing Two Lists

Figures 15.53 and 15.54 show a data set, criteria, and formulas. The goal of this formula is to extract the names in List 2 that are not in List 1. This is a classic "compare two lists" problem. The MATCH function compares the two lists and delivers an #N/A error when it does not find the name. You simply wrap the ISNA functions around that MATCH to get a TRUE whenever the MATCH delivers an #N/A.

> **Note:** To do the opposite—that is, to find the names in LIST 2 that are in List 1—use the ISNUMBER function in place of the ISNA function.

	A	B	C	D	E	F	G	H
1	Formula in E5: =SUMPRODUCT(--(ISNA(MATCH($C$5:$C$9,$A$5:$A$8,0))))							
2								
3	Extract Names in List 2 that are NOT in List 1							
4	List 1		List 2		Count			
5	Joe		Cynthia		3			
6	Cynthia		Gigi					
7	Mo		Timmy		Extract Area:			
8	Timmy		Omar		Names in List 2 that are NOT in List 1	SMALL requires Ctrl + Shift + Enter		
9			Tina		=IF(ROWS(E$9:E9)>$E$5,"",INDEX($C$5:$C$9,			
10					SMALL(IF(ISNA(MATCH($C$5:$C$9,$A$5:$A$8,0)),			
11					ROW($C$5:$C$9)-ROW($C$5)+1),ROWS(E$9:E9))))			

Figure 15.53 *A classic "compare two lists" formula.*

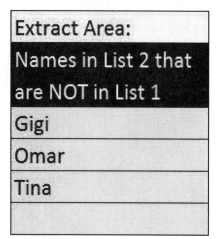

Extract Area:
Names in List 2 that are NOT in List 1
Gigi
Omar
Tina

Figure 15.54 *Three names are in list 2 that are not in List 1.*

Helper Columns in the Data Extract Area

Figures 15.55 shows a data set, criteria, and formulas. The goal of this formula is to extract records that are either from the West region OR East region. In this situation, you are not allowed to have a helper column in the data set area, but because you want to reduce formula calculation time, you decide instead to put a helper column in the data extraction area. As discussed earlier in this chapter, with helper cells, any time a formula element delivers the same item to the formula, repeating many times, you can remove it from the formula and place it in a cell so that it calculates only one time. In this case, the AGGREGATE (or SMALL, in other formulas) is delivering the same relative position throughout the entire row. The formula in cell L10 is copied down the column to create a helper column, and the results are referred to in the formula with a cell reference. This can reduce formula calculation time.

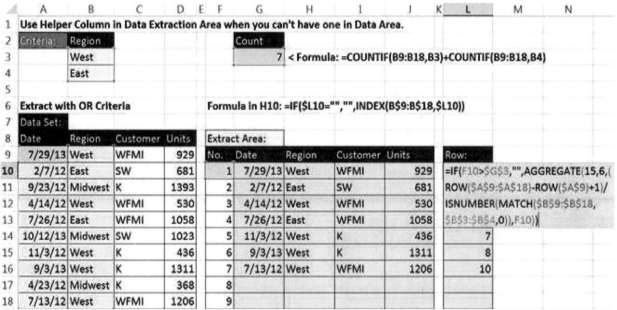

Figure 15.55 *The formula element that calculates the relative row position is removed from the formula and placed into a helper column. This means that formula element will calculate three fewer times per row.*

Dynamic Range Inside Array Formula to Extract Records

Sometimes you want your data extraction formula to pick up any new records entered into a table. One way to accomplish this is to create a defined name dynamic range formula, as you did in Chapter 13. Figure 15.56 shows two dynamic ranges created using the INDEX function and the "big number" concept. Figure 15.57 shows the data extraction formulas to extract data with two OR criteria.

Name	Refers To
ContactNames	='15-(56)'!$B$6:INDEX('15-(56)'!$B$6:$B$105,MATCH(9.99E+307,'15-(56)'!$C$6:$C$105))
ContactsTable	='15-(56)'!$A$6:INDEX('15-(56)'!$C$6:$C$105,MATCH(9.99E+307,'15-(56)'!$C$6:$C$105))

Figure 15.56 *Using INDEX and a "big number" to create two dynamic ranges.*

	A	B	C	D	E	F	G	H	I	J	K
1	Formula in I5: =SUMPRODUCT(--ISNUMBER(MATCH(ContactNames,$E$7:$E$11,0)))										
2											
3	Extract with OR Criteria and Defined Name Dynamic Range Formula										
4	Data Set:								Count		
5	Date	Name	Contacts		OR Criteria				4		
6	4/22/14	Mo	29		Name		Extract:				
7	5/2/14	Mo	10		Mo		Date	Name	Contacts		
8	5/4/14	Jane	51		Jane		=IF(ROWS(G$8:G8)>$I$5,"",INDEX(ContactsTable,				
9	5/10/14	Tina	14				AGGREGATE(15,6,(ROW(ContactNames)-ROW($B$6)+1)/				
10	5/10/14	Chin	42				ISNUMBER(MATCH(ContactNames,$E$7:$E$11,0)),				
11	5/10/14	Sue	2				ROWS(G$8:G8)),COLUMNS($G8:G8)))				
12	5/22/14	Jane	13								
13											
14											
15											

Figure 15.57 *The formulas use the defined name dynamic range formulas.*

Figure 15.58 shows the four records that the formulas should extract.

Extract:		
Date	Name	Contacts
4/22/14	Mo	29
5/2/14	Mo	10
5/4/14	Jane	51
5/22/14	Jane	13

Figure 15.58 *With the records entered as shown in Figure 15.57, you should get four extracted records.*

	A	B	C		E				Count	
4	Data Set:								Count	
5	Date	Name	Contacts		OR Criteria				6	
6	4/22/14	Mo	29		Name		Extract:			
7	5/2/14	Mo	10		Mo		Date	Name	Contacts	
8	5/4/14	Jane	51		Jane		4/22/14	Mo	29	
9	5/10/14	Tina	14				5/2/14	Mo	10	
10	5/10/14	Chin	42				5/4/14	Jane	51	
11	5/10/14	Sue	2				5/22/14	Jane	13	
12	5/22/14	Jane	13				5/23/14	Mo	43	
13	5/23/14	Mo	43				5/27/14	Jane	96	
14	5/27/14	Jane	96							
15										

Figure 15.59 *If you add new records, the defined name dynamic range formulas and the data extraction formulas should automatically extract the correct records.*

Comparing Methods for Extracting Data

The following table compares the different methods discussed in this chapter for extracting data.

Methods for Extracting Data		
Feature/ Formula	**Advantage**	**Disadvantage**
Filter	<ul><li>Easy to perform.</li><li>This method should be used when it is a one-time shot: You just need to extract and go.</li><li>Can use a helper column if a built-in feature won't work.</li><li>In some situations Filter may be a good alternative to formula solutions that take a long time to calculate.</li></ul>	<ul><li>Not automatic, like formulas.</li><li>Does not have all the capabilities of Advanced Filter or formulas.</li></ul>
Advanced Filter	<ul><li>Can see criteria in cells (not hidden behind AutoFilter drop-down arrows).</li><li>Can do OR criteria from two or more columns.</li><li>Can use formula criteria.</li><li>In some situations, Advanced Filter may be a good alternative to formula solutions that take a long time to calculate.</li></ul>	<ul><li>Not automatic, like formulas.</li><li>Not as quick as Filter.</li></ul>
Helper columns	<ul><li>Formulas automatically update when criteria or data changes.</li><li>Usually calculates *much* faster than array formulas.</li><li>More simple to create than array formulas.</li></ul>	<ul><li>Takes up space in the spreadsheet.</li></ul>
Array formula using SMALL	<ul><li>Formulas automatically update when criteria or data changes.</li><li>Does not require helper columns; is more self-contained that helper column solutions.</li></ul>	<ul><li>Usually much slower than helper columns.</li><li>Complicated to create.</li><li>Requires Ctrl+-Shift+Enter.</li></ul>
Array formula using AGGREGATE	<ul><li>Formulas automatically update when criteria or data changes.</li><li>Does not require helper columns; is more self-contained than helper column solutions.</li><li>Does not require Ctrl+Shift+Enter</li></ul>	<ul><li>Available only in Excel 2010 and later.</li><li>Usually much slower than helper columns.</li><li>Complicated to create.</li></ul>

Some Key Concepts for Data Extraction Formulas

In this chapter, you learned the following important information about data extraction:

- Use IF instead of IFERROR because the IFERROR function has to calculate in each cell, which can significantly increase formulas calculation time.

- AND criteria can be created with the IF function or Boolean math.

- OR criteria can be created with the IF function or Boolean math. Keep these two points in mind when using OR criteria:

  o For OR criteria operating on a single column, the ISNUMBER/MATCH combination tends to be easier to create and calculate faster than the Boolean OR addition calculation.

  o For OR criteria operating on multiple columns, remember to account for counts greater than 1.

- There are two helpful ways to think about data extraction formulas:

  o Extract records or data that match a set of criteria.

  o Return multiple items from one lookup value.

Chapter Summary

Wow!! This is quite a big chapter, all about how to create formulas to extract data with criteria. Later on, in Chapter 19, you will learn more about formulas for extracting data, such as extracting a unique list and creating formulas that sort. Before that, though, you must read Chapters 16, 17, and 18, which cover the FREQUENCY array function, unique counting formulas, and the MMULT array function, respectively.

Chapter 16: The FREQUENCY Array Function

Excel Files

To follow along with the examples in this chapter, you can download the accompanying files, as explained in the Introduction.

Array Functions from Earlier Chapters

Chapter 9 covered the fundamentals of array functions. The FREQUENCY array function will be our fourth example of an Array Function.

The FREQUENCY Array Function: Amazing, Powerful, and Versatile

The FREQUENCY array Function is very simple, yet very powerful and versatile. In this way it is sort of like the SUMPRODUCT function because it has its base use, and then there are many other ways people apply it to solve a myriad of problems. In this chapter you will learn the base use for the FREQUENCY function as well as details about how this function works. Then in Chapters 17 and 19 you will apply what you have learned in this chapter to provide amazing solutions to difficult problems.

The base use for FREQUENCY is to count how many numbers fall into a set of categories. As shown in Figure 16.1, the goal in this example is to count how many of the BMX racing times in the range A5:A17 fall into the categories shown in the range D5:D10.

> **Note:** The categories in the range D5:D10 are not part of the actual formula; they are shown for illustration purposes only.

You enter the FREQUENCY function into the range E5:E10 using Ctrl+Shift+Enter. It delivers a vertical array of numbers that reports the count of race times that fall within each category. For example, you can see that five kids got BMX racing times that were greater than 45 seconds and less than or equal to 50 seconds. There are two arguments for FREQUENCY: data_array contains the numbers to be counted in the range A5:A17, and bins_array contains the upper limits for each category in the range C5:C9. Notice that FREQUENCY delivers one more result than there are bins_array: there are six frequency numbers delivered by the FREQUENCY function, but only five upper limit numbers entered into the bins_array argument. This occurs because the people who programmed this function were being polite to the users of the function. They added the extra category in case you do not provide enough upper limits to count *all* the numbers in the data_array. As a user, you simply provide a set of upper limits, and an all-inclusive set of categories are automatically created. Notice the brilliance of the categories created:

- The first category counts all the values less than or equal the first upper limit.
- The middle categories count between a lower limit and an upper limit. The lower limit *is not* included in the category. The upper limit *is* included in the category. For example, 45 seconds would not be counted in the category 45 < Time <= 50, but would be counted in the category 40 < Time <=45.
- The last category catches all the values that are greater than the last upper limit.

| E5 | ▼ | : | ✕ | ✓ | ƒx | {=FREQUENCY(A5:A17,C5:C9)} |

▲	A	B	C	D	E	F
1	FREQUENCY Array Function: count how many numbers in each category.					
2	data_array		bins_array			
4	BMX racing times (sec)		Upper Limits	Category automatically created by FREQUENCY	Frequency	
5	65.52		40	Time <= 40	1	
6	52.1		45	40 < Time <= 45	3	
7	46.5		50	45 < Time <= 50	5	
8	39.4		55	50 < Time <= 55	2	
9	43.5		60	55 < Time <= 60	1	
10	46.8			60 < Time	1	
11	47.8					
12	48.1					
13	48					
14	43.5					
15	52.3					
16	56.35					
17	41.85					

Figure 16.1 *FREQUENCY counts numbers, given a set of category upper limits.*

The fact that you can type in any set of numbers into the range A5:A17 and have all the numbers accounted for in the frequency count means the function is robust.

Details of How the FREQUENCY Array Function Works

Here's what you need to know about how the FREQUENCY array function works:

- FREQUENCY counts how many numbers are in each category.
- The bins_array argument contains the upper values for the categories—numbers only.
- The data_array argument contains the values to count—numbers only.
- Keep in mind the following about categories:
  - Categories are automatically created. There is no visual indication of how the categories are organized.
  - The first category counts all the values less than or equal to the first upper limit.
  - The middle categories count between a lower limit and an upper limit. The lower limit *is not* included in the category. The upper limit *is* included in the category.
  - The last category catches all the values that are greater than the last upper limit.
  - There is always one more category than there are bins.
- FREQUENCY delivers a vertical array. If you need a horizontal array, use the TRANSPOSE function to convert a vertical array to a horizontal array.
- Because this is an array function, you must select the destination range before creating the formula and enter the formula with Ctrl+Shift+Enter. If you have n values in the bins_array argument, the selected destination range should contain n+ + 1 cells.

- FREQUENCY ignores empty cells and text.
- If there are duplicate bins, the duplicates get a count of zero. (You use this aspect utilized when you create formulas for unique counting.)
- After the FREQUENCY function has been entered into the destination range with Ctrl+Shift+Enter, the resultant array of values is considered a single unit and individual cells cannot be deleted. You can deleted all the values, but not just one.
- FREQUENCY can be used in larger array formulas and will deliver a vertical array.

Let's next look at an example of how to display the results from FREQUENCY in a row rather than a column.

Need Horizontal? Use TRANSPOSE Wrapped Around FREQUENCY

Figure 16.2 shows that if you enter the FREQUENCY function into a horizontal range, the cells display the first value in the resultant array in all the cells. Figure 16.3 shows the evaluated results of the FREQUENCY function. Notice the array syntax semicolons (semicolons mean go down a row). You cannot display a vertical array horizontally unless you convert the semicolons to commas (commas mean go to the next column), which then converts the vertical array to a horizontal array. Figure 16.4 shows how you can wrap the TRANSPOSE array function around FREQUENCY and convert the semicolons to commas. (Evaluate it by pressing F9 to see the commas.)

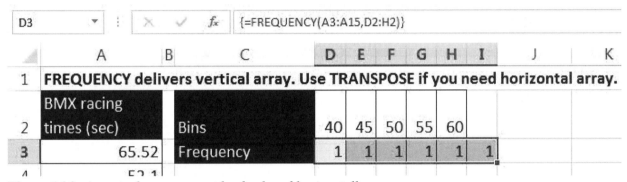

Figure 16.2 *A vertical array cannot be displayed horizontally.*

={1;3;5;2;1;1}

Figure 16.3 *FREQUENCY evaluates to a vertical resultant array with semicolons.*

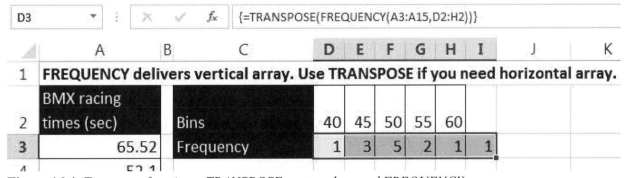

Figure 16.4 *Two array functions: TRANSPOSE wrapped around FREQUENCY.*

Empty Cells, Text, and Duplicate Bin Values

When you get to advanced uses for the FREQUENCY function in Chapters 17 and 19, it will be helpful if you know how the FREQUENCY function handles empty cells, text, and duplicate bin values. As shown in Figure 16.5, the FREQUENCY function ignores empty cells and text. The FREQUENCY function entered into the range F3:F8 ignores the empty A11 cell and the DQ text in cell A15. Figure 16.6 shows that duplicate bins_array values will get a count of zero. In formulas for counting or extracting unique values, the fact that the duplicate bin values get a zero will be particularly useful.

| F3 | ▼ | : | × | ✓ | *fx* | {=FREQUENCY(A3:A13,D3:D7)} |

	A	B	C	D	E	F
1	FREQUENCY ignores text and empty cells.					
2	BMX racing times (sec)	Rider		Bins	Category	Frequency
3	65.52	Brandon		40	Time <= 40	1
4	52.1	Hudson		45	40 < Time <= 45	2
5	46.5	Ella		50	45 < Time <= 50	3
6	39.4	Lucas		55	50 < Time <= 55	2
7	43.5	Rob		60	55 < Time <= 60	0
8	46.8	Logan			60 < Time	1
9	47.8	Collin				
10		Sioux				
11	52.3	Isaac				
12	DQ	Mike				
13	41.85	Walt				

Figure 16.5 *The FREQUENCY function ignores empty cells and text.*

	A	B	C	D	E
1	If you give FREQUENCY duplicate bins, it only counts in the first one.				
2	BMX racing times (sec)		Bins	Frequency	
3	65.52		40	1	<<== Only first duplicate gets a count.
4	52.1		40	0	<<== Duplicate bins gets no count, they are ignored
5	46.5		40	0	<<== Duplicate bins gets no count, they are ignored
6	39.4		45	2	
7	43.5		50	3	
8	46.8		55	2	
9	47.8		60	0	
10				1	
11	52.3				
12	DQ				
13	41.85				

Figure 16.6 *Duplicates in the bins_array argument get a count of zero.*

Creating Unambiguous Labels for Users

Figure 16.7 shows an example of how using the upper limits alone as labels for a report may be ambiguous. Figure 16.8 shows how you could add text formulas. Figure 16.9 shows a report that is clear and understandable.

	A	B	C	D
1	Upper limits only may be ambiguous			
2	BMX racing times (sec)		Upper Limits	Frequency
3	65.52		40	1
4	52.1		45	3
5	46.5		50	5
6	39.4		55	2
7	43.5		60	1
8	46.8			1
9	47.8			
10	48.1			
11	48			
12	43.5			
13	52.3			
14	56.35			
15	41.85			

Figure 16.7 *Having upper limits only may be unclear.*

	A	B	C	D	E	F
1	**Text formulas based on upper values can make report more clear**					
2	BMX racing times (sec)		Upper Limits	Frequency	Categories	Formulas in E column
3	65.52		40	1	Time <= 40	=" Time <= "&C3
4	52.1		45	3	40 < Time <= 45	=C3&" < Time <= "&C4
5	46.5		50	5	45 < Time <= 50	=C4&" < Time <= "&C5
6	39.4		55	2	50 < Time <= 55	=C5&" < Time <= "&C6
7	43.5		60	1	55 < Time <= 60	=C6&" < Time <= "&C7
8	46.8			1	60 < Time	=C7&" < Time"

Figure 16.8 *You can use text formulas to build clear labels.*

Categories for race times (sec)	Count within each category
Time <= 40	1
40 < Time <= 45	3
45 < Time <= 50	5
50 < Time <= 55	2
55 < Time <= 60	1
60 < Time	1

Figure 16.9 *This report is easier to understand because it has clear labels.*

Counting Between Upper and Lower Values: FREQUENCY, COUNTIF, or COUNTIFS?

When your goal is to count numbers between and upper and lower values, you have to consider how your categories will be constructed and whether the upper and lower values are included in the interval. If you have categories like the ones shown in Figure 16.10, using the FREQUENCY function is *much* easier than using COUNTIF or COUNTIFS. In Figure 16.10, you can see that you would have to create three different formulas if you were to use COUNTIF or COUNTIFS instead of FREQUENCY. There is no choice here: Use FREQUENCY because it is easy!

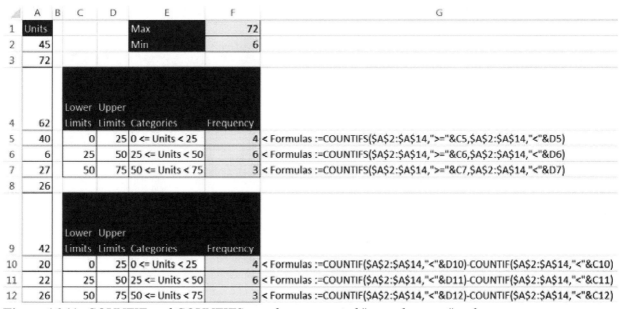

	A	B	C Upper Limits	D Categories	E Frequency	F
1	Units		Upper Limits	Categories	Frequency	
2	7		25	Units <= 25	3	< Formulas :{=FREQUENCY(A2:A14,C2:C4)}
3	34		50	25 < Units <= 50	6	< Formulas :{=FREQUENCY(A2:A14,C2:C4)}
4	4		75	50 < Units <= 75	3	< Formulas :{=FREQUENCY(A2:A14,C2:C4)}
5	9			75 < Units	1	< Formulas :{=FREQUENCY(A2:A14,C2:C4)}
6	31					
7	30		Upper Limits	Categories	Frequency	
8	28		25	Units <= 25	3	< Formulas :=COUNTIFS($A$2:$A$14,"<="&C8)
9	30		50	25 < Units <= 50	6	< Formulas :=COUNTIFS($A$2:$A$14,"<="&C9,$A$2:$A$14,">"&C8)
10	51		75	50 < Units <= 75	3	< Formulas :=COUNTIFS($A$2:$A$14,"<="&C10,$A$2:$A$14,">"&C9)
11	83			75 < Units	1	< Formulas :=COUNTIFS($A$2:$A$14,">"&C10)
12	44					
13	74		Upper Limits	Categories	Frequency	
14	58		25	Units <= 25	3	< Formulas :=COUNTIF($A$2:$A$14,"<="&C14)
15			50	25 < Units <= 50	6	< Formulas :=COUNTIF($A$2:$A$14,"<="&C15)-COUNTIF($A$2:$A$14,"<="&C14)
16			75	50 < Units <= 75	3	< Formulas :=COUNTIF($A$2:$A$14,"<="&C16)-COUNTIF($A$2:$A$14,"<="&C15)
17				75 < Units	1	< Formulas :=COUNTIF($A$2:$A$14,">"&C16)

Figure 16.10 *COUNTIF and COUNTIFS take a bit more effort than FREQUENCY.*

However, there are many types of intervals for counting between upper and lower values. Figure 16.11 shows an example of a different type of category that includes the lower limit but not the upper limit. In addition, because you calculated the max and min values before designing the categories, you can build uniform categories that will be all-inclusive and not require different rules for the first and last categories. If the requirement is to include the lower limit and not include the upper limit, FREQUENCY cannot do that, but COUNTIF and COUNTIFS can do that.

	A	B	C Lower Limits	D Upper Limits	E Categories	F Frequency	G
1	Units				Max	72	
2	45				Min	6	
3	72						
4	62		Lower Limits	Upper Limits	Categories	Frequency	
5	40		0	25	0 <= Units < 25	4	< Formulas :=COUNTIFS($A$2:$A$14,">="&C5,$A$2:$A$14,"<"&D5)
6	6		25	50	25 <= Units < 50	6	< Formulas :=COUNTIFS($A$2:$A$14,">="&C6,$A$2:$A$14,"<"&D6)
7	27		50	75	50 <= Units < 75	3	< Formulas :=COUNTIFS($A$2:$A$14,">="&C7,$A$2:$A$14,"<"&D7)
8	26						
9	42		Lower Limits	Upper Limits	Categories	Frequency	
10	20		0	25	0 <= Units < 25	4	< Formulas :=COUNTIF($A$2:$A$14,"<"&D10)-COUNTIF($A$2:$A$14,"<"&C10)
11	22		25	50	25 <= Units < 50	6	< Formulas :=COUNTIF($A$2:$A$14,"<"&D11)-COUNTIF($A$2:$A$14,"<"&C11)
12	26		50	75	50 <= Units < 75	3	< Formulas :=COUNTIF($A$2:$A$14,"<"&D12)-COUNTIF($A$2:$A$14,"<"&C12)

Figure 16.11 *COUNTIF and COUNTIFS can do more varied "count between" tasks.*

Chapter Summary

In this chapter you have learned the basics of the FREQUENCY array function. In Chapter 17 you will use the new knowledge about the FREQUENCY function to build formulas to count unique items in a list.

Chapter 17: Unique Counting Formulas and the Power of the FREQUENCY Function

Excel Files

To follow along with the examples in this chapter, you can download the accompanying files, as explained in the Introduction.

Unique Lists

In databases, the first column in a table is usually a unique list that is called the *primary key*, or *unique identifier*. It is used to verify that data collected for each unique identifier is located in one and only one location. There are no duplicates in a unique list.

In Excel, however, the raw data often comes in large data sets with many duplicates. If the goal is to use a formula to count the unique items in a list or extract a unique list, because there is no built-in function that can accomplish these two tasks, you must get creative with array formulas. This chapter looks at unique counting formulas, and Chapter 19 looks at extracting unique list formulas and sorting formulas.

In Excel, a *unique list* is a sublist that lists each item one time. There are no duplicates in a unique list.

Here are some typical examples of situations where you would have many duplicates and would need to count the unique items in a list:

- A table of transactional accounting records lists each invoice number multiple times. You need a count of unique invoices.
- A project time tracker has duplicate employee names, and you need to count how many unique employees worked on the project.
- A large table with customer transactions lists many duplicates, and you want to count how many unique customers there are.

In Chapter 16 you learned the basics of the FREQUENCY array function. Whereas in Chapter 16 you entered the FREQUENCY function's resultant array of values into multiple cells using Ctrl+-Shift+Enter, in this chapter you will use the FREQUENCY function's resultant array in larger array formulas that will help you count unique items from a list with duplicates. In addition, you will see how to use the resultant array of values from a COUNTIF function array operation to help with unique counting formulas.

> **Note:** I have to thank Excel master Aladin Akyurek for all the lessons he has given me about how to make unique counting formulas robust!

Using a Single-Cell Formula to Count Unique Numbers: FREQUENCY or COUNTIF?

Figure 17.1 shows an accounting data set that lists duplicate invoice numbers. The goal is to count the number of unique invoice numbers from the range A3:A8. Figure 17.1 shows two formulas that both correctly calculate a count of 3. This section examines each of these formulas in turn. First let's look at the FREQUENCY formula.

	A	B	C	D
1	**Count unique invoice numbers**			
2	Invoice #	Date	Amount	
3	1001	11/18/12	-$40.10	
4	1001	11/16/12	$500.25	
5	1012	11/16/12	$758.98	
6	1001	11/16/12	-$500.25	
7	1016	11/18/12	$1,045.10	
8	1016	11/18/12	-$1,045.10	
10	FREQUENCY		3	< Formula: =SUMPRODUCT(--(FREQUENCY(A3:A8,A3:A8)>0))
11	COUNTIF		3	< Formula: =SUMPRODUCT(1/COUNTIF(A3:A8,A3:A8))

Figure 17.1 *You need to count unique invoice numbers.*

As shown in Figure 17.2, the key unique counting concept in the FREQUENCY formula is that you use the same range of values in both the data_array (the numbers to count) and bins_array (the upper limits for categories) arguments.

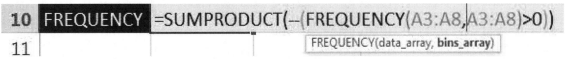

Figure 17.2 *You use the same range in both the data_array and bins_array arguments!*

Notes for the Formula =SUMPRODUCT(--(FREQUENCY(A3:A8,A3:A8)>0))

The following table shows the calculation process for this number unique count formula.

Calculation Notes:
1. =SUMPRODUCT(--(FREQUENCY(A3:A8,A3:A8)>0))
2. =SUMPRODUCT(--(FREQUEN CY({1001;1001;1012;1001;1016;1016},{1001;1001;1012;1001;1016;1016})>0))
• Because bins_array has all the numbers, the first occurrence of each number will have a count.   • Duplicate bin numbers will get a count of zero.
3. =SUMPRODUCT(--({3;0;1;0;2;0;0}>0))
• The FREQUENCY function delivers a resultant array that has a count for each unique invoice number and a zero for any duplicate number.   • For example, cell A3 gets a count of 3 because there are three invoices with the number 1001, but cells A4 and A6 each get a count of zero.   • Now you have a pattern that you can exploit to count unique numbers: "Any number greater than zero indicates the first occurrence of the invoice number."
4. =SUMPRODUCT(--{TRUE;FALSE;TRUE;FALSE;TRUE;FALSE;FALSE})
• You use a double negative because SUMPRODUCT can't "see" logicals.
5. =SUMPRODUCT({1;0;1;0;1;0;0}) = 3
• You use SUMPRODUCT (to avoid Ctrl+Shift+Enter) to add the results of three array operations (FREQUENCY, a comparative operator, and a double negative).

Now let's look at the COUNTIF formula. As shown in Figure 17.3, the key unique counting concept in the COUNTIF formula is that you use the same range of values in both the range (all the items to consider in the count) and criteria (the criteria for counting) arguments.

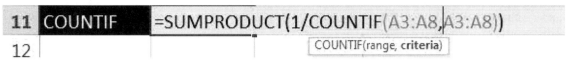

Figure 17.3 *You use the same range in both range and criteria arguments!*

Notes for the Formula =SUMPRODUCT(1/COUNTIF(A3:A8,A3:A8))

The following table shows the calculation process for this number unique count formula.

Calculation Notes:
1. =SUMPRODUCT(1/COUNTIF(A3:A8,A3:A8))
2. =SUMPRODUCT **(1/COUNTIF({1001;1001;1012;1001;1016;1016},{1001;1001;1012;1001;1016;1016}))**
• Because the criteria argument expects a single value and you instead give it more than one value, the COUNTIF function makes a function argument array operation.
• You are giving the criteria argument six criteria, and so the COUNTIF delivers six answers.
• Because you give COUNTIF the same items in both the range and criteria arguments, COUNTIF provides a count for each item in the criteria range, including repeating the count for any duplicate items. This is different from what FREQUENCY did when it ignored duplicate values.
• Remember: It is the range argument of COUNTIF that can't make array operations, but the criteria argument is capable of this array operation.
3. =SUMPRODUCT(1/{3;3;1;3;2;2})
• The COUNTIF function delivers an array of counts.
• For example, because invoice #1001 sits in cells A3, A4, and A6, the resultant array contains the count of 3 in those three corresponding positions.
• When you first see what COUNTIF delivers, it seems ridiculous because if you added them at this point, you would get a count that is way too big!
• But what if you made the array operation 1/array?
• Because 1/3+1/3+1/3 = 1, this will get you the unique count for invoice #1001.
4. =SUMPRODUCT({0.333;0.333;1;0.333;0.5;0.5}) = 3
• You use SUMPRODUCT to add the results of two array operations (COUNTIF and a double negative).

Timing FREQUENCY and COUNTIF Unique Counting Formulas for Numbers

The file for these timing results is named 23-UniqueCountFREQUENCYorCOUNTIF.xlsm, and it can be found in the Timing folder in the zipped files that accompany the book. To time your own formulas, see Chapter 2 for details. (Timing depends many factors, and your particular situation may have different timing results.)

From the worksheet tab sheet named Numbers, here are the two formulas I timed:

Formula [1]: =SUMPRODUCT(--(FREQUENCY(A2:A5001,A2:A5001)>0))

Formula [2]: =SUMPRODUCT(1/COUNTIF(A2:A5001,A2:A5001))

As shown in Figure 17.4, the FREQUENCY formula calculates dramatically faster than the COUNTIF formula. The test I did was on 5,000 rows. If you run the COUNTIF formula on 50,000 rows of numbers, it takes so long that it seems it is blowing up your computer (metaphorically speaking). The bottom line is, unless you are using small data sets, you shouldn't use the COUN-TIF formulas for counting unique items.

5000 rows of numbers. Time in seconds		
Time	FREQUENCY	COUNTIF
Time 1	0.03	1.81
Time 2	0.027	1.818
Time 3	0.03275	1.815
Ave	0.029916667	1.814333333
% Change	0.00%	5964.62%

Figure 17.4 *FREQUENCY is much faster than COUNTIF.*

Even though using the COUNTIF formula looks like a no-win solution, in the next example, you will see that if you have a small data set and you are counting unique text or mixed data items, the COUNTIF function formula for counting unique items is easier to create than the similar FRE-QUENCY function solution.

Using Single-Cell Formulas to Count Unique Text or Mixed Data Items: FREQUENCY or COUNTIF?

Figure 17.5 shows a project time tracker table that lists duplicate employee names. The goal is to count the number of unique employee names from the range C3:C9. Figure 17.5 shows two formulas that both correctly calculate a count of 3. You should immediately notice these things:

- The COUNTIF formula is exactly the same formula as the COUNTIF formula you used for numeric data (refer to Figure 17.3).

- The COUNTIF formula looks much simpler to create than the FREQUENCY formula.

- Using the FREQUENCY function to count non-numeric data requires the additional functions MATCH and ROW (as compared to the FREQUENCY formula for counting unique numbers, shown in Figure 17.2).

What if the data is not text, but instead it is mixed data? Guess what? You can use the same unique count formulas you used for text data on mixed data. Figure 17.6 shows a customer list with duplicates that contains both text and numeric data. The goal here is to count the unique customers. If you look closely at Figures 17.5 and 17.6, you will see that the formulas are the same.

	A	B	C	D
1	**Project time tracker**			
2	Date	Hours	Employee	
3	2/3/14	5	Sioux	
4	2/3/14	3	Chin	
5	2/4/14	4	Sioux	
6	2/6/14	3	Chin	
7	2/6/14	6	Sioux	
8	2/6/14	5	Gigi	
9	2/6/14	6	Gigi	
11	**Unique count of employees**			
12	3	< =SUMPRODUCT(--(FREQUENCY(MATCH(C3:C9,C3:C9,0),ROW(C3:C9)-ROW(C3)+1)>0))		
13	3	< =SUMPRODUCT(1/COUNTIF(C3:C9,C3:C9))		

Figure 17.5 *Formulas to count unique text or mixed data items. The Employee column contains text data.*

	A	B	C	D
1	**Customer sales table**			
2	Date	Sales	Customer	
3	2/10/14	53	Frontier	
4	2/25/14	1527	4369	
5	2/26/14	930	4369	
6	4/16/14	1910	EMI	
7	5/11/14	337	Frontier	
8	6/21/14	122	958641	
9	7/26/14	997	EMI	
11	**Unique count of customers**			
12	4	< =SUMPRODUCT(--(FREQUENCY(MATCH(C3:C9,C3:C9,0),ROW(C3:C9)-ROW(C3)+1)>0))		
13	4	< =SUMPRODUCT(1/COUNTIF(C3:C9,C3:C9))		

Figure 17.6 *Formulas to count unique text or mixed data items. The Customer column contains mixed data.*

Here is the kicker, though: Even though the FREQUENCY formula that is shown in Figures 17.5 and 17.6 is much longer and contains more functions than the COUNTIF formula, the formula calculation time is astonishingly faster!

Notes for the Formula
=SUMPRODUCT(--(FREQUENCY(MATCH(C3:C9,C3:C9,0),ROW(C3:C9)-ROW(C3)+1)>0))

The following table shows the calculation process for this number or text unique count formula.

Calculation Notes:
1. =SUMPRODUCT(--(FREQUENCY(MATCH(C3:C9,C3:C9,0),ROW(C3:C9)-ROW(C3)+1)>0))
• MATCH can help you get at the position of the first occurrence of each item by doing an exact match:
• If the data set is {"Frontier";4369;4369;"EMI";"Frontier";958641;"EMI"}, then positions 1, 2, 4, and 6 are the positions that contain the unique items.
• MATCH(C3:C9,C3:C9,0) creates the resultant array {1;2;2;4;1;6;4}.
• Notice that because you have an exact match, there are duplicate positions, but *only* the positions 1, 2, 4, and 6 are listed.
• You can now use the result from the MATCH as the data_array argument of FREQUENCY.
2. =SUMPRODUCT(--(FREQUENCY({1;2;2;4;1;6;4},ROW(C3:C9)-ROW(C3)+1)>0))
• If you calculate the ROW formula element, you can get all the relative positions and use that information in the bins_array argument of FREQUENCY.
• ROW(C3:C9)-ROW(C3)+1 creates the resultant array {1;2;3;4;5;6;7}.
• Now you have upper bins that can count the data_array.
3. =SUMPRODUCT(--(FREQUENCY({1;2;2;4;1;6;4},{1;2;3;4;5;6;7})>0))
• FREQUENCY({1;2;2;4;1;6;4},{1;2;3;4;5;6;7}) creates the resultant array {2;2;0;2;0;1;0;0}.
• Notice that in the data_array argument there are two 1 values. This is why the first element in the resultant array is 2. The 2 is the count.
• {2;2;0;2;0;1;0;0} gives you a pattern to exploit: "Numbers greater than zero indicate the first occurrence of an item."
4. =SUMPRODUCT(--({2;2;0;2;0;1;0;0}>0))
5. =SUMPRODUCT(--{TRUE;TRUE;FALSE;TRUE;FALSE;TRUE;FALSE;FALSE})
6) =SUMPRODUCT({1;1;0;1;0;1;0;0}) = 4
• You use SUMPRODUCT to add the results of five array operations (MATCH, ROW, FREQUENCY, a comparative operator, and a double negative).

Timing FREQUENCY and COUNTIF for Text or Mixed Data Unique Counting Formulas

The file for these timing results is named 23-UniqueCountFREQUENCYorCOUNTIF.xlsm, and it can be found in the Timing folder in the zipped files that accompany the book. To time your own formulas, see Chapter 2 for details. (Timing depends many factors, and your particular situation may have different timing results.)

From the Text Mixed worksheet tab sheet, here are the two formulas I timed:

Formula [1]: =SUMPRODUCT(--(FREQUENCY(MATCH(A2:A5001,A2:A5001,0),ROW(A2:A5001)-ROW(A2)+1)>0))

Formula [2]: =SUMPRODUCT(1/COUNTIF(A2:A5001,A2:A5001))

As shown in Figure 17.7, the FREQUENCY formula calculates dramatically faster than the COUNTIF formula.

5000 rows of numbers. Time in seconds		
Time	**FREQUENCY SUMPRODUCT**	**COUNTIF**
Time 1	0.01891	4.25
Time 2	0.01867	4.231
Time 3	0.01831	4.223
Ave	0.01863	4.234666667
% Change	0.00%	22630.36%

Figure 17.7 *You probably shouldn't use COUNTIF unless the data set is small.*

What if There Are Empty Cells in the Range?

This example uses the same table of customer sales as the last example, except that now there is an empty cell in the Customer column. Figure 17.8 shows the formulas to accommodate this added complication.

	A	B	C	D
1	Customer sales table			
2	Date	Sales	Customer	
3	2/10	53	Frontier	
4	2/25	1527	4369	
5	2/26	930	4369	
6	4/16	1910	EMI	
7	5/11	337	Frontier	
8	6/21	122		
9	7/26	997	EMI	
11	Unique count of customers			
12	3	< {=SUM(IF(FREQUENCY(IF(C3:C9<>"",MATCH(C3:C9,C3:C9,0)),ROW(C3:C9)-ROW(C3)+1),1))}		
13	3	< =SUMPRODUCT((C3:C9<>"")/COUNTIF(C3:C9,C3:C9&""))		

Figure 17.8 *These formulas count unique items if there are empty cells. These formula are not adversely affected by and do not count empty cells or formulas that delivered null text strings.*

Notes for the Formula
=SUM(IF(FREQUENCY(IF(C3:C9<>"",MATCH(C3:C9,C3:C9,0)),ROW(C3:C9)-ROW(C3)+1),1))

The following table shows the calculation process for this number or text or empty cell unique count formula.

Calculation Notes:
1. =SUM(IF(FREQUENCY(IF(C3:C9<>"",MATCH(C3:C9,C3:C9,0)),ROW(C3:C9)-ROW (C3)+1),1))
<ul><li>The first thing you should notice about this formula is that because you have an empty cell, the MATCH function array operation will produce an #N/A error, like this: MATCH(C3:C9,C3:C9,0) ➔ {1;2;2;4;1;#N/A;4}</li><li>To remove the error, you place MATCH into the IF function, like this: IF(C3:C9<>"",MATCH(C3:C9,C3:C9,0)) ➔ IF({T;T;T;T;T;FALSE;T},MATCH(C3:C9,C3:C9,0)) ➔ IF({T;T;T;T;T;FALSE;T},{1;2;2;4;1;#N/A;4}) ➔ {1;2;2;4;1;FALSE;4}</li><li>C3:C9<>"" is asking the question "Is anything in the range "not empty or a null text string?"</li><li>Because the IF function logical_test argument contains an array operation, this formula will require Ctrl+Shift+Enter, no matter what. This is why you use SUM instead of SUMPRODUCT, so the formula is less ambiguous (refer to Array Formula Efficiency Rule 14).</li><li>The IF/MATCH combo delivers the array {1;2;2;4;1;FALSE;4} to the data_array argument of the FREQUENCY function.</li></ul>
2. =SUM(IF(FREQUENCY({1;2;2;4;1;FALSE;4},ROW(C3:C9)-ROW(C3)+1),1))
3. =SUM(IF(FREQUENCY({1;2;2;4;1;FALSE;4},{1;2;3;4;5;6;7}),1))
<ul><li>The FREQUENCY function delivers an array of numbers like this: FREQUENCY({1;2;2;4;1;FALSE;4},{1;2;3;4;5;6;7}) ➔ {2;2;0;2;0;0;0;0}</li><li>These numbers can be understood by the logical_test argument of the IF function as TRUEs and FALSEs. Any nonzero number is TRUE; zero is FALSE.</li><li>FREQUENCY sits in the logical_test argument in order to deliver numbers or logical values like this: {2;2;0;2;0;0;0;0} = {TRUE;TRUE;FALSE;TRUE;FALSE;FALSE;FALSE;FALSE}</li></ul>
4. =SUM(IF({2;2;0;2;0;0;0;0},1))
5. =SUM(IF({TRUE;TRUE;FALSE;TRUE; FALSE; FALSE; FALSE; FALSE},1))
6. =SUM({1;1;FALSE;1;FALSE;FALSE;FALSE;FALSE})
7. The formula delivers a count of 3.

Notes for the Formula
=SUMPRODUCT((C3:C9<>"")/COUNTIF(C3:C9,C3:C9&""))

The following table shows the calculation process for this number or text or empty cell unique count formula.

Calculation Notes:
1. =SUMPRODUCT((C3:C9<>"")/COUNTIF(C3:C9,C3:C9&""))
• By itself, the COUNTIF function converts an empty cell to a zero in the criteria argument. If you evaluate COUNTIF alone, you get a count of zero in the location of the empty cell, like this: COUNTIF(C3:C9,C3:C9) ➜ {2;2;2;2;2;0;2}
• If you leave this in the formula, when you place the COUNTIF-delivered array in the denominator of the fraction, you get a "divide by zero" error, or #DIV/0! error.
• To remedy this, you can change the zero value in the criteria argument to a null text string by joining a null text string to the range C3:C9 in the criteria argument of COUNTIF, like this: COUNTIF(C3:C9,C3:C9&"") ➜ {2;2;2;2;2;1;2}
• After you join a null text string to the range C3:C9, you get a count of 1 in the denominator, which does not cause a #DIV/0! error.
2. =SUMPRODUCT((C3:C9<>"")/{2;2;2;2;2;1;2})
3. =SUMPRODUCT({TRUE;TRUE;TRUE;TRUE;TRUE;FALSE;TRUE}/{2;2;2;2;2;1;2})
Boolean division gives you this: {TRUE;TRUE;TRUE;TRUE;TRUE;FALSE;TRUE}/{2;2;2;2;2;1;2} ➜ {0.5;0.5;0.5;0.5;0.5;0;0.5}
4. =SUMPRODUCT({0.5;0.5;0.5;0.5;0.5;0;0.5})
5. The formula delivers a count of 3.

The timing results for these two formulas are similar to the earlier timing results: The COUNTIF formula is slower than the FREQUENCY formula.

Using a Single-Cell Formula to Count Unique Items with More Than One Condition

Sometimes you might have conditions for counting the unique elements in a list. Figure 17.8 shows survey results where voters were allowed to vote as many times as they wanted to vote. The goal here is to count the unique voter names (skipping over empty cells) where the income is greater than 40,000 and the vote was "Yes." The only difference between the formula shown in Figure 17.9 and the FREQUENCY formula shown in Figure 17.8 is that the Figure 17.9 formula has two extra IF functions to accommodate the two extra conditions. The formula calculates the correct count of 2 based on the name "Sioux" in cell A3 and "Han" in A12. Figures 17.10 and 17.11 show how to understand this formula.

	A	B	C	D	E	F	G
1	Vote multiple times okay.				Criteria:		
2	Name	Income	Vote		Income	Vote	
3	**Sioux**	**98,500**	**Yes**		40,000	Yes	
4	Gigi	54,205	No				
5	Phil	22,350	Yes				
6	Sioux	98,500	Yes				
7		65,200	Yes				
8	Tina	82,000	No				
9	Tina	82,000	No				
10	Gigi	54,205	No				
11	Chin	125,300	No				
12	**Han**	**43,100**	**Yes**				

14	**Count unique Yes voter names with income greater than 40,000**
15	2 < {=SUM(IF(FREQUENCY(IF(A3:A12<>"",IF(B3:B12>E3,
16	IF(C3:C12=F3,MATCH(A3:A12,A3:A12,0)))),
17	ROW(C3:C12)-ROW(C3)+1),1))}

Figure 17.9 *Counting unique "Yes" votes based on three conditions.*

Note: A COUNTIF formula like
=SUMPRODUCT(((A3:A12<>"")*(B3:B12>E3)*(C3:C12=F3))/COUN-
TIF(A3:A12,A3:A12&"")) has the potential of giving an incorrect answer. If you
were to type Sioux into cell A5, the result would be 1.67, whereas the FRE-
QUENCY function would still calculate 2.

```
=SUM(IF(
FREQUENCY(IF(A3:A12<>"",IF(B3:B12>E3,IF(C3:C12=F3,
MATCH(A3:A12,A3:A12,0)))),                    IF(logical_test, [value_if_true], [value_if_false])
ROW(C3:C12)-ROW(C3)+1),1))
```

Figure 17.10 *Because you have three conditions, you must run three IF functions before dumping the results of MATCH into the data_array argument.*

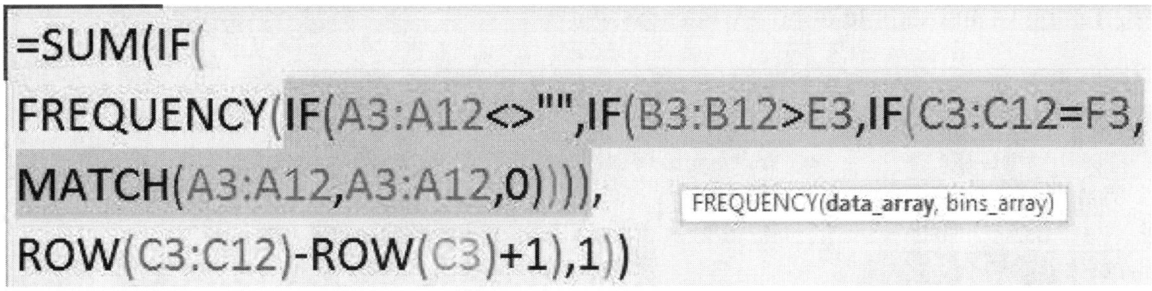

```
=SUM(IF(
FREQUENCY(IF(A3:A12<>"",IF(B3:B12>E3,IF(C3:C12=F3,
MATCH(A3:A12,A3:A12,0)))),
ROW(C3:C12)-ROW(C3)+1),1))
```

FREQUENCY(**data_array**, bins_array)

Figure 17.11 *The FREQUENCY function delivers an array of numbers to the logical_test argument: non-zero numbers = TRUE, zero = FALSE.*

Notes for the Formula =SUM(IF(FREQUENCY(IF(A3:A12<>"",IF(B3:B12>E3,IF(C3:C12=F3,MATCH(A3:A12,A3:A12,0)))),ROW(C3:C12)-ROW(C3)+1),1))

The following table shows the calculation process for this mixed data conditional unique count formula.

1. =SUM(IF(FREQUENCY(IF(A3:A12<>"",IF(B3:B12>E3,IF(C3:C12=F3,MATCH(A3:A12,A3:A12,0)))),ROW(C3:C12)-ROW(C3)+1),1))
• The three IFs help the MATCH function deliver only the relative positions that meet the three criteria.
2. =SUM(IF(FREQUENCY({1;FALSE;FALSE;1;FALSE;FALSE;FALSE;FALSE;FALSE;10},ROW(C3:C12)-ROW(C3)+1),1))
• FREQUENCY simply delivers numbers to the logical_test argument of IF. TRUE = a nonzero number. FALSE = zero.
3. =SUM(IF({2;0;0;0;0;0;0;0;1;0},1))
4. =SUM({1;F;F;F;F;F;F;F;1;F}) = 2

What About Wildcards?

Here is what the Microsoft help says about wildcards for the COUNTIF and MATCH functions:

- You can use the wildcard characters in criteria:
  - ? (question mark) matches any one character
  - * (asterisk) matches zero or more characters
- If you want to find an actual question mark or asterisk, type a tilde (~) before the character.

Figure 17.12 shows an example of how wildcards work.

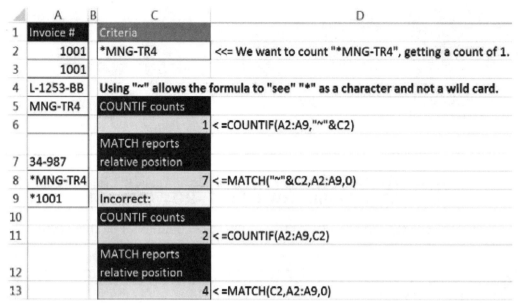

Figure 17.12 *Using "~" allows the formula to "see" * as a character and not as a wildcard.*

Figure 17.13 shows how you can create a unique count formula that treats wildcards as actual characters.

	A	B	C
1	**Count unique invoices**		
2	Names		
3	1001		
4	1001		
5	MNG-TR4		
6			
7	34-987		
8	*MNG-TR4		MNG-TR4 and *MNG-TR4 are not the same
9	*1001		1001 and *1001 are NOT the same.
10			
11	Count Unique		
12	5		
13	=SUM(IF(FREQUENCY(		
14	IF(A3:A9<>"",MATCH("~"&A3:A9,A3:A9&"",0)),		
15	ROW(A3:A9)-ROW(A3)+1),1))	FREQUENCY(**data_array**, bins_array)	

Figure 17.13 *Using "~" allows the formula to "see" * as a character and not a wildcard. The correct count is 5.*

> **Note:** If you were to try to create a COUNTIF formula like =SUMPRO-DUCT(--(A3:A9<>"")/COUNTIF("~"&A3:A9,A3:A9&"")), it would fail because the range argument in COUNTIF cannot handle the join array operation.

Notes for the Formula Element IF(A3:A9<>"",MATCH("~"&A3:A9,A3:A9&"",0))

The following table shows the calculation process for the MATCH formula element shown in Figure 17.13.

Calculation Notes:
1. IF(A3:A9<>"",MATCH("~"&A3:A9,A3:A9&"",0))
• In the MATCH lookup_value argument, you join the tilde to the lookup_value argument so that the lookup values can "see" the wildcards as charters.
• "~"&A3:A9 is a join array operation.
• "~"&A3:A9 ➔ {"~1001";"~1001";"~MNG-TR4";"~";"~34-987";"~*MNG-TR4";"~*1001"}
• The join operation converts all elements in the column to text values.
2. IF(A3:A9<>"",MATCH({"~1001";"~1001";"~MNG-TR4";"~";"~34-987";"~*MNG-TR4";"~*1001"},A3:A9&"",0))
• Because the lookup_value argument contains all text values and because there is an empty cell that will be considered a zero, you must convert the range of values in the criteria argument to text by joining it with a null text string.
• A3:A9&"" is a join array operation.
• A3:A9&"" ➔ {"1001";"1001";"MNG-TR4";"";"34-987";"*MNG-TR4";"*1001"}
3. IF(A3:A9<>"",MATCH({"~1001";"~1001";"~MNG-TR4";"~";"~34-987";"~*MNG-TR4";"~*1001"},{"1001";"1001";"MNG-TR4";"";"34-987";"*MNG-TR4";"*1001"},0))
• MATCH({"~1001";"~1001";"~MNG-TR4";"~";"~34-987";"~*MNG-TR4";"~*1001"},{"1001";"1001";"MNG-TR4";"";"34-987";"*MNG-TR4";"*1001"},0) ➔ {1;1;3;4;5;6;7}
4) IF(A3:A9<>"",{1;1;3;4;5;6;7})
5) {1;1;3;FALSE;5;6;7}
• {1;1;3;FALSE;5;6;7} gets delivered to the data_array argument in FREQUENCY.

Comparing Unique Counting Methods: FREQUENCY, COUNTIF, Helper Columns, PivotTables, and Advanced Filter

The following table compares the FREQUENCY and COUNTIF unique counting formulas shown in Figures 17.1 to 17.13.

Solutions for Counting Unique Items in a List		
Solution	**Advantages**	**Disadvantages**
Using FREQUENCY formulas	• Calculates very quickly compared to COUNTIF. • Can handle multiple conditions. • Can deal with wildcards.	• Formula can get complicated for non-numeric data.
Using COUNTIF formulas	• If there are no empty cells and the data set is small, this basic formula is easy to create: =SUMPRODUCT(1/COUNTIF(range,range)). • If there are empty cells you can use a formula like =SUMPRODUCT((range<>"")/COUNTIF(range,range)).	• Calculates very slowly compared to FREQUENCY. • Has a hard time with conditional unique counts. • Has a hard time with wildcard conditional counts.

Using Helper Column to Count Unique Items

Figure 17.14 shows that, if the goal is to count unique items in a column, you can use a helper column with the COUNTIF function and an expandable range. The unique counting formula is simply a second COUNTIF formula (cell B12 in Figure 17.14) that counts how many ones there are in the helper column. This solution is easy to create, it ignores the empty cell, and it counts different types of data. However, for large data sets, it takes a long time to calculate because the expandable range means there are many cell references for the calculation process to evaluate.

◢	A	B	C
1	**Helper Column to Count Unique Items**		
2	Items	Helper	
3	Jo	1	< =COUNTIF(A$3:A3,A3)
4	Jo	2	< =COUNTIF(A$3:A4,A4)
5	Phil	1	< =COUNTIF(A$3:A5,A5)
6		0	< =COUNTIF(A$3:A6,A6)
7	43	1	< =COUNTIF(A$3:A7,A7)
8	TRUE	1	< =COUNTIF(A$3:A8,A8)
9	Tris	1	< =COUNTIF(A$3:A9,A9)
10	Jo	3	< =COUNTIF(A$3:A10,A10)
11			
12	Count Unique	5	< =COUNTIF(B3:B10,1)

Figure 17.14 *Using COUNTIF and an expandable range in a helper column.*

Figure 17.15 shows an example of counting unique records in a data set when there are duplicates. Cell A11 shows the helper column formula, and cell A13 shows the single-cell formula.

◢	A	B	C	D	E
1	**Count unique records**				
2	Auto	ID	Owner	Helper	
3	Toyota	45-876	Jo	1	< =COUNTIFS(A$3:A3,A3,B$3:B3,B3,C$3:C3,C3)
4	Honda	23-46	Gigi	1	< =COUNTIFS(A$3:A4,A4,B$3:B4,B4,C$3:C4,C4)
5	Ford	G-876	Chin	1	< =COUNTIFS(A$3:A5,A5,B$3:B5,B5,C$3:C5,C5)
6	Toyota	45-876	Jo	2	< =COUNTIFS(A$3:A6,A6,B$3:B6,B6,C$3:C6,C6)
7	Ford	G-876	Chin	2	< =COUNTIFS(A$3:A7,A7,B$3:B7,B7,C$3:C7,C7)
8	Toyota	55-987	Gigi	1	< =COUNTIFS(A$3:A8,A8,B$3:B8,B8,C$3:C8,C8)
10	**Helper count**				
11	4	< =COUNTIF(D3:D8,1)			
12	**Single cell count**				
13	4	< {=SUM(IF(FREQUENCY(MATCH(A3:A8&B3:B8&C3:C8,A3:A8&B3:B8&C3:C8,0),ROW(C3:C8)-ROW(C3)+1),1))}			
14					
15	**Before 2007, helper could be:**	1	< =SUMPRODUCT(--(A$3:A3=A3),--(B$3:B3=B3),--(C$3:C3=C3))		

Figure 17.15 *Using a helper column and a single-cell formula to count unique records in a data set.*

Chapter Summary

In this chapter you have learn about formulas that can count unique items. Chapter 18 covers the MMULT array function, and Chapter 19 puts together what you have learned so far about array functions, showing how to create formulas to extract unique lists and sort data.

Chapter 18: The MMULT Array Function

Excel Files

To follow along with the examples in this chapter, you can download the accompanying files, as explained in the Introduction.

MMULT Array Function

MMULT stands for **m**atrix **mult**iplication. Matrix algebra?! I don't remember my matrix algebra from college! Even though this may be true for most of you as well (though not all of you), you need to re-remember how to multiply matrices. Why? Because multiplying matrices has some very practical uses.

In this chapter you will look at a total cost problem and solve it long hand, and then you will see how to use the MMULT array function to accomplish the same task more easily.

Using a Formula for Total Costs: MMULT

Figures 18.1 and 18.2 show an equipment order for bats, balls, and gloves for two different teams. Although the costs for the individual items are the same for each team, the quantities ordered by each team are different. The goal of this formula is to calculate the total costs for each team.

Figure 18.1 shows how you can calculate the total costs for the women's team. Notice that you are multiplying and then adding in succession the row of costs and the column of quantities for the women's team. Specifically, the formula is =A4*B9+B4*B10+C4*B11; you multiply a row by a column and then add. Figure 18.2 shows the men's team total cost formula. Notice that you are multiplying and then adding in succession the row of costs and the column of quantities for the men's team. Specifically, the formula is =A4*C9+B4*C10+C4*C11; you multiply a row by a column and then add.

Although you get the correct answers with these two formulas, there is a better way to do this. Rather than calculate the totals long hand, you can use the MMULT function to greatly simplify the formula. Before you can use MMULT, however, you need to learn two matrix multiplication rules:

- The number of columns in the first array must be equal to the number of rows in the second array.
- The size of the resultant array will be the number of rows in the first array times the number of columns in the second array.

Figure 18.3 illustrates these rules.

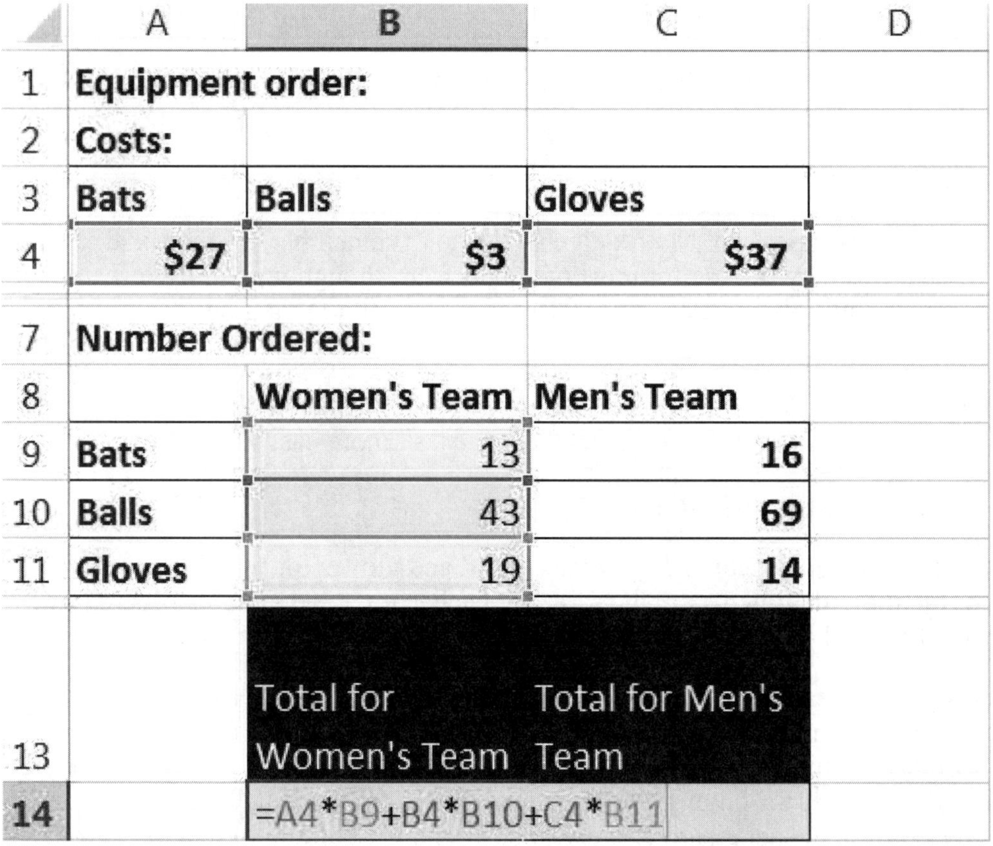

◢	A	B	C	D
1	**Equipment order:**			
2	**Costs:**			
3	**Bats**	**Balls**	**Gloves**	
4	**$27**	**$3**	**$37**	
7	**Number Ordered:**			
8		**Women's Team**	**Men's Team**	
9	**Bats**	13	**16**	
10	**Balls**	43	**69**	
11	**Gloves**	19	**14**	
13		Total for Women's Team	Total for Men's Team	
14		=A4*B9+B4*B10+C4*B11		

Figure 18.1 *Total for the women's team.*

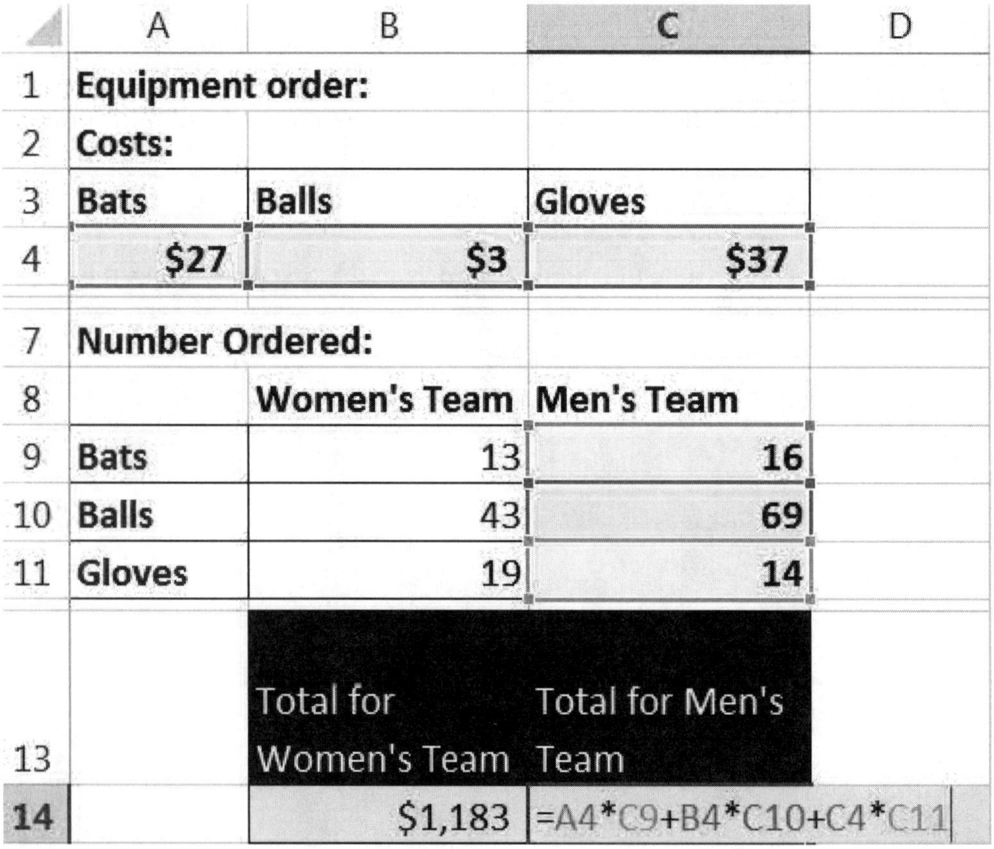

◢	A	B	C	D
1	**Equipment order:**			
2	**Costs:**			
3	**Bats**	**Balls**	**Gloves**	
4	**$27**	**$3**	**$37**	
7	**Number Ordered:**			
8		**Women's Team**	**Men's Team**	
9	**Bats**	13	**16**	
10	**Balls**	43	**69**	
11	**Gloves**	19	**14**	
13		Total for Women's Team	Total for Men's Team	
14		$1,183	=A4*C9+B4*C10+C4*C11	

Figure 18.2 *Total for the men's team.*

	A	B	C	D	E	F	G	H	I	J	K	L	M
1	Equipment order:		**Matrix 1**			**Rules for when you can multiply**							
2	Costs:		**Array 1**		**R x C = 1 x 3**	**arrays with MMULT:**							
3	**Bats**	**Balls**	**Gloves**			**Array 1:**				**Array 2:**			
4	$27	$3	$37			R	x	C		R	x	C	
5						1	x	3		3	x	2	
6			**Matrix 2**										
7	Number Ordered:		**Array 2**		**R x C = 3 x 2**			1) Must be equal					
8		Women's Team	Men's Team										
9	**Bats**	13	16					2) Size of resultant array					
10	**Balls**	43	69										
11	**Gloves**	19	14			**Resultant array =**							
12													

Figure 18.3 *Remember that the goal is to calculate two different totals: one for the women's team and one for the men's team. That is why a resultant array that is two cells wide will be perfect: One cell will give you the answer for the women's total costs, and the other will give you the answer for the men's total costs.*

Here is a test for you: Why couldn't you use the SUMPRODUCT function for this? The answer is that the two ranges do not have the same dimensions. For comparison purposes, take a look at Figure 18.4 to see how you could calculate the total costs for the woman's team, if both the ranges are horizontal.

	A	B	C	D
1		**Bats**	**Balls**	**Gloves**
2	Cost Each	$27	$3	$37
3	Quantity	13	43	19
5	**Total for Women's Team**	SUMPRODUCT(array1, [array2], [array3], [array4], …)		
6	=SUMPRODUCT(B2:D2,B3:D3)			
7	=SUMPRODUCT(B2:D2,B3:D3) = $1,183.00			

Figure 18.4 *If the ranges are orientated the same way, you can use SUMPRODUCT.*

Here are the reasons you are allowed to use the MMULT array function for this problem (refer to Figures 18.1 to 18.3):

- Because the number of columns in array 1 (the cost array) is equal to the number of rows in array 2 (the quantity array), you are allowed to perform matrix multiplication.
- The goal is to calculate the total costs and report them in a 1×2 array; this means the resultant array that is produced by multiplying a 1×3 array by a 3×2 array is exactly what you want.

These are the steps for creating the formula shown in Figure 18.5:

1. Make sure the cost array is the first array. Remember that when you get a calculation task like this, the boss does not say "This is array 1, and this is array 2." You have to figure it out. This is a mistake that I sometimes make when using MMULT, but if it doesn't work one way, I just try it the other way.

2. Determine how many cells to highlight. Because you have already figured out the dimensions of the resultant array, you know how many cells to highlight in advance. Remember that this is an array function that delivers more than one value, so to get it to work, you have to highlight one row and two columns.

3. Create your formula with the cost array as array 1 and the quantity array as array 2.

4. Because this is an array function, enter the array formula with Ctrl+Shift+Enter.

	A	B	C	D	E	F	G	H	I	J	K	L
1	Equipment order:		Matrix 1			Rules for when you can multiply						
2	Costs:		Array 1	R x C = 1 x 3		arrays with MMULT:						
3	Bats	Balls	Gloves			Array 1:				Array 2:		
4	$27		$3	$37			R	x	C	R	x	C
5							1	x	3	3	x	2
6			Matrix 2									
7	Number Ordered:		Array 2	R x C = 3 x 2					1) Must be equal			
8		Women's Team	Men's Team									
9	Bats	13	16					2) Size of resultant array				
10	Balls	43	69									
11	Gloves	19	14			Resultant array =						
12												
14		Total for Women's Team	Total for Men's Team									
15		=MMULT(A4:C4,B9:C11)										

Figure 18.5 *The cost array is array 1, and the quantity array is array 2.*

Figure 18.6 shows the resulting total costs. Using MMULT in this situation is easier than using the two formulas shown in Figures 18.1 and 18.2. Using MMULT would save even more time in terms of formula creation if you had 10 or 20 items rather than 3.

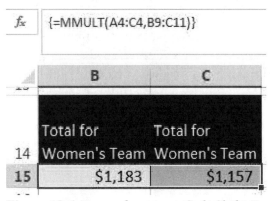

f_x	{=MMULT(A4:C4,B9:C11)}

	B	C
14	Total for Women's Team	Total for Women's Team
15	$1,183	$1,157

Figure 18.6 *Remember to use Ctrl+Shift+Enter.*

Using a Formula to Calculate Weighted Average: MMULT

As shown in Figure 18.7, you can use MMULT for calculating a weighted average when the two arrays have the same number of items but have different dimensions. Figure 18.7 shows a weighted grade example where array 1 (test scores in the range B4:E4) has a dimension of 1×4 and array 2 (weights in range $B$11:$B$14) has a dimension of 4×1. Enter this formula into the single cell F4 and then copy it down the column.

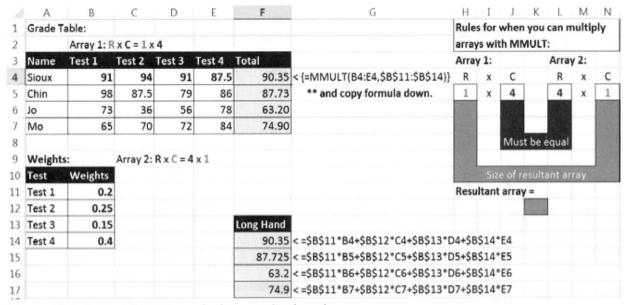

Figure 18.7 *Using MMULT to calculate weighted grades.*

Creating a Multiplication Table: MMULT

Figure 18.8 shows a silly multiplication table example.

| fx | {=MMULT(A2:A11,B1:K1)} |

⊿	A	B	C	D	E	F	G	H	I	J	K	L	M	N	O	P	Q	R	S
1		1	2	3	4	5	6	7	8	9	10	Array 2 = R x C = 1 x 10							
2	1	1	2	3	4	5	6	7	8	9	10								
3	2	2	4	6	8	10	12	14	16	18	20		Array 1:			Array 2:			
4	3	3	6	9	12	15	18	21	24	27	30		R	x	C	R	x	C	
5	4	4	8	12	16	20	24	28	32	36	40		10	x	1	1	x	10	
6	5	5	10	15	20	25	30	35	40	45	50								
7	6	6	12	18	24	30	36	42	48	54	60								
8	7	7	14	21	28	35	42	49	56	63	70			1) Equal = 1 x 1					
9	8	8	16	24	32	40	48	56	64	72	80								
10	9	9	18	27	36	45	54	63	72	81	90		2) Resultant Array = 10 x 10						
11	10	10	20	30	40	50	60	70	80	90	100								
12	Array 1 = R x C = 10 x 1																		

Figure 18.8 *An alternative would be to use mixed cell references formula.*

Finding the Expected Return for a Portfolio of Stocks: MMULT

Figure 18.9 shows the same example you saw in Chapter 10 for calculating expected returns for a portfolio of stocks. The goal of this formula is to multiply the ranges C3:D5*B3:B5*C1:D1 to calculate the expected return on the portfolio. In Chapter 10 you learned how to get around the SUM-PRODUCT function's requirement that the ranges all have the same dimensions by multiplying the ranges. However, if you ever have a situation where text is in the range C3:D5, the multiplication operation yields an error when it encounters text. Because there is no text in the other two ranges, you can use MMULT to multiply array 1 (the probability of economic state in range B3:B5) by array 2 (the weights in range C1:D1) to create an array that is the same size as the array of estimated returns in the range C3:D5. Then you can multiply those two ranges and take advantage of the fact that if you use the multiplication inherent in SUMPRODUCT (array1 comma array2), SUM-PRODUCT ignores text. (I learned this from Aladin Akyurek. Thanks, Aladin!)

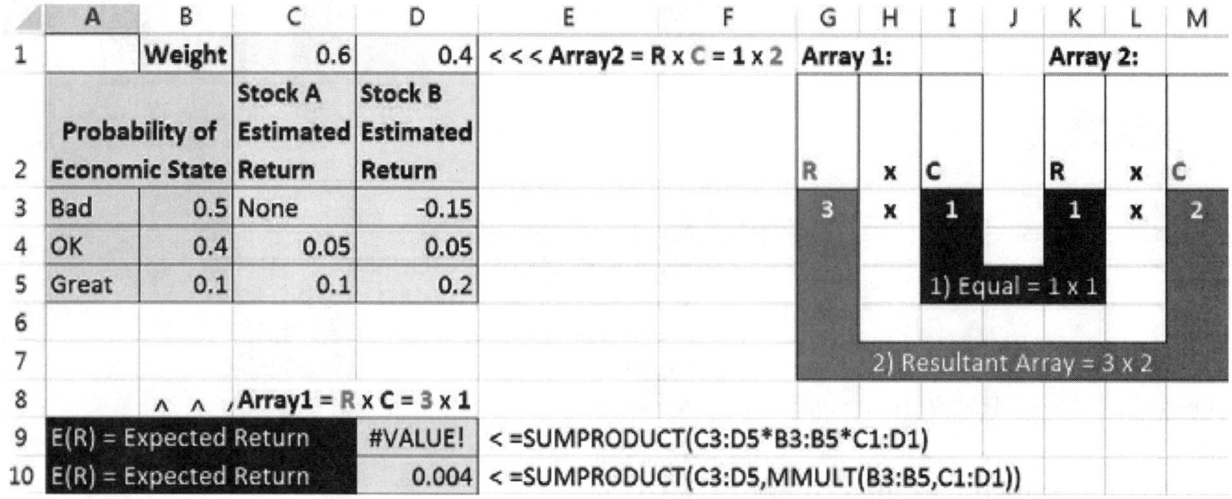

Figure 18.9 *Cell D10 contains a robust formula for calculating E(R).*

Notes for the Formula =SUMPRODUCT(C3:D5,MMULT(B3:B5,C1:D1))

The following table provides brief calculation steps for the formula in cell D10.

1. =SUMPRODUCT(C3:D5,MMULT(B3:B5,C1:D1))
2. =SUMPRODUCT(C3:D5,{0.3,0.2;0.24,0.16;0.06,0.04})
3. Formula result: 0.004

Parameters for the MMULT Array Function

Here is a list of parameters for the MMULT array function:

- Arrays can be cell ranges, array constants, or references.
- MMULT returns the #VALUE! error when:
  - Any cells are empty or contain text.
  - The number of columns in array 1 is not equal to the number of rows in array 2.
  - MMULT returns output that exceeds 5,460 cells.

Figure 18.10 shows what happens if one of the cells is empty.

	A	B	C	D	E	F	G	H	I	J	K	L	M
1	**Array 1:**						**Array 1:**				**Array 2:**		
2	1	5	2				R	x	C		R	x	C
3	1	1					2	x	3		3	x	5
4	**Array 2:**												
5	1	1	3	0	3								
6	2	3	3	2	1				1) Equal = 3 x 3				
7	2	1	1	1	3								
8									2) Resultant Array = 2 x 5				
9	**Resultant Array:**												
10	#VALUE!	#VALUE!	#VALUE!	#VALUE!	#VALUE!								
11	#VALUE!	#VALUE!	#VALUE!	#VALUE!	#VALUE!								

Figure 18.10 *Cell C3 is empty, and MMULT returns a #VALUE! error.*

The MINVERSE and MUNIT Array Functions

So far, all the examples you have seen for MMULT are practical examples that do not have much to do with matrix algebra. However, if you want to solve systems of equations using matrix algebra, it is helpful to learn about the MINVERSE and MUNIT array functions.

The MINVERSE and MUNIT array functions can help with matrix algebra when you are solving systems of equations.

> **Note:** I know that I intimated at the beginning of this chapter that you would stick to practical examples and not do much matrix algebra, but learning how to solve systems of equations may provide some benefit.

MINVERSE calculates the inverse of a square matrix (which has the same number of rows as columns) and the MUNIT (which is new in Excel 2013) calculates the identity, or unit, matrix.

When solving system of equations, it is helpful to calculate the inverse of a matrix. For example, as shown in Figure 18.11, if you assign the variable A for the square matrix A and A^{-1} for the inverse of A, then A^{-1} is the matrix such that:

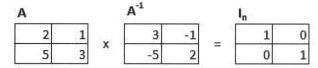

Figure 18.11 *A matrix times its inverse equals the identity, or unit, matrix (provided that the inverse exists).*

In Figure 18.11 the product of the square matrix and its inverse is called the identity, or unit, matrix, and it is denoted by I_n. Figure 18.12 shows how you can calculate the inverse of matrix A with the MINVERSE function. Figure 18.13 shows how you can prove that A^{-1} is the inverse of A by using the MMULT function to multiply A by A^{-1}. Both are entered with Ctrl+Shift+Enter.

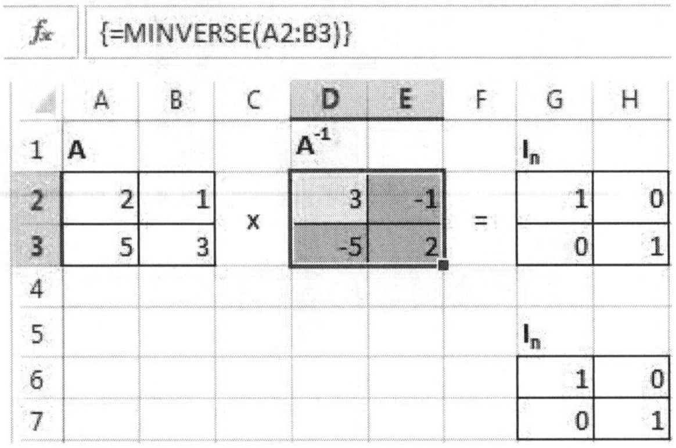

Figure 18.12 *The MINVERSE array function.*

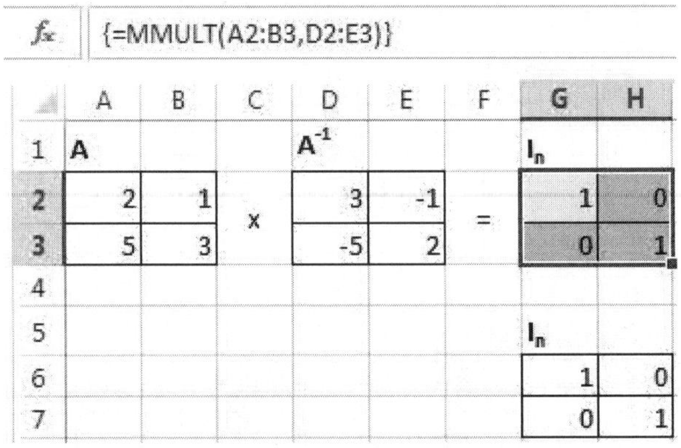

Figure 18.13 *The MMULT array function.*

If you have Excel 2013 or later, you can use the MUNIT array function, as shown in Figure 18.14, to solve for the identity matrix. For MUNIT, you highlight the same number of rows as columns and enter the dimension (which must be an integer greater than zero).

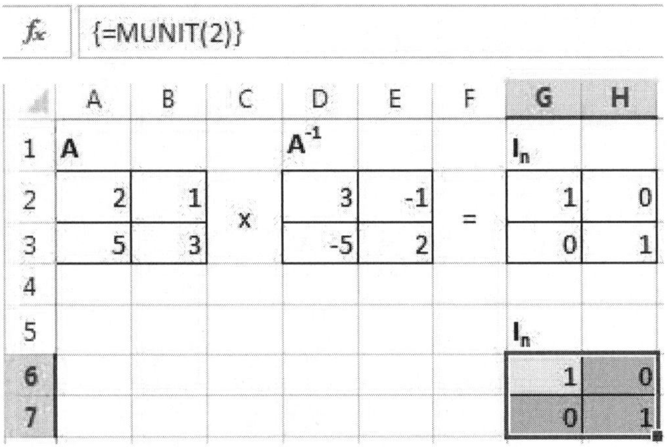

Figure 18.14 *MUNIT is a new array function that debuted in Excel 2013.*

Solving Systems of Equations Using MMULT

Here is a set of three linear equations with three x variables:

x_1	-	$2x_2$	+	x_3	=	4
		x_2	+	$2x_3$	=	4
$2x_1$	+	$3x_2$	-	$2x_3$	=	2

As shown in Figure 18.15, if you need to solve for the x values of x^1, x^2, and x^3 so that all three equations cross at the same point on a graph, you can use the MMULT and MINVERSE functions and complete the following steps:

1. Place the coefficients from the equations into a 3×3 array in the range I3:K5.

2. Place the constants from the equations into a 3×1 array in the range M3:M5.

3. Highlight the range Q3:Q5 (3×1) and enter the formula =MMULT(MIN-VERSE(I3:K5),M3:M5) or =MMULT(M3:M5,MINVERSE(I3:K5)), with Ctrl+-Shift+Enter.

4. Plug the results back into your equations and verify.

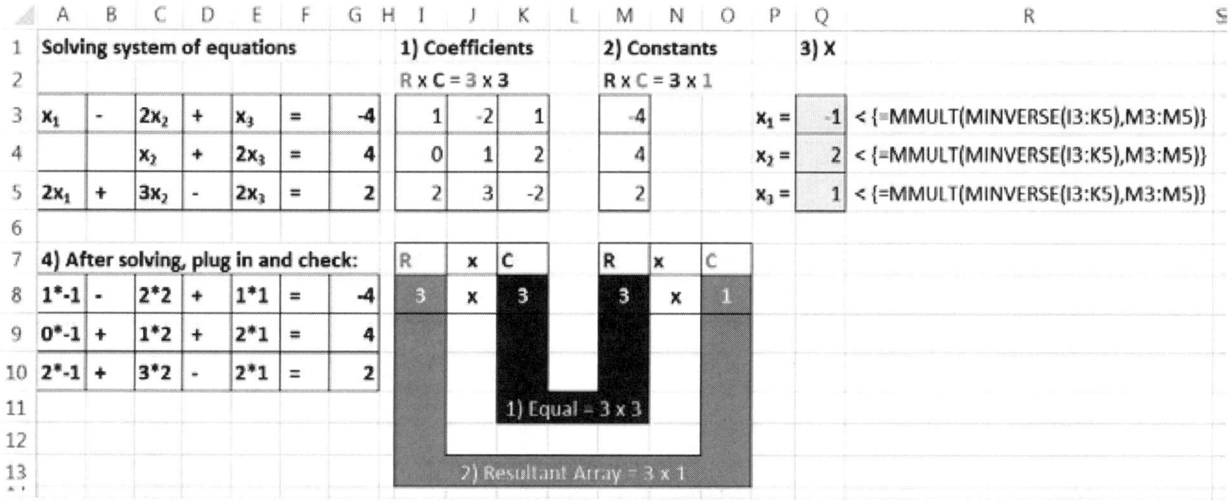

Figure 18.15 *Solving systems of equations with MMULT and MINVERSE.*

The last example in this chapter shows you how to condense a 14-cell solution into a single-cell solution, with the help of MMULT.

Using a Single-Cell Formula for Standard Deviation for a Portfolio of Stocks

In Chapter 3 you saw a great example of how to reduce a multiple-step solution for calculating the net cost to a single cell. As emphasized in Array Formula Efficiency Rules 9 and 10, sometimes less is more. Sometimes you do not need all the intermediate steps because all you want is the final answer. Whereas the example in Chapter 3 reduced 5 cells of calculations into one cell, in this example you will go from 14 cells to a single cell.

Calculating standard deviation (a measure of risk) for a portfolio of stocks is not something most people do, but the calculation provides a good example of how to condense a calculation process that spans many cells down to a single cell.

Figure 18.16 shows 14 cells that you want to reduce to a single cell. When you are in a situation like this, inventing a solution is daunting. Follow these steps, and you'll see how easy it really is:

1. Label the calculation steps (1 to 6).

2. Starting with calculation 1, construct a formula element that will simulate calculation 1 in the single cell. Verify that the numbers you see displayed in the multistep solution match the simulated numbers you create in the single cell.

3. Build calculation 2 around calculation 1, making sure that these two formula elements match the numbers you see displayed in the multistep solution.

4. Increment the building process, step-by-step, until all six calculations are in the single cell.

For this particular problem, the first part is the hardest to calculate, but MMULT comes to the rescue!

> **Note:** A number of years ago, I was trying to create a solution to this problem on my own, and I almost had an efficient solution. I then posted a question at the MrExcel Message Board, and Domenic helped me with this formula. Thanks, Domenic!!

	A	B	C	D	E	F	G	H	I	J
1		Weight	0.6	0.4		**Standard Deviation of Portfolio Calculations:**				
2		**Probability of Economic State**	**Stock A Estimated Return**	**Stock B Estimated Return**		Step 1) R,	Step 2) R, - E(R)	Step 3) (Rs - E(R))²	Step 4) (Rs - E(R))²*Prob	
3	Bad	0.5	0	-0.15		-0.0600	-0.0640	0.0041	0.0020	
4	OK	0.4	0.05	0.05		0.0500	0.0460	0.0021	0.0008	
5	Great	0.1	0.1	0.2		0.1400	0.1360	0.0185	0.0018	
6	E(R) = Expected Return for portfolio			0.0040			Var		0.0047	5) SUM
7	D6: =SUMPRODUCT(C3:D5,MMULT(B3:B5,C1:D1))						Standard deviation		0.0689	6) SQRT
8	Standard deviation for portfolio								I6: =SUM(I3:I5)	
9									I7: =SQRT(I6)	
10						F3: =SUMPRODUCT(C3:D3,$C$1:$D$1)	G3: =F3-$D$6	H3: =G3^2	I3: =H3*B3	
11						F4: =SUMPRODUCT(C4:D4,$C$1:$D$1)	G4: =F4-$D$6	H4: =G4^2	I4: =H4*B4	
12						F5: =SUMPRODUCT(C5:D5,$C$1:$D$1)	G5: =F5-$D$6	H5: =G5^2	I5: =H5*B5	

Figure 18.16 *14 cells of calculations: The final answer in cell I7 is 0.0689.*

The first step is to simulate the step 1 column of numbers, as shown in the range F3:F5 in Figure 18.16. You must create the array of numbers {-0.06;0.050;0.14} in cell D8. After selecting cell D8, you create the formula shown in Figure 18.17. If you evaluate this formula element, you can see that you do in fact simulate the column of numbers, as shown in Figure 18.18.

8	Standard deviation for portfolio	=MMULT(C1:D1*C3:D5,{1;1})
9		MMULT(**array1**, array2)

Figure 18.17 *To simulate step 1 use direct multiplication with multiplication operator between two ranges for array1 argument and a vertical array constant filled with two ones in the array2 argument.*

8	Standard deviation for portfolio	={-0.06;0.05;0.14}
9		

Figure 18.18 *Evaluate MMULT to see that you do in fact simulate the column of numbers needed from step 1.*

But wait a second! Why do you construct the formula like this? Before you proceed any further, you need to examine what is going on with this formula. The first thing to notice is that the array1 argument of MMULT contains the direct array multiplication operation C1:D1*C3:D5. You saw this sort of direct array multiplication operation on ranges with different dimensions back in Chapter 10. As shown in Figure 18.19, you can see the explicit calculation process that occurs when you directly multiply ranges with different dimensions. Each of the column header weights (range C1:D1) is multiplied by each of the returns (range C3:D5) in the respective columns.

C1:D1*C3:D5	→	C1 * C3	D1 * D3	→	0.6 * 0	0.4 * -0.15	→	Intermediate Array 1	
								0	-0.06
		C1 * C4	D1 * D4		0.6 * 0.05	0.4 * 0.05		0.03	0.02
		C1 * C5	D1 * D5		0.6 * 0.1	0.4 * 0.2		0.06	0.08

Figure 18.19 *A direct multiplication operation on different-dimensioned ranges.*

Array Formula Efficiency Rule 27

There are three different ways you can multiply arrays in Excel: direct array multiplication using the multiplication symbol, the SUMPRODUCT function and the MMULT function. Here is a description of the basic process for each:

- Directly multiplying column header numbers times a table of numbers will carry the respective column header number throughout the respective column to create a resultant array having the same dimensions as the table of numbers. A similar process can be used when there are row headers times a table, with the respective row numbers being carried through the respective row to create a resultant array having the same size as the table. Finally, direct multiplication can be performed on same-sized arrays, where each corresponding element in each array is multiplied to create a resultant array having the same size as the arrays being multiplied.

- You can use the SUMPRODUCT function on arrays that have the same dimensions where each corresponding element in each array is multiplied. Although there is a resultant array after the PRODUCT part of SUMPRODUCT performs the multiplication, the final answer of the multiplying is summed by the SUM part of the SUMPRODUCT to create a single number answer.

- You can use the MMULT array function on arrays where the number of columns of the first array is equal to the number of rows of the second array, and your goal is to perform matrix multiplication. The resultant array created by the MMULT has the dimensions rows of the first array by columns of the second array.

Now that you have the 3×2 intermediate array, you need to add the row elements, as shown in Figure 18.20. This will yield the final result, the R_s array, you are after.

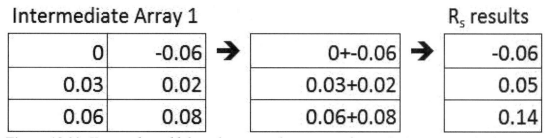

Figure 18.20 *You need to add the values in each row to go from a 3×2 array to a 3×1 array.*

The problem is that you can't directly add the rows and end up with a 3×1 column of answers unless you perform matrix multiplication, like this:

{0,-0.06;0.03,0.02;0.06,0.08} * {1;1} = {-0.06;0.05;0.14}

Why the array {1;1}? Figure 18.21 shows the process for determining that you needed the array {1;1}.

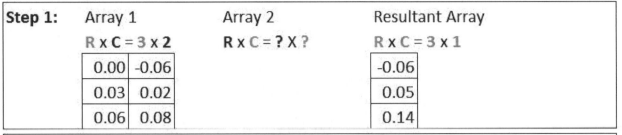

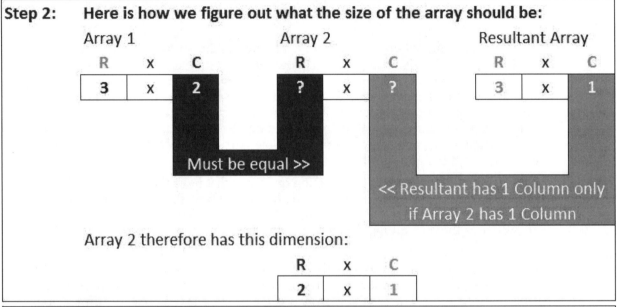

Step 1: Array 1   Array 2   Resultant Array

R x C = 3 x 2   R x C = ? X ?   R x C = 3 x 1

0.00	-0.06
0.03	0.02
0.06	0.08

-0.06
0.05
0.14

Step 2: **Here is how we figure out what the size of the array should be:**

Array 1   Array 2   Resultant Array

R	X	C
3	X	2

R	X	C
?	X	?

R	X	C
3	X	1

Must be equal >>

<< Resultant has 1 Column only
if Array 2 has 1 Column

Array 2 therefore has this dimension:

R	X	C
2	X	1

Step 3: **We need to add and so multiplying by 1 will do it:**

Array 1   Array 2   Resultant Array

R x C = 3 x 2   R x C = 2 X 1   R x C = 3 x 1

0.00	-0.06
0.03	0.02
0.06	0.08

1
1

-0.06
0.05
0.14

Figure 18.21 *The process for determining that you needed the array {1;1}*

Figure 18.22 shows the explicit matrix multiplication.

Intermediate Array 1 R_s results

0	-0.06
0.03	0.02
0.06	0.08

→

0*1+-0.06*1
0.03*1+0.02*1
0.06*1+0.08*1

→

-0.06
0.05
0.14

Figure 18.22 *3×2 times 2×1 equals 3×1, which gives you the R_s column.*

This is a lot of work to just get a single column of numbers! The rest of this array formula will be easy. Now that you have the R_s column of values in a single cell, you can go on to the step 2 calculation. As Figure 18.23 shows, you subtract the expected return from the R_s formula element.

If you evaluate this formula element, you can verify that the numbers in the formula element array (see Figure 18.24) are the same as the values in the step 2 column.

	A	B	C	D	E	F	G	H	I	J
1		Weight		0.6	0.4	**Standard Deviation of Portfolio Calculations:**				
2	Probability of Economic State		Stock A Estimated Return	Stock B Estimated Return		Step 1) R_s	Step 2) R_c - E(R)	Step 3) $(Rs - E(R))^2$	Step 4) $(Rs - E(R))^2$*Prob	
3	Bad	0.5	0	-0.15		-0.0600	-0.0640	0.0041	0.0020	
4	OK	0.4	0.05	0.05		0.0500	0.0460	0.0021	0.0008	
5	Great	0.1	0.1	0.2		0.1400	0.1360	0.0185	0.0018	
6	E(R) = Expected Return for portfolio			0.0040			Var		0.0047	5) SUM
7							Standard deviation		0.0689	6) SQRT
8	Standard deviation for portfolio			=MMULT(C1:D1*C3:D5,{1;1})-D6						

Figure 18.23 *Subtract the expected return from the R_s formula element.*

={-0.064;0.046;0.136}

Figure 18.24 *Evaluate to see if it creates the correct resultant array to simulate the step 2 column. It does!*

The step 3 column requires that you square the results from step 2. Figure 18.25 shows how you amend the formula to square the results from step 2 (parentheses force subtraction before an exponent), and Figure 18.26 shows that you can evaluate the formula element in order to verify that the formula element–delivered values are the same as in the step 3 column. (Remember that number formatting is applied to the cells but not the evaluated formula element.)

=(MMULT(C1:D1*C3:D5,{1;1})-D6)^2

Figure 18.25 *Formula to simulate step 3.*

={0.004096;0.002116;0.018496}

Figure 18.26 *Evaluation shows that the resultant array is correct.*

The step 4 column requires that you multiply the results from step 3 by the probabilities in the range B3:B5. As shown in Figure 18.27, because the two arrays are the same dimension, you simply multiply to get the resultant array as shown in Figure 18.28. (You do not need an extra set of parentheses because multiplying calculates before the exponent.)

=(MMULT(C1:D1*C3:D5,{1;1})-D6)^2*B3:B5

Figure 18.27 *Formula to simulate step 4.*

={0.002048;0.0008464;0.0018496}

Figure 18.28 *Evaluation shows that the resultant array is correct.*

Step 5 requires that you add the values from step 4 in order to calculate the variance. This is a simple sum, and so you wrap the SUMPRODUCT function around the step 4 formula element, as shown in Figure 18.29. You have used SUMPRODUCT to avoid Ctrl+Shift+Enter, even though the formula contains five array operations. The square root of the variance gives you the standard deviation, and so step 6 requires that you wrap the SQRT function around the SUMPRODUCT function, as shown in Figure 18.30.

=SUMPRODUCT((MMULT(C1:D1*C3:D5,{1;1})-D6)^2*B3:B5)

Figure 18.29 *For step 5 you use SUMPRODUCT to add resultant array.*

=SQRT(SUMPRODUCT((MMULT(C1:D1*C3:D5,{1;1})-D6)^2*B3:B5))

Figure 18.30 *For step 6 wrap SQRT around SUMPRODUCT.*

Figure 18.31 shows the final result.

	A	B	C	D	E	F	G	H	I	J
1		Weight	0.6	0.4		**Standard Deviation of Portfolio Calculations:**				
2	**Probability of Economic State**		**Stock A Estimated Return**	**Stock B Estimated Return**		Step 1) R_s	Step 2) $R_s - E(R)$	Step 3) $(Rs - E(R))^2$	Step 4) $(Rs - E(R))^2$*Prob	
3	Bad	0.5	0	-0.15		-0.0600	-0.0640	0.0041	0.0020	
4	OK	0.4	0.05	0.05		0.0500	0.0460	0.0021	0.0008	
5	Great	0.1	0.1	0.2		0.1400	0.1360	0.0185	0.0018	
6	E(R) = Expected Return for portfolio			0.0040			Var		0.0047	5) SUM
7							Standard deviation		0.0689	6) SQRT
8	Standard deviation for portfolio			0.0689						
9										
10	**Formula in cell D8: =SQRT(SUMPRODUCT((MMULT(C1:D1*C3:D5,{1;1})-D6)^2*B3:B5))**									
11	**Formula in cell D8 replaces everything in the range F1:J7**									

Figure 18.31 *Amazing single cell array formula!*

The formula that you just created is great. However, you did hard code the array constant, {1;1}, into the formula. If you did not want to hard code this into the formula, you could amend the formula and make it more robust, as shown in Figure 18.32.

=SQRT(SUM((MMULT(C1:D1*C3:D5,
TRANSPOSE(COLUMN(C1:D1)^0
))-D6)^2*B3:B5))   MMULT(array1, **array2**)

Figure 18.32 *Formula element to replace array constant makes the formula more robust. Because TRANSPOSE requires Ctrl+Shift+Enter no matter what function it is placed into, you also replace the SUMPRODUCT and with SUM. This formula requires Ctrl+Shift+Enter.*

To get the formula shown in Figure 18.32, you replace {1;1} with TRANSPOSE(-COLUMN(C1:D1)^0). Note the following:

- Because the information about the number of stocks you have in the portfolio (and therefore the information about how many 1 values you need) comes from the range C1:D1, which spans columns, you use the COLUMN function and point to the range C1:D1. By pointing to the range C1:D1, if you insert any new columns between cell C1 and D1 and add a new stock, this formula updates to reflect the additional stocks.
- COLUMN(C1:D1) creates the array {3,4}.
- Because you need {1,1} and not {3,4}, you use a zero exponent, like this: {3,4}^0 = {1,1}.

- Because you need the 1 values in rows and columns, you use the TRANSPOSE function like this: TRANSPOSE({1,1}) = {1;1}.

- You use the SUM function instead of SUMPRODUCT because TRANSPOSE is a finicky array function that requires Ctrl+Shift+Enter in most situations.

- Because you have added the TRANSPOSE function to the formula, this formula requires Ctrl+Shift+Enter.

The end result in an example involving the standard deviation for a portfolio of stocks is that you greatly reduce the amount of space used in the spreadsheet. Reducing the amount of space required to make a particular calculation can enhance the professional look of your calculations, as shown in Figure 18.33.

	A	B	C	D
1		**Weight**	0.6	0.4
2	**Probability**		**Stock A**	**Stock B**
3	Bad	0.5	0	-0.15
4	OK	0.4	0.05	0.05
5	Great	0.1	0.1	0.2
6				
7			E(R)	0.00400
8			SD	0.06888

Figure 18.33 *You need just two cells to get the numbers you need. It's clean and easy.*

Chapter Summary

In this chapter you have learned how to use the MMULT function to calculate practical results such as total costs, how to solve system of equations, and how to use MMULT to help reduce the number of cells required in a calculation-intensive process. Chapter 19 discusses how to use formulas to extract unique lists from data sets that contain duplicates.

Chapter 19: Extracting Unique Lists and Sorting Formulas

Excel Files

To follow along with the examples in this chapter, you can download the accompanying files, as explained in the Introduction.

Formulas to Do the Impossible

If you are excited by *really* complex array formulas, then you are going to love this chapter! It starts by looking at formulas to extract unique lists and then moves on to formulas that can sort. You will also place these mega-array-formulas in context by also looking at the built-in features that make these two tasks easy to accomplish.

> **Note:** Once again, I must thank some of the formula masters at the MrExcel Message Board for helping me learn about formulas to extract unique lists. Thanks, Aladin Akyurek and Domenic!!

Extracting Unique Lists from Lists or Tables with Duplicates

As you know by this point in the book, part of the reason formulas are so powerful is that they can be automatic and dynamic. If the goal is to extract a unique list of data and you do *not* need a process to be automatic or dynamic, you can use Advanced Filter or a PivotTable. If you need the process to be automatic and/or dynamic, you can accomplish it by using the following techniques that you have learned about in other chapters:

- Boolean logic (Chapter 11)
- Dynamic ranges (Chapter 13)
- Formulas to extract data with criteria (Chapter 15)
- Unique counting formulas (Chapter 17)

You will learn how to combine these techniques in new ways in this chapter, but that means you need to have already studied the techniques from these earlier chapters.

Advanced Filter: Extracting a Unique List from a Single Column

I very often use Advanced Filter to extract unique records. This is one of the features I used most in Excel because I often get data sets with many duplicates, and I need a unique list of data that I can use as criteria for formulas. For example, Figure 19.1 shows a data set with the field names Date, Race Track, and Place. Because you need a unique list and you need the data set to remain intact, you cannot use the Remove Duplicates feature in the Data Ribbon, but you can use Advanced Filter. To open the Advanced Filter dialog box, you press Alt, A, Q (or, in Excel 2003 or before, Alt, D, F, A). As shown in Figure 19.1, in the Advanced Filter dialog, you check the Unique Records Only check box and complete the other entries. Figure 19.2 shows that you get a unique list, including a field name in the range E1:E6. If you do not include the field name in the List Range text box in the Advanced Filter dialog, Excel will treat the first item as a field name, and you run the risk of having a duplicate. Figure 19.3 shows one of many potential uses for a unique list.

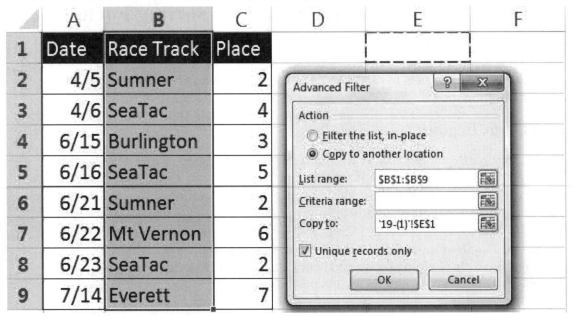

	A	B	C	D	E	F
1	Date	Race Track	Place			
2	4/5	Sumner	2			
3	4/6	SeaTac	4			
4	6/15	Burlington	3			
5	6/16	SeaTac	5			
6	6/21	Sumner	2			
7	6/22	Mt Vernon	6			
8	6/23	SeaTac	2			
9	7/14	Everett	7			

Figure 19.1 *The Unique Records Only option in Advanced Filter.*

	A	B	C	D	E	F
1	Date	Race Track	Place		Race Track	
2	4/5	Sumner	2		Sumner	
3	4/6	SeaTac	4		SeaTac	
4	6/15	Burlington	3		Burlington	
5	6/16	SeaTac	5		Mt Vernon	
6	6/21	Sumner	2		Everett	
7	6/22	Mt Vernon	6			
8	6/23	SeaTac	2			
9	7/14	Everett	7			

Figure 19.2 *Excel dumps the field name and a unique list into cell E1 and below.*

E	F	G
Race Track	# races	
Sumner	2	< Formula: =COUNTIF($B$2:$B$9,E2)
SeaTac	3	< Formula: =COUNTIF($B$2:$B$9,E3)
Burlington	1	< Formula: =COUNTIF($B$2:$B$9,E4)
Mt Vernon	1	< Formula: =COUNTIF($B$2:$B$9,E5)
Everett	1	< Formula: =COUNTIF($B$2:$B$9,E6)

Figure 19.3 *The unique list can become criteria in formulas.*

Advanced Filter: Extracting Unique Records with Criteria

In the last example you extracted a unique list from a single column. Advanced Filter can also extract a unique set of records from multiple columns, including situations where you have criteria.

Figures 19.4 and 19.5 show a situation where you need to extract unique records where the company is equal to ABC. You can create a formula for this, as you will see later in this chapter. However, if you do not need the process to be automatic, you can use the Advanced Filter method, which is amazingly easy compared to the formula method. This is one of the reasons I like Advanced Filter so much: It is flat-out *easy*! And you can extend this technique to include any of the Advanced Filter criteria examples shown in Chapters 11 and 15, including the formula criteria examples.

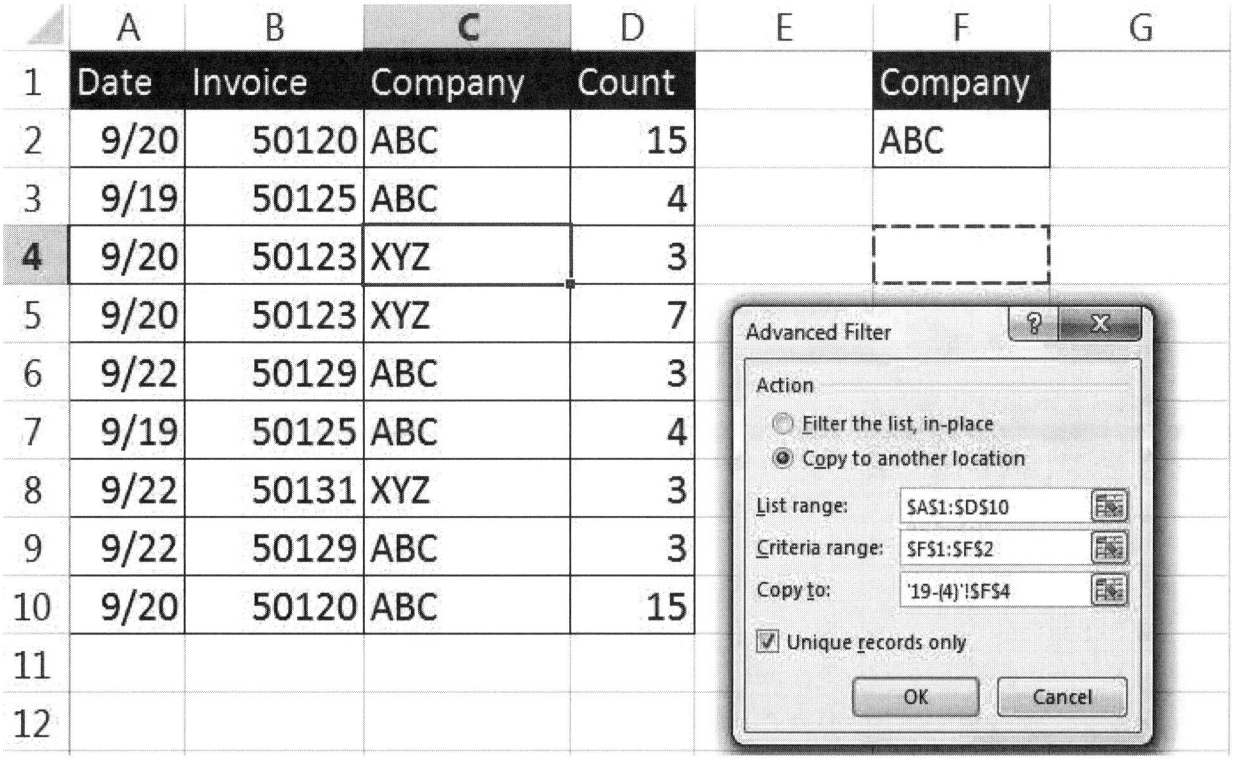

	A	B	C	D	E	F	G
1	Date	Invoice	Company	Count		Company	
2	9/20	50120	ABC	15		ABC	
3	9/19	50125	ABC	4			
4	9/20	50123	XYZ	3			
5	9/20	50123	XYZ	7			
6	9/22	50129	ABC	3			
7	9/19	50125	ABC	4			
8	9/22	50131	XYZ	3			
9	9/22	50129	ABC	3			
10	9/20	50120	ABC	15			
11							
12							

Figure 19.4 *You need the unique records for ABC.*

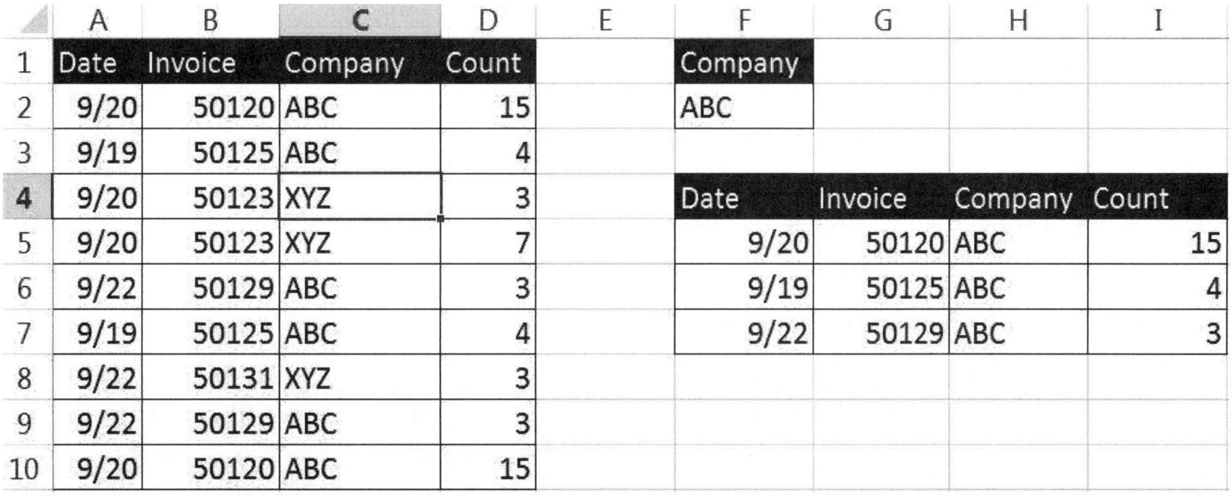

	A	B	C	D	E	F	G	H	I
1	Date	Invoice	Company	Count		Company			
2	9/20	50120	ABC	15		ABC			
3	9/19	50125	ABC	4					
4	9/20	50123	XYZ	3		Date	Invoice	Company	Count
5	9/20	50123	XYZ	7		9/20	50120	ABC	15
6	9/22	50129	ABC	3		9/19	50125	ABC	4
7	9/19	50125	ABC	4		9/22	50129	ABC	3
8	9/22	50131	XYZ	3					
9	9/22	50129	ABC	3					
10	9/20	50120	ABC	15					

Figure 19.5 *Using Advanced Filter for unique records with criteria is* much *easier than using the alternative formula methods. However, the extracted records will not automatically update if the criteria in cell F2 is changed unless you run Advanced Filter again.*

PivotTable: Extracting a Unique List from a Single Column

If you use PivotTables often, then you already know that any time you drop a field from the field list into a row or column area, you automatically get a unique list. Sometimes people use this technique to extract a unique list; because the values are located in a PivotTable, which has limitations, you can then copy the unique list in the PivotTable and use Paste Special Values to place the list outside the PivotTable. The steps go something like this:

1. Click in a single cell in the data set.

2. In Excel 2003, press Alt, D, P; in Excel 2007 and 2010, press Alt N, V, T; and in Excel 2013, press Alt N, V.

3. From the Field List, drag and drop the desired field into Row area.

4. Use the Filter for the field in the Row Area to remove any blanks (empty cells).

5. Copy and paste special values.

6. Delete the PivotTable.

Figure 19.6 shows how you can quickly create a unique list of race track names and then count the number of visits made to each track.

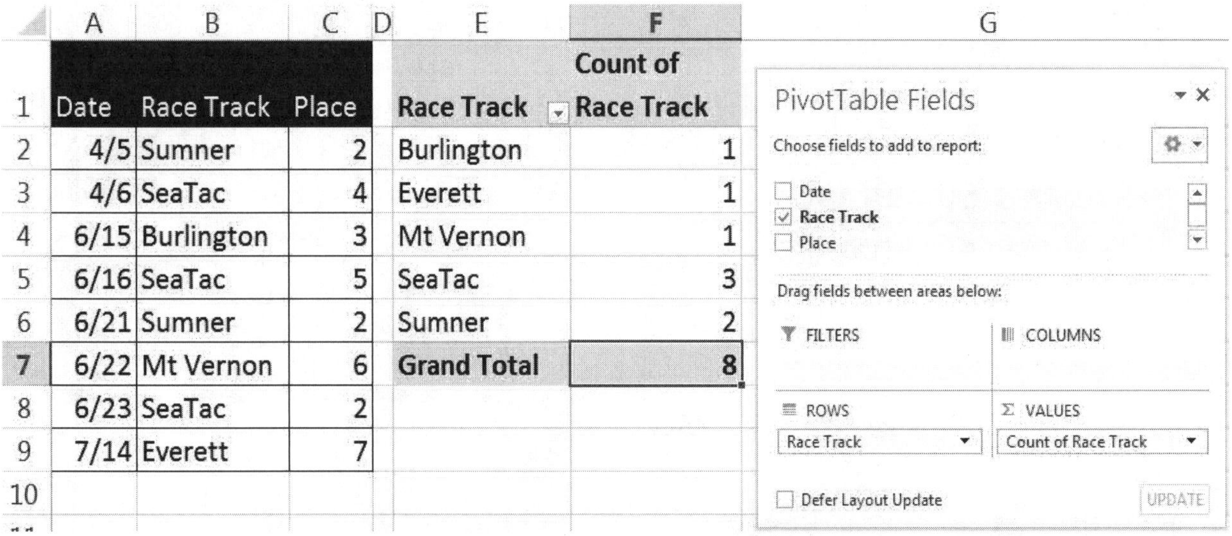

Figure 19.6 *Using a PivotTable is easy when you need a unique list and a calculation based on the unique list.*

Although you can use a PivotTable to extract a unique list from a single column, a PivotTable is not a good tool for extracting unique records with criteria. The next section looks at some formula solutions for extracting a unique list.

Helper Column Formula: Extracting a Unique List from a Single Column

Using helper column formula solutions for extracting unique data is much easier than using array formula methods. Figure 19.7 shows the formulas you use to extract a unique list of race track names from the range B2:B9. This example combines what you learned about using the COUNTIF function for a unique count from Chapter 17 and what you learned about helper columns for extracting records with criteria from Chapter 15. If the data were to change in the Race Track column, the formula would immediately pick it up.

	A	B	C	D	E
1	Date	Race Track	Place	Helper	
2	4/5	Sumner	2	1	< Formula: =SUM(COUNTIF(B$2:B2,B2)=1,D1)
3	4/6	SeaTac	4	2	** Copy formula down
4	6/15	Burlington	3	3	
5	6/16	SeaTac	5	3	
6	6/21	Sumner	2	3	
7	6/22		6	3	
8	6/23	SeaTac	2	3	
9	7/14	Everett	7	4	
11				Unique Count	
12				4	< Formula: =MAX(D2:D9)
14			No	Race Track	
15			1	Sumner	< Formula: =IF(C15>D$12,"",INDEX(B$2:B$9,MATCH(C15,$D$2:$D$9,0)))
16			2	SeaTac	** Copy formula down
17			3	Burlington	
18			4	Everett	
19			5		
20			6		
21			7		

Figure 19.7 *Using a helper column and an INDEX lookup formula to show unique list.*

Array Formula: Extracting a Unique List from a Single Column, Using SMALL

In this section, you'll combine techniques that you have already studied. Even so, array formulas for extracting unique lists can get kind of big and hard to understand. Because the formulas can get so big, I first create the formula to do the unique counting (see Chapter 17); then because that formula is the "heart" of the data extracting formula, I copy and paste it into the data extracting formula (see Chapter 15). Figure 19.8 shows the unique counting formula that you enter using Ctrl+Shift+Enter. Notice two important facts about this unique counting formula:

1. Figure 19.8 shows how the FREQUENCY function sits in the logical_test argument of the IF function. Figure 19.9 shows that the FREQUENCY function is delivering an array of numbers, where nonzero equals TRUE and zero equals FALSE. This formula counts the unique track names in the range B2:B9.

2. In both of these figures, the value_if_false argument in the IF function contains a 1. In the data extracting formula (next example), you have to replace the 1 value with the formula element for all the relative positions: ROW($B$2:$B$9)-ROW($B$2)+1.

	A	B	C	D	E	F	G
1	Date	Race Track	Place		Unique Count		
2	4/5	Sumner	2		=SUM(IF(FREQUENCY(IF(B2:B9<>"",		
3	4/6	SeaTac	4		MATCH(B2:B9,B2:B9,0)),		
4	6/15	Burlington	3		ROW(B2:B9)-ROW(B2)+1),1))		
5	6/16	SeaTac	5		IF(logical_test, [value_if_true], [value_if_false])		
6	6/21	Sumner	2				
7	6/22		6				
8	6/23	SeaTac	2				
9	7/14	Everett	7				

Figure 19.8 *FREQUENCY sits in the logical_test argument of IF.*

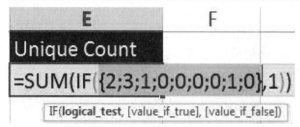

Figure 19.9 *FREQUENCY delivers a resultant array of frequency counts to the logical_test argument. Any non-zero number is TRUE and zero is FALSE.*

Next, you need to consider how to create the unique list extracting formula. Figure 19.10 shows the array of relative positions that you need in the array argument of the SMALL function.

	A	B	C	D	E	F	G	H
1	Date	Race Track	Place		Unique Count			
2	4/5	Sumner	2		5			
3	4/6	SeaTac	4					
4	6/15	Burlington	3		Race Track			
5	6/16	SeaTac	5		=IF(ROWS(E$5:E5)>$E$2,"",INDEX($B$2:$B$9,			
6	6/21	Sumner	2		SMALL({1;2;3;FALSE;FALSE;6;FALSE;8;FALSE},			
7	6/22	Mt Vernon	6		ROWS(E$5:E5)))) SMALL(array, k)			

Figure 19.10 *This is the array of relative positions of the unique items that you need to sit in the array argument of the SMALL function.*

You can create the resultant array {1;2;3;FALSE;FALSE;6;FALSE;8;FALSE} by taking the IF formula element from the unique count formula and replacing the 1 value in the value_if_false argument with ROW($B$2:$B$9)-ROW($B$2)+1.

You would have to go from this:

IF(FREQUENCY(IF($B$2:$B$9<>"",MATCH($B$2:$B$9,$B$2:$B$9,0)),ROW($B$2:$B$9)-ROW($B$2)+1),**1**)

To this:

IF(FREQUENCY(IF($B$2:$B$9<>"",MATCH($B$2:$B$9,$B$2:$B$9,0)),ROW($B$2:$B$9)-ROW($B$2)+1), **ROW($B$2:$B$9)-ROW($B$2)+1**)

This looks big and scary, but if you just do a bit of copying and pasting, it makes a seemingly impossible formula easier to create.

This formula element:

IF(FREQUENCY(IF($B$2:$B$9<>"",MATCH($B$2:$B$9,$B$2:$B$9,0)),ROW($B$2:$B$9)-ROW($B$2)+1), ROW($B$2:$B$9)-ROW($B$2)+1)

then creates the array that the SMALL array argument needs:

{1;2;3;FALSE;FALSE;FALSE;FALSE;8;FALSE}

Now the formula becomes what is shown in Figure 19.11. The rest of the formula outside the SMALL function array argument formula element is the same basic data extracting formula you have seen before. Because there are array operations in the IF function, you must enter the formula with Ctrl+Shift+Enter. Figures 19.12 and 19.13 show the formula results.

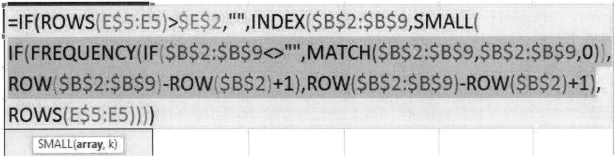

```
=IF(ROWS(E$5:E5)>$E$2,"",INDEX($B$2:$B$9,SMALL(
IF(FREQUENCY(IF($B$2:$B$9<>"",MATCH($B$2:$B$9,$B$2:$B$9,0)),
ROW($B$2:$B$9)-ROW($B$2)+1),ROW($B$2:$B$9)-ROW($B$2)+1),
ROWS(E$5:E5))))
```

SMALL(**array**, k)

Figure 19.11 *The SMALL function array argument formula element is the key. When you enter this array formula into cell E5 use Ctrl+Shift+Enter (IF function mandates that you use Ctrl+Shift+Enter).*

	A	B	C	D	E
1	Date	Race Track	Place		Unique Count
2	4/5	Sumner	2		4
3	4/6	SeaTac	4		
4	6/15	Burlington	3		Race Track
5	6/16	SeaTac	5		Sumner
6	6/21	Sumner	2		SeaTac
7	6/22		6		Burlington
8	6/23	SeaTac	2		Everett
9	7/14	Everett	7		

Figure 19.12 *Using a formula to extract a unique list.*

	A	B	C	D	E
1	Date	Race Track	Place		Unique Count
2	4/5	Sumner	2		5
3	4/6	SeaTac	4		
4	6/15	Burlington	3		Race Track
5	6/16	SeaTac	5		Sumner
6	6/21	Sumner	2		SeaTac
7	6/22	Mt Vernon	6		Burlington
8	6/23	SeaTac	2		Mt Vernon
9	7/14	Everett	7		Everett

Figure 19.13 *If the data changes, the formula immediately updates. Filter and Advanced Filter can't update like this without VBA intervention.*

Figure 19.13 shows how if you change the data, the formulas update. But what about if you added new records? Next you will see how to create these same formulas with a dynamic range.

Array Formula: Using a Dynamic Range and Extracting a Unique List from a Single Column

In this example you will combine what you saw in the last example with what you learned about formulas to create defined name dynamic ranges in Chapter 13. Figure 19.14 shows the formula you use for the defined name RaceTrack. This formula assumes that you will never enter records past row 51. Once you have the RaceTrack defined name, you can simply copy and paste the defined name in all the places in the formulas that show column B. Figure 19.15 shows the unique counting formula, and Figure 19.16 shows the extracting formula. Notice that instead of using the IF function logical_test argument range<>"" (range not empty or null text string), you use the ISTEXT function (any text yields a TRUE). When you use ISTEXT, if you type a number, or any non-text, the formula does not pick it up. Figure 19.17 shows that the formulas automatically extract any new track names and ignore numbers.

Defined Name:	RaceTrack	=$B$2:INDEX($B$2:$B$51,MATCH("Ω",$B$2:$B$51))

Figure 19.14 *Using a defined name dynamic range formula for text items.*

	A	B	C	D	E	F	G
1	Date	Race Track	Place		Unique Count		
2	4/5	Sumner	2		=SUM(IF(FREQUENCY(IF(ISTEXT(RaceTrack),		
3	4/6	SeaTac	4		MATCH(RaceTrack,RaceTrack,0)),		
4	6/15	Burlington	3		ROW(RaceTrack)-ROW($B$2)+1),1))		
5	6/16	SeaTac	5		Sumner	IF(logical_test, [value_if_true], [value_if_false])	

Figure 19.15 *Using a unique counting formula with a defined name dynamic range.*

```
=IF(ROWS(E$5:E5)>$E$2,"",INDEX(RaceTrack,SMALL(
IF(FREQUENCY(IF(ISTEXT(RaceTrack),MATCH(RaceTrack,RaceTrack,0)),
ROW(RaceTrack)-ROW($B$2)+1),ROW(RaceTrack)-ROW($B$2)+1),
ROWS(E$5:E5))))       SMALL(array, k)
```

Figure 19.16 *Using an extracting formula with a defined name dynamic range.*

	A	B	C	D	E
1	Date	Race Track	Place		Unique Count
2	4/5	Sumner	2		5
3	4/6	SeaTac	4		
4	6/15	Burlington	3		Race Track
5	6/16	SeaTac	5		Sumner
6	6/21	Sumner	2		SeaTac
7	6/22		6		Burlington
8	6/23	SeaTac	2		Everett
9	7/14	Everett	7		Redmond
10	7/20	Redmond	8		
11		2			
12					

Figure 19.17 *New records are extracted, and numbers are ignored.*

Creating a Unique List Formula for a Data Validation Drop-Down List

Building on the example you just completed, for this next example you want the second defined name dynamic range formula to be pointing to the formula extracting range E5:E14. Because the range E5:E14 has extracted text values and null text strings, you use the wildcards *? (which means at least one character) for the MATCH function lookup_value argument and -1 in the match_type argument of MATCH. -1 allows MATCH to find the last text item in the column that is one character or greater in length. As shown in Figure 19.18, you can then use the defined name in the Source text box when you use a data validation list. The drop-down list can expand and contract as new data is added or removed from the original race track names in column B.

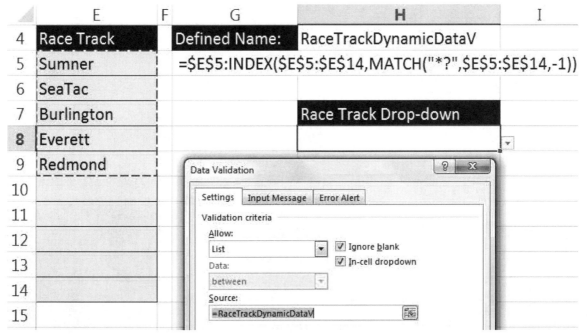

Figure 19.18 *Using a defined name dynamic formula for a data validation drop-down.*

Treating Wildcards as Characters

As you learned in Chapter 17, wildcards sometimes need to be treated as characters. Figure 19.18 shows how you can amend formulas in such cases. For the MATCH function, you join a tilde to the front of the range in the lookup_value argument and join a null text string to the back of the range in the lookup_array argument.

	A	B	C	D	E	F
1	ID	Date	# Calls		Unique Count	
2	100-456	11/18	115		5	< {=SUM(IF(FREQUENCY(IF($A$2:$A$9<>"",
3	10987	11/19	112			MATCH("~"&$A$2:$A$9,$A$2:$A$9&"",0)),
4	10987	11/19	112			ROW($A$2:$A$9)-ROW($A$2)+1),1))}
5	100-456	11/19	126		ID	
6		11/19	126		100-456	< {=IF(ROWS(E$5:E5)>$E$2,"",INDEX($A$2:$A$9,
7	*Sioux	11/23	112		10987	SMALL(IF(FREQUENCY(IF($A$2:$A$9<>"",
8	10907	11/24	36		*Sioux	MATCH("~"&$A$2:$A$9,$A$2:$A$9&"",0)),
9	Sioux	11/23	112		10907	ROW($A$2:$A$9)-ROW($A$2)+1),
10					Sioux	ROW($A$2:$A$9)-ROW($A$2)+1),
11						ROWS(E$5:E5))))}

Figure 19.19 *Wildcards are treated as characters with these formulas.*

Using a Helper Column or an Array Formula to Extract Unique Records with Criteria

As you saw earlier in this chapter, if you want to extract unique records based on criteria, using Advanced Filter is a great way to go! If you have to do this with formulas, you can use a helper column formula or an array formula. Figure 19.20 shows a great COUNTIFS helper column formula. (See Chapter 17 for similar formulas that work in Excel 2003 or before.)

	A	B	C	D	E	F	G	H
1	Date	Invoice	Company	Count	Helper			
2	9/20	50120	ABC	15	1	< =SUM(AND(		
3	9/19	50125	ABC	4	2		COUNTIFS(A$2:A2,A2,B$2:B2,B2,C$2:C2,C2,D$2:D2,D2)=1,	
4	9/20	50123	XYZ	3	2	C2=G$10),E1)		
5	9/20	50123	XYZ	7	2		** Copy formula down	
6	9/22	50129	ABC	3	3			
7	9/19	50125	ABC	4	3			
8	9/22	50131	XYZ	3	3		Criteria:	
9	9/22	50129	ABC	3	3		Company	
10	9/20	50120	ABC	15	3		ABC	
11								
12	Count	3	< =MAX(E2:E10)					
13	Formula in A15: =IF(ROWS(A$15:A15)>$B$12,"",INDEX(A$2:A$10,MATCH(ROWS(A$15:A15),$E$2:$E$10,0)))							
14	Date	Invoice	Company	Count		** Copy through range A15:D18.		
15	9/20	50120	ABC	15				
16	9/19	50125	ABC	4				
17	9/22	50129	ABC	3				
18								

Figure 19.20 *Using a helper column to extract unique records with one condition.*

Figure 19.21 shows the formula results for the following two array formulas necessary to extract unique records, based on one condition:

1. You enter the following formula in cell B12 with Ctrl+Shift+Enter:
   =SUM(IF(FREQUENCY(IF(C2:C10=F2,**MATCH(A2:A10&B2:B10&C2:C10&D2:D1 0,A2:A10&B2:B10&C2:C10&D2:D10,0)**),ROW(A2:A10)-ROW(A2)+1),1))

2. You enter the following formula in cell A15 with Ctrl+Shift+Enter and copy it through the range A15:D18:
   =IF(ROWS(A$15:A15)>$B$12,"",INDEX(A$2:A$10,SMALL(IF(FREQUEN-CY(IF($C$2:$C$10=$F$2,
   MATCH($A$2:$A$10&$B$2:$B$10&$C$2:$C$10&$D$2:$D$10,$A$2:$A$10&B 2:$B$10&$C$2:$C$10&$D$2:$D$10,0)
   ),ROW($A$2:$A$10)-ROW($A$2)+1),ROW($A$2:$A$10)-ROW($A$2)+1),ROWS(A$15:A15))))

The only difference between these two formulas and the other ones you have seen in this chapter is that all the columns in the data set are mashed together with a join array operation in both the lookup_value and lookup_array arguments in the MATCH function (MATCH function and join operation are highlighted in bold).

	A	B	C	D	E	F
1	Date	Invoice	Company	Count		Company
2	9/20	50120	ABC	15		ABC
3	9/19	50125	ABC	4		
4	9/20	50123	XYZ	3		
5	9/20	50123	XYZ	7		
6	9/22	50129	ABC	3		
7	9/19	50125	ABC	4		
8	9/22	50131	XYZ	3		
9	9/22	50129	ABC	3		
10	9/20	50120	ABC	15		
11						
12	Count	3				
13						
14	Date	Invoice	Company	Count		
15	9/20	50120	ABC	15		
16	9/19	50125	ABC	4		
17	9/22	50129	ABC	3		
18						

Figure 19.21 Array formulas to extract unique records based on one condition.

Dynamic Formulas to Extract Customer Names and Subtotals from a Transactional Data Set

The formulas shown in Figure 19.22 create a solution that automatically lists all customer names and subtotals, based on a transactional data set. For example, if a new record is added for TT Trucks in row 17, the SUMIF formula in cell F15 automatically includes the new amount in the subtotal. In addition, if new customers are added, the unique list extracting formula in column E displays the new customer, and the SUMIF formula in column F shows a new subtotal for the new customer. Notice that the SUMIF sum_range argument contains a single cell. When this happens, the SUMIF function bases the number of cells it uses to add the height of the customer range in the range argument of SUMIF, and the function becomes volatile and recalculates often. The formulas entered into cells E15 and F15 are copied down the respective columns.

	A	B	C	D	E	F	G
1	Customer Defined Name: =$B$10:INDEX($B$10:$B$34,MATCH(REPT("z",255),$B$10:$B$34))						
2	Formula in E13: {=SUM(IF(FREQUENCY(IF(Customer<>"",						
3			MATCH(Customer,Customer,0)),ROW(Customer)-ROW($B$10)+1),1))}				
4	Formula in E15: {=IF(ROWS(E$15:E15)>E$13,"",INDEX(Customer,SMALL(IF(FREQUENCY(						
5			IF(Customer<>"",MATCH(Customer,Customer,0)),				
6			ROW(Customer)-ROW($B$10)+1),ROW(Customer)-ROW($B$10)+1),				
7			ROWS(E$15:E15)))}				
8	Formula in F15: =IF(E15="","",SUMIF(Customer,E15,$C$10))						
9	Date	Customer	Sales				
10	3/29/2013	TT Trucks	493				
11	3/29/2013	Van Inc.	134				
12	3/29/2013	Fran's	949		Count		
13	3/30/2013	Fran's	188			4	
14	3/30/2013	TT Trucks	984		Customer	Sales	
15	3/30/2013	Mad Dog	888		TT Trucks	1477	
16	3/31/2013	Mad Dog	183		Van Inc.	134	
17					Fran's	1137	
18					Mad Dog	1071	
19							

Figure 19.22 *Using one defined name formula, two array formulas, and a SUMIF formula to create a dynamic extract solution that shows subtotals for customers and also automatically shows any new customers.*

Formulas for Sorting

Creating formulas to sort can be fairly easy—as for sorting numbers—or insanely hard—as for sorting mixed data. For this reason, if you do not need to sort with a formula, you can make life easier and just use the sort feature. The following sections show examples of sorting formulas.

Formulas for Sorting Numbers

Figure 19.23 shows two number-sorting formulas. You can use the SMALL and ROWS functions to sort smallest to biggest, or you can use the LARGE and ROWS functions to sort biggest to smallest. As you have seen numerous times through this book, knowing how to create a number incrementor like ROWS(B$3:B3) is very useful.

	A	B	C
1	**Sort numbers with formula.**		
2	**Smallest To Biggest**		
3	4	2	< Formula: =SMALL($A$3:$A$5,ROWS(B$3:B3))
4	2	3	** **Copy formula down**
5	3	4	
7	**Biggest To Smallest**		
8	4	4	< Formula: =LARGE($A$8:$A$10,ROWS(B$8:B8))
9	2	3	** **Copy formula down**
10	3	2	

Figure 19.23 *Using SMALL and LARGE with formula number incrementors to sort numbers.*

Using a Helper Column Formula to Sort (Ascending) Records Based on a Numeric Column

If the goal is to sort records based on numeric values, you can accomplish this with a helper column. Figure 19.24 shows how you can use the RANK and COUNTIF functions in a helper column. Notice that the COUNTIF function has an expandable range that looks one row above so that it does not get a count of one until it encounters the second occurrence of the number. Since RANK assigns the same number for ties, the extra count when COUNTIF "sees" the second occurrence helps RANK to fill the column with sequential numbers and no ties. This sequential numbering establishes the order in which the INDEX, MATCH, and ROWS functions can extract the records.

	A	B	C	D	E
1	**Helper column formula to sort (ascending) records based on numeric column.**				
2	Item	Count	Helper		
3	Bellen	22	3	< Formula: =RANK(B3,$B$3:$B$6,1)+COUNTIF($B$2:B2,B3)	
4	Carlota	20	1	** **Copy formula down**	
5	Bellen	20	2		
6	Quad	35	4		
8	Item	Count			
9	Carlota	20	< Formula in cell A9: =INDEX(A$3:A$6,MATCH(ROWS(A$9:A9),$C$3:$C$6,0))		
10	Bellen	20	** **Copy through range A9:B12**		
11	Bellen	22			
12	Quad	35			

Figure 19.24 *Using RANK and COUNTIF in a helper column to deliver sequential numbers.*

Using an Array Formula to Sort (Ascending) Records Based on a Numeric Column

If you cannot have a helper column to help establish the order in which to extract records, you can accomplish the same thing with a number-sorting formula and an array formula to extract the remaining items based on the sorted number column.

As shown in Figure 19.25, cell A11 contains the number-sorting formula, and cell B11 contains the array formula that is entered with Ctrl+Shift+Enter. Notice that in the array formula, the COUNTIF function with an expandable range is used in the k argument of the SMALL function.

	A	B	C
1	Array formula to sort (ascending) records based on numeric column.		
2	Item	Count	
3	Bellen	22	
4	Carlota	20	
5	Bellen	20	
6	Quad	35	
7			
8	Formula in cell A11: =SMALL($B$3:$B$6,ROWS(A$11:A11))		
9	Formula in cell B11: {=INDEX($A$3:$A$6,SMALL(IF($B$3:$B$6=A11,ROW($B$3:$B$6)-ROW($B$3)+1),COUNTIF($A$11:A11,A11)))}		
10	Count	Item	** Copy formulas down
11	20	Carlota	
12	20	Bellen	
13	22	Bellen	
14	35	Quad	

Figure 19.25 *If you cannot use a helper column, you can use a number-sorting formula (cell A11) and an array formula (cell B11).*

Using a Formula to Extract the Top Three Scores and Names Associated with Scores (Including Ties)

A common goal of formulas in business and sports is to extract the top *n* values along with the names associated with those top values. The formulas to accomplish this are the same basic formulas used in the last example. The difference here is that rather than sorting and showing all the values, you want just the top values. As shown in Figure 19.26, you start the solution by creating a COUNTIF formula in cell A11 that will determine the number of records to show. Notice that the criteria for COUNTIF is greater than or equal to the third-largest number. This allows you to pick up any ties. (Remember that Chapter 7 discusses this type of formula.) You can then use that hurdle in the formula to show only the top three scores and names, including ties. The extracting formula in this example uses the Excel 2010 function AGGREGATE. You can use SMALL in place of AGGREGATE if you do not have Excel 2010 or later.

	A	B	C	D	E
1	Extract top 3 score and name associated with score (including ties).				
2	Names	Score			
3	Jo	22			
4	Hal	15			
5	Chin	12			
6	Sioux	15		Criteria:	
7	Joe	22		Top 3	
8	Phil	10		3	
10	Count				
11	4	Formula in cell A11: =COUNTIF(B3:B8,">="&LARGE(B3:B8,D8))			
13	Formula in cell A16: =IF(ROWS(A$16:A16)>A$11,"",LARGE($B$3:$B$8,ROWS(A$16:A16)))				
14	B16: =IF(A16="","",INDEX($A$3:$A$8,AGGREGATE(15,6,(ROW($B$3:$B$8)-ROW($B$3)+1)/				
15	Score	Names		($B$3:$B$8=A16),COUNTIF($A$16:A16,A16))))	
16	22	Jo		** Copy formulas down	
17	22	Joe			
18	15	Hal			
19	15	Sioux			
20					
21					

Figure 19.26 *Using a formula to show the top* n *scores and the names of the people who earned the scores. If you change the* n *in cell D8, the extract formulas will update!*

Using a Helper Column Formula to Sort (Ascending) Records Based on a Text Column

If you would like to sort based on a text column and you can have a helper column, Figure 19.27 shows a great COUNTIF formula that can help solve this problem. Notice that the criteria in the first COUNTIF function in cell C3 is asking how many are less than the item (in terms of sorting).

> **Note:** Comparative operators operate on text in this example. Whether or not one character or word is bigger or smaller than another character or word is based on Excel's default sorting hierarchy. The next section of this book discusses this topic in more detail.

To see how this formula works, consider the formula result in cell C3. Because there are no text items less than Bellen, the first COUNTIF gets a count of zero, but then the second COUNTIF adds a one.

	A	B	C	D	E
1	Helper column formula to sort (ascending) records based on text column.				
2	Item	Count	Helper		
3	Bellen	22	1	< Formula: =COUNTIF($A$3:$A$6,"<"&A3)+COUNTIF($A$3:A3,A3)	
4	Carlota	20	3	** Copy formula down	
5	Bellen	33	2		
6	Quad	35	4		
7					
8	Item	Count			
9	Bellen	22	< Formula in cell A9: =INDEX(A$3:A$6,MATCH(ROWS(A$9:A9),$C$3:$C$6,0))		
10	Bellen	33	** Copy through range A9:B12		
11	Carlota	20			
12	Quad	35			

Figure 19.27 *Using a helper column to create sequential numbers for sorted text items.*

The last few examples have shown four sorting formulas for numbers and one for text items. But what if you have mixed data? The following section looks at what you do in that case.

Using an Array Formula to Extract a Unique List and Sort Mixed Data

You have created some pretty big array formulas in this book so far. But none of them have been as big as the one you are about to create. You are going to throw the kitchen sink at this formula and use ideas from most of the chapters you have already studied in the book.

Figure 19.28 shows the completed formula. This formula takes a list of mixed data and extracts a unique list; then it sorts the results.

> **Note:** This formula is from Domenic at the MrExcel Message Board. Absolutely amazing, Domenic!!

Because the formula is so big, it is best if you build the formula step by step. Let's start by considering how the standard Excel sorting feature works.

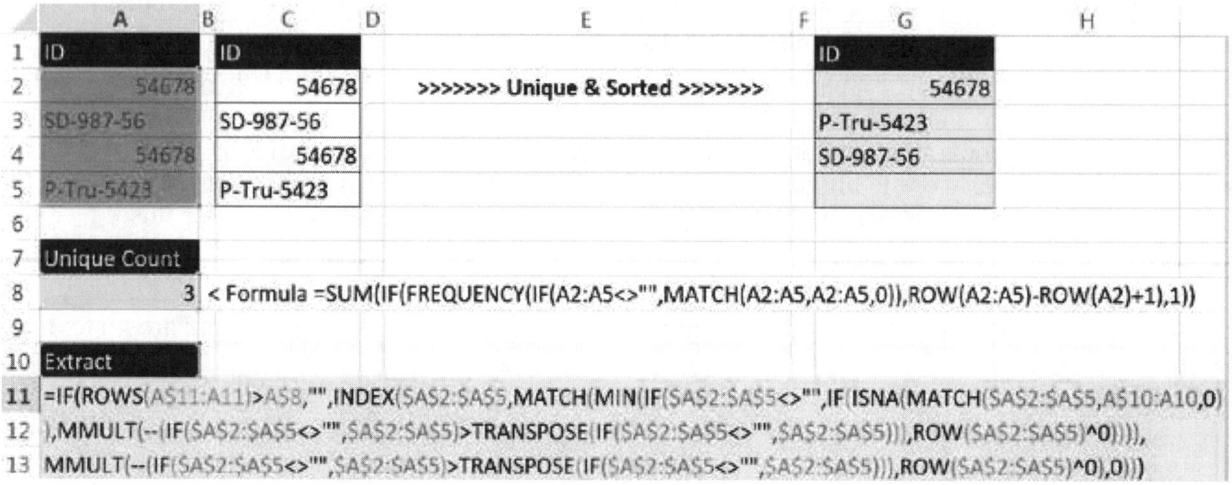

Figure 19.28 *Using a formula that extracts a unique list and sorts the results.*

When you sort a column, the sorted results are based Excel's sort order (For sorting ascending, Numbers are listed first, then Text (including null text strings), then FALSE, then TRUE, then Errors in the order they occur, then empty cells) and on ASCII characters. There are 255 ASCII characters, each of which corresponds with a number 1 to 255. The following table shows examples of a few ASCII characters and their corresponding numbers. For example, the ASCII character 5 corresponds to the ASCII number 53, and the ASCII character S corresponds to the ASCII number 83. If you were to sort a column smallest to biggest (ascending) that contained the number 5 and the letter S, the number 5 would be above S because 53 is smaller than 83.

ASCII Number	ACSII Character	ASCII Number	ACSII Character
45	–	65	A
47	/	66	B
48	0	67	C
49	1	83	S
50	2	84	T
51	3	85	U
52	4	97	a
53	5	98	b
54	6	99	c
55	7	100	d
56	8	101	e
57	9	102	f

Figure 19.29 shows the data set in the range A2:A5. For illustration purposes, the sorted data (ascending) is shown in the range G2:G5. This sorted list will help you understand the numbers in the range C2:C5. Each number in the range C2:C5 answers the question "If the list is sorted, how many of the other items in the list are above you?" For example, if you ask this question of the ID in cell A2 (54678), the answer is zero because if the list is sorted, the ID 54678 would be at the top of the sorted list, and none would be above it. On the other hand, the ID SD-987-56 would have three above it. If you could invent a formula element that would create these numbers, you would have one of the necessary parts for the formula.

	A	B	C	D	E	F	G
1	ID		How many are above you?		Count # greater than you.		Sorted results
2	54678		0		0		54678
3	SD-987-56		3		3		54678
4	54678		0		0		P-Tru-5423
5	P-Tru-5423		2		2		SD-987-56

Figure 19.29 *If you were to sort the ID list, the ID P-Tru-5423 would have two items above it.*

To create the numbers as shown in the range C2:C5, you start by making some calculations off to the side that will help you understand what is going on with the formula. First, you highlight the range E1:H1 and enter the formula =TRANSPOSE(A2:A5) with Ctrl+Shift+Enter, as shown in Figure 19.30. As shown in Figure 19.31, next, you highlight the range E2:H5 and create the formula =A2:A5>E1:H1. You enter this formula using Ctrl+Shift+Enter. Figure 19.32 shows the result. This result is a rectangular array of TRUEs and FALSEs that correspond to each cell in the resultant array, asking the question "Is the column header less than the row header?" For example, the calculation that occurs in cell E3 is SD-987-56 > 54678. Because 54678 is less than SD-987-56, in terms of sorting, the answer is TRUE. Notice that in the range E3:H3, there are three TRUE values and one FALSE value. If you were to add the three TRUE values, you would get the number 3. Looking back at Figure 19.29, you can see that the number three is the number you are after because it indicates that three values are above it.

	A	B	C	D	E	F	G	H
1	ID				=TRANSPOSE(A2:A5)			
2	54678							
3	SD-987-56							
4	54678							
5	P-Tru-5423							

Figure 19.30 *In the range E1:H1, enter the array function =TRANSPOSE(A2:A5) with Ctrl+Shift+Enter.*

	A	B	C	D	E	F	G	H
1	ID				54678	SD-987-56	54678	P-Tru-5423
2	54678				=A2:A5>E1:H1			
3	SD-987-56							
4	54678							
5	P-Tru-5423							

Figure 19.31 *In the range E2:H5 enter the array formula =A2:A5>E1:H1 with Ctrl+Shift+Enter.*

	A	B	C	D	E	F	G	H
1	ID				54678	SD-987-56	54678	P-Tru-5423
2	54678				FALSE	FALSE	FALSE	FALSE
3	SD-987-56				TRUE	FALSE	TRUE	TRUE
4	54678				FALSE	FALSE	FALSE	FALSE
5	P-Tru-5423				TRUE	FALSE	TRUE	FALSE

Figure 19.32 *Each cell in the resultant array, asks the question "Is the column header less than (in terms of sorting) the row header?"*

As shown in Figures 19.33 and 19.34, you can convert the TRUEs and FALSEs to ones and zeros by amending the formula with a double negative and then entering it with Ctrl+Shift+Enter. Now that you have the zeros and ones, if you add the rows, you have the numbers you are after: {0;3;0;2}. Because you need to add the rows and have the result displayed in a 4×1 array, you can use the MMULT function (discussed in Chapter 18), as shown in Figure 19.35. You enter MMULT by using Ctrl+Shift+Enter (see Figure 19.36). Now, instead of using the range E2:H5 in MMULT, you want to create a formula element to replace it.

	A	B	C	D	E	F	G	H
1	ID				54678	SD-987-56	54678	P-Tru-5423
2	54678				=--(A2:A5>E1:H1)		FALSE	FALSE
3	SD-987-56				TRUE	FALSE	TRUE	TRUE
4	54678				FALSE	FALSE	FALSE	FALSE
5	P-Tru-5423				TRUE	FALSE	TRUE	FALSE

Figure 19.33 *Convert TRUEs and FALSEs to ones and zeros with double negative.*

	A	B	C	D	E	F	G	H
1	ID				54678	SD-987-56	54678	P-Tru-5423
2	54678				0	0	0	0
3	SD-987-56				1	0	1	1
4	54678				0	0	0	0
5	P-Tru-5423				1	0	1	0

Figure 19.34 *Instead of TRUEs and FALSEs you get ones and zeros.*

	A	B	C	D	E	F	G	H
1	ID					54678	SD-987-56	54678	P-Tru-5423
2	54678	=MMULT(E2:H5,{1;1;1;1})			0	0	0
3	SD-987-56				1	0	1	1
4	54678				0	0	0	0
5	P-Tru-5423				1	0	1	0

Figure 19.35 *You can use MMULT to add the ones and zeros*

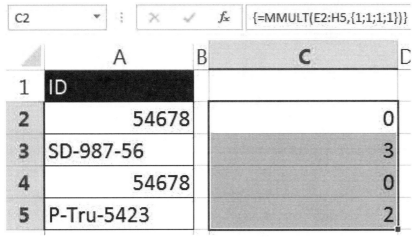

Figure 19.36 *After entering MMULT with Ctrl+Shift+Enter, you get your column of numbers that say "how many are above the ID in a sorted list".*

As shown in Figure 19.37, you replace the range E2:H5 with the formula element --(A2:A5>TRANSPOSE(A2:A5)).

	A	B	C	D	E	F
1	ID					
2	54678		=MMULT(--(A2:A5>TRANSPOSE(A2:A5)),{1;1;1;1})			
3	SD-987-56			MMULT(**array1**, array2)		
4	54678					
5	P-Tru-5423					

Figure 19.37 *Replace the range with a formula element.*

Figure 19.38 shows how you can replace the array constant with the formula element ROW(A2:A5)^0. (This formula element is discussed in detail in Chapter 18.)

Figure 19.38 *Replace the array constant with a formula element.*

Next, because you do not want the formula to fail if there are empty cells, Figure 19.39 shows how you can replace the range A2:A5 with the formula element IF(A2:A5<>"",A2:A5).

=MMULT(--(IF(A2:A5<>"",A2:A5)>TRANSPOSE(IF(A2:A5<>"",A2:A5))),ROW(A2:A5)^0)

Figure 19.39 *To deal with potential empty cells replace all instances of A2:A5 with the formula element IF-(A2:A5<>"",A2:A5). ROW does not need the IF because it considers cell address rather than cell content.*

Because the final formula will be copied to other cells, you need to make all the ranges absolute. Figure 19.40 shows the formula with absolute cell references. Figure 19.41 shows the resultant numbers if you enter the formula with Ctrl+Shift+Enter.

=MMULT(--(IF($A$2:$A$5<>"",$A$2:$A$5)>TRANSPOSE(IF($A$2:$A$5<>"",$A$2:$A$5))),ROW($A$2:$A$5)^0)

Figure 19.40 *Because the formula will be copied, make all ranges absolute.*

	A	B	C
1	ID		
2	54678		0
3	SD-987-56		3
4	54678		0
5	P-Tru-5423		2

Figure 19.41 *Enter the formula with Ctrl+Shift+Enter.*

Because this formula element is long and will be used twice in the formula, you can save it as a defined name and then use the defined name in the formula. As shown in the New Name dialog in Figure 19.42, name the formula HMA, which stands for "How Many Above?"

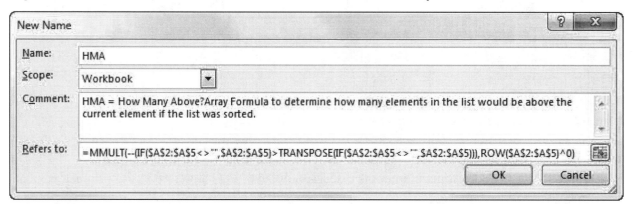

Figure 19.42 *Because the formula element will be used in the formula more than once, save formula as a defined name.*

Next, you need to create the extracting data part of the formula.

As shown in Figure 19.43, you start the extract-sorting formula in cell A11. The formula so far has these elements:

1. The INDEX array argument contains the range with the items you need to look up.

2. This first MATCH function tells INDEX the relative position of the item is you are looking up.

3. For now you leave the lookup_value argument empty.

4. The defined name, HMA, is in the lookup_array argument of MATCH because as you copy the formula down, you first look up the position of 0, then 2, then finally 3.

5. A zero is in the match_type argument to force an exact match lookup because there are duplicate IDs.

	A	B	C	D	E
1	ID				
2	54678		0		
3	SD-987-56		3		
4	54678		0		
5	P-Tru-5423		2		
7	Unique Count				
8	3				
10	Extract				
11	=INDEX($A$2:$A$5,MATCH(,HMA,0))				
12		MATCH(**lookup_value**, lookup_array, [match_type])			

Figure 19.43 *You start the extract-sorting formula in cell A11. The lookup_array argument in MATCH is still left empty.*

Before you can create the lookup_value for MATCH, you have to think about what it should be. There are three unique items to be sorted, so you need three numbers for lookup_value as the formula is copied down in order for MATCH to deliver the correct relative position to the INDEX:

1. In cell A11, the MATCH function needs to look up the number 0 and report the relative position 1 from the defined name HMA.

2. When the formula is copied down to cell A12, the MATCH function needs to look up the number 2 and report the relative position 4 from the defined name HMA.

3. In cell A13, the MATCH function needs to look up the number 3 and report the relative position 2 from the defined name HMA.

A pattern emerges when you think about what the lookup_value must be as you copy the formula down is: "Give me the minimum number from the defined name that has not already been used." As shown in Figure 19.44, the formula element MIN(IF(ISNA(-MATCH($A$2:$A$5,A$10:A10,0)),HMA)) delivers that minimum number perfectly as the formula is copied down. The reason it works is that the ISNA and MATCH combination, ISNA(-MATCH($A$2:$A$5,A$10:A10,0)), is a formula element to compare two lists (see Chapter 15). Notice the expandable range, A$10:A10, in the lookup_array argument. In cell A11, the ISNA and MATCH combination helps deliver all the HMA numbers to the MIN function. However, when the formula gets down to cell A12, the ID that has already been delivered to cell A11 is now in the expandable range and can be found in the range $A$2:$A$5. This triggers a FALSE from the ISNA and eliminates the 0 value from the defined name HMA. To see this more clearly, you can enter the formula into cell A11 with Ctrl+Shift+Enter and copy the formula down.

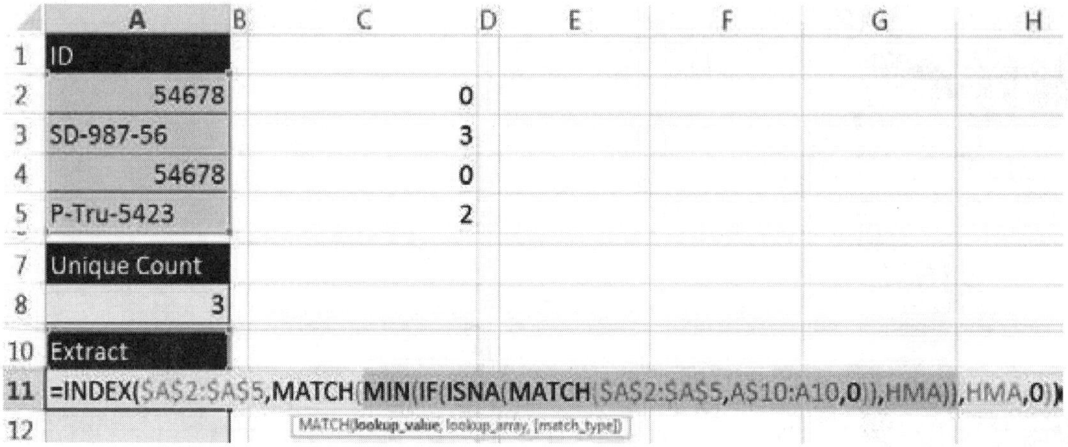

Figure 19.44 *The formula element in the lookup_value argument of MATCH asks: "Give me the minimum number from the defined name that has not already been used."*

After you copy the formula down, now you can put the formula in cell A12 in Edit mode. Figure 19.45 shows the expandable range, and you can see that the ISNA and MATCH combination will now find the ID 54678 in the range $A$2:$A$5. To further understand how this formula works, Figures 19.46 to 19.49 show how the MATCH formula element in the row_num argument of the INDEX function works.

Figure 19.45 *The expandable range now includes the first ID.*

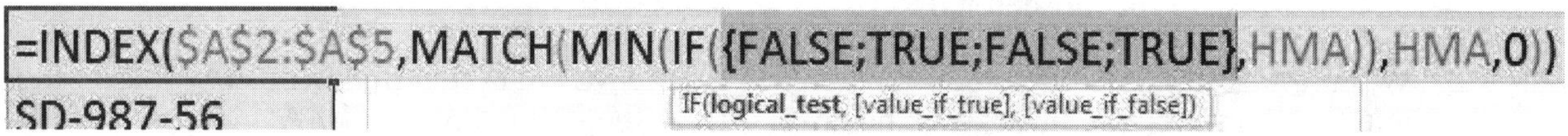

Figure 19.46 *This figure shows that the ISNA and MATCH combination delivers an array of logical values. The two FALSE values eliminate the zero values from the defined name HMA.*

Figure 19.47 *This figure shows that the zeros are eliminated and only the numbers 3 and 2 remain. The number 2 is the smallest and represents the next sorted item to be extracted.*

Figure 19.48 *This figure shows that MIN selects the number 2. The MIN function has fulfilled the request "Give me the minimum number from the defined name that has not already been used." The MATCH can now find the correct relative position for the INDEX function.*

Figure 19.49 *This figure shows that INDEX can now look up the fourth ID in the list.*

Now, going back to cell A11, you can add one more condition to the MIN calculation so that empty cells do not adversely affect the formula. Figure 19.50 shows the formula with another IF condition.

```
=INDEX($A$2:$A$5,MATCH(MIN(
IF($A$2:$A$5<>"",
IF(ISNA(MATCH($A$2:$A$5,A$10:A10,0)),
HMA))),HMA,0))
```

Figure 19.50 *Inside the MIN the first IF asks: "Are any cells not empty?" The second IF asks: "Have you not already been used?"*

Figure 19.51 shows the final formula with a condition to show nothing after that last sorted unique item has been displayed. Figure 19.52 shows the final results in the range A11:A15, including an empty cell (cell A3) in the source data range (to test whether the condition for empty cells is working).

```
=IF(ROWS(A$11:A11)>A$8,"",INDEX($A$2:$A$5,MATCH(MIN(
IF($A$2:$A$5<>"",
IF(ISNA(MATCH($A$2:$A$5,A$10:A10,0)),
HMA))),HMA,0)))
```

Figure 19.51 *The final formula.*

	A	B
1	ID	
2	54678	
3		
4	54678	
5	P-Tru-5423	
7	Unique Count	
8	2	
10	Extract	
11	54678	
12	P-Tru-5423	
13		
14		
15		

Figure 19.52 *Formula is working even if there are empty cells.*

That has been an amazing chapter! You have seen that it can sometimes be quite difficult to get formulas to do what you want them to do.

Chapter Summary

In this chapter you have learned about formulas to extract unique lists and to do sorting. Chapters 20, 21, and 22 are short chapters about conditional formatting, data tables, and the LINEST array function.

Chapter 20: Conditional Formatting with Array Formulas

Excel Files

To follow along with the examples in this chapter, you can download the accompanying files, as explained in the Introduction.

Conditional Formatting with Formulas, Including Array Formulas

Conditional formatting is fun, especially when you use formulas and link the conditions for formatting to cells.

Here are the important facts you need to know about conditional formatting with formulas:

- Conditional formatting means that formatting will be applied if a condition is met.
- A logical test that evaluates to TRUE or FALSE is applied to a range of cells.
- For each cell in a range, the test is evaluated. If the test is TRUE, the cell gets the formatting. If the test is FALSE, the cell does not get the formatting.
- Logical formulas that evaluate to TRUE or FALSE can be used to create conditional formatting.
- Conditional formatting can be used with non-array formulas and array formulas.
- Conditional formatting is volatile: It recalculates often and can slow overall spreadsheet calculation time.
- These are the steps in creating conditional formatting with formulas:

1. Highlight the range of cells. Make a metal note of which cell is the active cell in the highlighted range. (The active cell is the light-colored cell.)

2. Open the Conditional Formatting Rules Manager dialog box by pressing Alt, O, D (or from the Home Ribbon tab, select the Styles group and then select Manage Rules from the Conditional Formatting drop-down).

3. Open the New Formatting Rule dialog box by pressing Alt+N (or by clicking the New Rule button).

4. Select Use a Formula to Determine Which Cells to Format from the "Select a Rule Type" list. (To get there using the keyboard, press the down-arrow key five times, or just hold down the down-arrow key until the cursor gets to the bottom of the list.)

5. Click the Format Values Where This Formula Is True text box.

6. Create your formula from the point of view of the active cell in the highlighted range. That is, build the formula as if you were placing it into the active cell and then copying it down and over. Remember, whatever the conditional test is that you are creating must be evaluated for each cell to determine whether each cell in the range gets the formatting—yes or no. So, even if the formula is not actually going into the active cell, the dialog box will copy it throughout the range in memory as if the formula were in the cells in the highlighted range.

7. Click the Format button and select any combination of formatting you want from the four tabs (Number, Font, Border, and Fill).

8. Click OK in the Format Cells dialog box.

9. Click OK in the New Formatting Rule dialog box.

10. Click OK in the Conditional Formatting Rules Manager dialog box.

Let's look at two examples that illustrate conditional formatting with array formulas.

The first example, Figure 20.1, shows how to highlight the row that contains the smallest value for the city name that is typed into cell A11. Notice the mixed cell reference, $B3, that allows each cell in the row to compare the minimum value for the city to the time value in column B. Notice that the array calculation in this formula calculates the same value in each cell. This is a lot of repeat calculating. The volatile nature of conditional formatting compounds the problem. To get around this repeat calculating, it would be beneficial if you used a helper cell. The second example, Figure 20.2, shows a conditional formatting example that uses a helper cell.

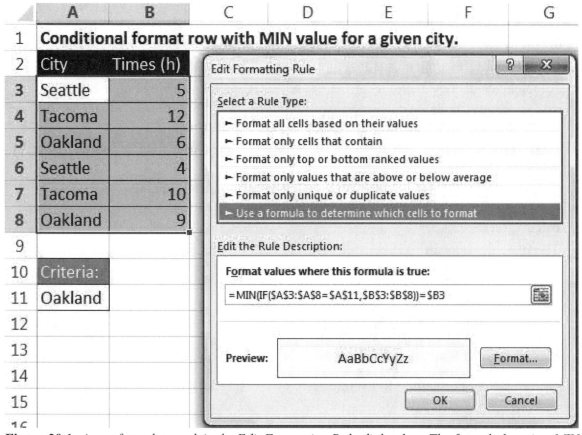

Figure 20.1 *Array formulas work in the Edit Formatting Rule dialog box. The formula here is =MIN(IF($A $3:$A$8=$A$11,$B$3:$B$8))=$B3.*

The formatting goal for Figure 20.2 is to highlight the row that contains a racers two fastest times. The racer's name is in cell A17. The hurdle for number of times to show is in cell B17. (You want to show the two fastest times, so you place a 2 in cell B17.) The array formulas for calculating the second fastest time for the racer are in D18 and D19 (either one of the formulas can be used). The formula =AND($A3=$A$17,$B3<=$D$18) tests whether the row has the racer's name and whether it has a value less than or equal to the second-fastest time. The helper cells prevent repeat calculating for the second-fastest time formula (cell D18).

Conditional format row with racer's 2 fastest times using helper cell.

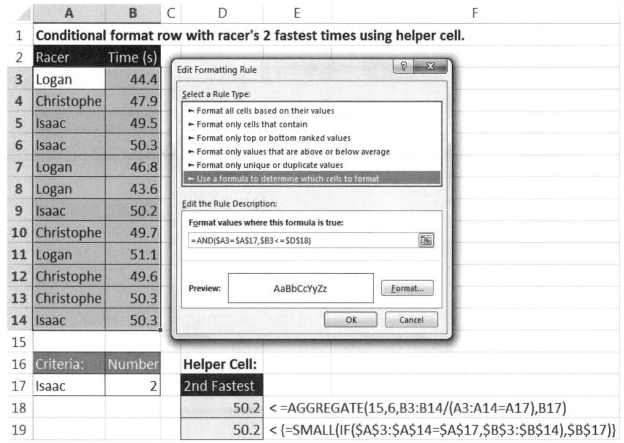

	A	B	C	D	E	F
2	Racer	Time (s)				
3	Logan	44.4				
4	Christophe	47.9				
5	Isaac	49.5				
6	Isaac	50.3				
7	Logan	46.8				
8	Logan	43.6				
9	Isaac	50.2				
10	Christophe	49.7				
11	Logan	51.1				
12	Christophe	49.6				
13	Christophe	50.3				
14	Isaac	50.3				
15						
16	Criteria:	Number		Helper Cell:		
17	Isaac	2		2nd Fastest		
18				50.2	< =AGGREGATE(15,6,B3:B14/(A3:A14=A17),B17)	
19				50.2	< {=SMALL(IF($A$3:$A$14=$A$17,$B$3:$B$14),$B$17)}	

Edit Formatting Rule

Select a Rule Type:

- Format all cells based on their values
- Format only cells that contain
- Format only top or bottom ranked values
- Format only values that are above or below average
- Format only unique or duplicate values
- **Use a formula to determine which cells to format**

Edit the Rule Description:

Format values where this formula is true:

=AND($A3=$A$17,$B3<=$D$18)

Preview: AaBbCcYyZz   [Format...]

[OK]   [Cancel]

Figure 20.2 *A helper cell can prevents repeat calculating of the array formula.*

Chapter Summary

In this chapter you have taken a quick look at array formulas and conditional formatting. Chapter 21 takes a look at the data table feature, which uses the TABLE array function.

Chapter 21: Data Tables

Excel Files

To follow along with the examples in this chapter, you can download the accompanying files, as explained in the Introduction.

Data Tables

This chapter takes a look at the data table feature, which creates an array of results with the TABLE function (not a function that you can manually enter into a cell). Using a data table is a quick and easy way to do what-if analysis for formulas that use formula inputs. This feature allows you to change one or two of the formula inputs and display multiple what-if results. Let's start by looking at the one variable data tables.

> **Note:** Back in Chapters 4, 5, and 10 you saw some brief examples of data tables being used in combination with D-functions. In those examples, the D-function and data table examples had formula calculation times that were much faster than the related array formula calculation times.

Using One-Variable Data Tables for One-Formula What-If Analysis

Figure 21.1 shows a PMT function in cell B6 that is using formula inputs. If you were to change the input in cell B2 (annual rate), the PMT function would update. The goal, however, is to change that input to five different rates and display all five PMT results. Although this would be easy to accomplish by creating your own formula, the data table feature can be advantageous for two reasons:

1. Data tables can have faster formula calculation times than alternative formula solutions. (You saw timing results in Chapters 4 and 5.)

2. When you use data tables to replace many formulas (as you'll see in the next example), formula creation time can be faster.

For the PMT example, these are the steps you need to perform to get the data table to create the solution:

1. Highlight the range A10:B15. You do this because cell B10 contains a formula that refers to the formula on which you want to perform what-if analysis. Also, the range A11:A15 contains the new what-if formula inputs for the PMT function. These are the five values you want to "substitute" into the PMT function in order to produce five new values.

2. Open the Data Table dialog by pressing Alt D, T (or, from the Data Ribbon tab, select the Data Tools group and then select Data Table from the What-If Analysis drop-down).

3. Because the "substitute" values are in a column, click the Column Input Cell text box and select the original formula input that the PMT function in cell B6 is pointing to, which is cell B2. (Notice that PMT is indirectly pointing to B2.) Here you are telling the data table feature to remove the value from cell B2 in the PMT calculation process and instead substitute into the formula the values in the range A11:A15.

4. Click OK.

	A	B	C	D	E
1	Loan Amount	$225,000.00	< = Direct formula input.		
2	Annual Rate	4.0%	< = Indirect formula input.		
3	Month Rate	0.3333%	< =B2/12, direct formula input.		
4	Years	30	< = Indirect formula input.		
5	# Months	360	< =B4*12, direct formula input.		
6	Monthly PMT	$1,074.18	< =-PMT(B3,B5,B1).		
7					
8	1 Variable Data Table				
9	Annual Rate	Monthly PMT			
10		$1,074.18	< =B6	< This refers up to the cell with the	
11	2.0%	$831.64		PMT function that you want to	
12	3.0%	$948.61		perform what-if analysis on.	
13	4.0%	$1,074.18			
14	5.0%	$1,207.85			
15	6.0%	$1,348.99			

Figure 21.1 *Cell B6 contains a formula that indirectly uses the formula input from cell B2.*

If you highlight the range B11:B15 and look in the formula bar, you can see the array formula TABLE function with a column input that the data table feature entered into the range B11:B15. The TABLE function is not a function that you can type out yourself; instead, it is automatically created and entered when you use the Data Table dialog.

⋮	×	✓	*fx*	{=TABLE(,B2)}

	A	B
11	2.0%	$831.64
12	3.0%	$948.61
13	4.0%	$1,074.18
14	5.0%	$1,207.85
15	6.0%	$1,348.99

Figure 21.2 *The TABLE function entered through the Data Table dialog box.*

Using One-Variable Data Tables to Replace Many Formulas with One Formula

In Figure 21.3 each of the cells in the range E3:I3 contains a different formula that directly or indirectly refers to the formula input for units sold in cell B3. By using a data table, you can perform what-if analysis based on the units in the range D4:D12 for these five formulas.

	A	B	C	D	E	F	G	H	I
1				Units	**Formula in E3:** =B3*B4	**Formula in F3:** =B3*B5	**Formula in G3:** =E3-F3	**Formula in H3:** =E3-F3-B6	**Formula in I3:** =F3+B6
2	Formula Inputs			Units	Sales	Variable Cost	Contribution	Net Income	Total Costs
3	Units sold	5000			$150,000	$68,450	$81,550	$2,300	$147,700
4	Price per unit	$30		0	$0	$0	$0	-$79,250	$79,250
5	Variable cost per unit	$13.69		2000	$60,000	$27,380	$32,620	-$46,630	$106,630
6	Fixed costs	$79,250		4000	$120,000	$54,760	$65,240	-$14,010	$134,010
7				6000	$180,000	$82,140	$97,860	$18,610	$161,390
8				8000	$240,000	$109,520	$130,480	$51,230	$188,770
9				10000	$300,000	$136,900	$163,100	$83,850	$216,150
10				12000	$360,000	$164,280	$195,720	$116,470	$243,530
11				14000	$420,000	$191,660	$228,340	$149,090	$270,910
12				16000	$480,000	$219,040	$260,960	$181,710	$298,290

Data Table dialog box:
- Row input cell:
- Column input cell: $B$3

Figure 21.3 *A one-variable data table can work on more than one formula.*

Using Two-Variable Data Tables

The goal of the formula in this example is to create a cross-tabulated table that shows the minimum value based on two criteria. You can use a two-variable data table to obtain this goal. As shown in Figure 21.4, you can create a two-variable data table by using both the Row Input Cell and Column Input Cell text boxes in the Data Table dialog box. The only potential drawback is that you must place a formula in the upper-left corner of the data table, which shows a "rogue" value that doesn't really fit with the layout of the table. One solution is to hide the rogue value by using the custom number format ;;; (three semicolons in a row). In this example, the DMIN formula and data table solution replace this array formula:

=MIN(IF($B$2:$B$19=$F9,IF($C$2:$C$19=G$8,$D$2:$D$19)))

The DMIN and data table solution calculates more quickly than the array formula solution.

	A	B	C	D	E	F	G	H	I	J
1	Date	Region	Sales Rep	Units		Region	Sales Rep	Min		
2	7/29	West	Joplin	18707		West	Joplin	12731	< =DMIN(B1:D19,"Units",F1:G2)	
3	7/30	East	Phylis	9939						
4	7/31	Midwest	Chrissy	10493		Formula in cell F8: =H2.				
5	8/1	West	Chrissy	5806						
6	8/2	East	Joplin	20035						
7	8/3	Midwest	Phylis	112						
8	8/4	West	Phylis	10776		12731	Chrissy	Joplin	Phylis	
9	8/5	East	Phylis	9185		East	10452	8692	9185	
10	8/6	Midwest	Joplin	4497		Midwest	10493	4497	112	
11	8/7	West	Chrissy	8353		West	5806	12731	10718	
12	8/8	East	Chrissy	10452						
13	8/9	Midwest	Chrissy	14032						
14	8/10	West	Phylis	10718						
15	8/11	East	Joplin	16978						
16	8/12	Midwest	Phylis	665						
17	8/13	West	Joplin	12731						
18	8/14	East	Joplin	8692						
19	8/15	Midwest	Chrissy	21000						

Data Table dialog box:
- Row input cell: $G$2
- Column input cell: $F$2

Figure 21.4 *A two-variable data table can replace an array formula if you don't mind the formula in the upper-left corner.*

Figure 21.5 shows a second example of a two-variable data table replacing this array formula:

=INDEX($C$2:$C$15,MATCH($E9&F$8,$A$2:$A$15&$B$2:$B$15,0))

You saw this example of a two-value lookup back in Chapter 5, with a join array operation. The DGET and data table solution calculates more quickly than the join array operation formula.

	A	B	C	D	E	F	G	H
1	Product Code	L/R?	Qty				Qty	
2	2A45-2A46	R	18		Product Code	L/R?	Qty	
3	2A39-2A40	L	36		2A38-2A39	R	36	◄ =DGET(A1:C15,G2,E2:F3)
4	2A35-2A36	L	30					
5	2A38-2A39	R	36		Formula in cell E8: =G3.			
6	2A44-2A45	L	18					
7	2A48-2A49	L	20				Qty	
8	2A45-2A46	L	24		36	L	R	
9	2A48-2A49	R	24		2A35-2A36	30	35	
10	2A44-2A45	R	28		2A38-2A39	30	36	
11	2A46-2A47	L	30		2A39-2A40	36	35	
12	2A38-2A39	L	30		2A44-2A45	18	28	
13	2A35-2A36	R	35		2A45-2A46	24	18	
14	2A39-2A40	R	35		2A46-2A47	30	36	
15	2A46-2A47	R	36		2A48-2A49	20	24	

Data Table — Row input cell: $F$3 — Column input cell: $E$3 — OK / Cancel

Figure 21.5 *Using a two-variable data table to create a cross-tabulated table that replaces a two-value lookup array formula.*

One final note about data tables: There is a setting that allows you to calculate a formula automatically, except for data tables. To get to this option, you go to the File Ribbon tab, click Options, click the Formulas tab, go to Calculation Options/Workbook Calculations, and select the Automatic Except for Data Tables button.

Chapter Summary

In this chapter you have learned about the data table feature. Chapter 22 discusses the LINEST array function.

Chapter 22: The LINEST Array Function

Excel Files

To follow along with the examples in this chapter, you can download the accompanying files, as explained in the Introduction.

An Array Function for Many Statistics at Once

Statistics, anyone? If you are calculating statistics associated with an *x-y* straight-line data set, you will love the LINEST function! The LINEST function can calculate many statistics when you are fitting data to a straight line using the least-squares method. Here are some of the statistics that it can calculate:

1. Coefficient of determination

2. Degrees of freedom

3. F statistic

4. Intercept

5. Slope

6. Standard error for intercept

7. Standard error for slope

8. Standard error of *y*

9. Sum of squares regression

10. Sum of squares residual

You can highlight a range of cells, enter the LINEST function, highlight the *x-y* data set, and press Ctrl+Shift+Enter and instantly calculate many statistics.

In this book I do not discuss what all the statistics mean; rather, I simply show how to get the LINEST array function to calculate the statistics and how to display the results neatly. For more details about this function, use Excel's function help and search for LINEST. (There is fairly useful information in the Microsoft help article.) In addition, Conrad Carlberg, an Excel MVP and statistics master, has written a great book for Que Publishing, *Statistical Analysis: Microsoft Excel 2010*, which has some great tips about the LINEST function and the statistics that it generates.

The LINEST function takes four arguments		
Argument	**Description**	**Notes**
known_y's	The set of y values in the relationship $y = mx+b$.	• If the range of known_y's is in a single column, each column of known_x's is interpreted as a separate variable. • If the range of known_y's is contained in a single row, each row of known_x's is interpreted as a separate variable.
[known_x's]	The set of x values in the relationship $y = mx+b$. This argument is optional.	• The range of known_x's can include one or more sets of variables. If only one variable is used, known_y's and known_x's can be ranges of any shape, as long as they have equal dimensions. If more than one variable is used, known_y's must be a vector (that is, a range with a height of one row or a width of one column). • If known_x's is omitted, it is assumed to be the array {1,2,3,...} that is the same size as known_y's.
[const]	A logical value that specifies whether to force the constant b to equal 0. This argument is optional.	• If const is TRUE or omitted, b is calculated normally. • If const is FALSE, b is set equal to 0 and the m-values are adjusted to fit $y = mx$.
[stats]	A logical value that specifies whether to return additional regression statistics. This argument is optional.	• If stats is TRUE, LINEST returns the additional regression statistics beyond just slope (m) and intercept (b). • If stats is FALSE or omitted, LINEST returns only the slope (m) and intercept (b).

Using LINEST to Deliver Slope and Intercept to a Horizontal Range

Let's look at an example of how to get the LINEST functions to deliver just two statistics: the slope and intercept for a data set with one x value (one independent variable). Figure 22.1 shows the data set. (You saw this same data set in Chapter 9, when we discussed the SLOPE, INTERCEPT, FORECAST, and TREND functions.) Because LINEST is an array function and you want to display both values, you follow these steps:

1. Highlight the range D2:E2. LINEST delivers an array of two values displayed horizontally, in two columns.

2. Enter known y values. These are scores that students earned on a final test. This is past data.

3. Enter known x values. These are the number of hours that students said they studied for the final test. This is past data.

4. Omit the [const] argument. If you leave out this argument, the default (TRUE) is to calculate the intercept normally.

5. Omit the [stats] argument. If you leave out this argument, the default (FALSE) is to calculate only slope and intercept.

6. Enter the formula with Ctrl+Shift+Enter.

	A	B	C	D	E	F
1	Hours Studying for test - x	Score on Final - y		Slope = m Intercept = b		
2	2	75		=LINEST(B2:B12,A2:A12)		
3	15	91		LINEST(known_y's, **[known_x's]**, [const], [stats])		
4	5	79				
5	1	70				
6	6	65				
7	9	98				
8	25	100				
9	41	100				
10	10	82				
11	6	79				
12	2	60				

Figure 22.1 *Using LINEST to deliver slope and intercept to a horizontal range.*

Figure 22.2 shows the result. The slope is 0.8842, and the intercept is 71.9207.

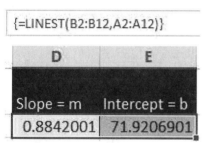

{=LINEST(B2:B12,A2:A12)}

D	E
Slope = m	Intercept = b
0.8842001	71.9206901

Figure 22.2 *Using the single array function LINEST instead of using the two separate functions SLOPE and INTERCEPT.*

Using LINEST to Deliver Slope and Intercept to a Vertical Range

Because the resultant array from the LINEST array function displays values in columns, if you try to enter LINEST into a vertical range, you see only the first value in the resultant array. Figure 22.3 shows a formula to display the two values horizontally.

m	0.88420007	< Formula: =INDEX(LINEST($B$2:$B$12,$A$2:$A$12),ROWS(E$5:E5))
b	71.9206901	< Formula: =INDEX(LINEST($B$2:$B$12,$A$2:$A$12),ROWS(E$5:E6))

Figure 22.3 *LINEST delivers a 1×2 horizontal resultant array. You can display the values vertically with this formula.*

Using LINEST to Deliver 10 Statistics for One x Variable

This example shows how to display addition statistics beyond just the slope and intercept. To determine how many cells to highlight before entering the LINEST array function when you are delivering extra stats, follow this rule: Highlight one more column than there are x variables and highlight five rows.

As shown in Figure 22.4, because you have one *x* variable (there are many *x* values, but only one *x* variable), you highlight the range E2:F6 (2 columns by 5 rows) because:

- You have 1 *x* variable, so 1+1 = 2 columns.
- You always highlight 5 rows when you are delivering the extra stats.

Figure 22.4 shows that you enter the *y* values, *x* values, TRUE for the [const] argument because you want *b* to be calculated normally, and TRUE for the [stats] argument because you want the extra stats. After you enter the array function with Ctrl+Shift+Enter, the results should match the ones shown in Figure 22.5.

Figure 22.4 *When you want the extra stats for 1* x *variable, highlight a 2×5 range. LINEST will deliver 10 statistics.*

Slope	0.8842001	71.9206901 Intercept
Standard Error m	0.2498316	3.99872472 Standard Error b
Coefficient of Determination	0.5818976	9.56208704 Standard Error y
F	12.525826	9 df
SS Regression	1145.2802	822.901576 SS Residual

Figure 22.5 *It's amazing that LINEST delivers 10 statistics!*

Using a Formula to List LINEST Table Results in a Vertical Column

In Chapter 8 you saw how to use formula number incrementors and the INDEX function to take results shown in a table and display them vertically. Figure 22.6 shows a formula to take the 5×2 resultant array of values that the LINEST function delivers and display them vertically.

These are the formula elements to enter into the three INDEX function arguments:

- array argument = LINEST($B$2:$B$12,$A$2:$A$12,TRUE,TRUE). LINEST delivers an array of values with five rows and two columns.
- row_num argument = MOD(ROWS(E$1:E1)-1,5)+1. This formula element delivers the values 1,2,3,4,5,1,2,3,4,5 as you copy it down.
- column_num argument = INT((ROWS(E$1:E1)-1)/5)+1. This formula elements delivers the numbers 1,1,1,1,1,2,2,2,2,2 as you copy it down.

D	E	F	G	H	I
Slope	0.8842001	< =INDEX(LINEST($B$2:$B$12,$A$2:$A$12,TRUE,TRUE),			
Standard Error m	0.2498316	MOD(ROWS(E$1:E1)-1,5)+1,			
Coefficient of Determination	0.5818976	INT((ROWS(E$1:E1)-1)/5)+1)			
F	12.525826	** Copy down column			
SS Regression	1145.2802				
Intercept	71.92069				
Standard Error b	3.9987247				
Standard Error y	9.562087				
df	9				
SS Residual	822.90158				

Figure 22.6 *Using a formula to display values from a 5×2 resultant array in a vertical column.*

The completed formula that is entered with Ctrl+Shift+Enter into cell E1 and then copied down the column is:

=INDEX(LINEST($B$2:$B$12,$A$2:$A$12,TRUE,TRUE),MOD(ROWS(E$1:E1)-1,5)+1,INT((ROWS(E$1:E1)-1)/5)+1)

Using LINEST to Deliver 12 Statistics for Two *x* Variables (Multiple Regression)

Each of the last two examples has a single *x* variable. In this example, you want to use LINEST to calculate statistics based on two *x* variables. As shown in Figure 22.7, you have collected past data about scores on student's tests. The x and y variables that are being considered in Figure 22.7 are described here:

- y values = dependent variable = score on final test = D column.
- X_1 values = independent variable 1 = homework scores = B column.
- X_2 values = independent variable 2 = hours studied for final test = C column.

These are the keys to getting LINEST to calculate the statistics:

- Notice that the x_1 values are listed in the column *before* the x_2 values.
- The number of columns you must highlight before entering the function is 2 (Number × Variables) + 1 = 3 columns.
- Highlight the 5×3 range B3:D7.
- Create the formula: =LINEST(D13:D23,B13:C23,TRUE,TRUE). For the known_x's argument, be sure to highlight both columns of *x* values from the range B13:C23.
- Enter the function with Ctrl+Shift+Enter.
- Notice that even though you highlighted the x_1 values *before* the x_2 values in the range B13:C23, the slope values are listed as m_2 and then m_1, m_2 *after* m_1.

Figure 22.7 shows the resultant array of statistics.

	fx	{=LINEST(D13:D23,B13:C23,TRUE,TRUE)}			
	A	B	C	D	E
1			C3 = Slope x_1		
2			C4 = Standard Error x_1		
3	B3 = Slope x_2	0.504932928	0.600728442	24.98327247	D3 = Intercept
4	B4 = Standard Error x_2	0.206372691	0.180969295	14.40495975	D4 = Standard Error b
5	B5 = Coefficient of Determination	0.824133781	6.577772188	#N/A	
6	B6 = F	18.74456124	8	#N/A	
7	B7 = SS Regression	1622.045123	346.1366956	#N/A	
8			C5 = Standard Error y		
9			C6 = df		
10			C7 = SS Residual		
12		Homework scores out of 100 (X_1)	Hours Studying for test (X_2)	Score on Final (Y)	
13		82	2	75	
14		95	15	91	
15		87	5	79	
16		85	1	70	
17		52	6	65	
18		97.5	9	98	
19		100	25	100	
20		99	41	100	
21		80	10	82	
22		84	6	79	
23		75	2	60	

Figure 22.7 *For two* x *variables, LINEST performs multiple regression.*

If you do not want to show the #N/A errors, you can wrap the IFERROR function around the LINEST function and deliver a null text string to the cell rather than an #N/A error. Figure 22.8 shows this completed formula (entered with Ctrl+Shift+Enter):

=IFERROR(LINEST(D13:D23,B13:C23,TRUE,TRUE),"")

	fx	{=IFERROR(LINEST(D13:D23,B13:C23,TRUE,TRUE),"")}			
	A	B	C	D	E
1			C3 = Slope x_1		
2			C4 = Standard Error x_1		
3	B3 = Slope x_2	0.504932928	0.600728442	24.98327247	D3 = Intercept
4	B4 = Standard Error x_2	0.206372691	0.180969295	14.40495975	D4 = Standard Error b
5	B5 = Coefficient of Determination	0.824133781	6.577772188		
6	B6 = F	18.74456124	8		
7	B7 = SS Regression	1622.045123	346.1366956		
8			C5 = Standard Error y		
9			C6 = df		
10			C7 = SS Residual		

Figure 22.8 *You can put LINEST in IFERROR to show nothing instead of #N/A errors.*

Using LINEST to Deliver 14 Statistics for Three *x* Variables (Multiple Regression)

Figure 22.9 shows an example with three *x* variables.

✓	*fx*	{=IFERROR(LINEST(E13:E23,B13:D23,TRUE,TRUE),"")}

⟋	A	B	C	D	E	F
1			C3 = Slope x$_2$	D3 = Slope x$_1$		
2			C4 = Standard Error x$_2$	D4 = Standard Error x$_1$		
3	B3 = Slope x$_3$	7.835932699	0.341793341	0.301173879	27.64805488	E3 = Intercept
4	B4 = Standard Error x$_3$	3.878950265	0.193054477	0.213618663	12.31055883	E4 = Stand. Error b
5	B5 = C. of Determination	0.888901926	5.589035302			
6	B6 = F	18.66913097	7			
7	B7 = SS Regression	1749.520609	218.6612093			
8			C5 = Standard Error y			
9			C6 = df			
10			C7 = SS Residual			
12		Homework scores out of 100 (X$_1$)	Hours Studying for test (X$_2$)	Grade from Pre Req (x3)	Score on Final (Y)	
13		82	2	2	75	
14		95	15	3.8	91	
15		87	5	3.1	79	
16		85	1	2.8	70	
17		52	6	1.9	65	
18		97.5	9	4	98	
19		100	25	3.9	100	
20		99	41	4	100	
21		80	10	3.8	82	
22		84	6	3.2	79	
23		75	2	2.1	60	

Figure 22.9 *LINEST can create statistics for three* x *variables using the formula: =IFERROR(LINEST(E13 :E23,B13:D23,TRUE,TRUE),"")*

Chapter Summary

In this chapter you have learned how to use the LINEST function. In Chapter 23 you will see a number of fun concluding array formulas.

Chapter 23: Can You Figure Out How the Huge Array Formula Works?

Excel Files

To follow along with the examples in this chapter, you can download the accompanying files, as explained in the Introduction.

Figuring Out How an Array Formula Works

Throughout this book, most of the time I have laid out the logic of how a particular array formula works. But what if you have a huge array formula, and can't figure out how it works? What do you do then? You have already seen many techniques for figuring out why a formula is doing what it is doing. Array Formula Efficiency Rule 28 lists them.

Array Formula Efficiency Rule 28

Tips for figuring out the logic of how a particular array formula is working:

- Break the formula into the smallest possible pieces and place each piece is a separate cell. This allows you to see how each part is working. It gives you a different perspective than looking at the whole formula in a single cell. This is especially true when the formula element changes as the formula is copied. If you place a formula element like this in a cell and copy it, you can explicitly see what the part is doing.

- While the formula is in a single cell, run the Evaluate Formula feature (by pressing Alt, M, V or selecting Evaluate Formula from the Formula Auditing group of the Formula Ribbon tab). The Evaluator Formula feature is great for seeing the steps that Excel goes through when calculating a formula. There are two drawbacks to this feature: (1) Sometimes the evaluated formula element is too big for the Evaluate Formula dialog box; and (2) sometimes this dialog does not show all the steps or it shows a different result from using the F9 key when the formula is in Edit mode.

- Use the Evaluate Formula Element trick (see Array Formula Efficiency Rule 5). Press the F9 key to evaluate each separate part of the formula while the formula is in Edit mode in the cell. You can see this trick throughout the book. This is an invaluable trick for learning how a formula does what it does. After you evaluate the formula element with the F9 key, immediately undo it with Ctrl+Z. If you do not undo and you evaluate two or more times in a row, you will not be able to undo it all back to the beginning. This is because there is only one undo while in Edit mode. If the formula elements evaluates to more than 8,192 characters, you will get an error message. 8,192 is the maximum number of characters that a cell can display. One advantage that the F9 key has over the Evaluate Formula feature is that the F9 method sometimes shows what a formula element evaluates to, whereas the Evaluate Formula feature does not.

- Read Microsoft's function help. The function help articles reveal many of the hidden powers of functions.

- Watch the ScreenTips to see which argument is highlighted in bold to help you understand where a particular formula element is sitting in the larger formula. To highlight a particular formula element, you can click the argument name in the ScreenTip; this highlights the complete formula element that sits in the function argument.

- Use the combination of the Evaluate Formula Element trick (by pressing F9) and reading the function argument name in the ScreenTip to "see" what each formula element is delivering to the given function argument.

- After entering the completed formula and then putting the cell in Edit mode, you can press the F9 key to evaluate each part of the formula. When you are done looking at what each formula element evaluates to, press the Esc key to revert to the formula you had in the cell before you put the cell into Edit mode. Be careful: If you press Enter after using the F9 key, the evaluated values will be hard coded into the formula. (You can use Ctrl+Z to undo it, though.)

- Don't give up if you don't figure it out right away. Over the years, a few formulas have taken me days to figure out. It is worth the fight when you get it.

Now let's look at how to put these techniques into use with an example.

Looking Up the First Item in a Row with Empty Cells

Figure 23.1 shows an array formula that looks up the first non-empty cell in a row. (This is one of the many formulas that I learned from Aladin Akyurek at the MrExcel Message Board.)

	A	B	C	D	E	F	G
1	Lookup first number in row when there may be some empty cells.						
2	11/27	11/28	11/29	11/30	Stock	First	
3	$23	$15			ABC	$23	< {=IF(COUNT(A3:D3),INDEX(A3:D3,MATCH(TRUE,A3:D3<>"",0)),"")}
4					DDR		** Copy down
5		$65		$67	MWII	$65	

Figure 23.1 *Looking up the first non-empty cell in a row.*

Here is the formula:

=IF(COUNT(A3:D3),INDEX(A3:D3,MATCH(TRUE,A3:D3<>"",0)),"")

If you don't know how this formula is doing what it is doing, you can start by copying the formula and pasting it into the cell. While the formula is in Edit mode, click through the formula and see which formula elements are sitting in which function arguments. As shown in Figure 23.2, you can start off with the first argument in the first function in the formula. By clicking the logical_test argument name in the ScreenTip, you can highlight the formula element that sits in that argument. You can see that the COUNT function is sitting in this argument. If you press the F9 key, you can see that COUNT evaluates to the number 2. Quickly undo the evaluation by using Ctrl+Z. This means that COUNT delivers a 2 to the logical_test argument of the IF function. Because the logical_test argument interprets any nonzero number as TRUE and zero as FALSE, the COUNT function works perfectly for the logical_test argument.

=IF(COUNT(A3:D3),INDEX(A3:D3,MATCH(TRUE,A3:D3<>"",0)),"")

IF(**logical_test**, [value_if_true], [value_if_false])

Figure 23.2 *Clicking the logical_test argument name in the ScreenTip for the IF function in order to highlight the formula element.*

Next you can click the value_if_true argument name in the ScreenTip, as shown in Figure 23.3, and see that the INDEX function is sitting in this argument. You can press the F9 key in this formula element to see that INDEX is delivering the first value, 23. (Remember to press Ctrl+Z to undo the evaluation.) If you look through the IF function ScreenTip, you can also see that a null text string sits in the value_if_false argument. At this point you are still just hunting around in the formula and seeing what is going on. Next you want to look at the MATCH formula element.

=IF(COUNT(A3:D3),INDEX(A3:D3,MATCH(TRUE,A3:D3<>"",0)),"")

IF(logical_test, [**value_if_true**], [value_if_false])

Figure 23.3 *INDEX sits in the value_if_true argument of the IF function.*

Now, with the formula in Edit mode, click somewhere in the INDEX function to expose the IN-DEX function ScreenTip. Then, as shown in Figure 23.4, click the row_num argument name in the ScreenTip in order to highlight the MATCH function. If you press the F9 key in this formula element, you see that it is delivering the relative position 1 to the row_num argument. (Remember to undo the evaluation by pressing Ctrl+Z.)

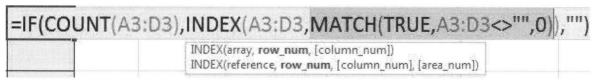

Figure 23.4 *MATCH sits in the row_num argument of the INDEX function.*

Next you will look at the array operation in the lookup_array argument of the MATCH function. Figures 23.5 and 23.6 show that the array comparative operation evaluates to an array of TRUEs and FALSEs. If you are trying to figure out how the formula is finding the first non-empty cell, this array operation is the key. You can see that there are two TRUE values. So how does the MATCH function figure out which one to select? For this you can go to the Microsoft function help.

Figure 23.5 *Clicking the lookup_array argument name in the MATCH function ScreenTip to highlight the array operation.*

Figure 23.6 *Pressing the F9 key to see what the array operation evaluates to. (Remember to then press Ctrl+Z to undo the evaluation.)*

If you click the MATCH function name in the MATCH function ScreenTip, the Microsoft help for the MATCH function appears, as shown in Figure 23.7. If you read through the help, you will find the section that says that if you use an exact match (0 in the match_type argument), "MATCH finds the first value that is exactly equal to lookup_value." This is great because you can use this fact to help you find the first TRUE in the array of logical values.

MATCH(TRUE,A3:D3<>"",0)),"")

MATCH(lookup_value, lookup_array, [match_type])

Figure 23.7 *Clicking on the function name in the ScreenTip will open up the Help article for the function.*

The final thing that might be helpful in understanding how this formula works is to copy and paste the MATCH function formula element, MATCH(TRUE,A3:D3<>"",0), into the cells and see how this individual part of the formula is working. Figure 23.8 shows that MATCH correctly delivers the relative position of the first number in each row. When there are no numbers entered in the row, you can see the #N/A error. For #N/A, the COUNT function delivers a zero to the logical_test argument of the IF function, and the null text string is delivered to the cell instead of the results from the INDEX function.

G3	▼	:	✕	✓	*fx*	{=MATCH(TRUE,A3:D3<>"",0)}

	A	B	C	D	E	F	G
1	Lookup first number in row when there may be som
2	11/27	11/28	11/29	11/30	Stock	First	
3	$23	$15			ABC	$23	1
4					DDR		#N/A
5		$65		$67	MWII	$65	2

Figure 23.8 *Placing just the MATCH formula element into a cell and then copying the formula down the column helps you understand how the formula is working.*

After you examine the formula and formula elements in Edit mode, you might want to run the Evaluate Formula feature to see how Excel steps through and calculates the formula.

Another great trick for understanding how the formula is working is to press the F9 key to evaluate each formula element, one after the other, and then press the Esc key when you are done. However, because the Esc key brings the cell back to its original state before you put the cell into Edit mode, you must enter the completed formula into the cell and then put the cell back into Edit mode before you start this trick. Figure 23.9 shows an example of this.

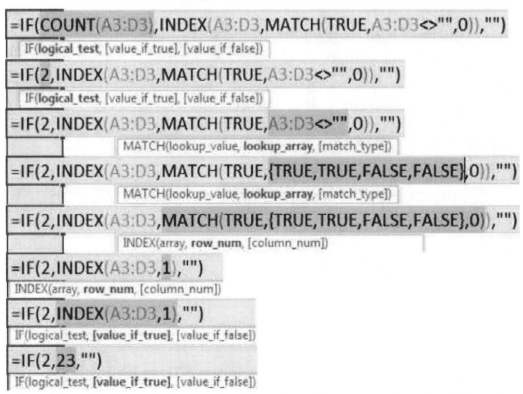

Figure 23.9 *After entering the completed formula and then putting the cell in Edit mode, you can press the F9 key to evaluate each part of the formula; then you press the Esc key to revert back to the formula you had in the cell before you put the cell into Edit mode.*

The techniques you've already seen in this chapter can go a long way toward helping you decipher a huge array formula that someone gives you. Because these tips are so important, I repeat them here in a more abbreviated form:

1. Break the formula into the smallest possible pieces and see what each piece does.

2. Run the Evaluate Formula feature to see how Excel steps through the calculation process.

3. Press the F9 key to evaluate a formula element to see what a particular piece is delivering to the formula.

4. Read Microsoft's function help to learn about a particular function argument or function.

5. Read the function argument names in the ScreenTips to "see" where a particular formula element is sitting.

6. Use both F9 and ScreenTips to see what a formula element is delivering to a function argument.

7. Enter the completed formula, enter Edit mode, press F9 for each formula element, and press Esc after you are done evaluating each element.

8. Don't give up!

Now that you've seen an example of how to figure out how array formulas work, you'll see some examples to try it out yourself. The following array formula examples do not give much explanation for how the formulas work. I leave it up to you to apply what you have learned and figure out how these formulas are working. However, if you really want an explanation for how any of these array formulas work, watch video 24 on the *Ctrl+Shift+Enter: Mastering Excel Array Formulas* DVD.

A Formula to Look Up Column Headers Associated with the First Non-empty Cell in a Row

Figure 23.10 shows a formula that looks up the date from the column headers associated with the first non-empty cell in a row. The only difference between this formula and the one shown in Figure 23.1 is that the array argument of the INDEX function is pointing at the date column headers and is absolute instead of relative.

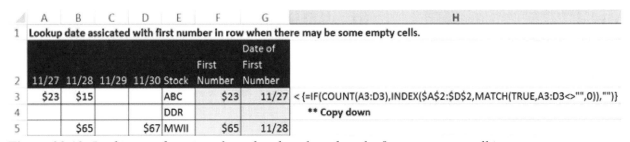

	A	B	C	D	E	F	G	H
1	Lookup date assicated with first number in row when there may be some empty cells.							
2	11/27	11/28	11/29	11/30	Stock	First Number	Date of First Number	
3	$23	$15			ABC	$23	11/27	< {=IF(COUNT(A3:D3),INDEX($A$2:$D$2,MATCH(TRUE,A3:D3<>"",0)),"")}
4					DDR			** Copy down
5		$65		$67	MWII	$65	11/28	

Figure 23.10 *Looking up dates in column headers, based on the first non-empty cell in a row.*

A Formula to Look Up a Column and Then Match a Condition in the Column and Extract Data

Figure 23.11 shows a great formula solution that first looks up a column (Day 3) and then, within that column, matches the condition (Job 4) and then retrieves the employee names and display them vertically. Several interesting things are going on in this formula:

- COUNTIF can accept ranges created by INDEX in range argument (see Chapters 10 and 13).
- INDEX looks up a whole column or row (see Chapter 13).
- Formulas extract data (see Chapter 15).

	A	B	C	D	E
1	Lookup Column of Data, Match Criterion, Display Items Vertically.				
2	Employee	Day 1	Day 2	Day 3	
3	Lesley Baronne	Job 2	Job 2	Job 3	
4	Ellsworth Chanofsky	Job 3	Job 1	Job 4	
5	Hobert Linkon	Job 3	Job 2	Job 4	
6	Malcom Gunzenhause	Job 3	Job 4	Job 1	
7	Darell Gaviria	Job 1	Job 1	Job 2	
8	Patricia Glowski	Job 3	Job 2	Job 4	
9	Manual Inbody	Job 3	Job 1	Job 4	
11	Column to lookup:	Criteria	Count		
12	Day 3	Job 4		4	< =COUNTIF(INDEX($B$3:$D$9,,MATCH($A$12,$B$2:$D$2)),B12)
14	Extracted Employees	** Copy down			
15	Ellsworth Chanofsky	< {=IF(ROWS(A$15:A15)>$C$12,"",INDEX($A$3:$A$9,SMALL(IF(			
16	Hobert Linkon	INDEX($B$3:$D$9,,MATCH($A$12,$B$2:$D$2))=$B$12,			
17	Patricia Glowski	ROW($A$3:$A$9)-ROW($A$3)+1),ROWS(A$15:A15))))}			
18	Manual Inbody	or			
19		< =IF(ROWS(A$15:A15)>C$12,"",INDEX($A$3:$A$9,AGGREGATE(15,6,			
20		(ROW($A$3:$A$9)-ROW($A$3)+1)/			
21		(INDEX($B$3:$D$9,0,MATCH($A$12,$B$2:$D$2,0))=B$12),ROWS(A$15:A15))))			

Figure 23.11 *Formula to look up a column, match criteria, and extract names.*

A Formula to Look Up the Longest Word in a Column

Figure 23.12 shows a formula that looks up the item in the column with the largest number of characters. It works on text and numbers. The LEN function is making a function argument array operation.

	A	B
1	Lookup Longest Word.	
2	Lookup	
3	excelisfun	< {=INDEX(A6:A9,MATCH(MAX(LEN(A6:A9)),LEN(A6:A9),0))}
5	Words	
6	rad	
7	cool	
8		
9	excelisfun	

Figure 23.12 *Looking up the item with the longest length. This works whether the item is text or a number.*

A Formula to Calculate Percentile with One Condition

Figure 23.13 shows how to calculate the CPA score that corresponds to the 90th percentile. The calculated score is the marker that divides the data set so that 90% of the values are below the marker and 10% are above. Cells D4 and D5 calculate the percentile marker for all the CPA data. Formulas in cells E11 and E17 calculate the percentile marker with one condition (each school's name). In Excel 2010, the new AGGREGATE function provides function 18, the PERCENTILE. EXC function (excluded 0% and 100%), which is perfect for the array calculation necessary to make the percentile with one condition calculation.

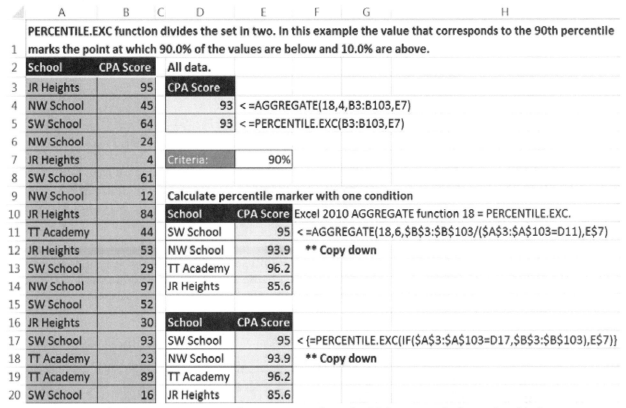

Figure 23.13 *Calculating a CPA score that corresponds to the 90th percentile for each school.*

The *Ctrl+Shift+Enter: Mastering Excel Array Formulas* DVD does not include the example shown in Figure 23.13 (I forgot to include it when I filmed the videos).

A Formula to Rank Values with One Condition

Sometimes you need to rank with a condition. Because there is no RANKIF function, you can make an array calculation inside the SUMPRODUCT function, as shown in Figure 23.14. This formula ranks the scores for each department.

	A	B	C	D	E
1	**RANK Score with condition from Department column**				
2	Student	Score	Department	RANKIF	
3	Tameka Eastep	68	Finance	2	< =SUMPRODUCT(--($C$3:$C$11=C3),--($B$3:$B$11>B3))+1
4	Noreen Bley	78	Finance	1	** Copy down
5	Hugh Vasques	66	Operations	3	
6	Noemi Kinghorn	78	Marketing	2	
7	Odessa Paille	94	Operations	1	
8	Carlene Meisinger	93	Marketing	1	
9	Selena Pulice	75	Operations	2	
10	Lonnie Plaisance	72	Marketing	3	
11	Hugh Garceau	66	Finance	3	

Figure 23.14 *Ranking the scores for each department.*

A Formula to Calculate the Maximum Two-Day Running Total

The goal in Figure 23.15 is to calculate the maximum two-day running total over a seven-day period. The formula must choose between the six available two-day totals. The OFFSET function is used inside the SUBTOTAL function to create the six two-day subtotals, which the MAX function can then choose from. This is a formula that I learned from Domenic at the MrExcel Message Board.

> **Hint:** If you run the Evaluate Formula feature, you see that parts of the formula show errors, but if you evaluate the same parts using the F9 key, you do not see errors. This is an example of why it is useful to have both the F9 key evaluation method and the Evaluate Formula feature.

	A	B	C	D	E	F	G	H	I	J	K
1									Days	2	
2	**Max of 2 day running total - SUBTOTAL, OFFSET and MAX function.**										
3	Day 1	Day 2	Day 3	Day 4	Day 5	Day 6	Day 7	Max of 2 day running subtotal	** Copy down		
4	4	2	1	8	3	6	2	11	< {=MAX(SUBTOTAL(9,OFFSET(A4,,		
5	4	4	10	8	9	6	3	18	ROW(INDIRECT("1:"&COLUMNS(A4:G4)-$J$1+1))-1,1,$J$1)))}		
6	6	8	1	6	10	10	9	20	or		
7	5	8	6	1	3	6	10	16	=MAX(SUBTOTAL(9,OFFSET(A4,,{0,1,2,3,4,5},1,$J$1)))		

Figure 23.15 *Calculating the maximum two-day total over a seven-day period.*

A Formula to Calculate Net Cost Equivalent, Based on Variable-Length Series Discounts

Figure 23.16 shows a single-cell formula to calculate the net cost equivalent. For example, in cell D3 the formula must make this calculation: 0.8*0.95*0.9*0.8. When the formula is copied down to cell D4, the formula must calculate this: 0.9*0.9.

	Retail	Series	Net Cost	
Product	Price	Discount	Equivalent	

Extract Numbers From Text String and calculate Net Cost Equivalent.

Product	Retail Price	Series Discount	Net Cost Equivalent	** Copy down
Quad	$30.25	20/05/10/20	0.5472	< {=PRODUCT(1-MID(C3,
Bellen	$25.25	10/10	0.81	CHOOSE(LEN(C3)-LEN(SUBSTITUTE(C3,"/",""))+1,1,{1,4},{1,4,7},{1,4,7,10}),
Carlota	$21.95	15/10/16	0.6426	2)/100)}
Sunset	$23.95	05	0.95	

Figure 23.16 *Calculating net cost equivalent, based on variable-length series discounts.*

A Formula to Maximize Consecutive Appearances in Bowl Games, Win or Lose

The last formula, shown in Figure 23.17, is one of my favorites. This solution uses the amazing FREQUENCY function. Here is a hint about this formula: The OR criteria helps you count in either one column or the other. The AND criteria helps you ensure that both teams are *not* equal to the team of interest (criteria).

> **Note:** This formula is based on a formula I learned from pgc01 at the MrExcel Message Board. Thanks, pgc01!

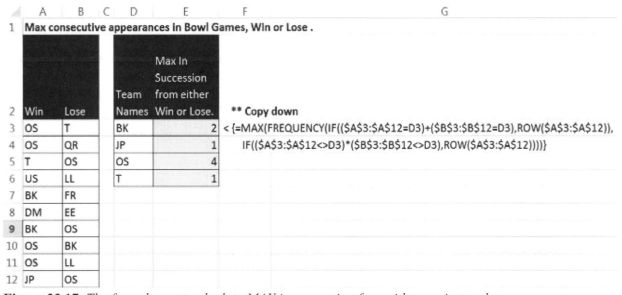

Max consecutive appearances in Bowl Games, Win or Lose .

Win	Lose	Team Names	Max In Succession from either Win or Lose.	** Copy down
OS	T	BK	2	< {=MAX(FREQUENCY(IF(($A$3:$A$12=D3)+($B$3:$B$12=D3),ROW($A$3:$A$12)),
OS	QR	JP	1	IF(($A$3:$A$12<>D3)*($B$3:$B$12<>D3),ROW($A$3:$A$12)))))}
T	OS	OS	4	
US	LL	T	1	
BK	FR			
DM	EE			
BK	OS			
OS	BK			
OS	LL			
JP	OS			

Figure 23.17 *The formula must calculate MAX in succession from either a win or a loss.*

Before I finish the book I must mention two last important array formula facts in the last two sections.

An Array Formula Cannot Calculate on an Entire Column

This comes straight from Microsoft Help:

- This is the "entire column" rule: Although you can create very large arrays in Excel, you cannot create an array that uses a whole column or multiple columns of cells. Because recalculating an array formula that uses a whole column of cells is time-consuming, Excel does not allow you to create this kind of array in a formula.

> **Note:** There are 65,536 cells in a column in Microsoft Office Excel 2003 and earlier versions of Excel. There are 1,048,576 cells in a column in Microsoft Office Excel 2007 and later.

For more information, check out http://support.microsoft.com/kb/166342.

Using Defined Names to Avoid Ctrl+Shift+Enter

Back in Chapter 13, I said that if you create a defined name that contains a formula that requires Ctrl+Shift+Enter, and then place that defined name in a cell formula, the formula will not require Ctrl+Shift+Enter. However, I did not give an example of this. I would like to give an example of a cool trick now.

If you have an array formula that requires Ctrl+Shift+Enter, you can save it as a defined name, and when you use the defined name in a formula, you won't have to use Ctrl+Shift+Enter. Figure 23.18 shows three AND criteria in cells B3, C3, and D3. The goal of this formula is to extract the records that match the three criteria (you saw this example in Chapter 15). The difference in this example is that you take the part of the formula that requires Ctrl+Shift+Enter and store it in a defined name. Then when you use the defined name in a cell formula, the formula does not re-quire Ctrl+Shift+Enter. In Figure 23.18 you can see that the defined name RP is a formula element that creates an array of relative positions that match the three AND criteria. This formula element requires Ctrl+Shift+Enter if used directly in a cell. But as the formula in cell F13 shows, if you use the defined name RP in a formula, the formula does not require Ctrl+Shift+Enter.

▲	A	B	C	D	E	F	G	H	I	J
1	**Extract records, AND Criteria**									
2	Criteria:	Date	Date	Region						
3		6/1/12	5/31/13	West						
5	Count									
6	2	< Formula =COUNTIFS(A14:A23,">="&B3,A14:A23,"<="&C3,B14:B23,D3)								
7										
8	Defined Name = RP =IF($A$14:$A$23>=$B$3,IF($A$14:$A$23<=$C$3,IF($B$14:$B$23=$D$3,									
9		ROW($A$14:$A$23)-ROW($A$14)+1)))								
10										
11	Formula in F13: =IF(ROWS(F$15:F15)>$A$6,"",INDEX(A$14:A$23,SMALL(RP,ROWS(F$15:F15))))									
12	Data Set:									
13	Date	Region	Customer	Units		Extract Area:				
14	7/29/13	West	WFMI	929		Date	Region	Customer	Units	
15	2/7/12	East	SW	681		11/3/12	West	K	436	
16	9/23/12	Midwest	K	1393		7/13/12	West	WFMI	1206	
17	4/14/12	West	WFMI	530						
18	7/26/12	East	WFMI	1058						
19	10/12/13	Midwest	SW	1023						
20	11/3/12	West	K	436						
21	9/3/13	West	K	1311						
22	4/23/12	Midwest	K	368						
23	7/13/12	West	WFMI	1206						

Figure 23.18 *If an array formula that requires Ctrl+Shift+Enter is stored as a defined name, when the defined name is used in a formula, the formula does not require Ctrl+Shift+Enter.*

Array Formula Efficiency Rule 29

If you create a defined name that contains a formula that requires Ctrl+-Shift+Enter and then place that defined name in a cell formula, the formula does not require Ctrl+Shift+Enter.

Conclusion

Haven't you had a lot of fun with array formulas? Armed with a complete set of Array Formula Efficiency Rules (listed back in chapter 14), you are ready to go out and create useful solutions! See you at YouTube for more fun with Excel!

Index